I SAW YOU...

ALSO BY JULIA WERTZ

The Fart Party

THREE RIVERS PRESS

NEW YORK

I SAW YOU...

Comics Inspired By Real-Life Missed Connections

filled with near misses, brief encounters, strange sightings, lusty longings, and a little hope for love

Edited by Julia Wertz

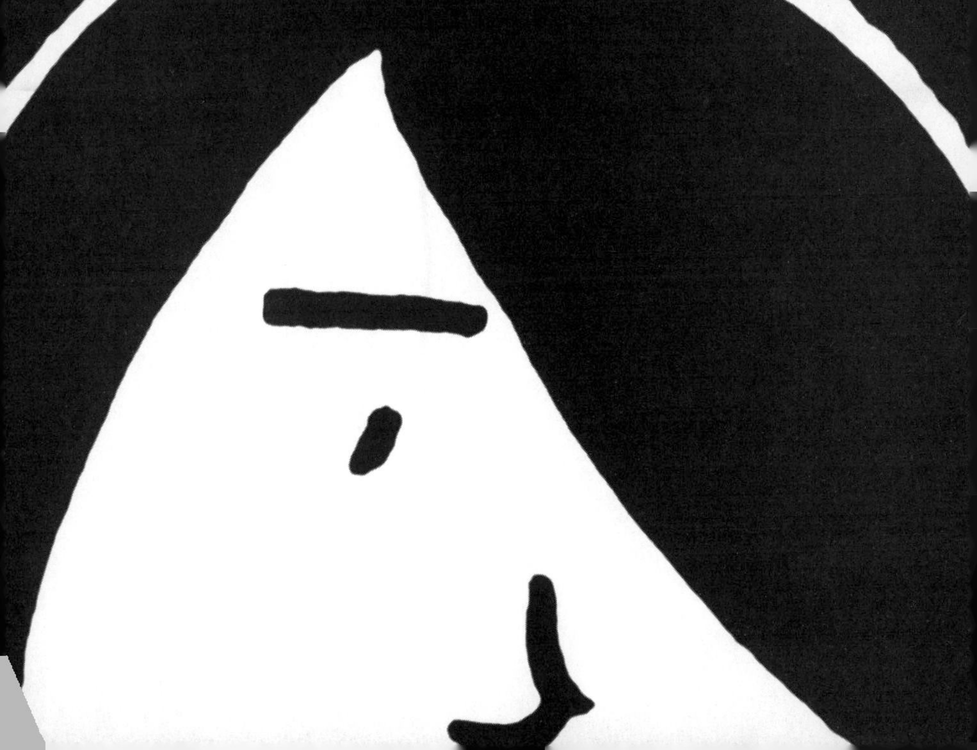

Published in the United States by Three Rivers Press, an imprint of the
Crown Publishing Group, a division of Random House, Inc., New York.
www.crownpublishing.com

Three Rivers Press and the Tugboat design are registered trademarks of
Random House, Inc.

Library of Congress Cataloging-in-Publication Data

I saw you : comics inspired by real-life missed connections / [compiled by]
Julia Wertz.
    p. cm.
1. Comic books, strips, etc.   I. Wertz, Julia.
PN6726.I24 2009
741.5'973—dc22   2008027896

ISBN 978-0-307-40853-2

Printed in the United States of America

Design by Maria Elias

Frontispiece: Laura Park

10 9 8 7 6 5 4 3 2 1

First Edition

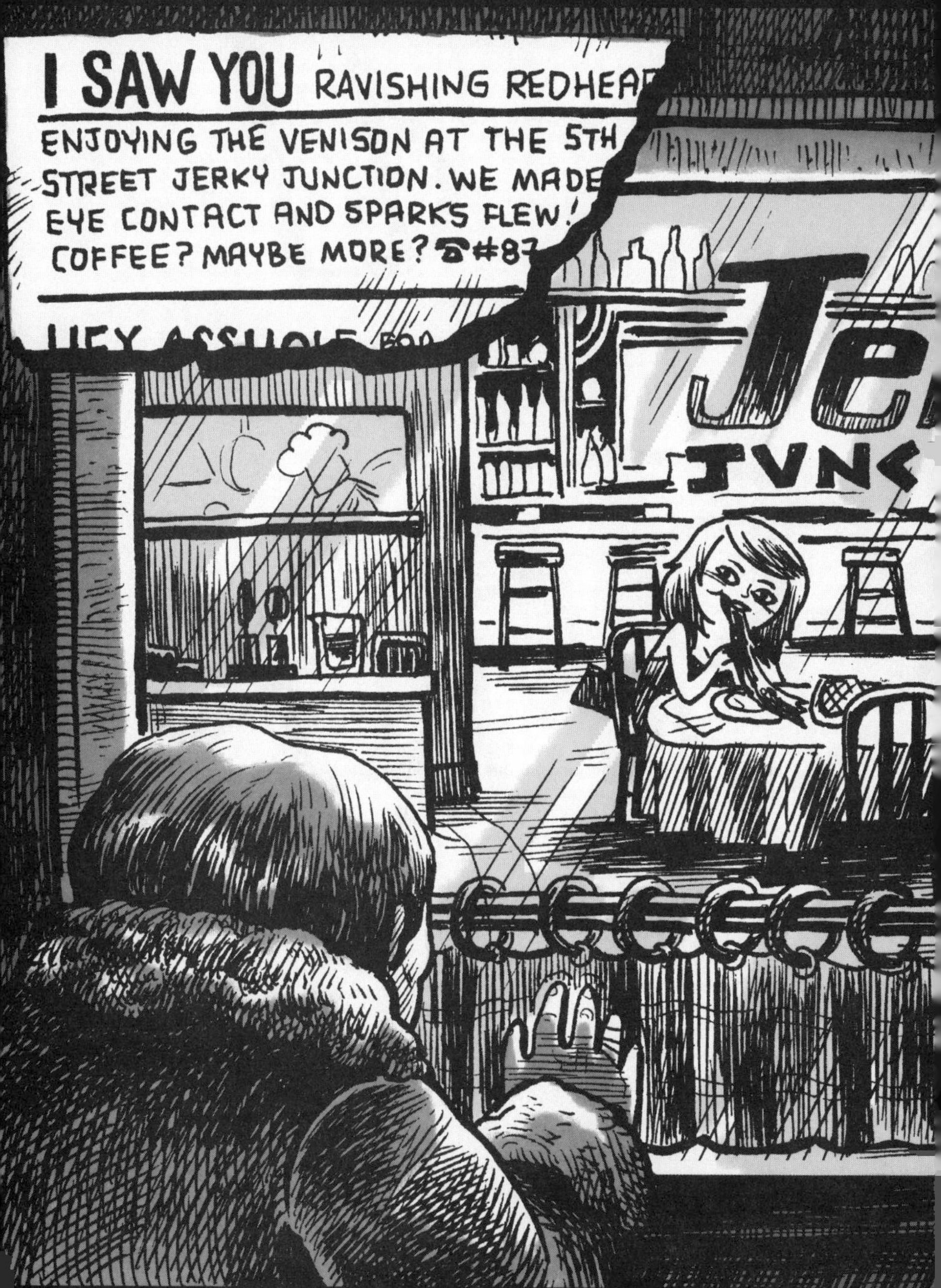
I SAW YOU RAVISHING REDHEA
ENJOYING THE VENISON AT THE 5TH STREET JERKY JUNCTION. WE MADE EYE CONTACT AND SPARKS FLEW! COFFEE? MAYBE MORE? ☎#87

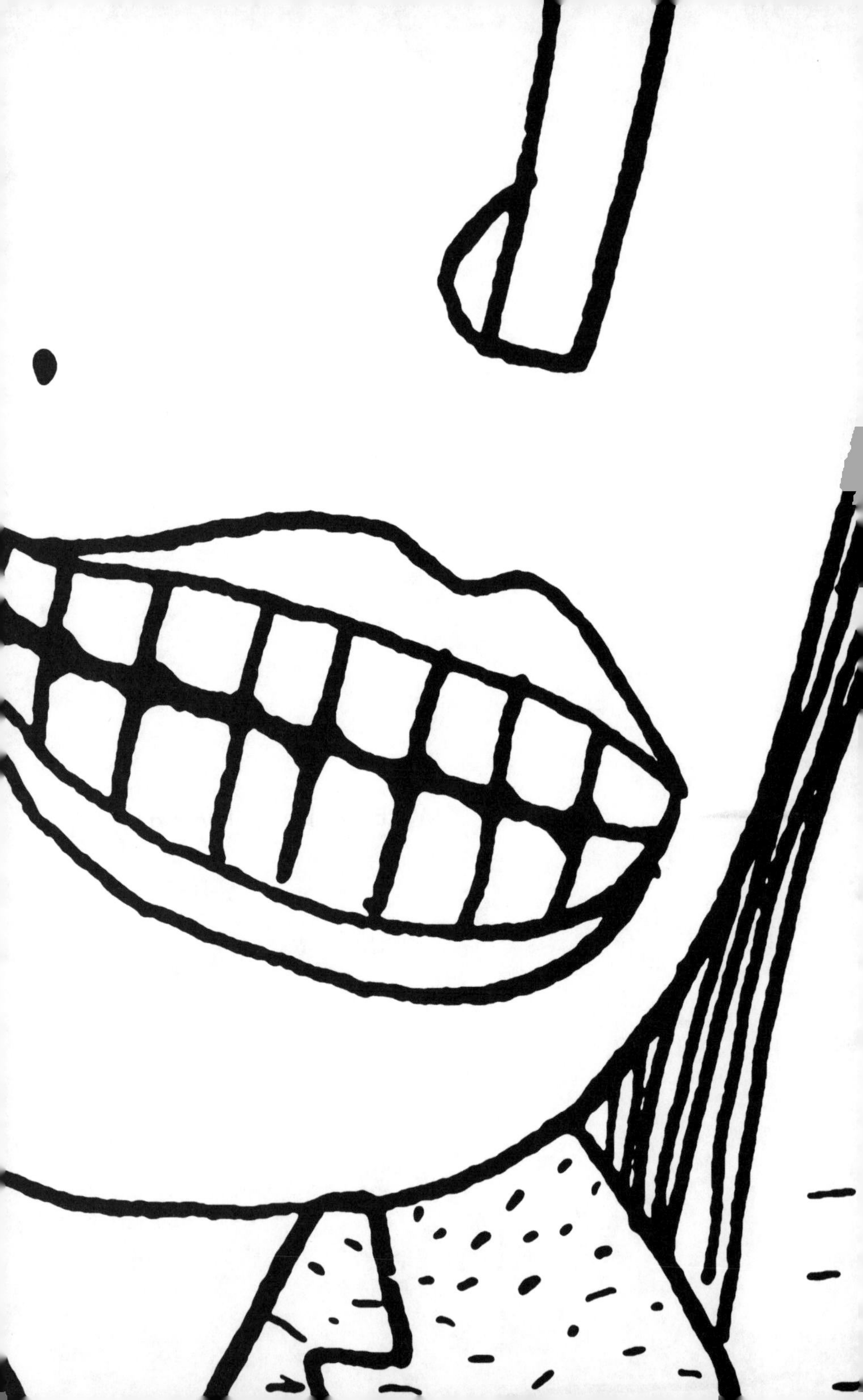

Contents

EDITOR'S NOTE

WHEN I FIRST STARTED READING missed connection ads on Craigslist, it was merely out of procrastination while job hunting. But what began as a distraction turned into a secret obsession that I'm sure I share with many others. I would take my laptop to a café, tilt the screen so no one could see me log onto Craigslist, and type in the places I had gone and stores I had been in, wondering if anyone had left a missed connection. Being a short, average-looking girl, I knew it was an exercise in futility. Most missed connections are left for "striking" and "beautiful" women or men but, nevertheless, I still checked.

But part of me wasn't really looking for an ad for myself, I was reading them out of sheer curiosity of the nature of those who left missed connection ads. I became intrigued with the concept of a subculture of people who feel they missed something great because they didn't have the courage to speak up. I found it even more peculiar that there were many people who think that strangers they spotted in a passing car or on the other side of the bus must surely be the loves of their lives. Having never been much of a romantic myself, I found it inconceivable that these people felt such deep connections with complete strangers. In short, I didn't really understand people who left missed connection ads, yet I was oddly drawn to them on a purely observatory level. And, being a cartoonist, combining the two seemed like a nifty little idea.

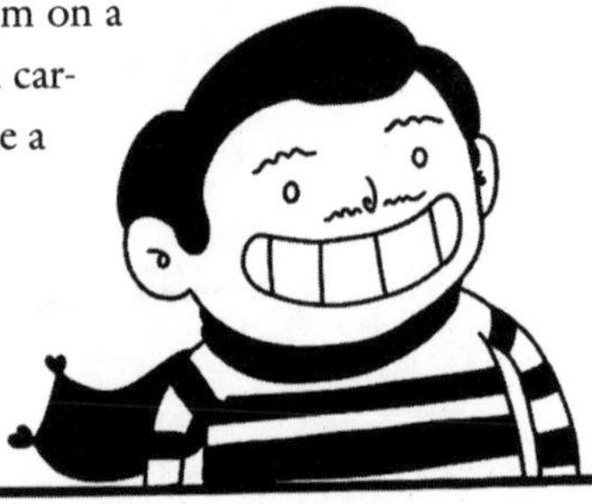

So, around fall of 2006, I put up a blog calling for submissions to a comics anthology based on missed connection ads. I didn't expect much more than a few submissions, mostly from my cartoonist friends. But I underestimated the draw of missed connection ads and soon my e-mail was flooded with submissions. I took the first fifteen submissions and turned them into a mini comicbook, which I sold at the Alternative Press Expo in San Francisco in spring of 2007.

Shortly after the expo, I got a phone call from an agent in New York expressing interest in representing the book. At first I thought it was utterly ridiculous. An agent? In New York? For a mini comic? I said no. I said no at least three more times until she convinced me to send her just a few copies of the comic. I relented and mailed a few to her. Within a week, she called to say she'd found a publisher and sold the book.

So, what followed was par for the course: I flew to New York, had lunch, shook some hands, signed some papers, and flew back home. I used the advance money to expand the book and get more contributors. I wanted the book to showcase not only the quirky nature of missed connection ads, but also the growing scene of alternative comics. I'm very grateful to Three Rivers Press for giving me the opportunity to put this book out and further my agenda of putting comics into the hands of the general public.

Coincidentally, while I was working on this book, I had a missed connection of my own. After a concert at Bottom of the Hill in San Francisco, I dropped my wallet while getting out of the cab. I didn't even notice it was gone until I received a phone call from the person who had found it. He had gotten my phone number from my optometrist, as I had been carrying my glasses prescription with me and that was the only number in my wallet. We made plans to meet up during his lunch break the following day.

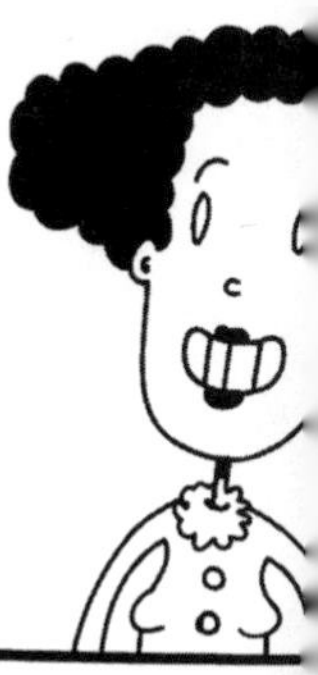

When I arrived, I found an average-looking man who appeared to be around thirty. Our interaction was perfunctory: he handed me the wallet, I said thank you, and we parted ways. But while riding the bus back to my apartment, I realized that he, under no obligation to return the wallet, had not only left everything intact but had taken the time to hunt down my phone number. I wasn't carrying ID with me at the time, so for all he knew, I could have been an eighty-year-old woman instead of a twenty-four-year-old girl. I mean, carrying around a glasses prescription isn't exactly characteristic of a younger woman. Which meant his intentions were nothing beyond simple benevolence.

Later that night, while indulging in the guilty pleasure of perusing Craigslist missed connections, I was surprised to find that my mysterious good Samaritan had left one for me. It was short and simple and read: "To the dark-haired girl who lost her wallet, I returned it to you today and didn't have the courage to ask you out at that time but I would love to take you out to dinner." This part of the story is where I should have called him back, gone out to dinner, and fallen in love. That's how these things go, right?

However, I did not call him back. Not because I didn't want to go out with him, but because I simply chickened out and by the time I resolved to contact him, the ad had expired. And, as I assume happens with these things, I eventually forgot about it.

But now, two years later, I am twenty-six and living in New York, which has a notorious reputation for being hard on single women. It seems the larger a city, the lonelier its occupants. And I'm pretty sure no one in New York would return a lost wallet. So, anonymous man from San Francisco, if you're reading this, I just want to say thank you, and when I return to my hometown, I'd like to take you out to dinner.

Julia Wertz

PART I.

JUST ONE MORE CHANCE . . .

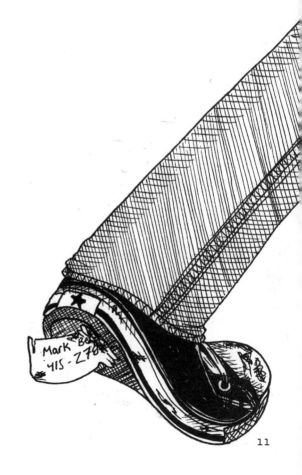

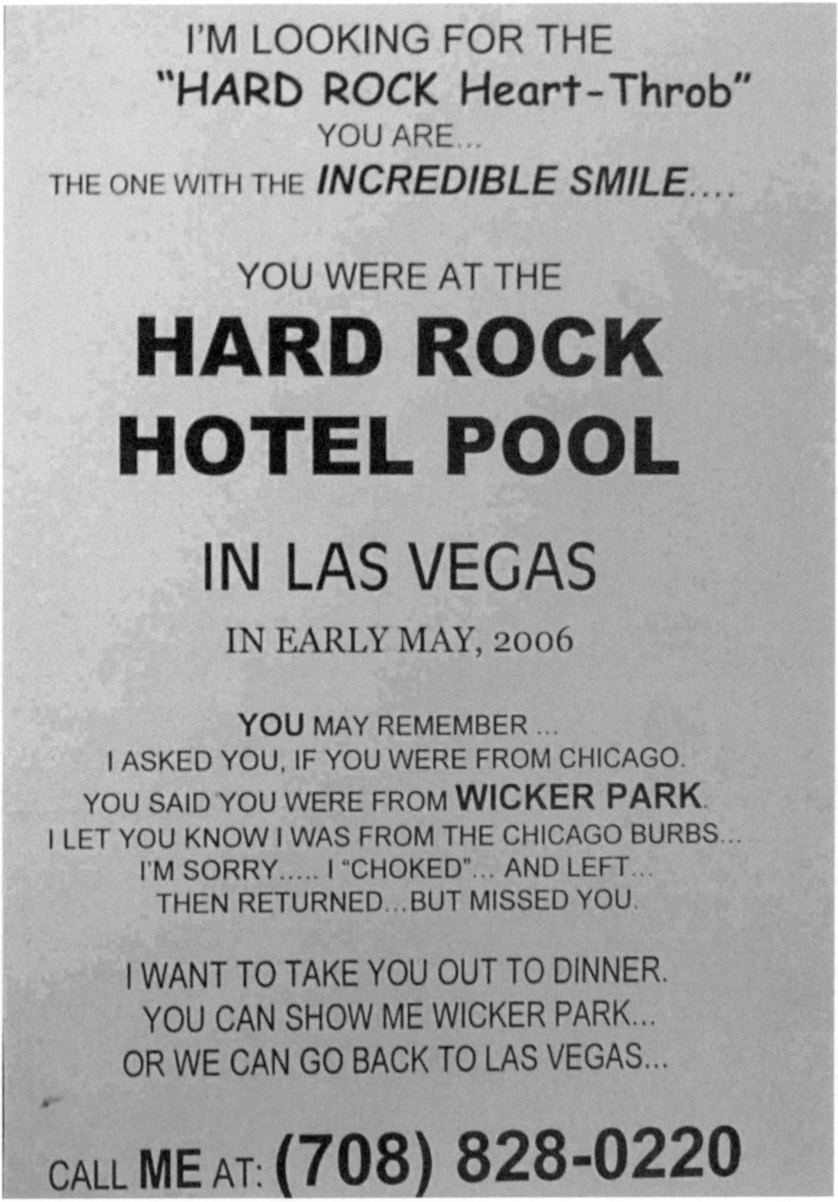
I'M LOOKING FOR THE
"HARD ROCK Heart-Throb"
YOU ARE...
THE ONE WITH THE INCREDIBLE SMILE....
YOU WERE AT THE
HARD ROCK
HOTEL POOL
IN LAS VEGAS
IN EARLY MAY, 2006
YOU MAY REMEMBER ...
I ASKED YOU, IF YOU WERE FROM CHICAGO.
YOU SAID YOU WERE FROM WICKER PARK.
I LET YOU KNOW I WAS FROM THE CHICAGO BURBS...
I'M SORRY..... I "CHOKED"... AND LEFT...
THEN RETURNED...BUT MISSED YOU.
I WANT TO TAKE YOU OUT TO DINNER.
YOU CAN SHOW ME WICKER PARK...
OR WE CAN GO BACK TO LAS VEGAS...
CALL ME AT: (708) 828-0220

by **Lucy Knisley**

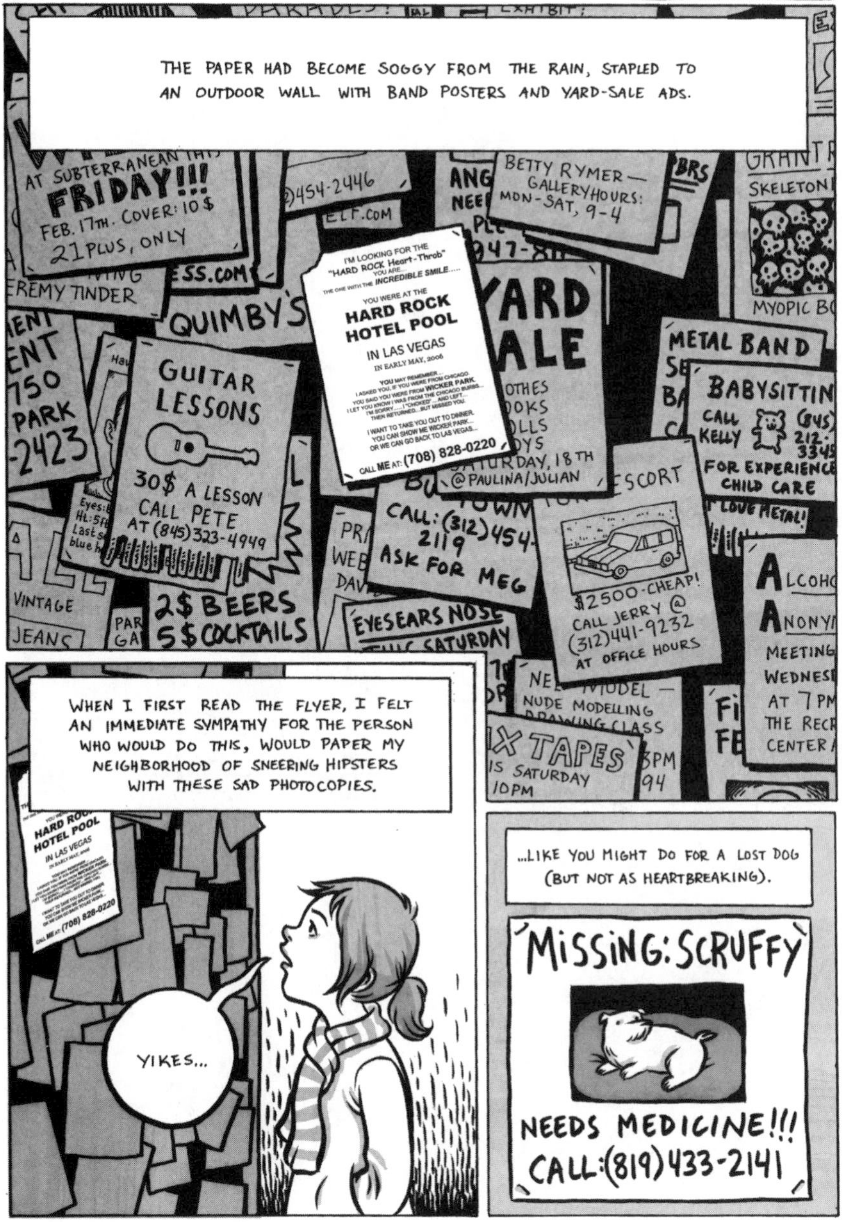
THE PAPER HAD BECOME SOGGY FROM THE RAIN, STAPLED TO AN OUTDOOR WALL WITH BAND POSTERS AND YARD-SALE ADS.
I'M LOOKING FOR THE "HARD ROCK Heart-Throb" YOU ARE... THE ONE WITH THE INCREDIBLE SMILE.....
YOU WERE AT THE HARD ROCK HOTEL POOL IN LAS VEGAS IN EARLY MAY, 2006
YOU MAY REMEMBER... I ASKED YOU, IF YOU WERE FROM CHICAGO. YOU SAID YOU WERE FROM WICKER PARK. I LET YOU KNOW I WAS FROM THE CHICAGO BURBS... I'M SORRY..... I "CHOKED" ... AND LEFT... THEN RETURNED... BUT MISSED YOU.
I WANT TO TAKE YOU OUT TO DINNER. YOU CAN SHOW ME WICKER PARK... OR WE CAN GO BACK TO LAS VEGAS...
CALL ME AT: (708) 828-0220
AT SUBTERRANEAN FRIDAY!!! FEB. 17TH. COVER: 10$ 21 PLUS, ONLY
BETTY RYMER — GALLERY HOURS: MON-SAT, 9-4
GUITAR LESSONS 30$ A LESSON CALL PETE AT (845) 323-4949
YARD SALE CLOTHES BOOKS DOLLS TOYS SATURDAY, 18TH @ PAULINA/JULIAN
METAL BAND
BABYSITTIN CALL KELLY (GUS) FOR EXPERIENCED CHILD CARE
CALL: (312) 454-2119 ASK FOR MEG
ESCORT $2500-CHEAP! CALL JERRY @ (312) 441-9232 AT OFFICE HOURS
2$ BEERS 5$ COCKTAILS
EYES EARS NOSE THIS SATURDAY
NUDE MODELLING DRAWING CLASS
ALCOHOLICS ANONYMOUS MEETING WEDNESDAY AT 7PM THE REC CENTER
WHEN I FIRST READ THE FLYER, I FELT AN IMMEDIATE SYMPATHY FOR THE PERSON WHO WOULD DO THIS, WOULD PAPER MY NEIGHBORHOOD OF SNEERING HIPSTERS WITH THESE SAD PHOTOCOPIES.
YIKES...
...LIKE YOU MIGHT DO FOR A LOST DOG (BUT NOT AS HEARTBREAKING).
MISSING: SCRUFFY
NEEDS MEDICINE!!! CALL: (819) 433-2141

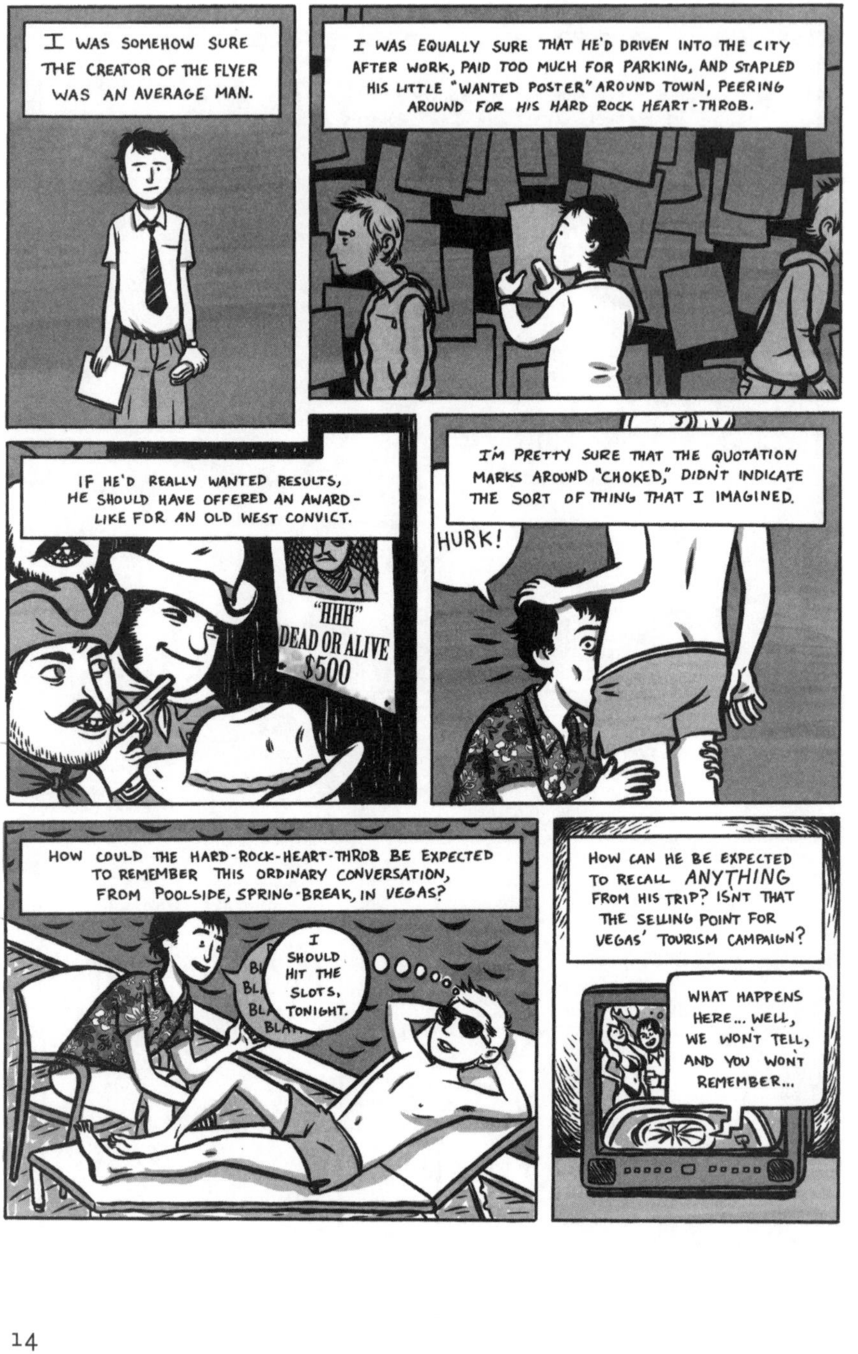

I WAS SOMEHOW SURE THE CREATOR OF THE FLYER WAS AN AVERAGE MAN.
I WAS EQUALLY SURE THAT HE'D DRIVEN INTO THE CITY AFTER WORK, PAID TOO MUCH FOR PARKING, AND STAPLED HIS LITTLE "WANTED POSTER" AROUND TOWN, PEERING AROUND FOR HIS HARD ROCK HEART-THROB.
IF HE'D REALLY WANTED RESULTS, HE SHOULD HAVE OFFERED AN AWARD-LIKE FOR AN OLD WEST CONVICT.
"HHH"
DEAD OR ALIVE
$500
I'M PRETTY SURE THAT THE QUOTATION MARKS AROUND "CHOKED," DIDN'T INDICATE THE SORT OF THING THAT I IMAGINED.
HURK!
HOW COULD THE HARD-ROCK-HEART-THROB BE EXPECTED TO REMEMBER THIS ORDINARY CONVERSATION, FROM POOLSIDE, SPRING-BREAK, IN VEGAS?
I SHOULD HIT THE SLOTS, TONIGHT.
HOW CAN HE BE EXPECTED TO RECALL ANYTHING FROM HIS TRIP? ISN'T THAT THE SELLING POINT FOR VEGAS' TOURISM CAMPAIGN?
WHAT HAPPENS HERE... WELL, WE WON'T TELL, AND YOU WON'T REMEMBER...

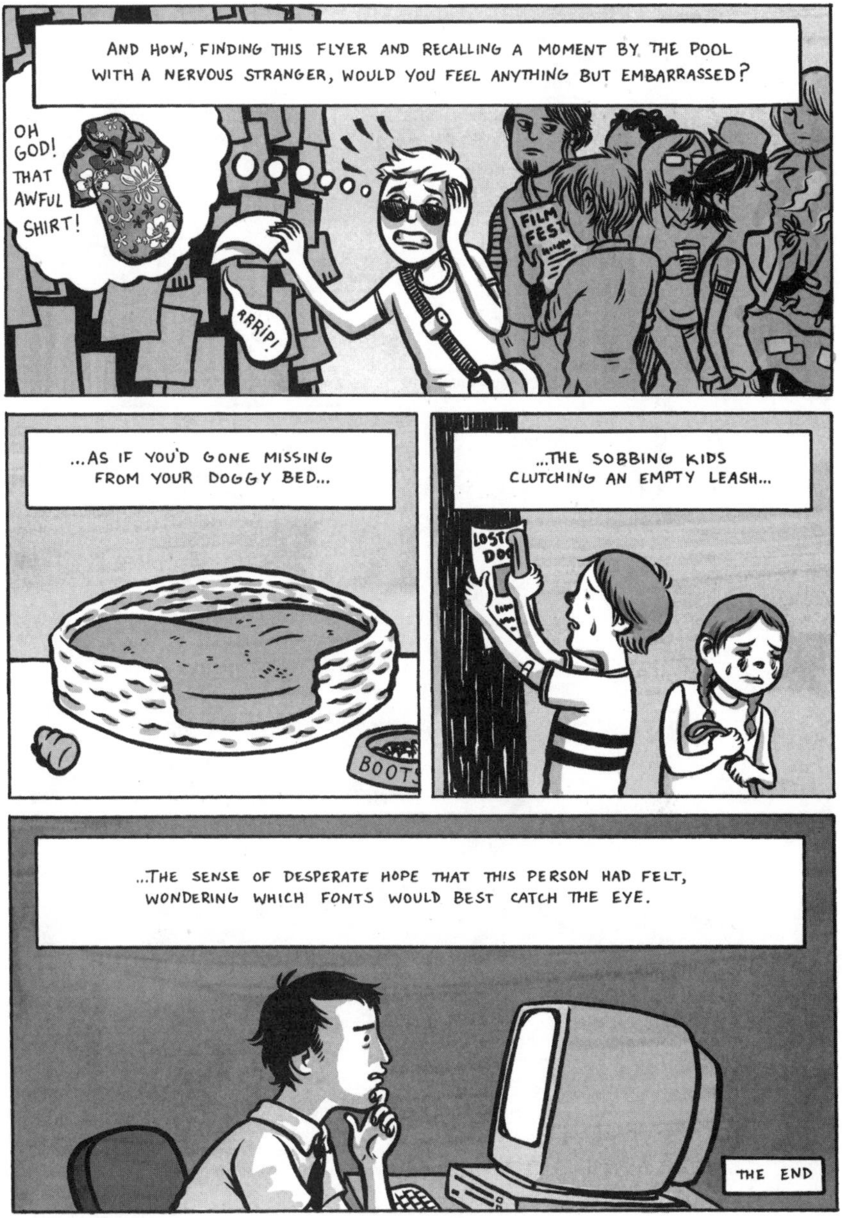
AND HOW, FINDING THIS FLYER AND RECALLING A MOMENT BY THE POOL WITH A NERVOUS STRANGER, WOULD YOU FEEL ANYTHING BUT EMBARRASSED?
OH GOD! THAT AWFUL SHIRT!
ARRIP!
FILM FEST
...AS IF YOU'D GONE MISSING FROM YOUR DOGGY BED...
BOOTS
...THE SOBBING KIDS CLUTCHING AN EMPTY LEASH...
LOST DOG
...THE SENSE OF DESPERATE HOPE THAT THIS PERSON HAD FELT, WONDERING WHICH FONTS WOULD BEST CATCH THE EYE.
THE END

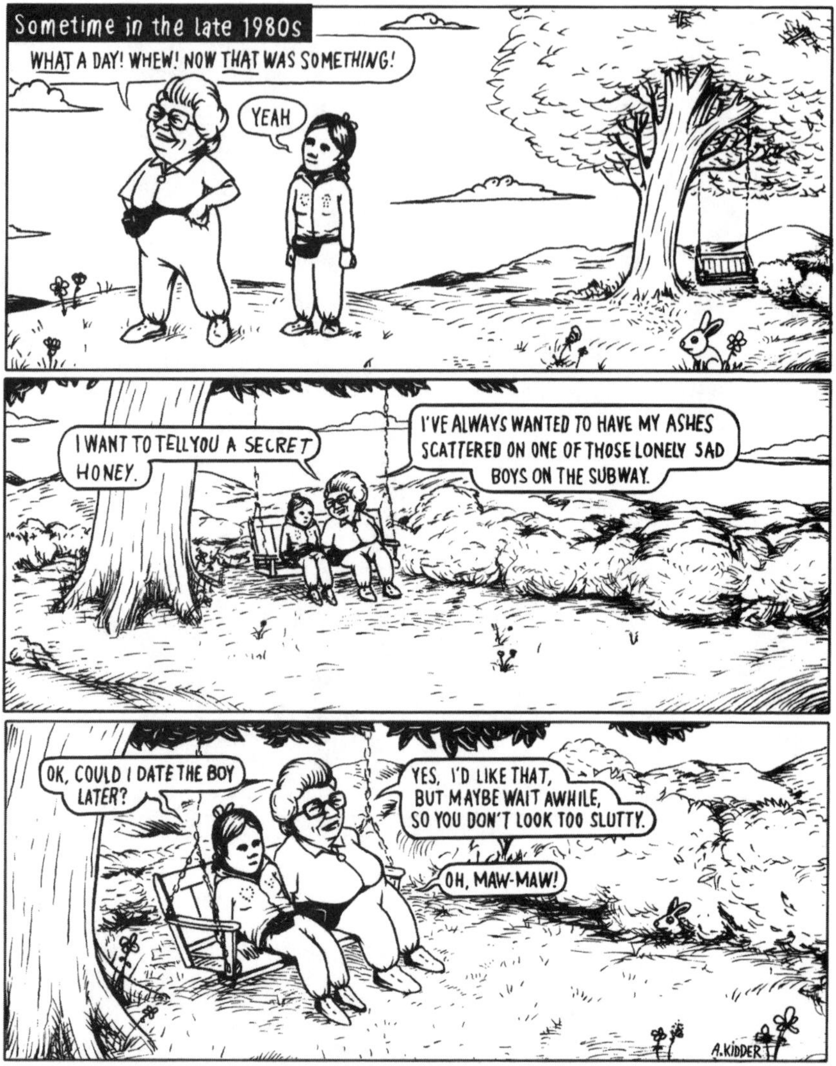
Sometime in the late 1980s
WHAT A DAY! WHEW! NOW THAT WAS SOMETHING!
YEAH
I WANT TO TELL YOU A SECRET HONEY.
I'VE ALWAYS WANTED TO HAVE MY ASHES SCATTERED ON ONE OF THOSE LONELY SAD BOYS ON THE SUBWAY.
OK, COULD I DATE THE BOY LATER?
YES, I'D LIKE THAT, BUT MAYBE WAIT AWHILE, SO YOU DON'T LOOK TOO SLUTTY.
OH, MAW-MAW!
A. KIDDER

—YEARS LATER⟶ I spilled grandma on you around spadian station - w4m

You: unsuspecting lonley sad looking boy on subway

Me: Girl with blue Urn

I spilled my grandmother on you, im sure you remember, If you see this we should do lunch ...this time without grandma

by **Adam Kidder**

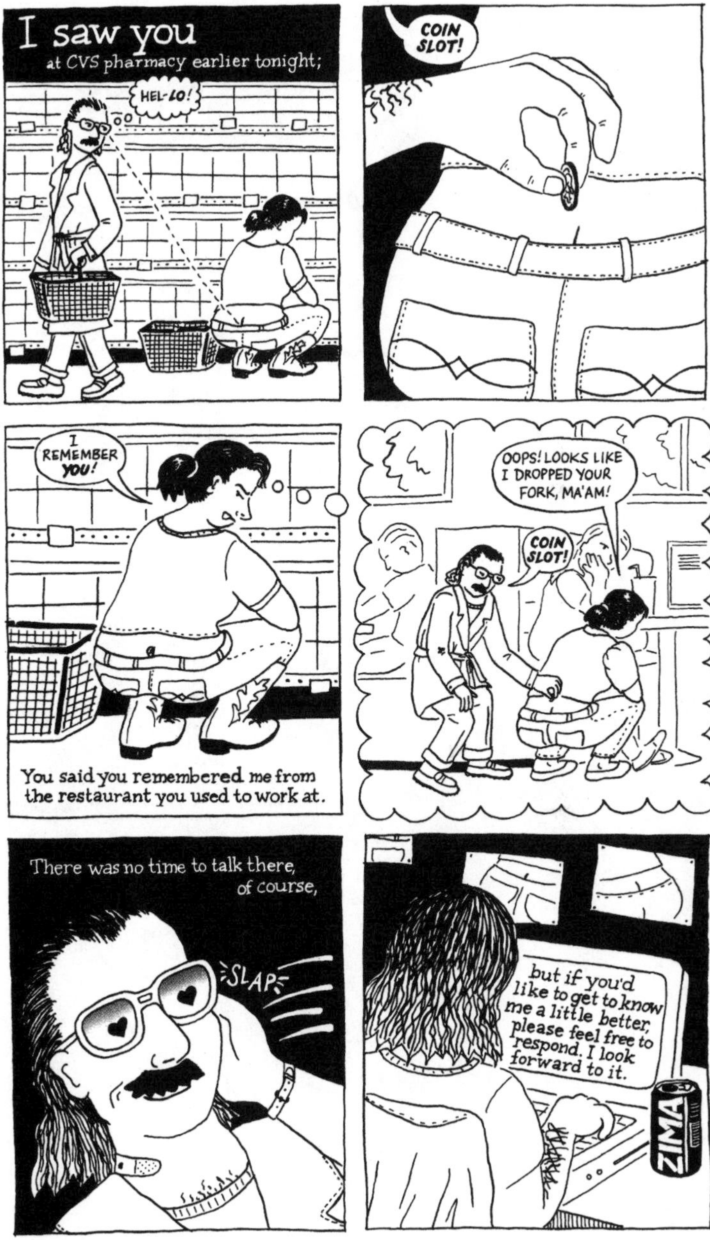

I saw you
at CVS pharmacy earlier tonight;
HEL-LO!
COIN SLOT!
I REMEMBER YOU!
You said you remembered me from the restaurant you used to work at.
OOPS! LOOKS LIKE I DROPPED YOUR FORK, MA'AM!
COIN SLOT!
There was no time to talk there, of course,
SLAP
but if you'd like to get to know me a little better, please feel free to respond. I look forward to it.
ZIMA

by **Minty Lewis**

hello there Doctor Love,

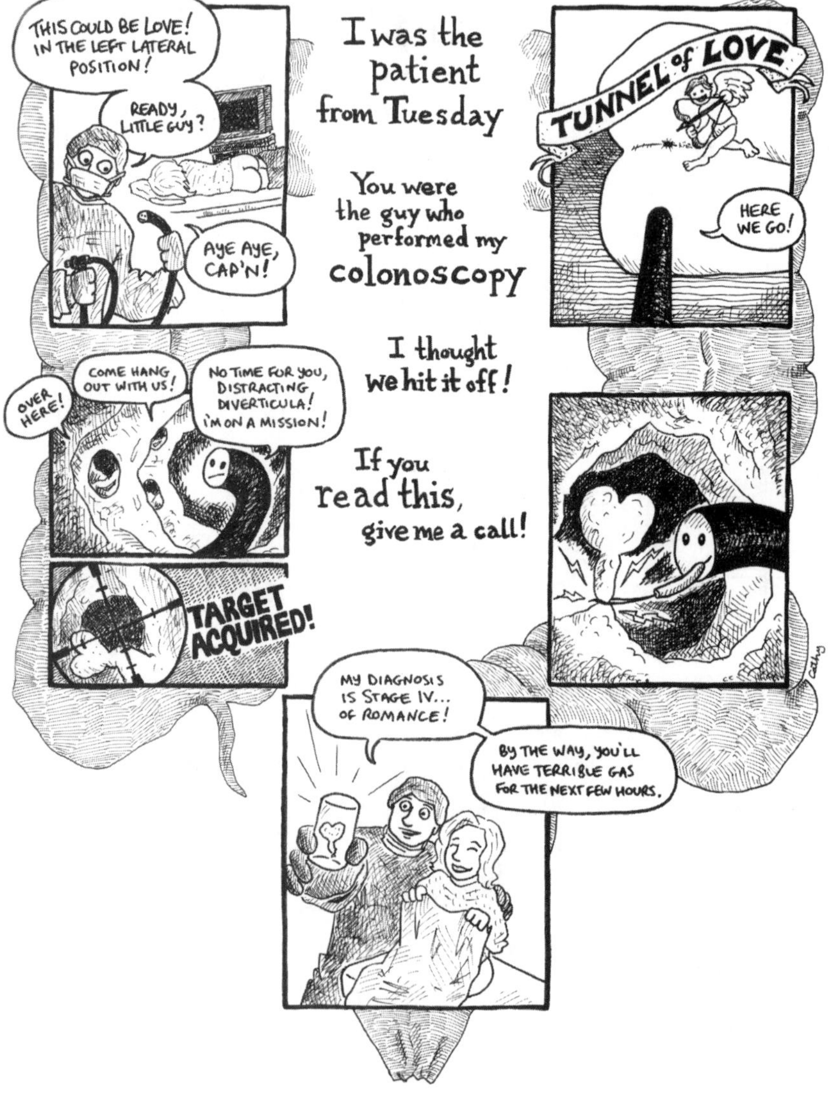
THIS COULD BE LOVE! IN THE LEFT LATERAL POSITION!
READY, LITTLE GUY?
AYE AYE, CAP'N!
I was the patient from Tuesday
TUNNEL of LOVE
HERE WE GO!
You were the guy who performed my colonoscopy
OVER HERE!
COME HANG OUT WITH US!
NO TIME FOR YOU, DISTRACTING DIVERTICULA! I'M ON A MISSION!
I thought we hit it off!
TARGET ACQUIRED!
If you read this, give me a call!
MY DIAGNOSIS IS STAGE IV... OF ROMANCE!
BY THE WAY, YOU'LL HAVE TERRIBLE GAS FOR THE NEXT FEW HOURS.

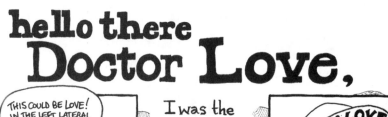

by **Cathy Leamy**

I JUST HAD TO TELL YOU

a heartfelt story from a 29-year-old male

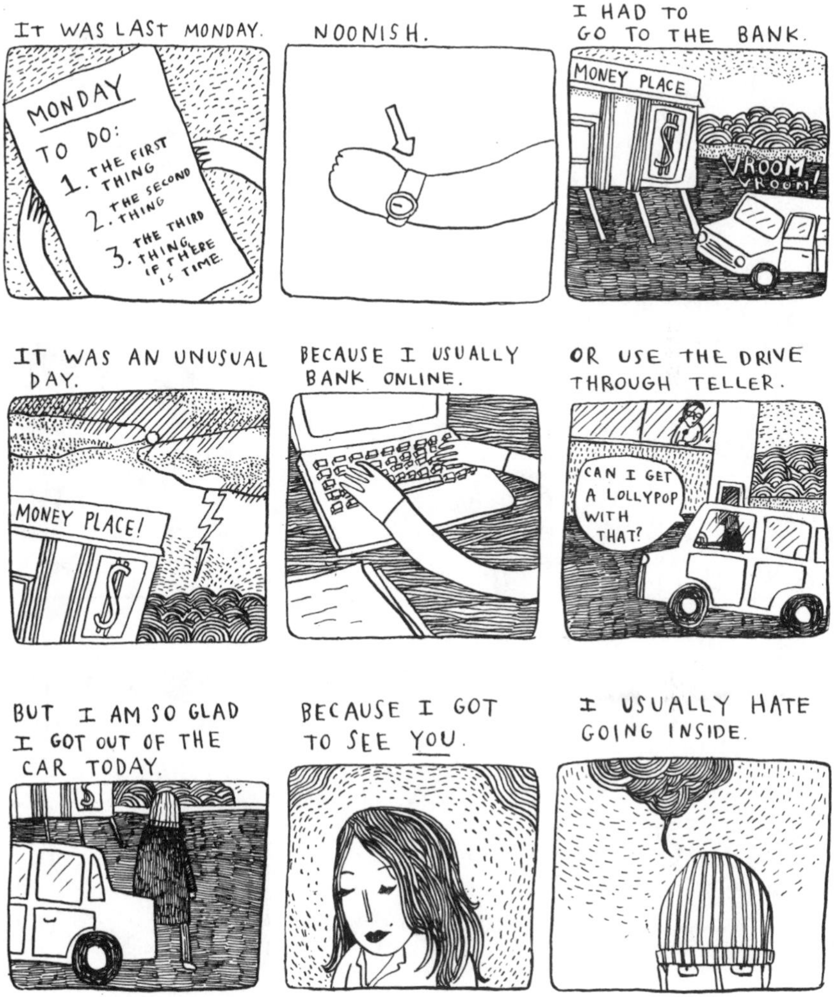
IT WAS LAST MONDAY.
MONDAY
TO DO:
1. THE FIRST THING
2. THE SECOND THING
3. THE THIRD THING IF THERE IS TIME.
NOONISH.
I HAD TO GO TO THE BANK.
MONEY PLACE
VROOM VROOM!
IT WAS AN UNUSUAL DAY.
MONEY PLACE!
BECAUSE I USUALLY BANK ONLINE.
OR USE THE DRIVE THROUGH TELLER.
CAN I GET A LOLLYPOP WITH THAT?
BUT I AM SO GLAD I GOT OUT OF THE CAR TODAY.
BECAUSE I GOT TO SEE YOU.
I USUALLY HATE GOING INSIDE.

by **Corinne Mucha**

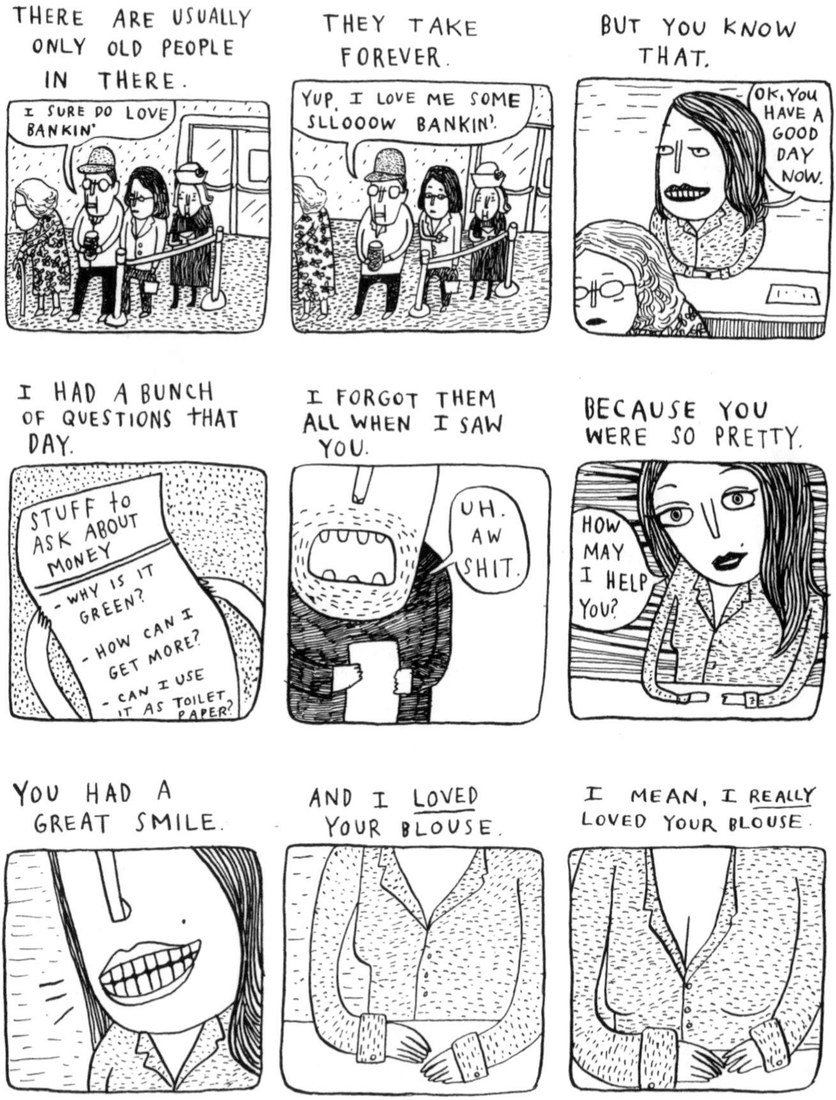
THERE ARE USUALLY ONLY OLD PEOPLE IN THERE.
I SURE DO LOVE BANKIN'
THEY TAKE FOREVER.
YUP, I LOVE ME SOME SLLOOOW BANKIN'.
BUT YOU KNOW THAT.
OK, YOU HAVE A GOOD DAY NOW.
I HAD A BUNCH OF QUESTIONS THAT DAY.
STUFF to ASK ABOUT MONEY
- WHY IS IT GREEN?
- HOW CAN I GET MORE?
- CAN I USE IT AS TOILET PAPER?
I FORGOT THEM ALL WHEN I SAW YOU.
UH. AW SHIT.
BECAUSE YOU WERE SO PRETTY.
HOW MAY I HELP YOU?
YOU HAD A GREAT SMILE.
AND I LOVED YOUR BLOUSE.
I MEAN, I REALLY LOVED YOUR BLOUSE.

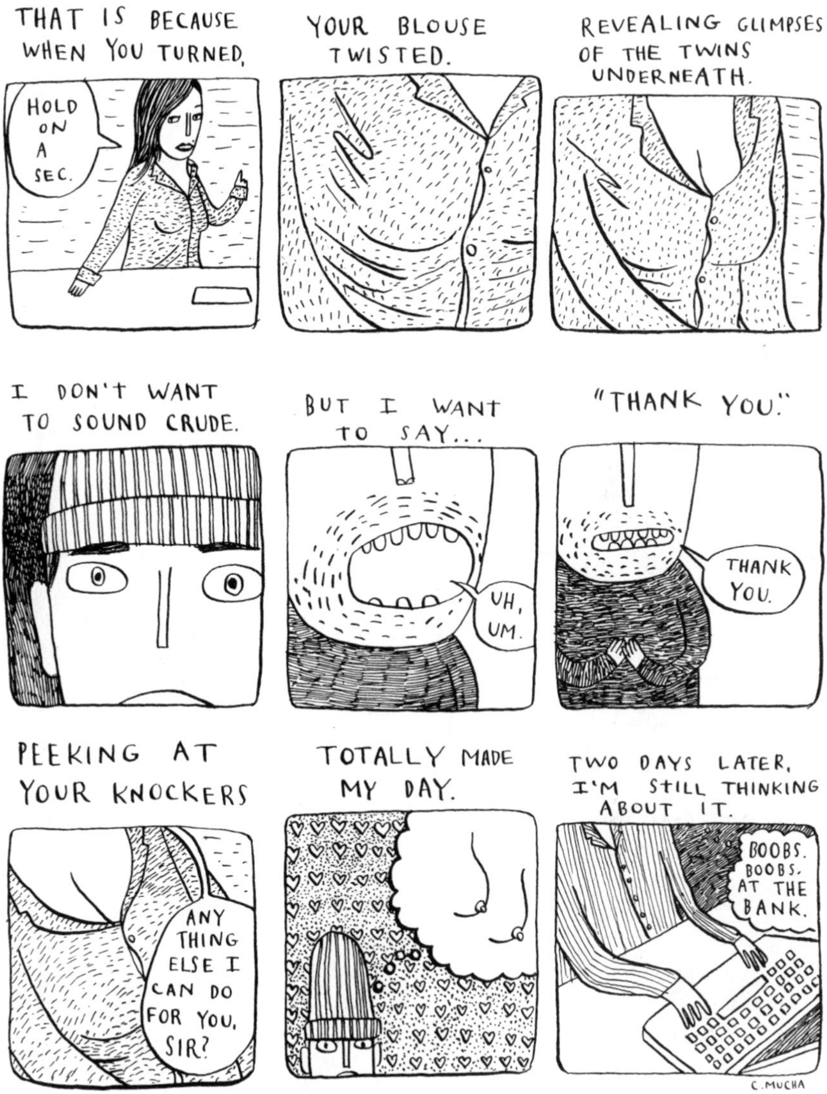
THAT IS BECAUSE WHEN YOU TURNED,
HOLD ON A SEC.
YOUR BLOUSE TWISTED.
REVEALING GLIMPSES OF THE TWINS UNDERNEATH.
I DON'T WANT TO SOUND CRUDE.
BUT I WANT TO SAY...
UH, UM.
"THANK YOU."
THANK YOU.
PEEKING AT YOUR KNOCKERS
ANY THING ELSE I CAN DO FOR YOU, SIR?
TOTALLY MADE MY DAY.
TWO DAYS LATER, I'M STILL THINKING ABOUT IT.
BOOBS. BOOBS. AT THE BANK.
C. MUCHA

Whitmore Ave

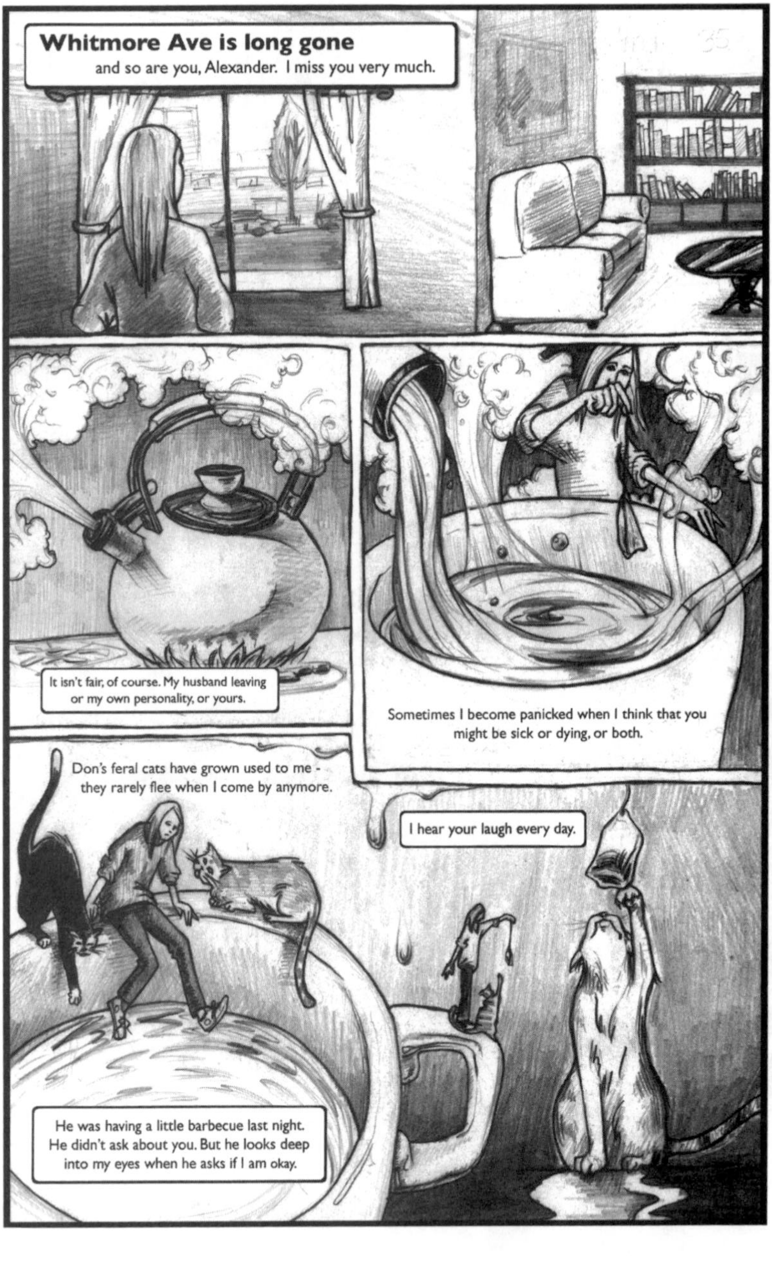

Whitmore Ave is long gone
and so are you, Alexander. I miss you very much.
It isn't fair, of course. My husband leaving or my own personality, or yours.
Sometimes I become panicked when I think that you might be sick or dying, or both.
Don's feral cats have grown used to me - they rarely flee when I come by anymore.
I hear your laugh every day.
He was having a little barbecue last night. He didn't ask about you. But he looks deep into my eyes when he asks if I am okay.

by **Maria Sequeira**

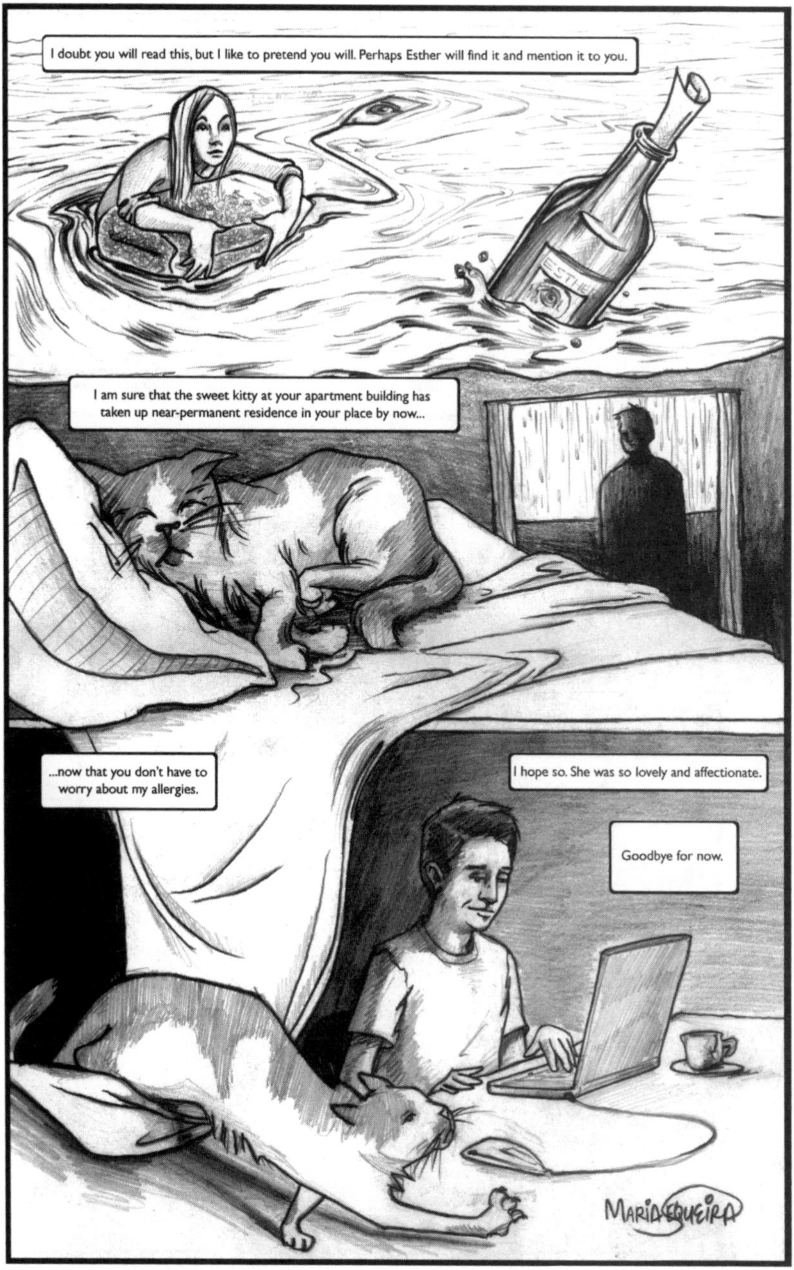
I doubt you will read this, but I like to pretend you will. Perhaps Esther will find it and mention it to you.
ESTHER
I am sure that the sweet kitty at your apartment building has taken up near-permanent residence in your place by now...
...now that you don't have to worry about my allergies.
I hope so. She was so lovely and affectionate.
Goodbye for now.
MARIA SEQUEIRA

m4m- "Hi" Again... (Castro/ Upper Market)

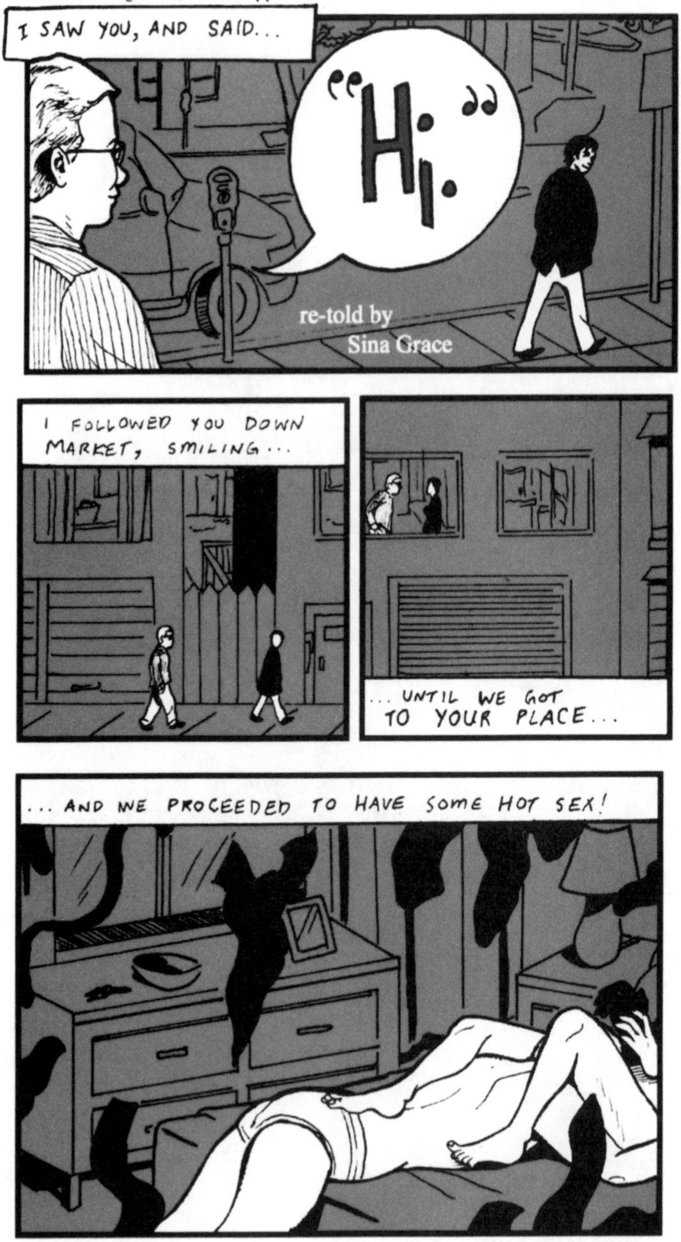
I SAW YOU, AND SAID...
"Hi."
re-told by Sina Grace
I FOLLOWED YOU DOWN MARKET, SMILING...
... UNTIL WE GOT TO YOUR PLACE...
... AND WE PROCEEDED TO HAVE SOME HOT SEX!

by **Sina Grace**

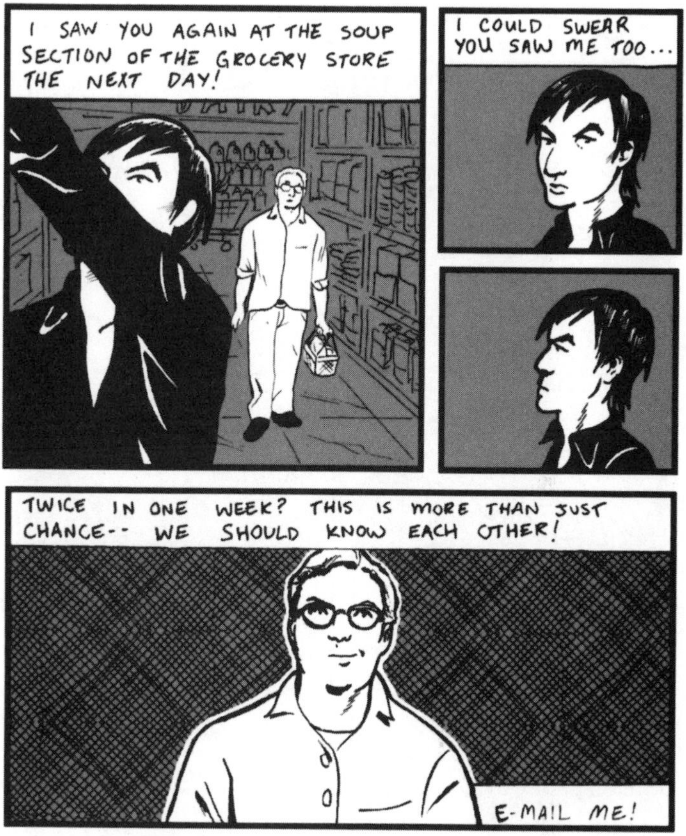
I SAW YOU AGAIN AT THE SOUP SECTION OF THE GROCERY STORE THE NEXT DAY!
I COULD SWEAR YOU SAW ME TOO...
TWICE IN ONE WEEK? THIS IS MORE THAN JUST CHANCE-- WE SHOULD KNOW EACH OTHER!
E-MAIL ME!

it's NOT ok to contact this poster with services or other commercial interests.

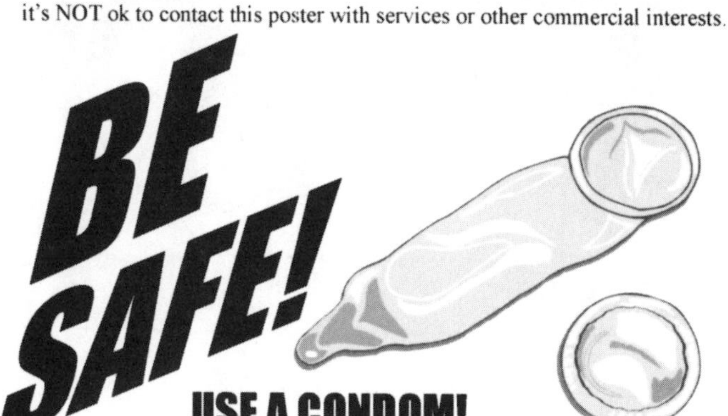
BE SAFE!
USE A CONDOM!

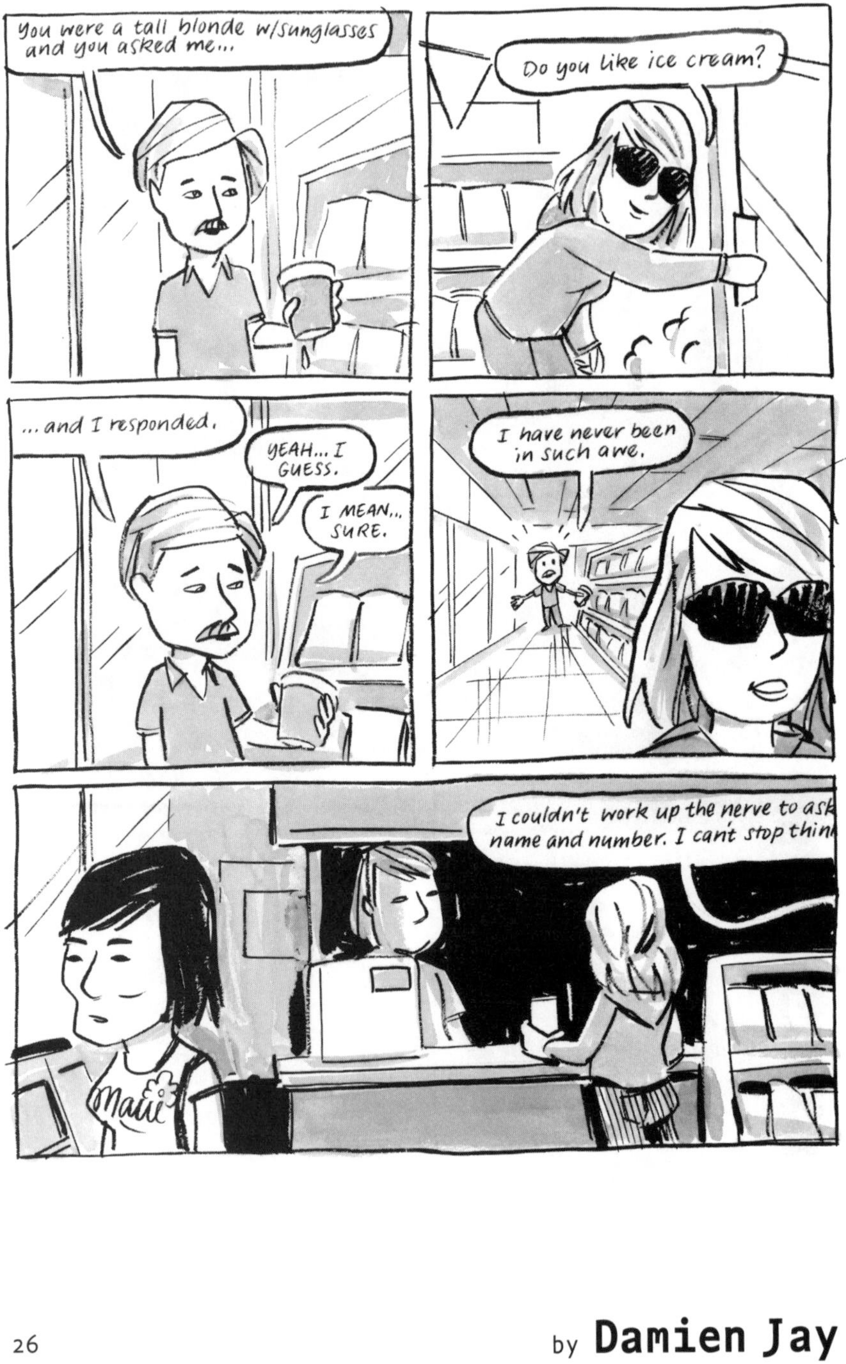
You were a tall blonde w/sunglasses and you asked me...
Do you like ice cream?
... and I responded.
YEAH... I GUESS.
I MEAN... SURE.
I have never been in such awe.
I couldn't work up the nerve to ask
name and number. I can't stop think

by **Damien Jay**

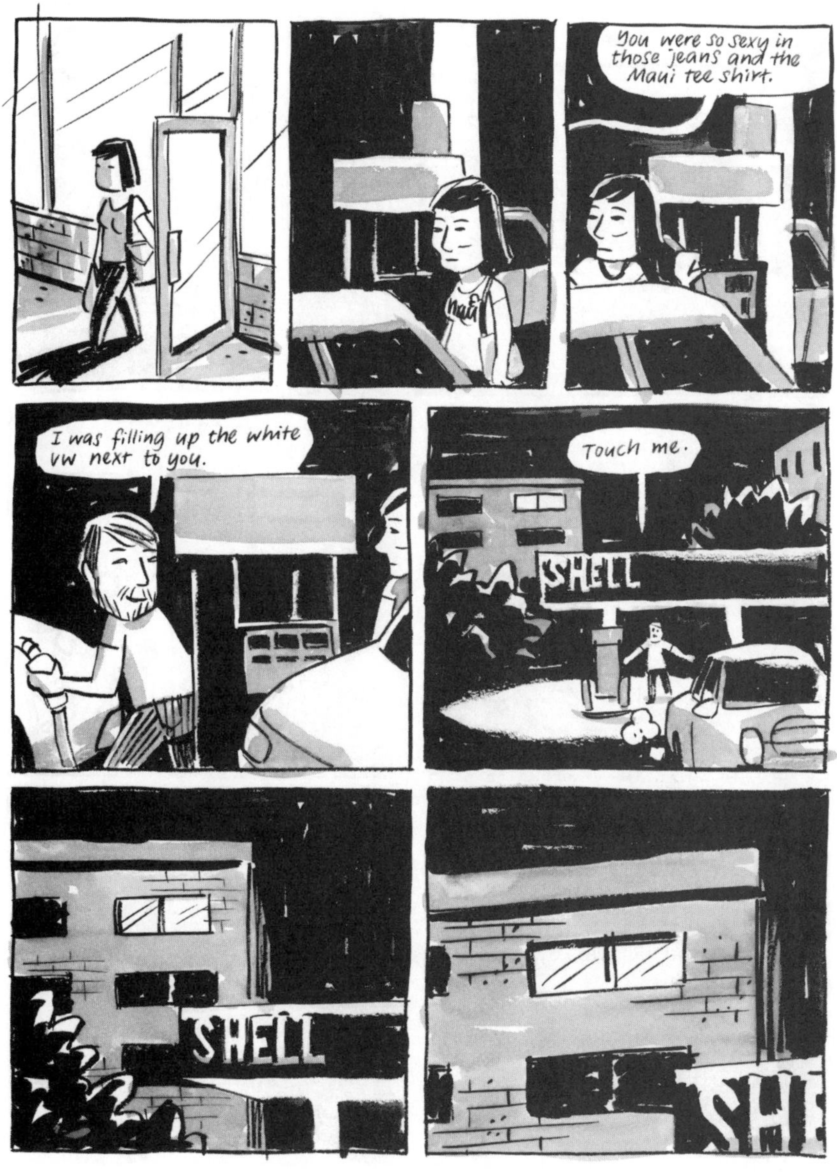
You were so sexy in those jeans and the Maui tee shirt.
I was filling up the white VW next to you.
Touch me.
SHELL
SHELL
SHE

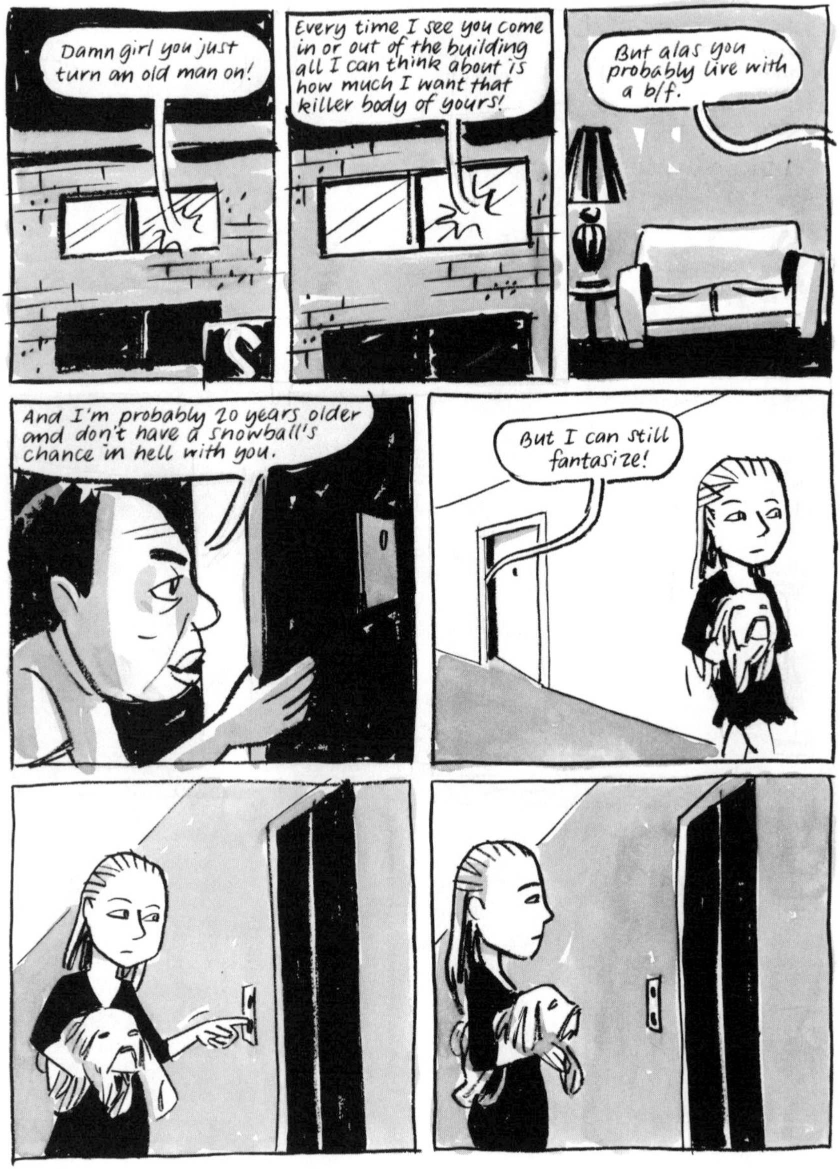
Damn girl you just turn an old man on!
Every time I see you come in or out of the building all I can think about is how much I want that killer body of yours!
But alas you probably live with a b/f.
And I'm probably 20 years older and don't have a snowball's chance in hell with you.
But I can still fantasize!

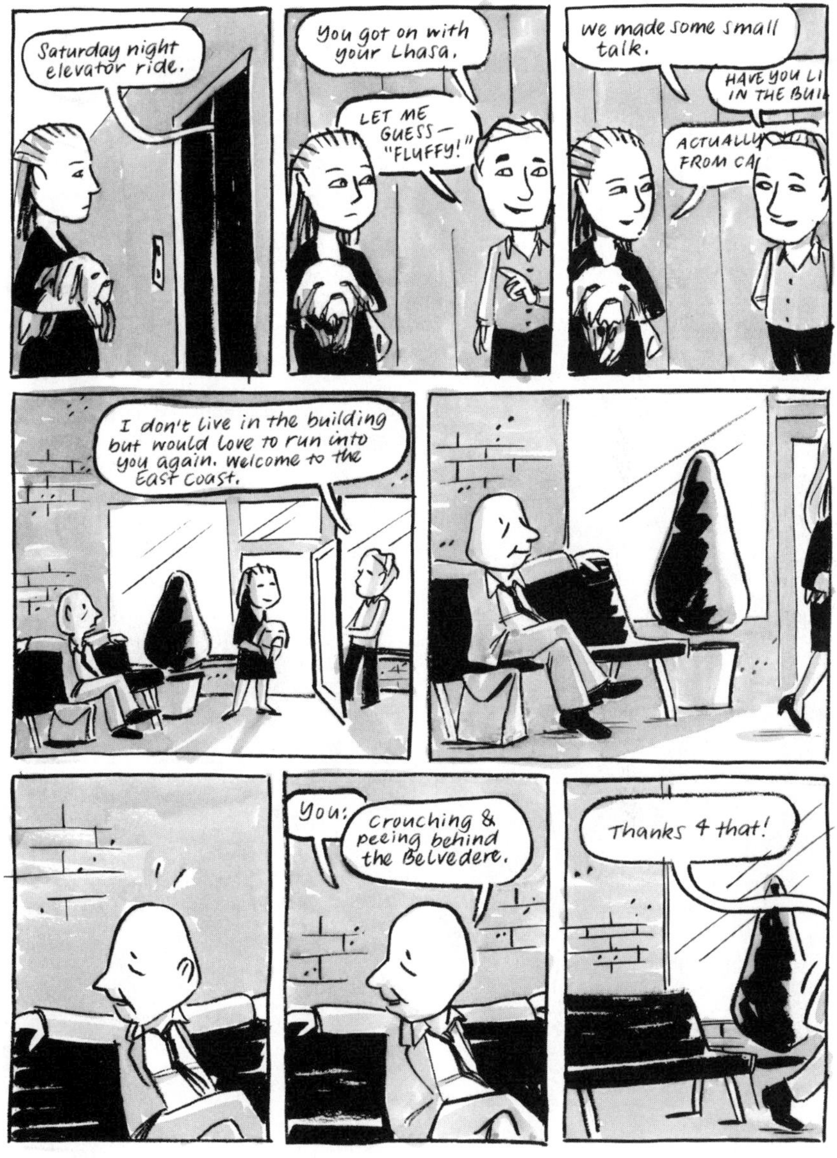
Saturday night elevator ride.
You got on with your Lhasa.
LET ME GUESS— "FLUFFY!"
We made some small talk.
HAVE YOU LI
IN THE BUI
ACTUALLY
FROM CA
I don't live in the building but would love to run into you again. Welcome to the East Coast.
You:
Crouching & peeing behind the Belvedere.
Thanks 4 that!

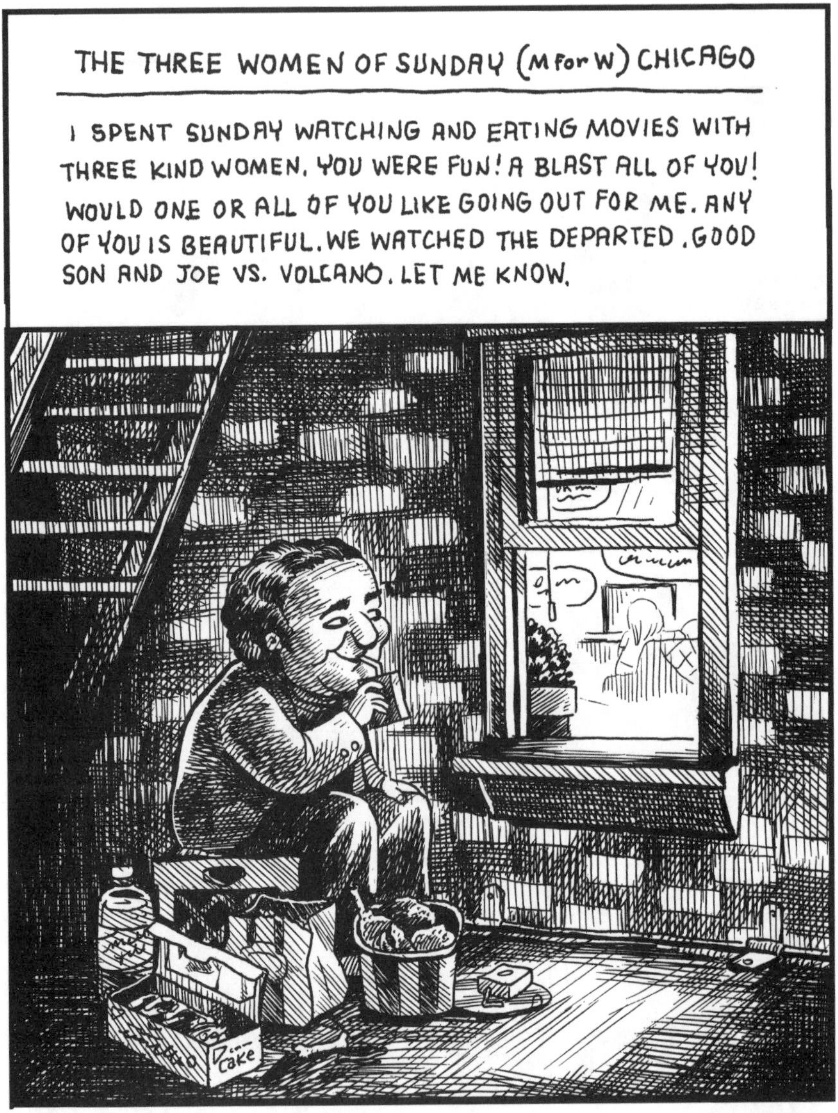
THE THREE WOMEN OF SUNDAY (M for W) CHICAGO
I SPENT SUNDAY WATCHING AND EATING MOVIES WITH THREE KIND WOMEN. YOU WERE FUN! A BLAST ALL OF YOU! WOULD ONE OR ALL OF YOU LIKE GOING OUT FOR ME. ANY OF YOU IS BEAUTIFUL. WE WATCHED THE DEPARTED. GOOD SON AND JOE VS. VOLCANO. LET ME KNOW.

by **Laura Park**

MAY 20, 1987
WHEELER'S
SHE WAS A GORGEOUS SKINNY BLONDE, WITH BIG BROWN EYES + AMAZING HAIR
CELEBRATING HER 38TH BIRTHDAY WITH FRIENDS AT THE LOCAL DIVE BAR
YOUR FACE HERE
DURAN DURAN
YOU WERE ABOUT 25 YEARS OLD...
THE CHEMISTRY WAS WILD...
HER NAME WAS RIO
AND YOUR ANTICS ON THE DANCEFLOOR
GET A ROOM!
SOON GOT THE CROWDS TALKING
SHE TOOK YOU HOME
AND PRETENDED TO BE ASLEEP THE NEXT MORNING WHEN YOU LEFT. SOUND FAMILIAR?
THERE ARE A FEW KEY PIECES
TO THE PUZZLE THAT ONLY MY REAL DAD WOULD KNOW
SO IF YOU ARE THE REAL DEAL
CALL ME NOW!
ARCH

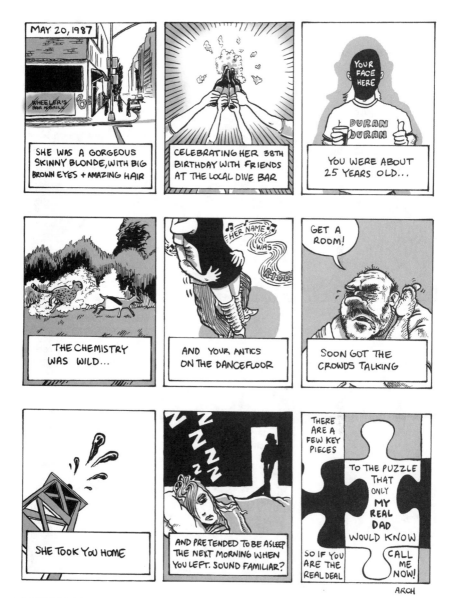

by **Dan Archer**

you had sideburns and a mullet and a hat with a wild pony on it - w4m

Shaenon K. Garrity

THE MAN THE LEGEND

I'm reposting this because I saw you again recently in our shared yard, painting hooker clothes on religious statues. Here are a few of the things that intrigue me about you:

1. The first time I saw you, you were sitting on a washing machine whistling xmas carols and whittling a piece of wood into the shape of a lady's shoe.

2. Once I saw you wearing sunglasses and balancing a jug on your head.

3. I heard you and your girlfriend arguing over whether there are still bobcats in the wilderness.

4. Also, I heard you tell your roommate you were going to walk across the U.S.A. and never come back.

by Shaenon K. Garrity

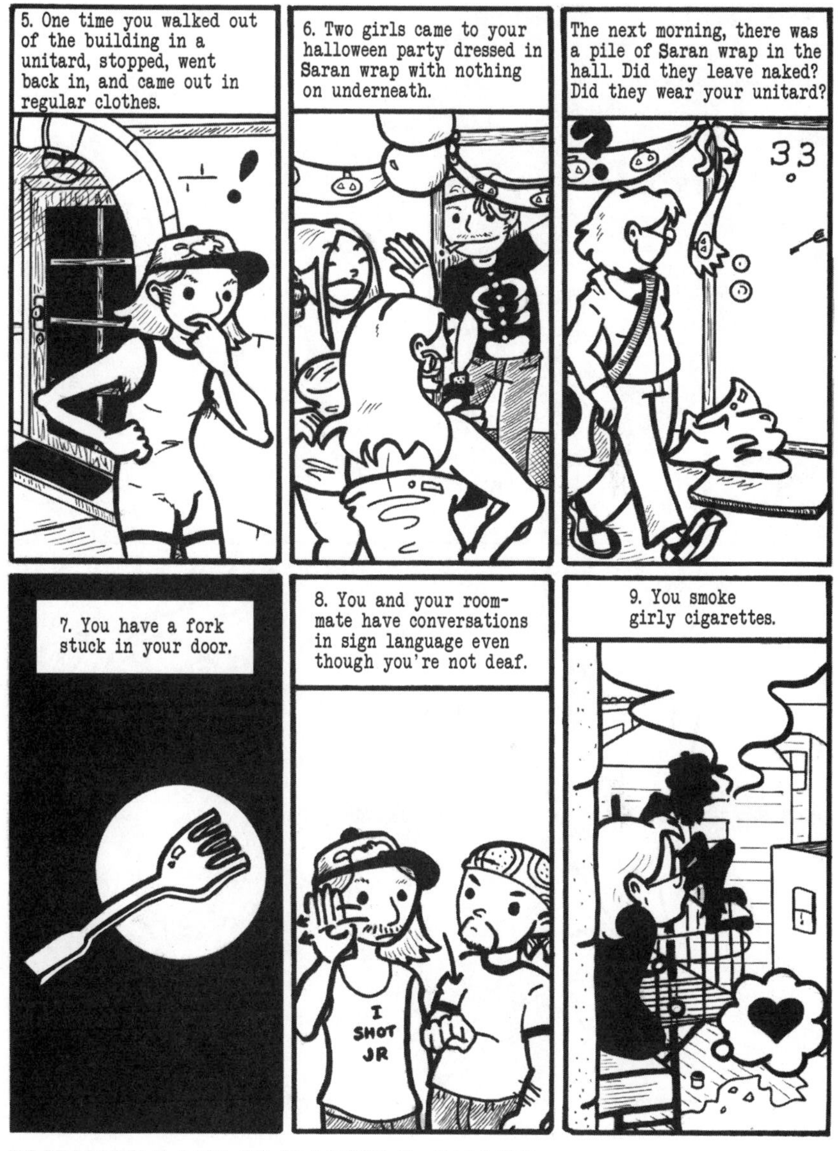
5. One time you walked out of the building in a unitard, stopped, went back in, and came out in regular clothes.
6. Two girls came to your halloween party dressed in Saran wrap with nothing on underneath.
The next morning, there was a pile of Saran wrap in the hall. Did they leave naked? Did they wear your unitard?
33
7. You have a fork stuck in your door.
8. You and your roommate have conversations in sign language even though you're not deaf.
I SHOT JR
9. You smoke girly cigarettes.

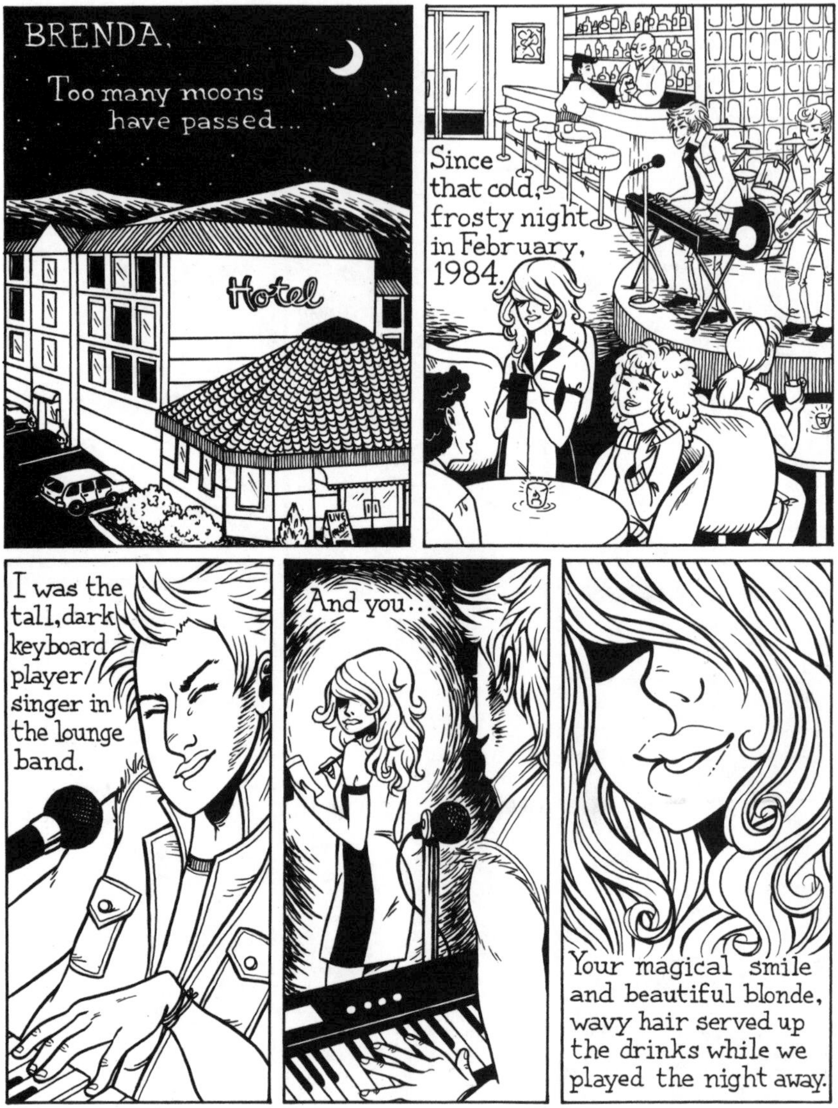
BRENDA,
Too many moons have passed...
Hotel
Since that cold, frosty night in February, 1984.
I was the tall, dark keyboard player/ singer in the lounge band.
And you...
Your magical smile and beautiful blonde, wavy hair served up the drinks while we played the night away.

by **Daniel Barlow and Megan Baehr**

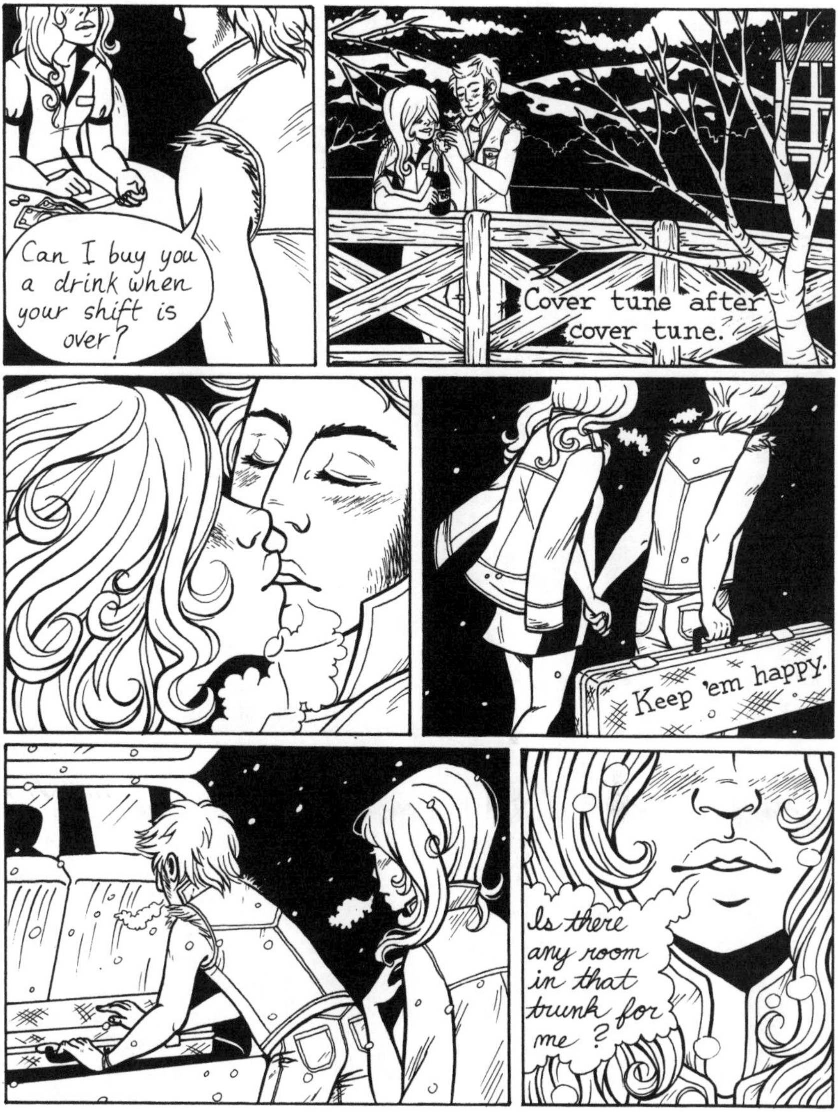
Can I buy you a drink when your shift is over?
Cover tune after cover tune.
Keep 'em happy.
Is there any room in that trunk for me?

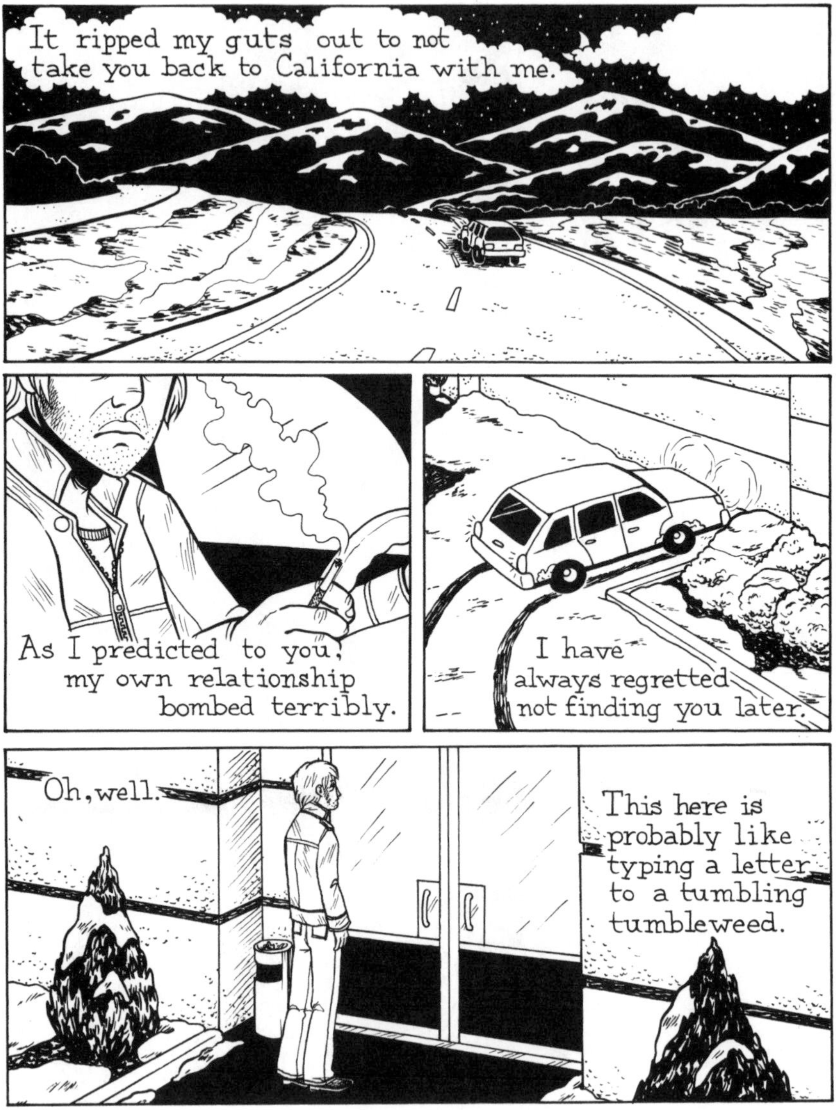
It ripped my guts out to not take you back to California with me.
As I predicted to you, my own relationship bombed terribly.
I have always regretted not finding you later.
Oh, well.
This here is probably like typing a letter to a tumbling tumbleweed.

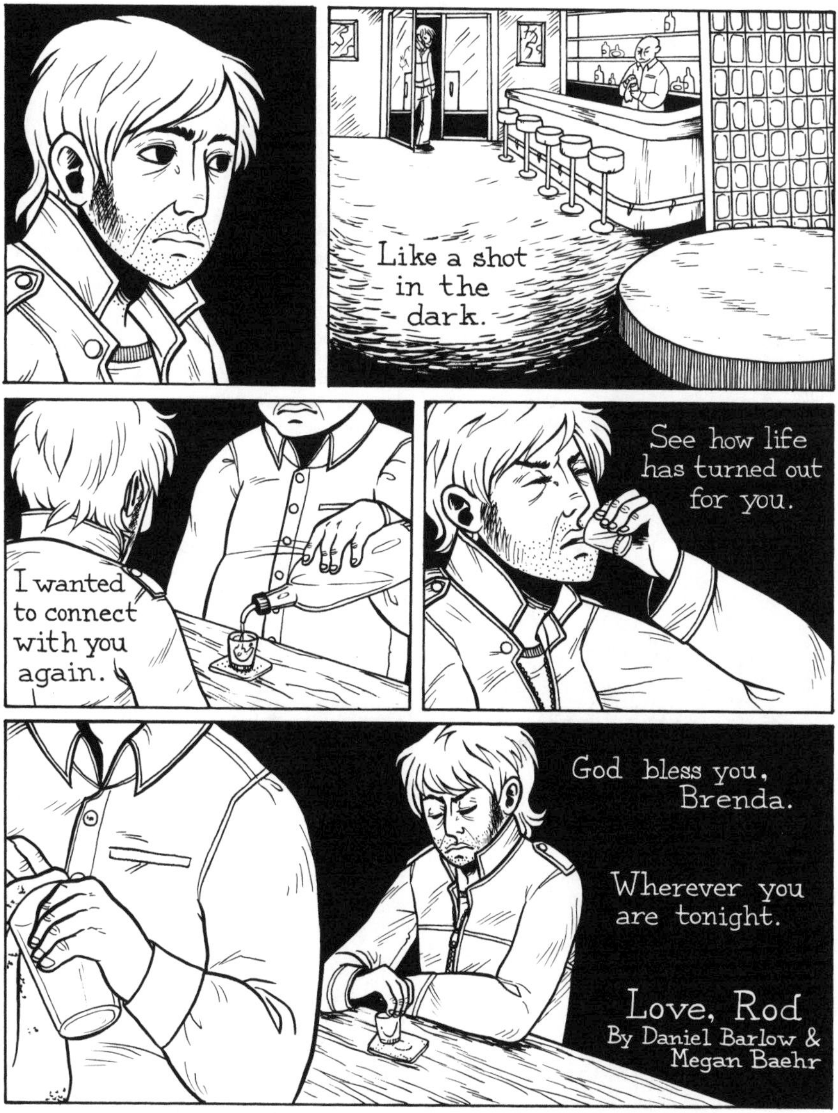
Like a shot in the dark.
I wanted to connect with you again.
See how life has turned out for you.
God bless you, Brenda.
Wherever you are tonight.
Love, Rod
By Daniel Barlow & Megan Baehr

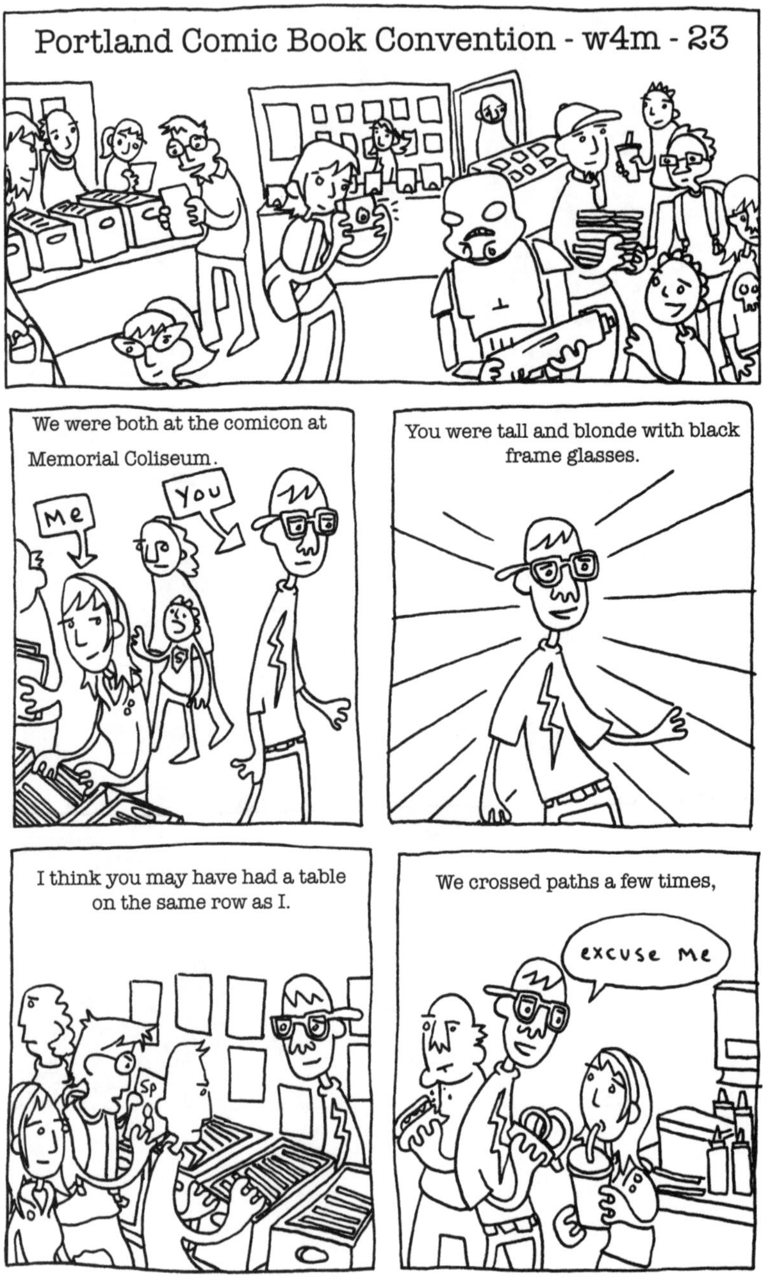
Portland Comic Book Convention - w4m - 23
We were both at the comicon at Memorial Coliseum.
Me
You
You were tall and blonde with black frame glasses.
I think you may have had a table on the same row as I.
We crossed paths a few times,
excuse me

by **Greg Means**

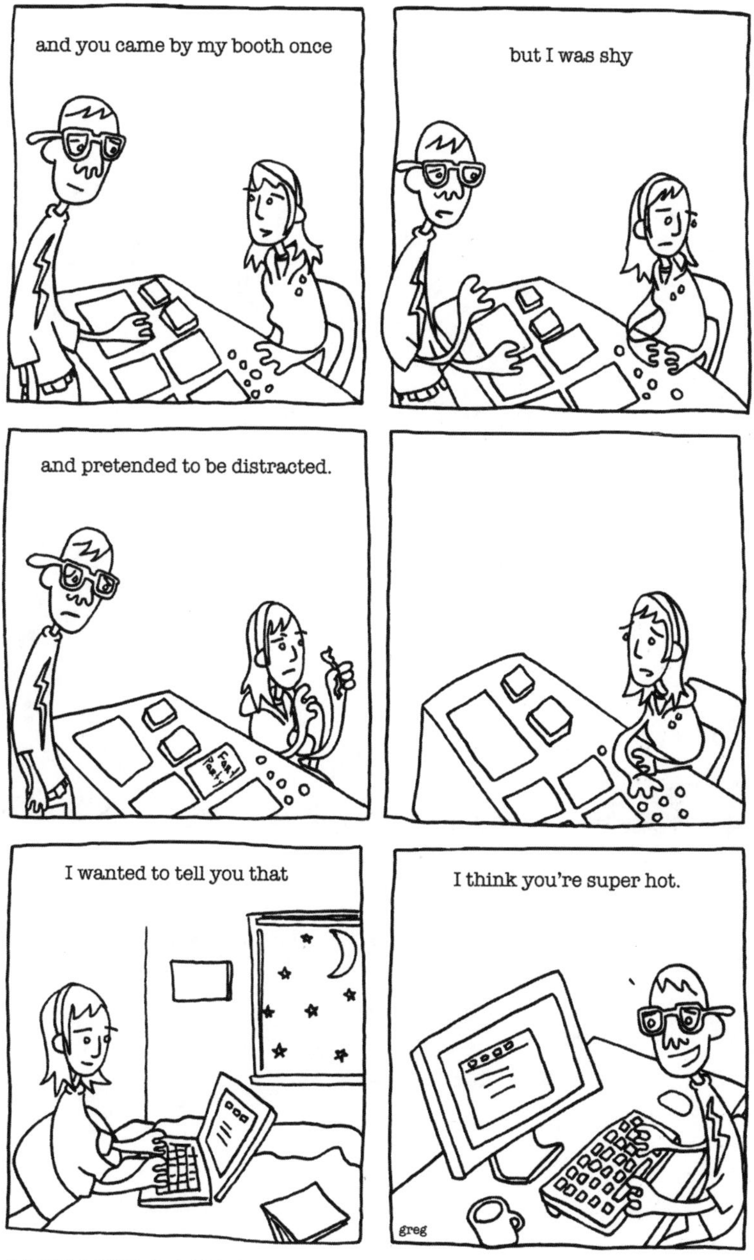
and you came by my booth once
but I was shy
and pretended to be distracted.
I wanted to tell you that
I think you're super hot.
greg

OCD with a red skirt

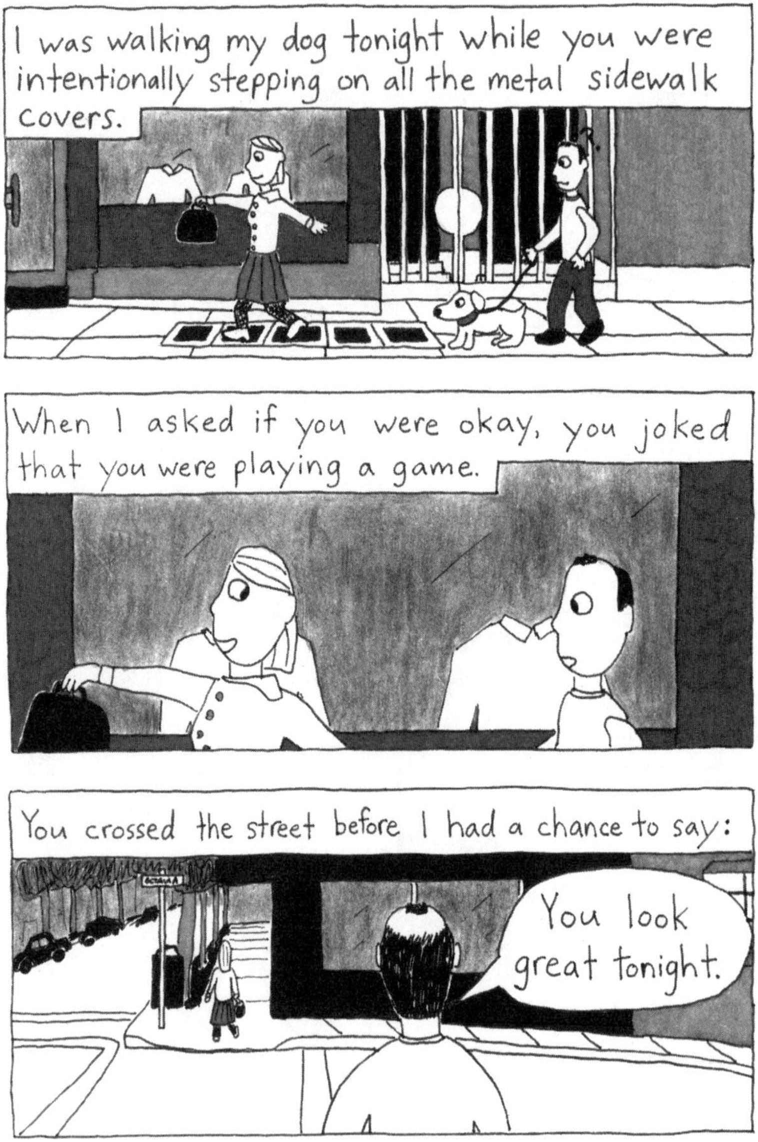
I was walking my dog tonight while you were intentionally stepping on all the metal sidewalk covers.
When I asked if you were okay, you joked that you were playing a game.
You crossed the street before I had a chance to say:
You look great tonight.

by **Jason Martin**

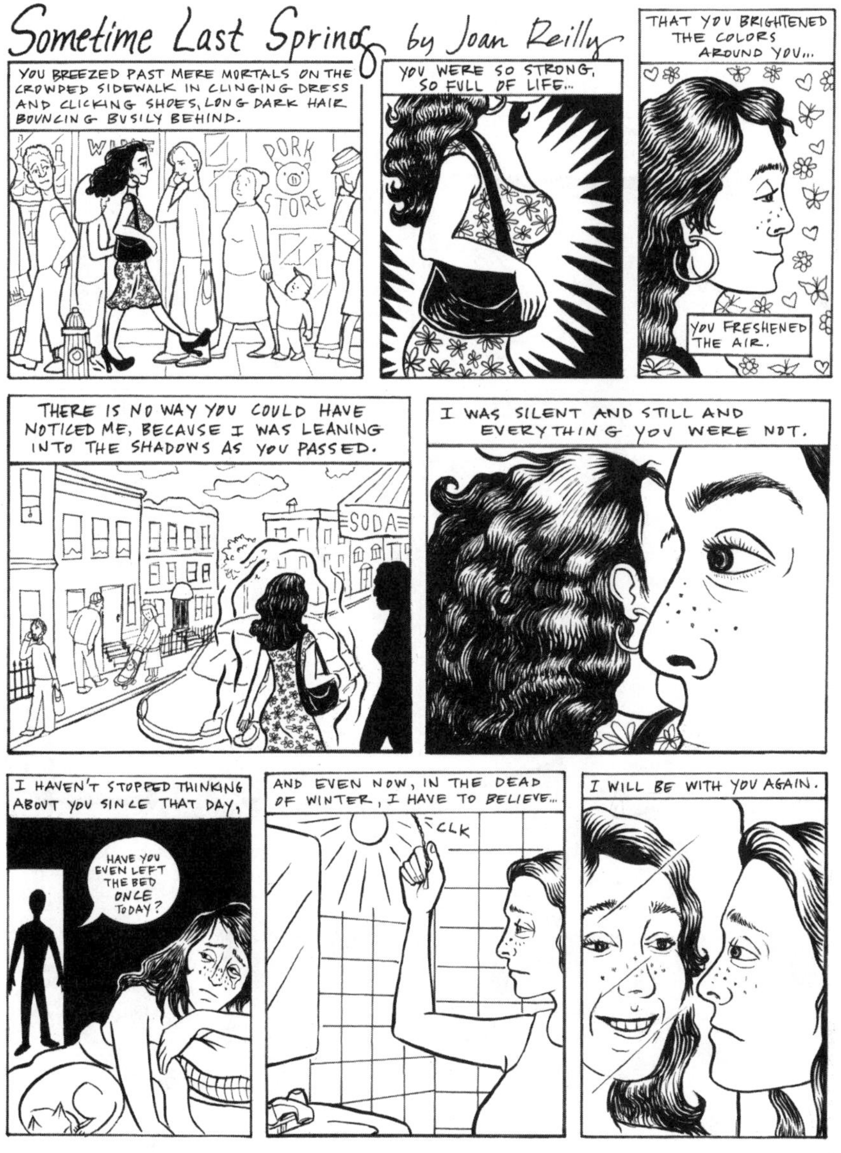
Sometime Last Spring by Joan Reilly
YOU BREEZED PAST MERE MORTALS ON THE CROWDED SIDEWALK IN CLINGING DRESS AND CLICKING SHOES, LONG DARK HAIR BOUNCING BUSILY BEHIND.
PORK STORE
YOU WERE SO STRONG, SO FULL OF LIFE...
THAT YOU BRIGHTENED THE COLORS AROUND YOU...
YOU FRESHENED THE AIR.
THERE IS NO WAY YOU COULD HAVE NOTICED ME, BECAUSE I WAS LEANING INTO THE SHADOWS AS YOU PASSED.
SODA
I WAS SILENT AND STILL AND EVERYTHING YOU WERE NOT.
I HAVEN'T STOPPED THINKING ABOUT YOU SINCE THAT DAY,
HAVE YOU EVEN LEFT THE BED ONCE TODAY?
AND EVEN NOW, IN THE DEAD OF WINTER, I HAVE TO BELIEVE...
CLK
I WILL BE WITH YOU AGAIN.

by **Joan Reilly**

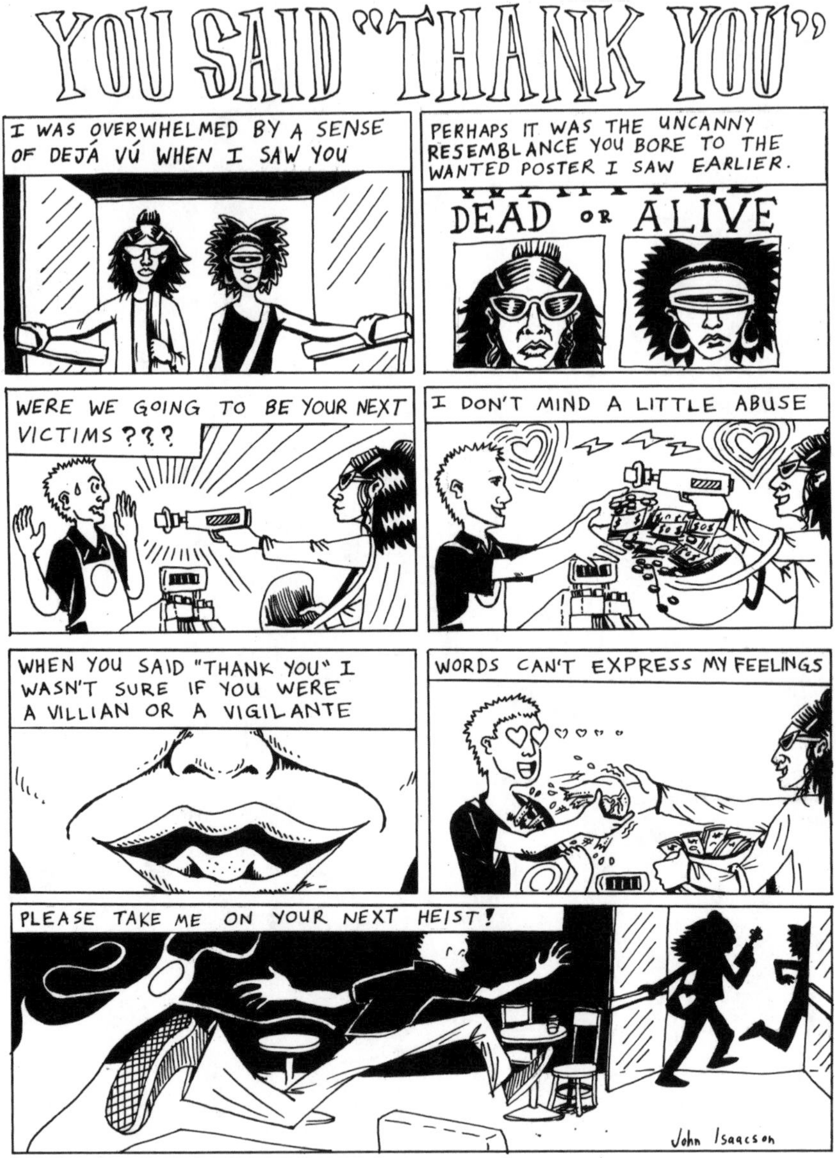
YOU SAID "THANK YOU"
I WAS OVERWHELMED BY A SENSE OF DEJÁ VÚ WHEN I SAW YOU
PERHAPS IT WAS THE UNCANNY RESEMBLANCE YOU BORE TO THE WANTED POSTER I SAW EARLIER.
DEAD OR ALIVE
WERE WE GOING TO BE YOUR NEXT VICTIMS???
I DON'T MIND A LITTLE ABUSE
WHEN YOU SAID "THANK YOU" I WASN'T SURE IF YOU WERE A VILLIAN OR A VIGILANTE
WORDS CAN'T EXPRESS MY FEELINGS
PLEASE TAKE ME ON YOUR NEXT HEIST!
John Isaacson

by **John Isaacson**

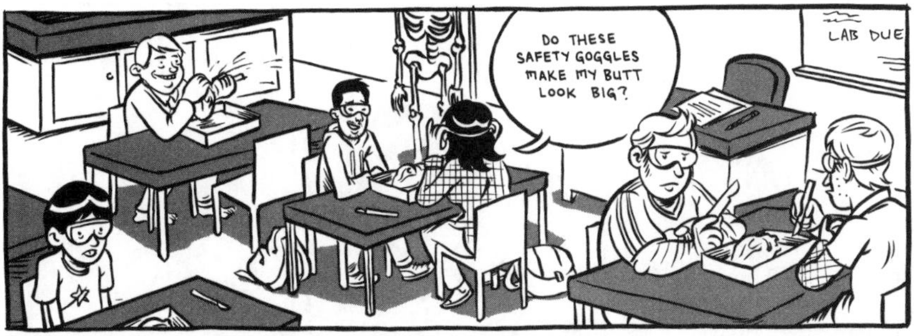
LAB DUE
DO THESE SAFETY GOGGLES MAKE MY BUTT LOOK BIG?

i miss talking to you in biology

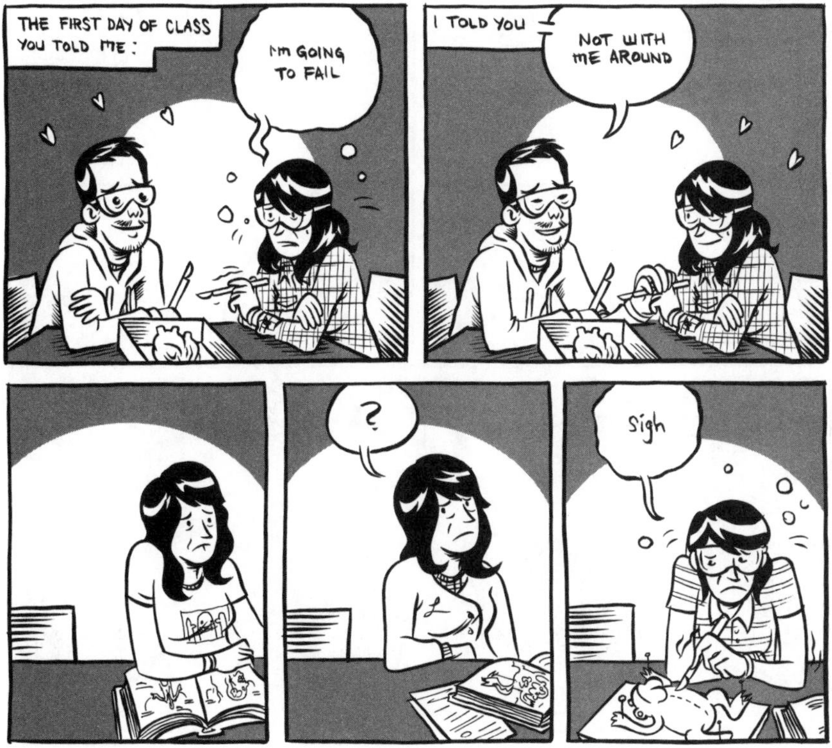
THE FIRST DAY OF CLASS YOU TOLD ME:
I'M GOING TO FAIL
I TOLD YOU
NOT WITH ME AROUND
?
Sigh

by **Jonathan Hill**

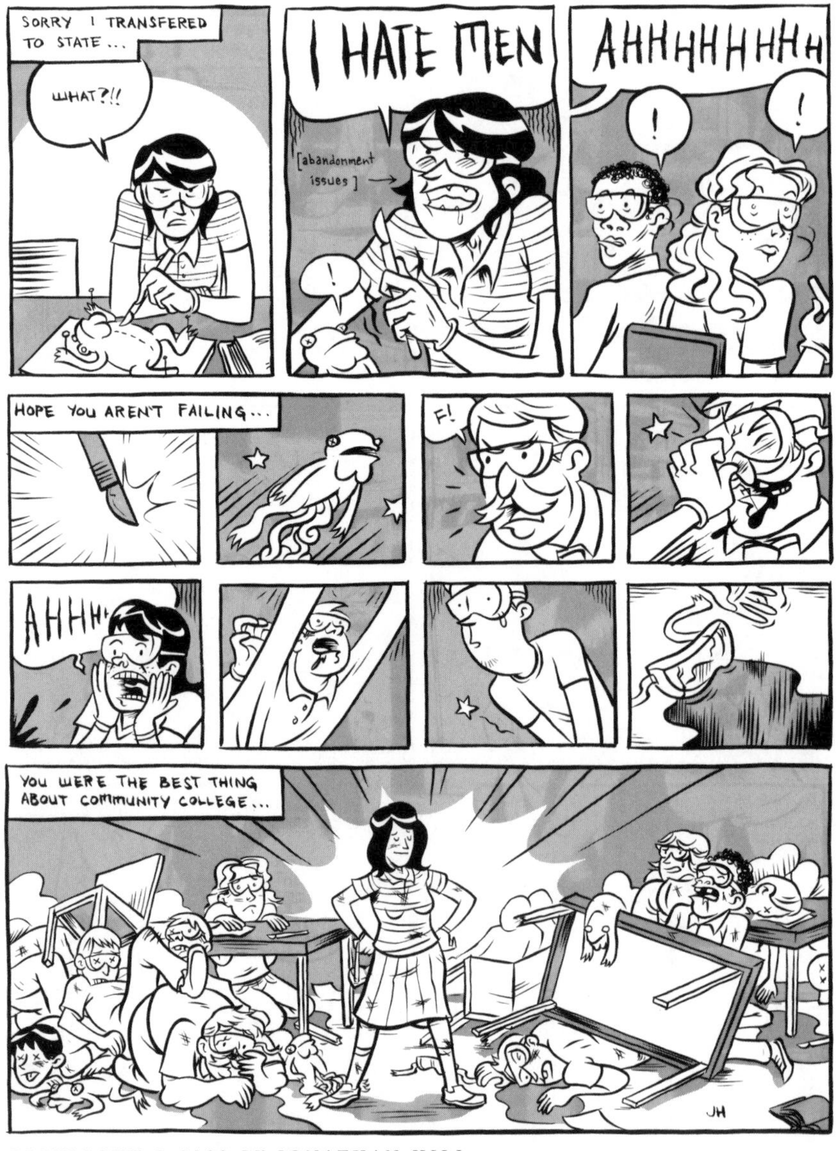
SORRY I TRANSFERED TO STATE...
WHAT?!!
I HATE MEN
[abandonment issues] →
!
AHHHHHHHH
!
!
HOPE YOU AREN'T FAILING...
F!
AHHH
YOU WERE THE BEST THING ABOUT COMMUNITY COLLEGE...
JH

M4W: I SAW YOU ON PAGE AND DIVISADERO...

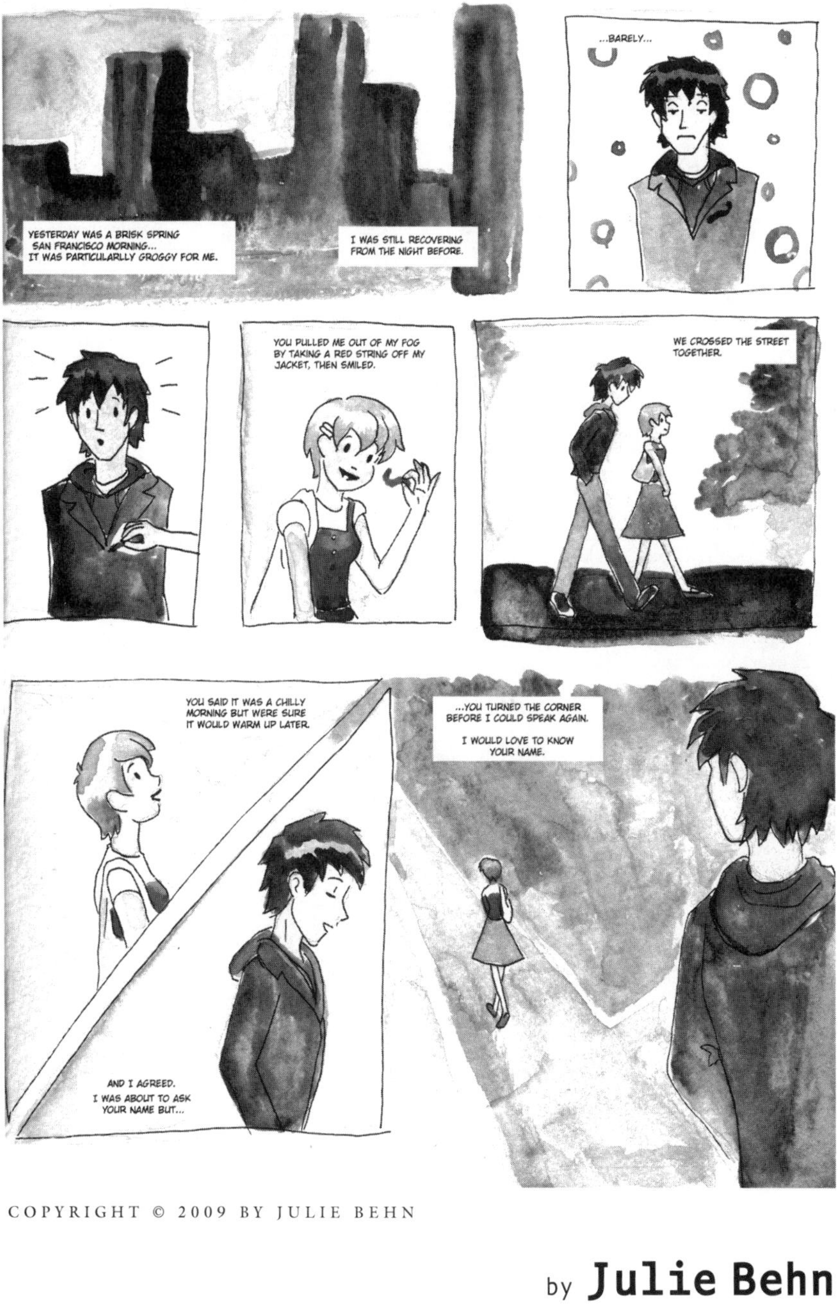

YESTERDAY WAS A BRISK SPRING SAN FRANCISCO MORNING... IT WAS PARTICULARLLY GROGGY FOR ME.
I WAS STILL RECOVERING FROM THE NIGHT BEFORE.
...BARELY...
YOU PULLED ME OUT OF MY FOG BY TAKING A RED STRING OFF MY JACKET, THEN SMILED.
WE CROSSED THE STREET TOGETHER.
YOU SAID IT WAS A CHILLY MORNING BUT WERE SURE IT WOULD WARM UP LATER.
AND I AGREED. I WAS ABOUT TO ASK YOUR NAME BUT...
...YOU TURNED THE CORNER BEFORE I COULD SPEAK AGAIN.
I WOULD LOVE TO KNOW YOUR NAME.

by **Julie Behn**

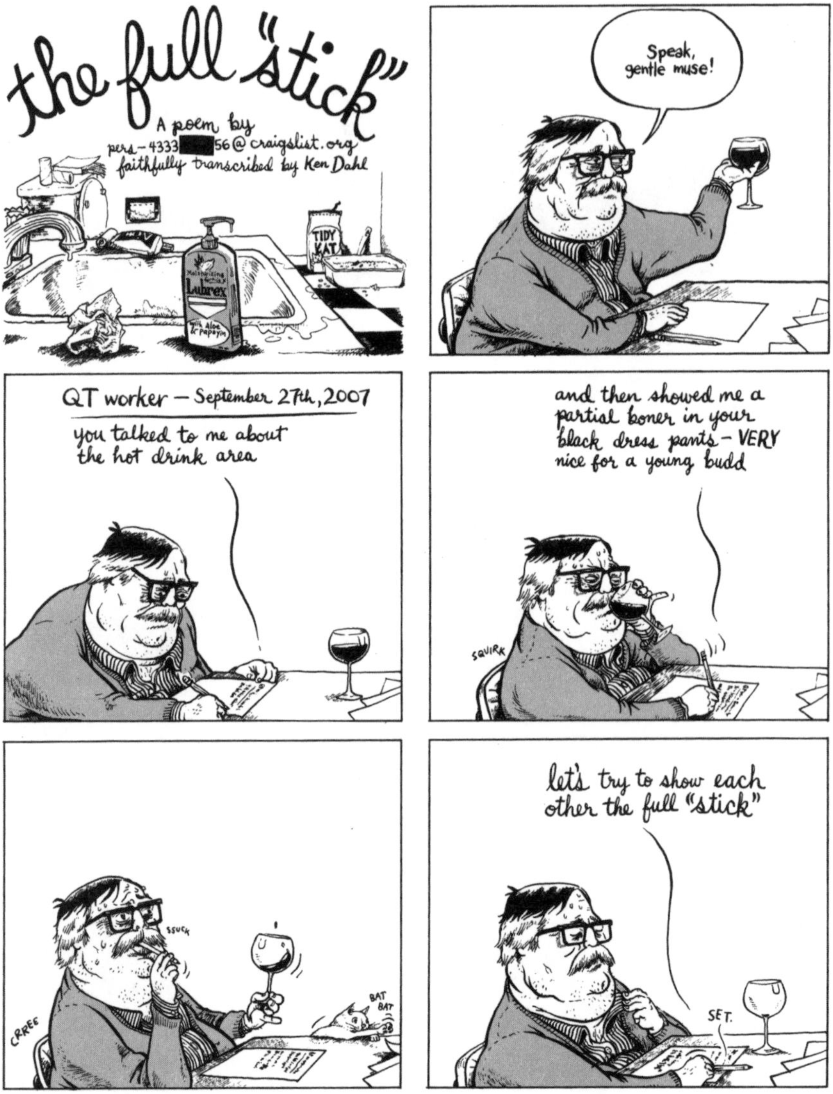
the full "stick"
A poem by
pers-4333[redacted]56@craigslist.org
faithfully transcribed by Ken Dahl
Lubrex
TIDY KAT
Speak, gentle muse!
QT worker — September 27th, 2007
you talked to me about the hot drink area
and then showed me a partial boner in your black dress pants - VERY nice for a young budd
SQUIRK
SSUCK
CRREE
BAT BAT
let's try to show each other the full "stick"
SET.

by **Ken Dahl**

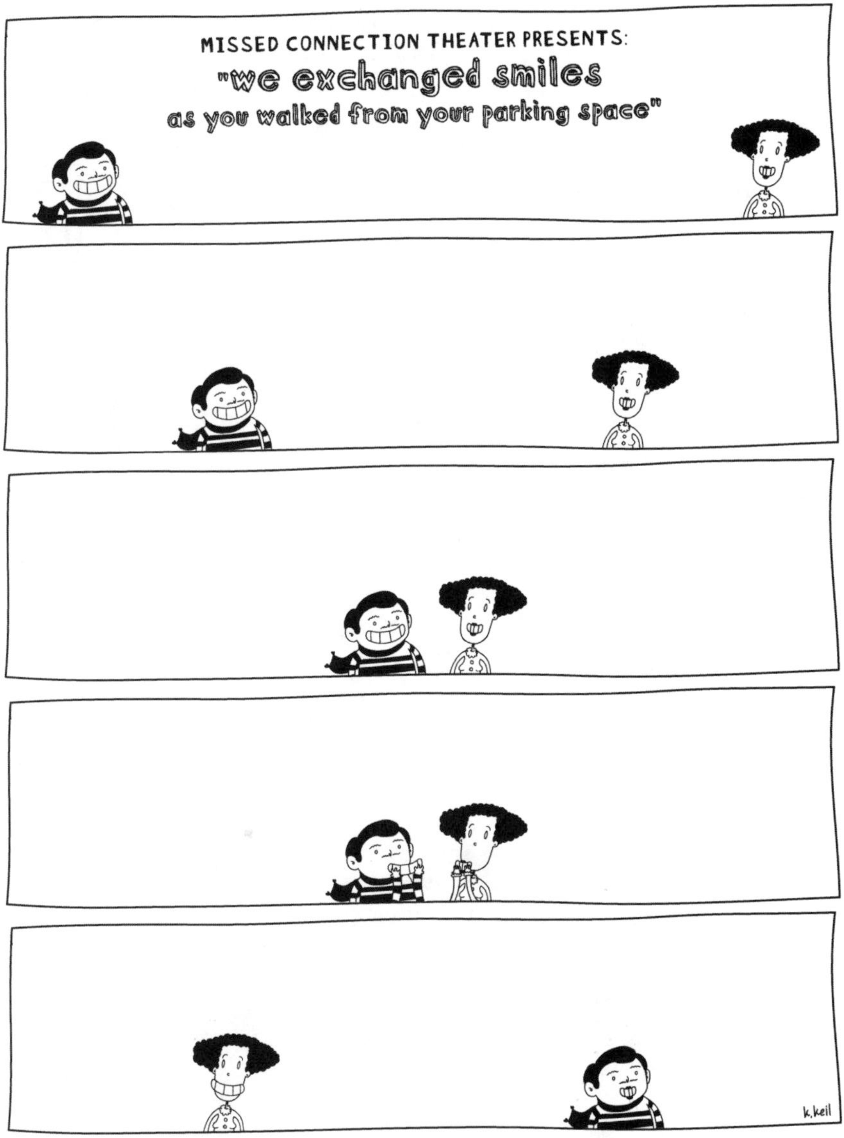
MISSED CONNECTION THEATER PRESENTS:
"we exchanged smiles
as you walked from your parking space"
k.keil

by **Kenny Keil**

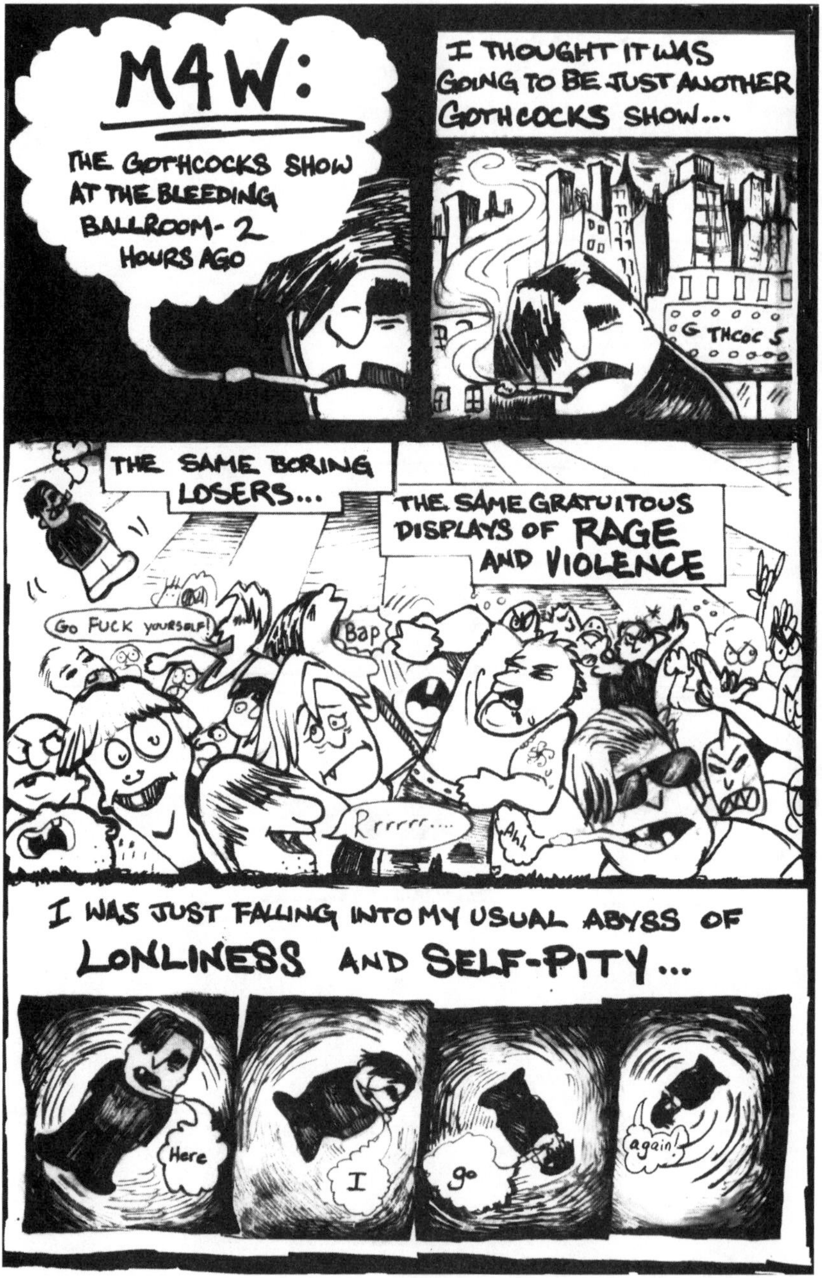
M4W:
THE GOTHCOCKS SHOW AT THE BLEEDING BALLROOM- 2 HOURS AGO
I THOUGHT IT WAS GOING TO BE JUST ANOTHER GOTHCOCKS SHOW...
THE SAME BORING LOSERS...
THE SAME GRATUITOUS DISPLAYS OF RAGE AND VIOLENCE
Go FUCK yourself!
Bap
Rrrrrr....
Ah!
I WAS JUST FALLING INTO MY USUAL ABYSS OF LONLINESS AND SELF-PITY...
Here
I
go
again!

by **Marlene Kryza**

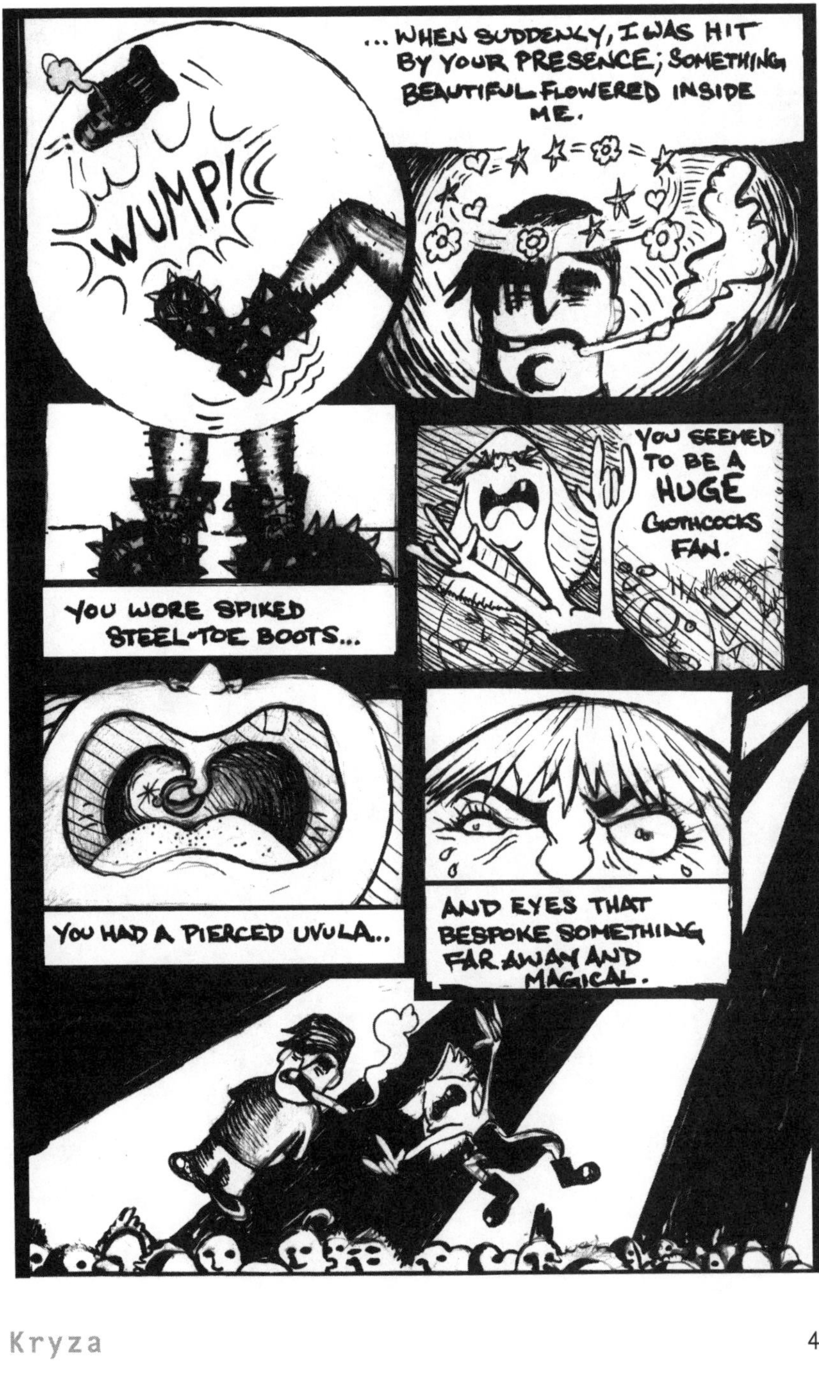
...WHEN SUDDENLY, I WAS HIT BY YOUR PRESENCE; SOMETHING BEAUTIFUL FLOWERED INSIDE ME.
WUMP!
YOU WORE SPIKED STEEL-TOE BOOTS...
YOU SEEMED TO BE A HUGE GOTHCOCKS FAN.
YOU HAD A PIERCED UVULA...
AND EYES THAT BESPOKE SOMETHING FAR AWAY AND MAGICAL.

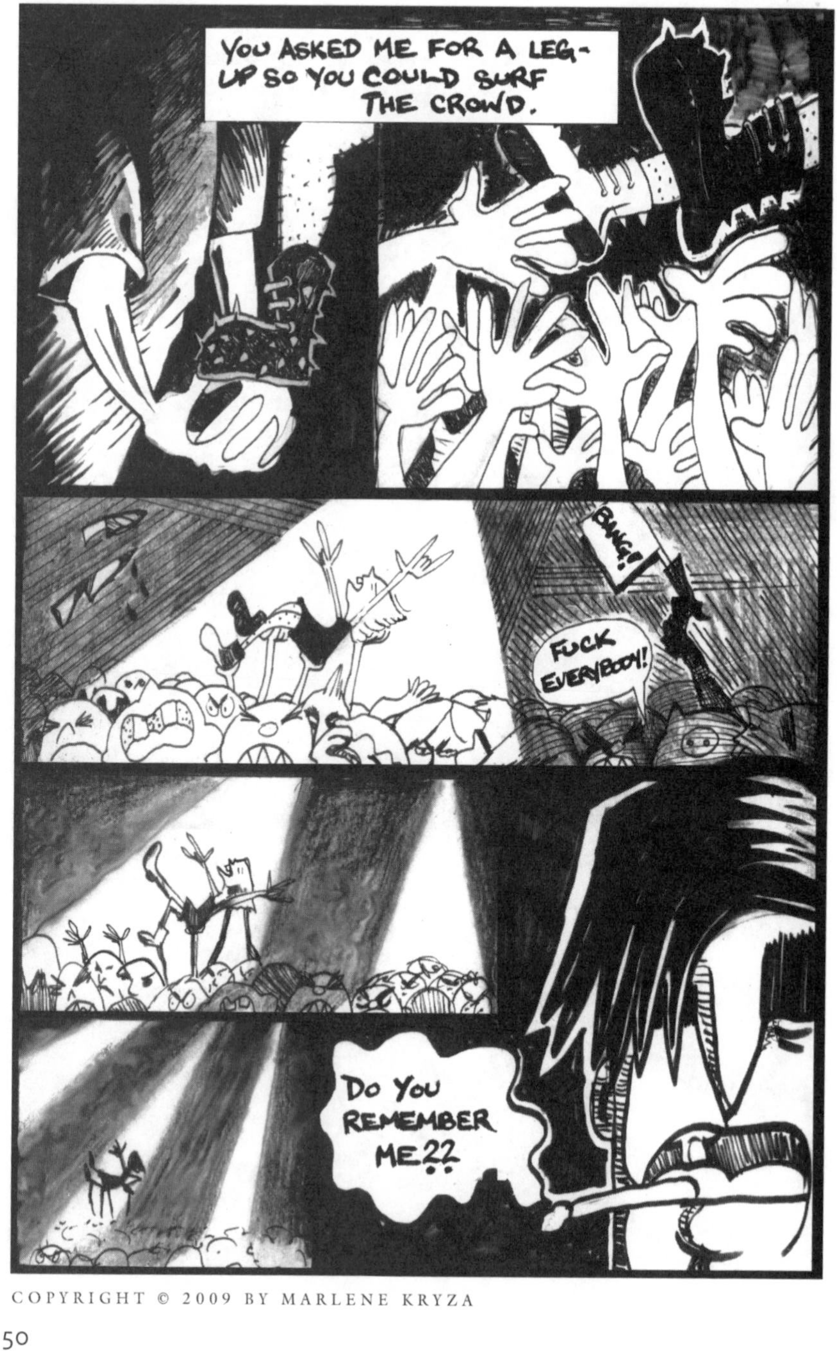
YOU ASKED ME FOR A LEG-UP SO YOU COULD SURF THE CROWD.
BANG!
FUCK EVERYBODY!
DO YOU REMEMBER ME??

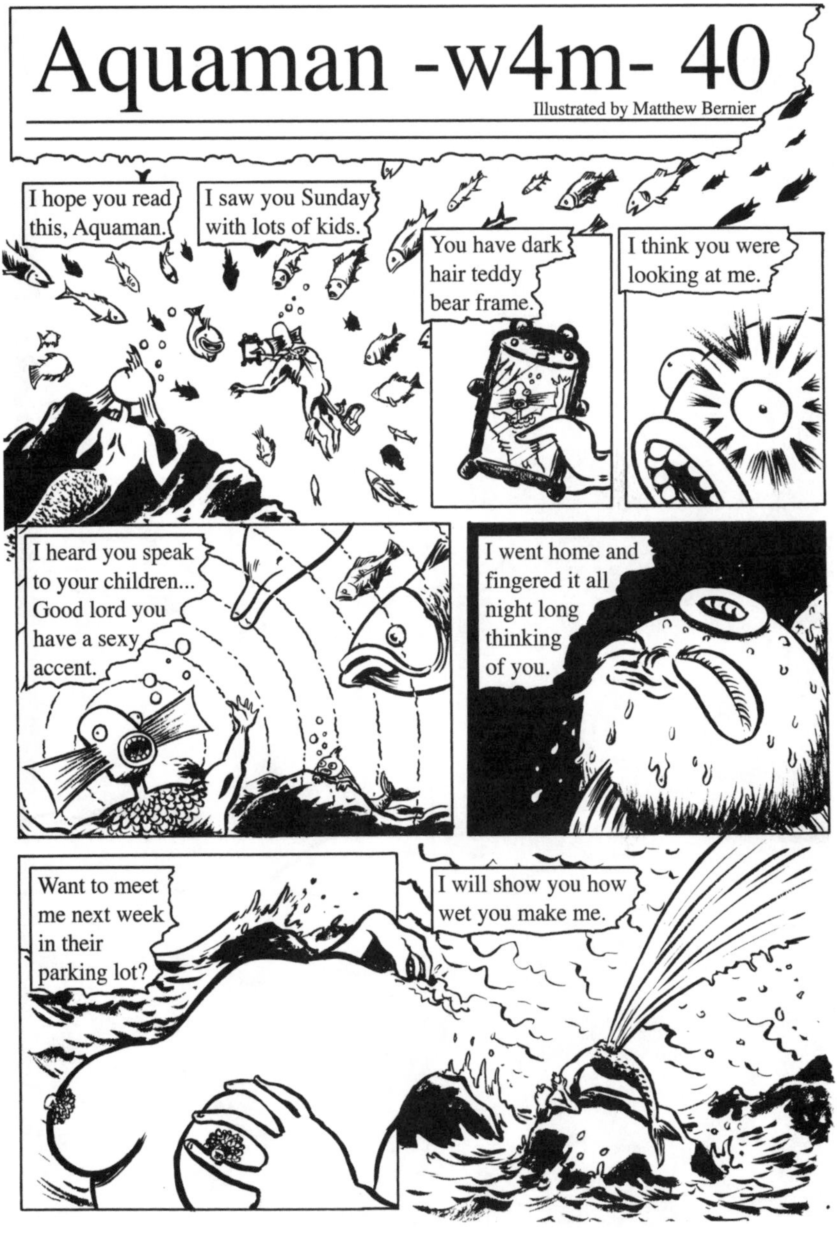
Aquaman -w4m- 40
Illustrated by Matthew Bernier
I hope you read this, Aquaman.
I saw you Sunday with lots of kids.
You have dark hair teddy bear frame.
I think you were looking at me.
I heard you speak to your children... Good lord you have a sexy accent.
I went home and fingered it all night long thinking of you.
Want to meet me next week in their parking lot?
I will show you how wet you make me.

by **Matthew Bernier**

RE: Aquaman – m4w

Illustrated by Matthew Bernier

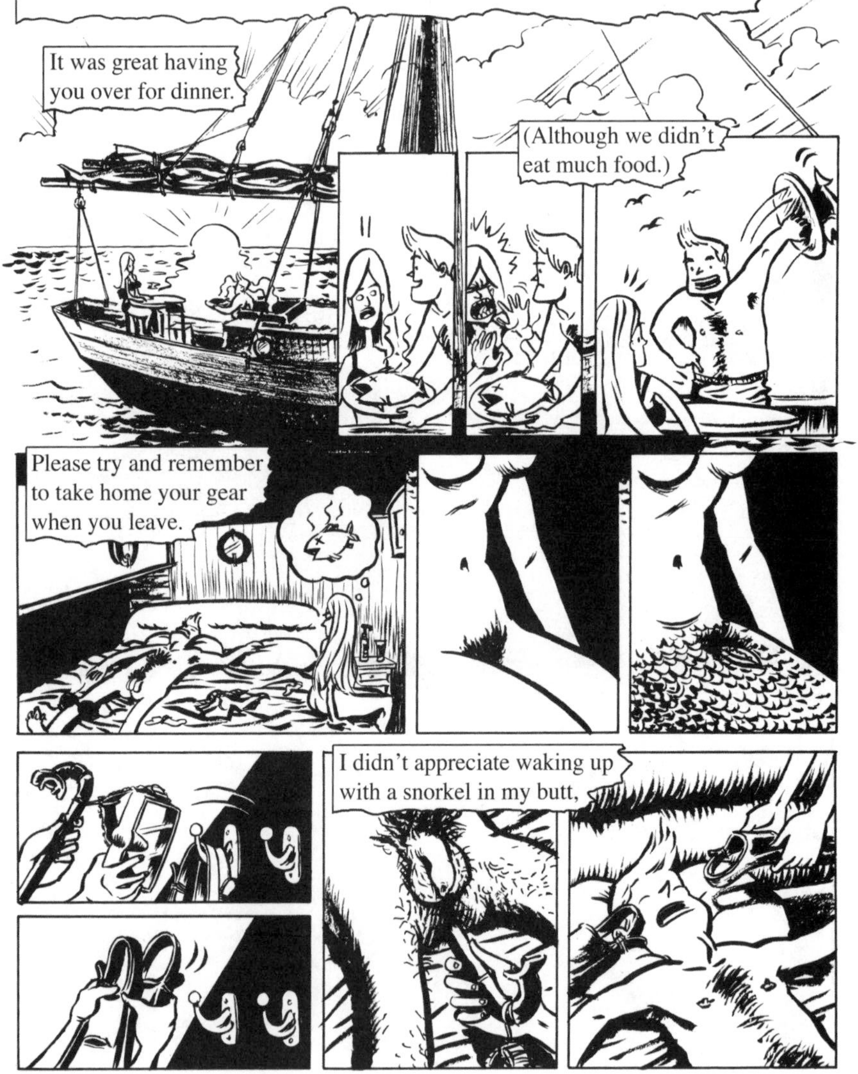
It was great having you over for dinner.
(Although we didn't eat much food.)
Please try and remember to take home your gear when you leave.
I didn't appreciate waking up with a snorkel in my butt,

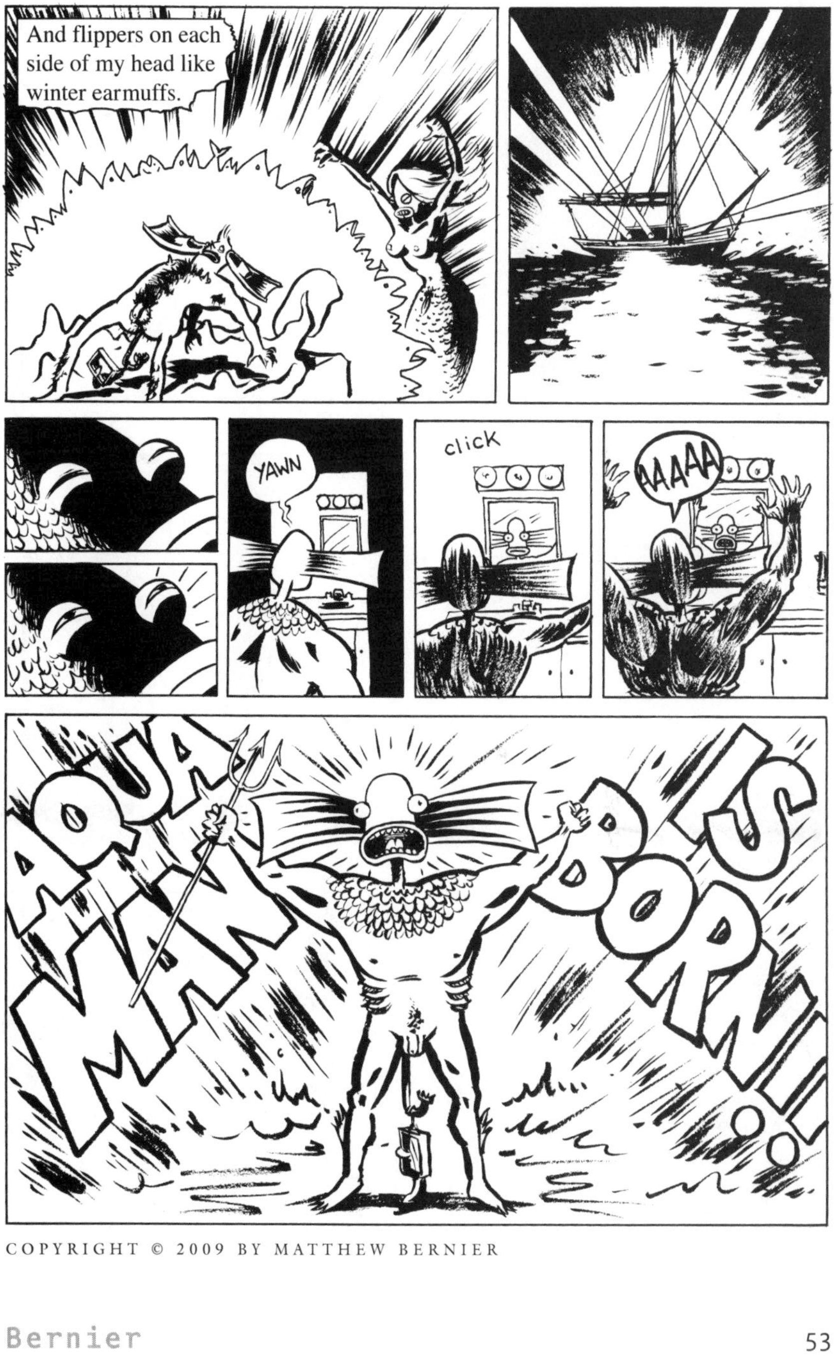
And flippers on each side of my head like winter earmuffs.
YAWN
click
AAAAA
AQUA MAN IS BORN!!

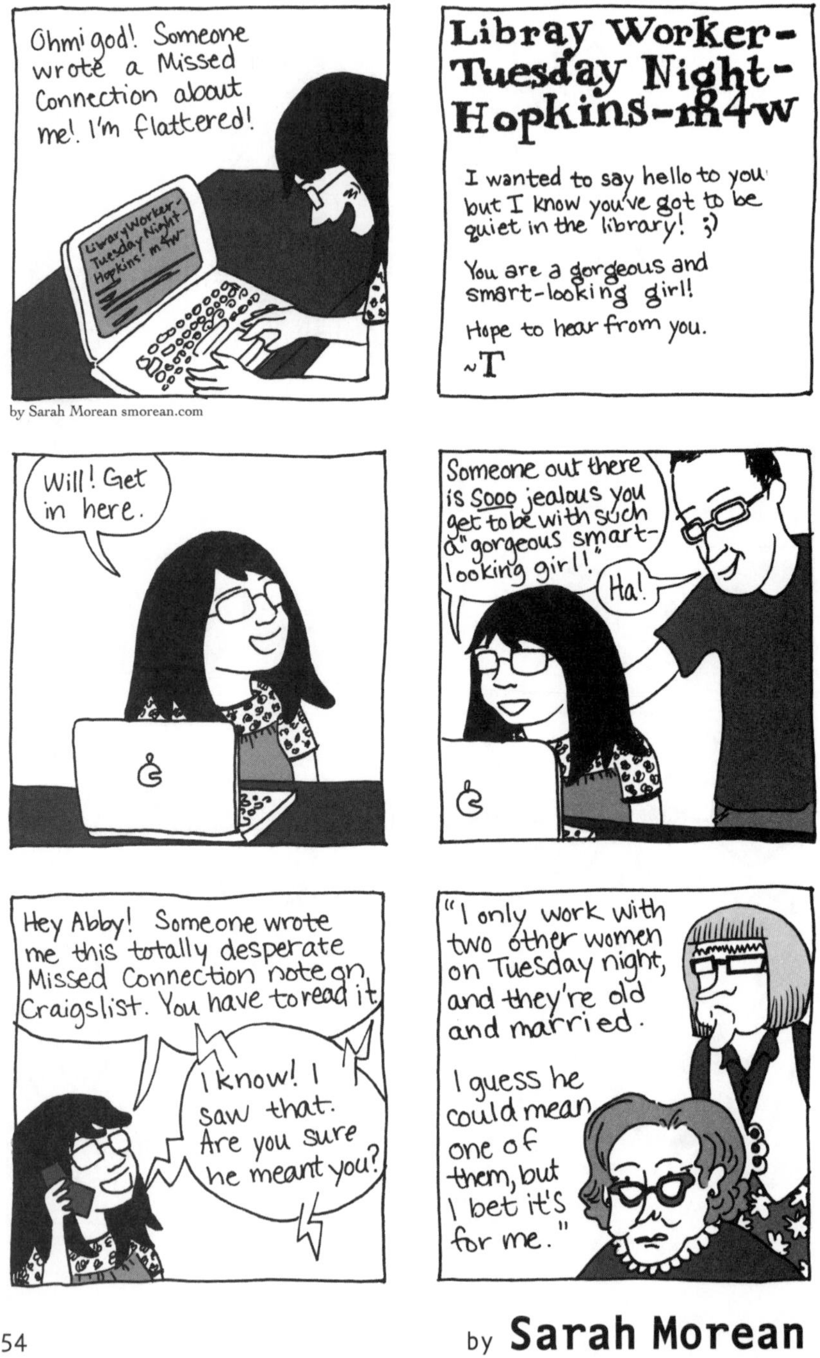
Ohmigod! Someone wrote a Missed Connection about me! I'm flattered!
LibraryWorker-Tuesday Night-Hopkins: m4w-
Libray Worker-Tuesday Night-Hopkins-m4w
I wanted to say hello to you but I know you've got to be quiet in the library! ;)
You are a gorgeous and smart-looking girl!
Hope to hear from you.
~T
by Sarah Morean smorean.com
Will! Get in here.
Someone out there is Sooo jealous you get to be with such a "gorgeous smart-looking girl!"
Ha!
Hey Abby! Someone wrote me this totally desperate Missed Connection note on Craigslist. You have to read it.
I know! I saw that. Are you sure he meant you?
"I only work with two other women on Tuesday night, and they're old and married.
I guess he could mean one of them, but I bet it's for me."

by **Sarah Morean**

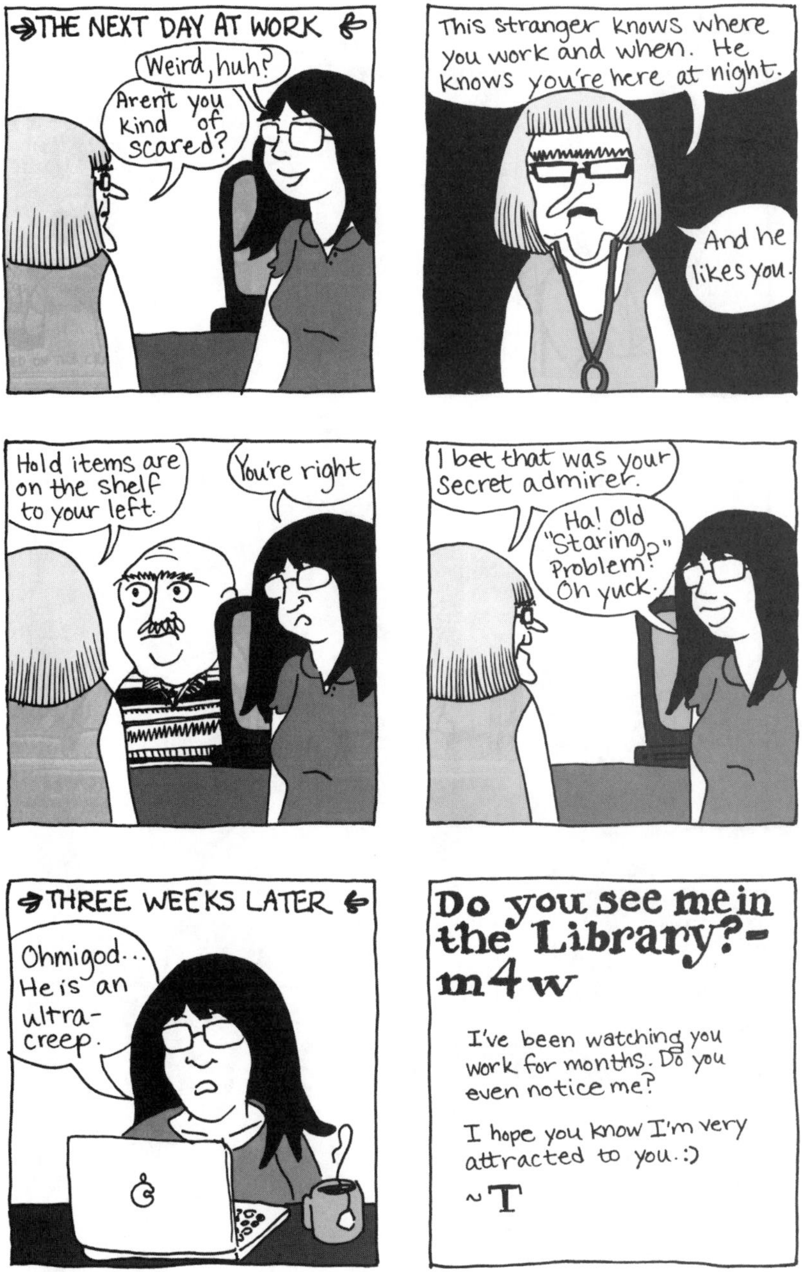
THE NEXT DAY AT WORK
Weird, huh?
Aren't you kind of scared?
This stranger knows where you work and when. He knows you're here at night.
And he likes you.
Hold items are on the shelf to your left.
You're right
I bet that was your secret admirer.
Ha! Old "Staring Problem?" Oh yuck.
THREE WEEKS LATER
Ohmigod... He is an ultra-creep.
Do you see me in the Library? - m4w
I've been watching you work for months. Do you even notice me?
I hope you know I'm very attracted to you. :)
~T

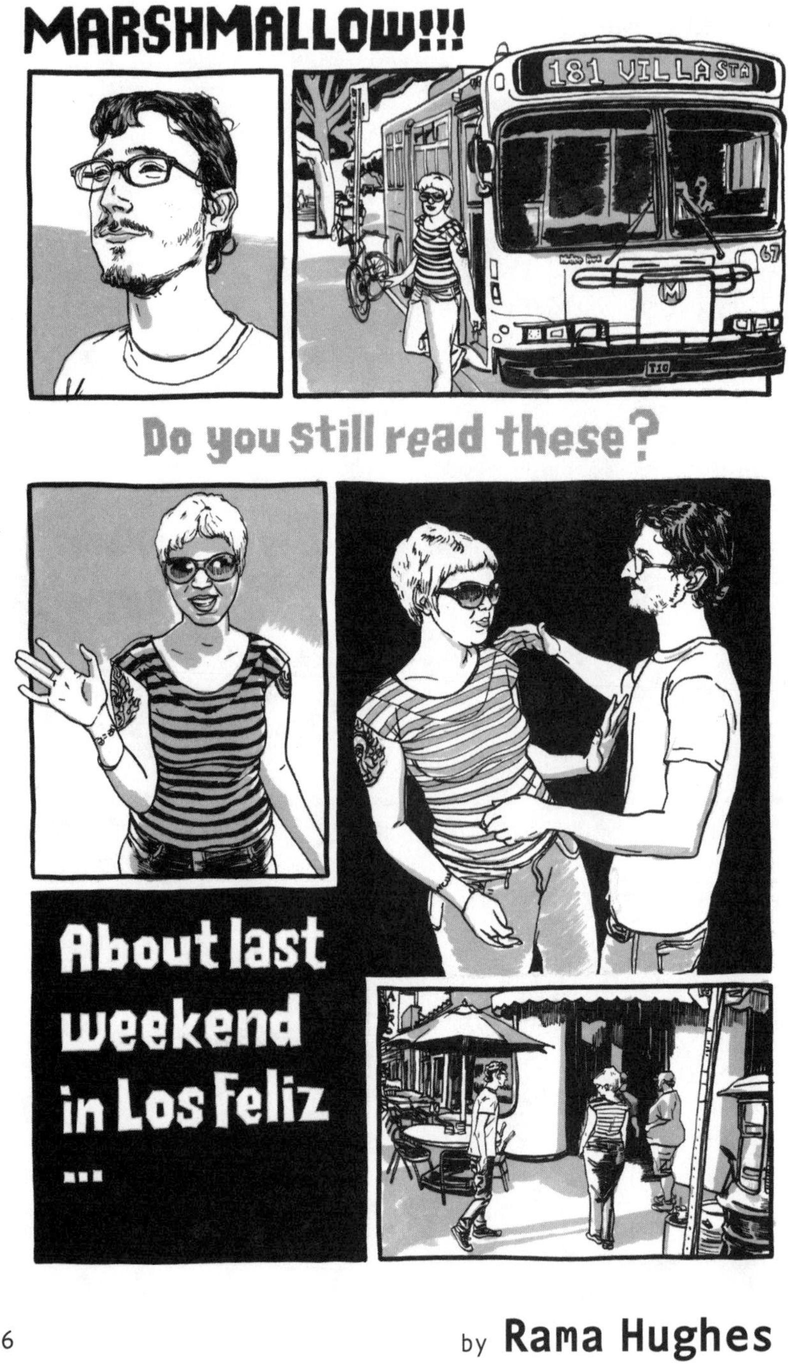
MARSHMALLOW!!!
181 VILLA STA
Do you still read these?
About last weekend in Los Feliz ...

by **Rama Hughes**

I was going to ask you for one last chance

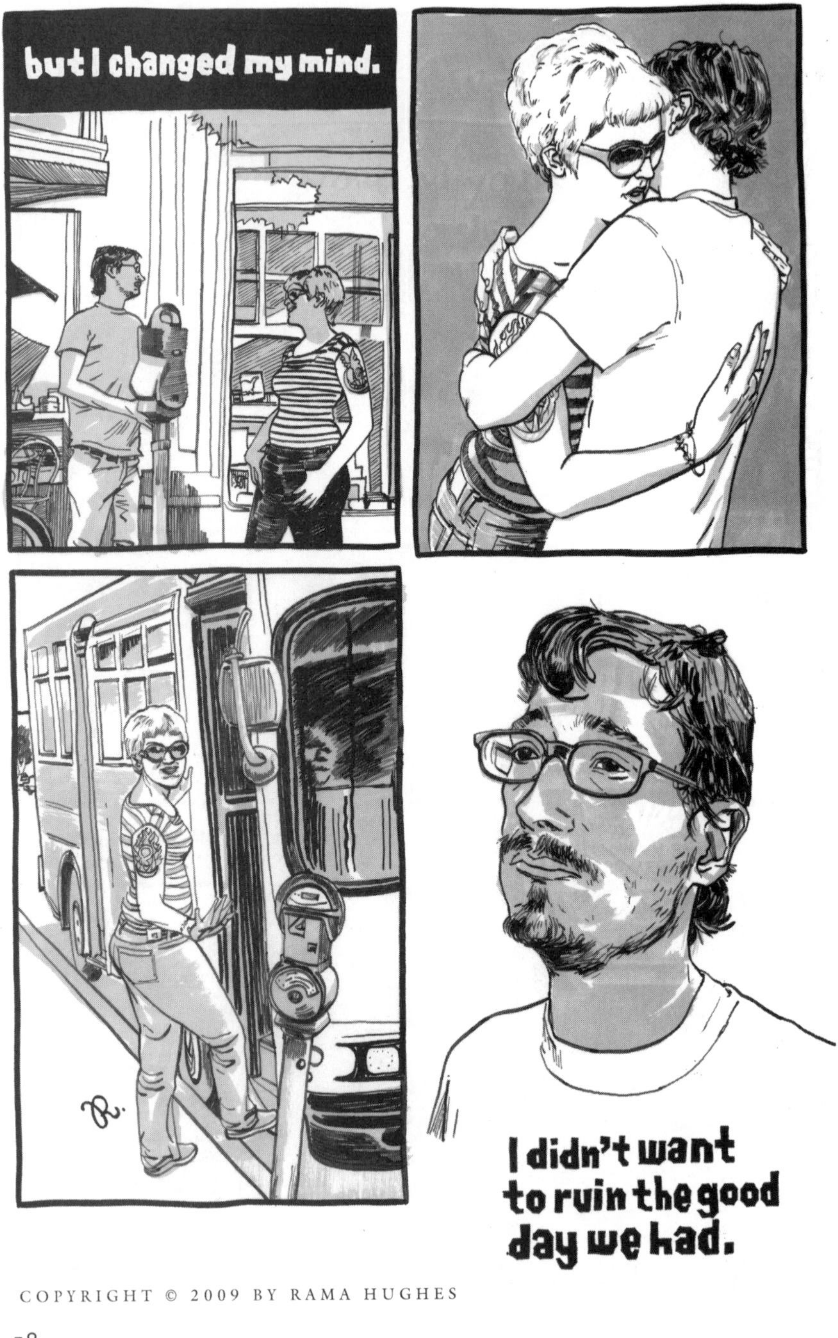
but I changed my mind.
I didn't want to ruin the good day we had.

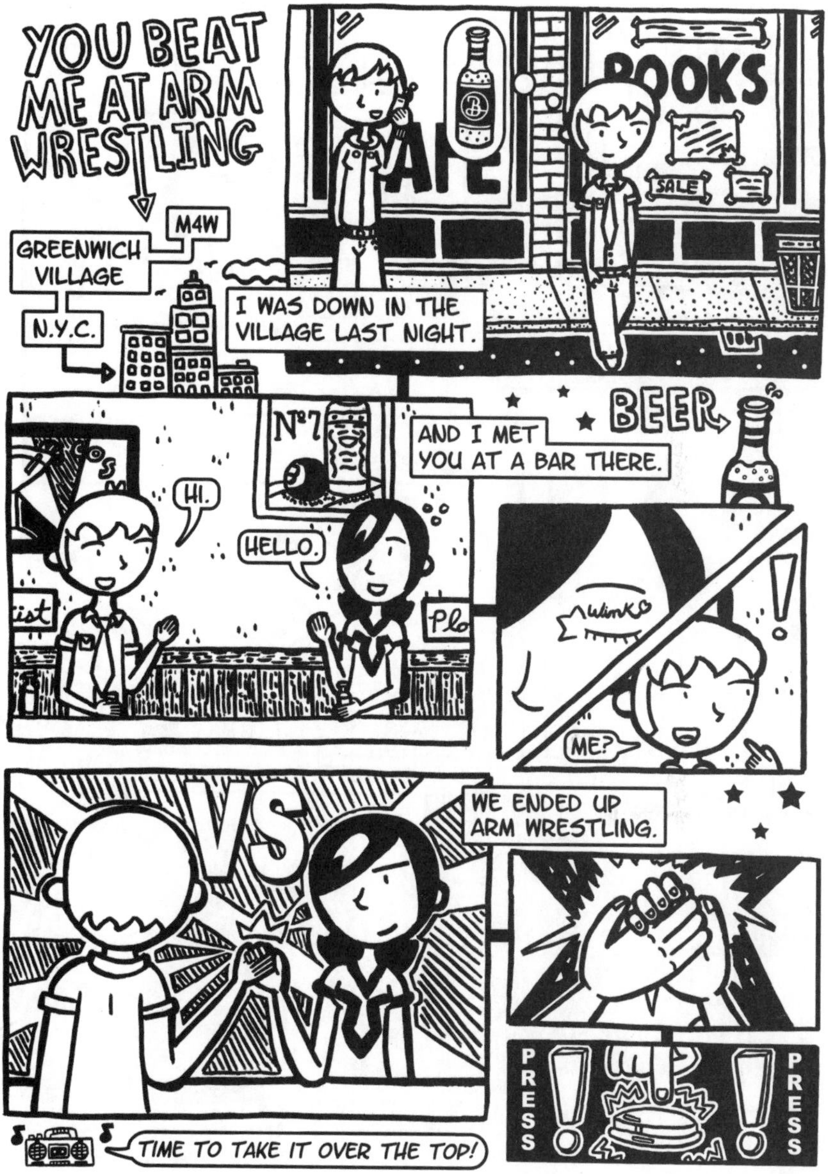
YOU BEAT ME AT ARM WRESTLING
M4W
GREENWICH VILLAGE
N.Y.C.
I WAS DOWN IN THE VILLAGE LAST NIGHT.
SALE
AND I MET YOU AT A BAR THERE.
BEER
HI.
HELLO.
Wink
ME?
VS
WE ENDED UP ARM WRESTLING.
TIME TO TAKE IT OVER THE TOP!
PRESS
PRESS

by **Robin Enrico**

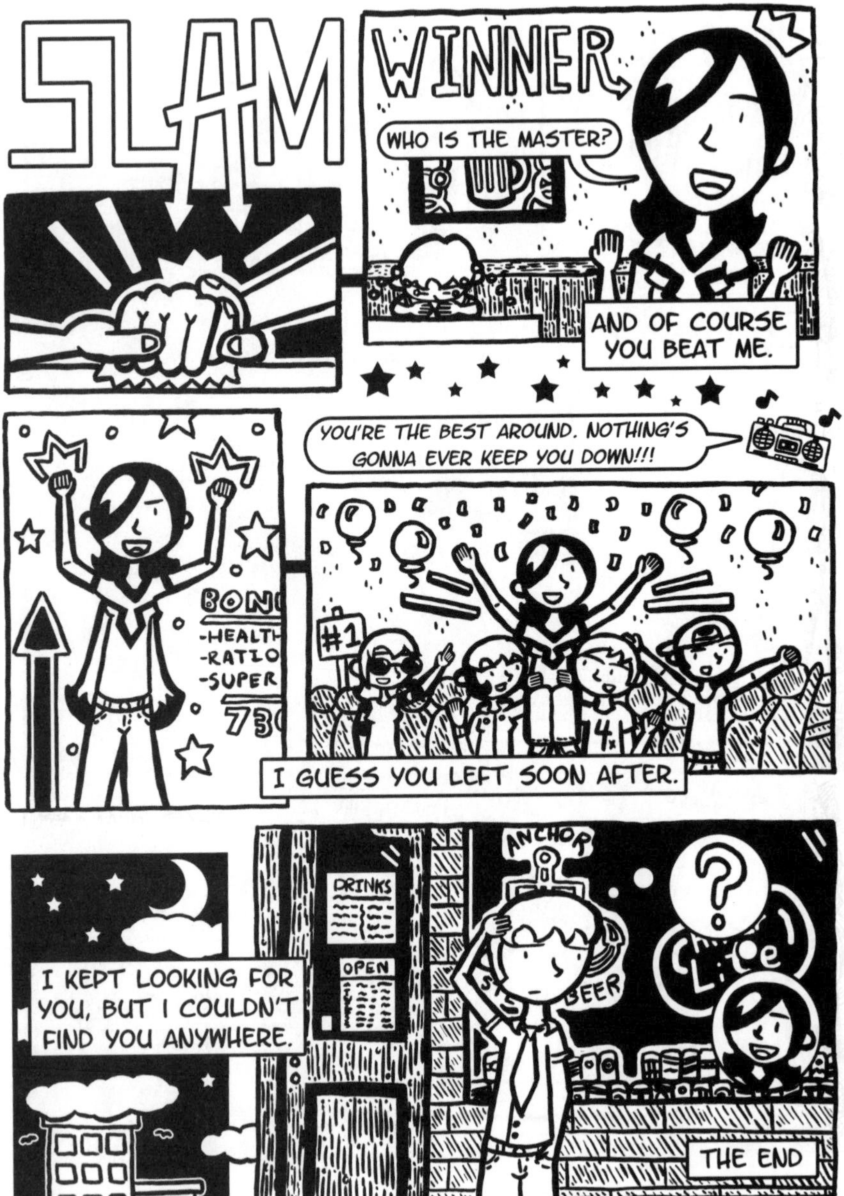
SLAM
WINNER
WHO IS THE MASTER?
AND OF COURSE YOU BEAT ME.
YOU'RE THE BEST AROUND. NOTHING'S GONNA EVER KEEP YOU DOWN!!!
-HEALTH
-RATIO
-SUPER
#1
I GUESS YOU LEFT SOON AFTER.
I KEPT LOOKING FOR YOU, BUT I COULDN'T FIND YOU ANYWHERE.
DRINKS
OPEN
ANCHOR
BEER
THE END

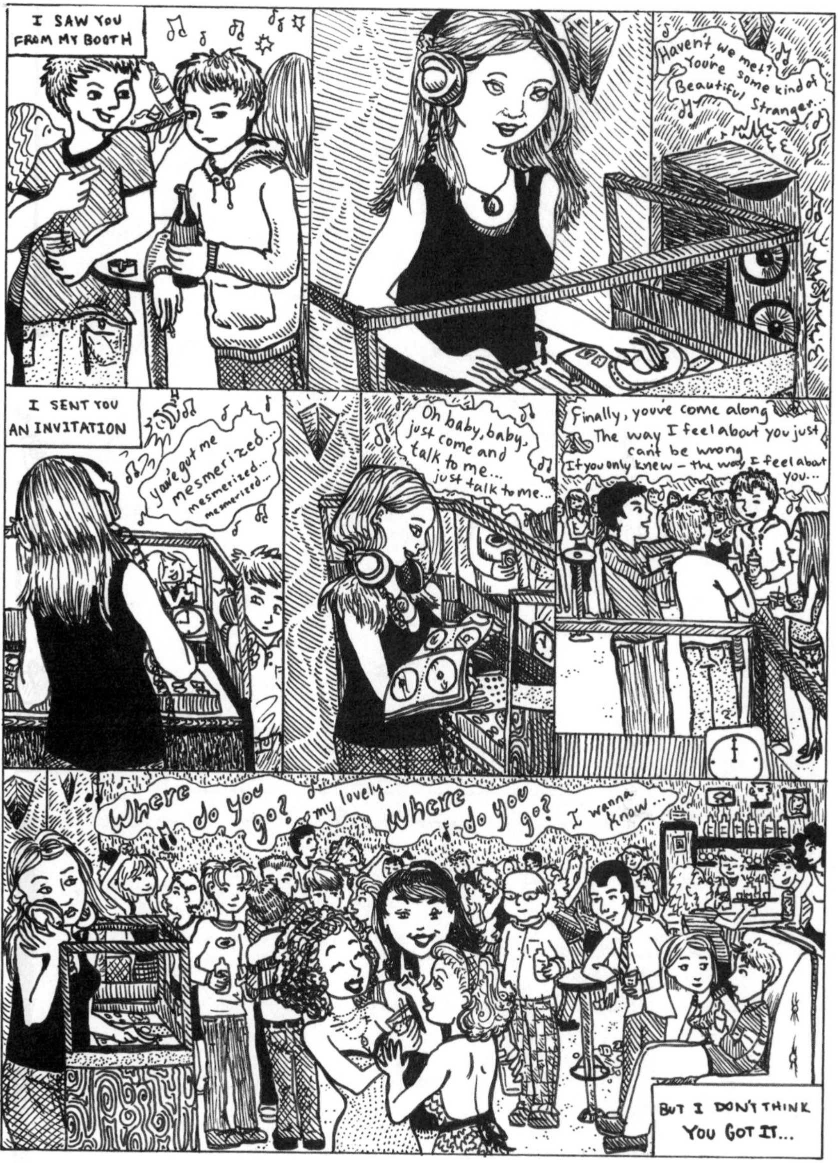
I SAW YOU FROM MY BOOTH
Haven't we met? You're some kind of Beautiful Stranger...
I SENT YOU AN INVITATION
you've got me mesmerized... mesmerized... mesmerized...
Oh baby, baby, just come and talk to me... just talk to me...
Finally, you've come along The way I feel about you just can't be wrong If you only knew – the way I feel about you...
Where do you go? my lovely... Where do you go? I wanna know...
BUT I DON'T THINK YOU GOT IT...

by **Sara Pecherek**

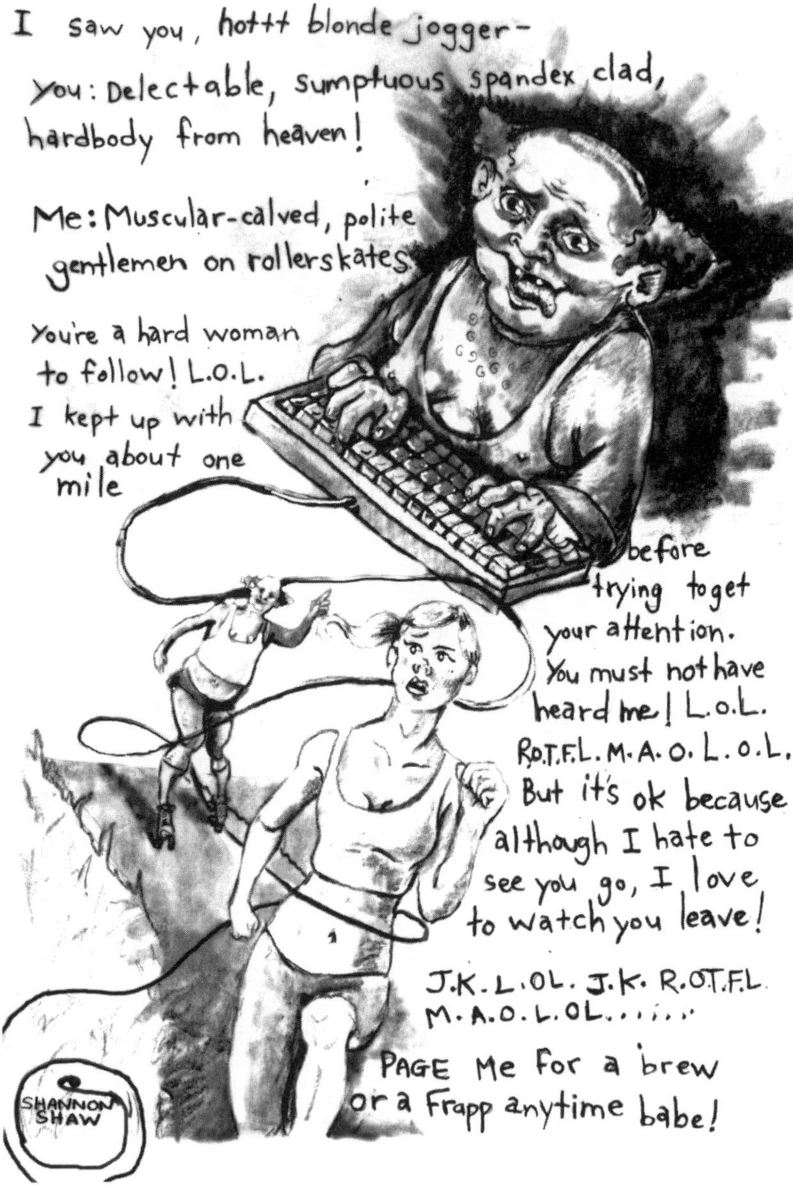
I saw you, hottt blonde jogger-
you: Delectable, sumptuous spandex clad, hardbody from heaven!
Me: Muscular-calved, polite gentlemen on rollerskates
You're a hard woman to follow! L.O.L.
I kept up with you about one mile
before trying toget your attention.
You must not have heard me! L.o.L.
R.O.T.F.L.M.A.O. L.O.L.
But it's ok because although I hate to see you go, I love to watch you leave!
J.K. L.OL. J.K. R.O.T.F.L M.A.O.L.OL.......
PAGE Me for a brew or a Frapp anytime babe!
SHANNON SHAW

by **Shannon Shaw**

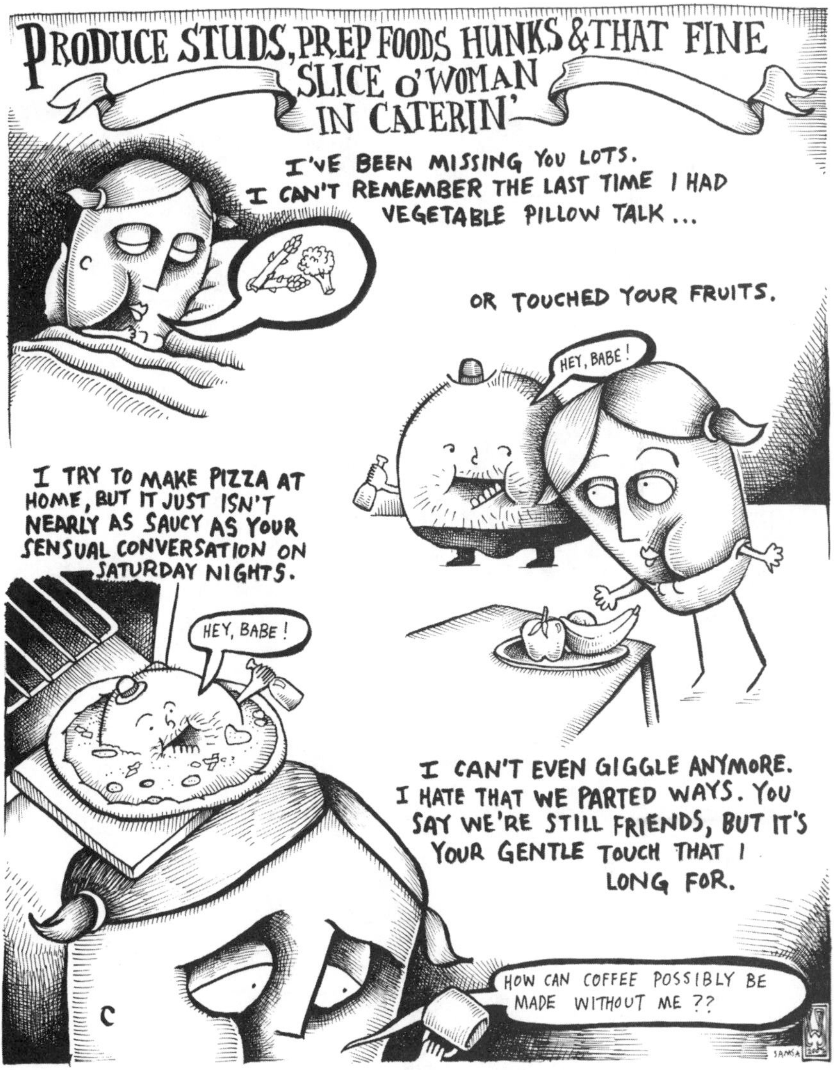
PRODUCE STUDS, PREP FOODS HUNKS & THAT FINE SLICE O' WOMAN IN CATERIN'
I'VE BEEN MISSING YOU LOTS. I CAN'T REMEMBER THE LAST TIME I HAD VEGETABLE PILLOW TALK...
OR TOUCHED YOUR FRUITS.
HEY, BABE!
I TRY TO MAKE PIZZA AT HOME, BUT IT JUST ISN'T NEARLY AS SAUCY AS YOUR SENSUAL CONVERSATION ON SATURDAY NIGHTS.
HEY, BABE!
I CAN'T EVEN GIGGLE ANYMORE. I HATE THAT WE PARTED WAYS. YOU SAY WE'RE STILL FRIENDS, BUT IT'S YOUR GENTLE TOUCH THAT I LONG FOR.
HOW CAN COFFEE POSSIBLY BE MADE WITHOUT ME ??

by **William Schaff**

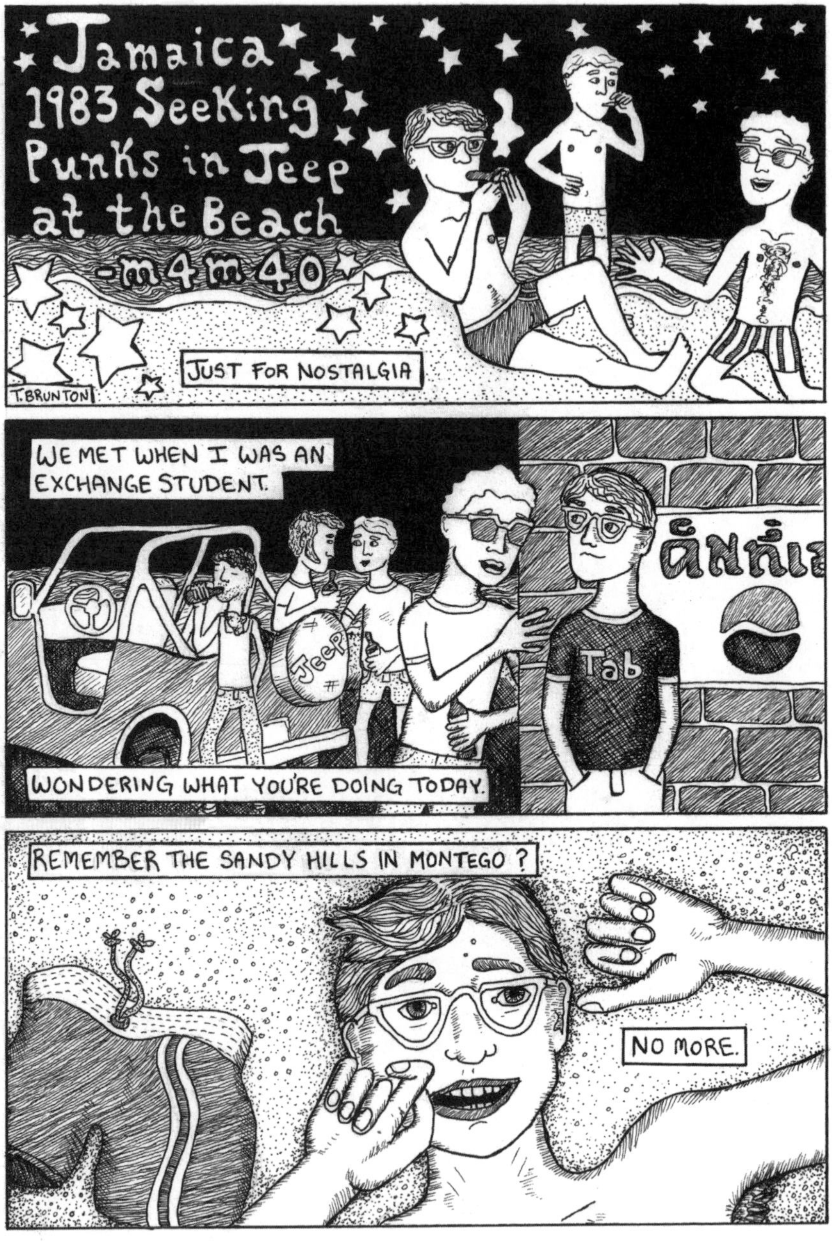
Jamaica 1983 SeeKing Punks in Jeep at the Beach -m4m 40
JUST FOR NOSTALGIA
T. BRUNTON
WE MET WHEN I WAS AN EXCHANGE STUDENT.
Jeep
Tab
WONDERING WHAT YOU'RE DOING TODAY.
REMEMBER THE SANDY HILLS IN MONTEGO ?
NO MORE.

by **Tessa Brunton**

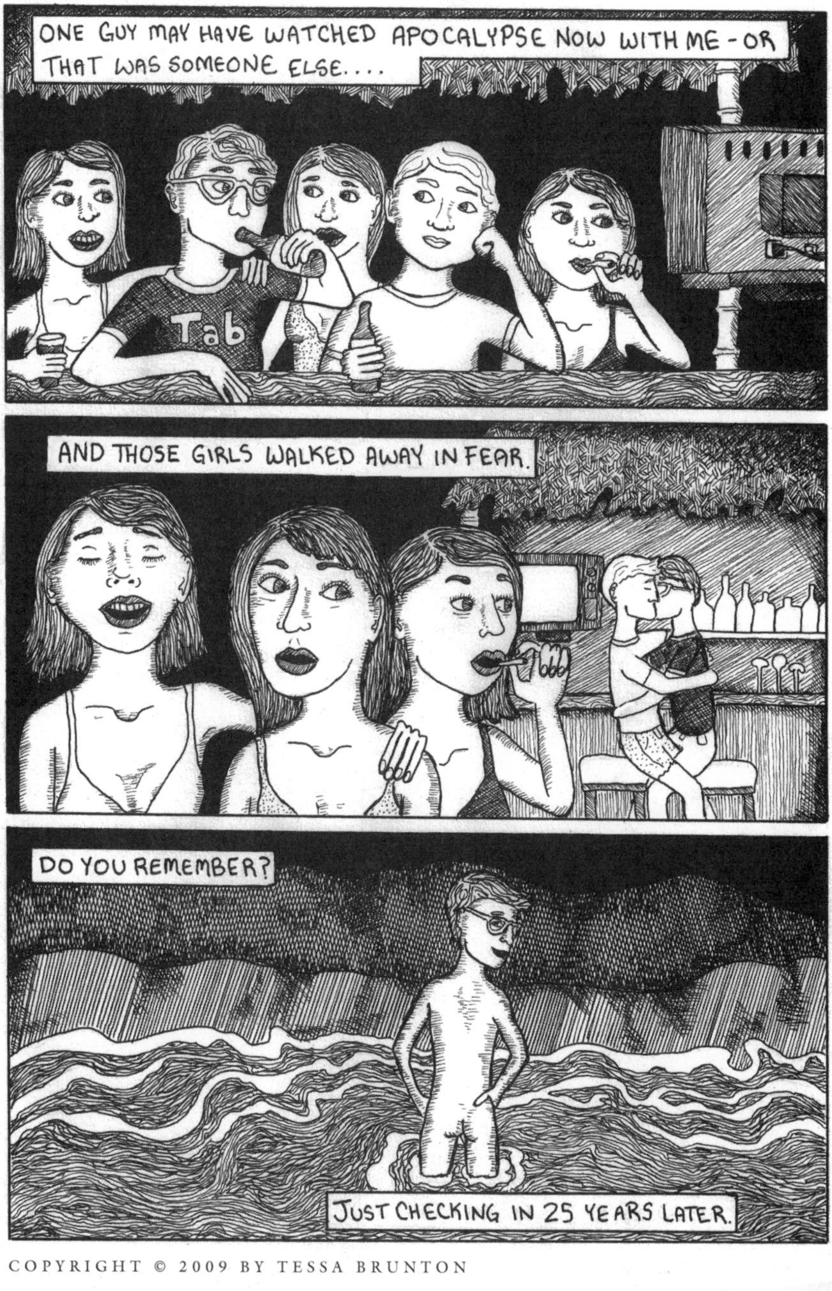
ONE GUY MAY HAVE WATCHED APOCALYPSE NOW WITH ME - OR THAT WAS SOMEONE ELSE....
Tab
AND THOSE GIRLS WALKED AWAY IN FEAR.
DO YOU REMEMBER?
JUST CHECKING IN 25 YEARS LATER.

PART 2.

LOVE ON THE ROAD

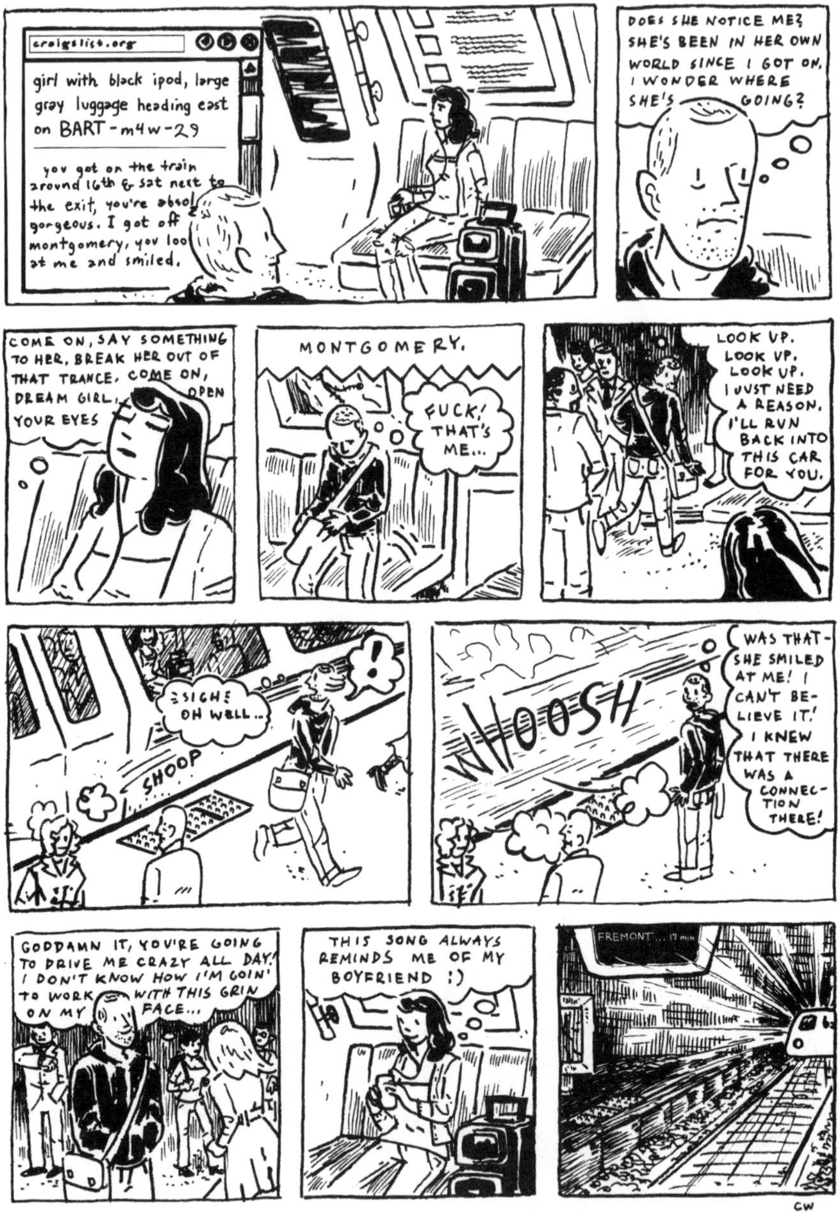
craigslist.org
girl with black ipod, large gray luggage heading east on BART - m4w - 29
you got on the train around 16th & sat next to the exit, you're absol gorgeous. I got off montgomery, you loo at me and smiled.
DOES SHE NOTICE ME? SHE'S BEEN IN HER OWN WORLD SINCE I GOT ON. I WONDER WHERE SHE'S GOING?
COME ON, SAY SOMETHING TO HER. BREAK HER OUT OF THAT TRANCE. COME ON, DREAM GIRL, OPEN YOUR EYES
MONTGOMERY.
FUCK! THAT'S ME...
LOOK UP. LOOK UP. LOOK UP. I JUST NEED A REASON. I'LL RUN BACK INTO THIS CAR FOR YOU.
!
SIGH OH WELL...
SHOOP
WHOOSH
WAS THAT- SHE SMILED AT ME! I CAN'T BE-LIEVE IT! I KNEW THAT THERE WAS A CONNEC-TION THERE!
GODDAMN IT, YOU'RE GOING TO DRIVE ME CRAZY ALL DAY! I DON'T KNOW HOW I'M GOIN' TO WORK WITH THIS GRIN ON MY FACE...
THIS SONG ALWAYS REMINDS ME OF MY BOYFRIEND :)
FREMONT ... 17 min
CW

by **Calvin Wong**

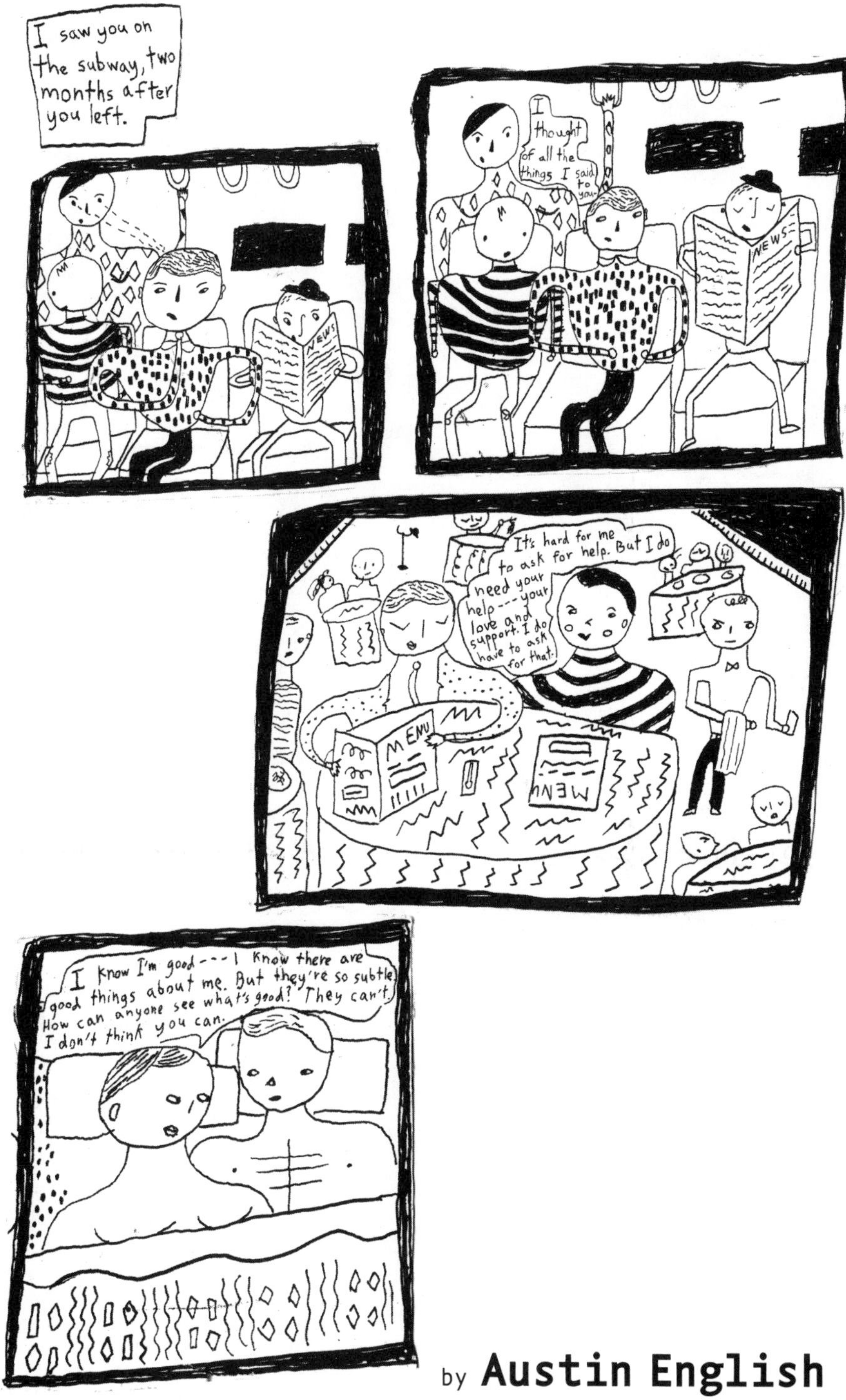
I saw you on the subway, two months after you left.
NEWS
I thought of all the things I said to you.
NEWS
It's hard for me to ask for help. But I do need your help---your love and support. I do have to ask for that.
MENU
MENU
I know I'm good---I know there are good things about me. But they're so subtle. How can anyone see what's good? They can't. I don't think you can.

by **Austin English**

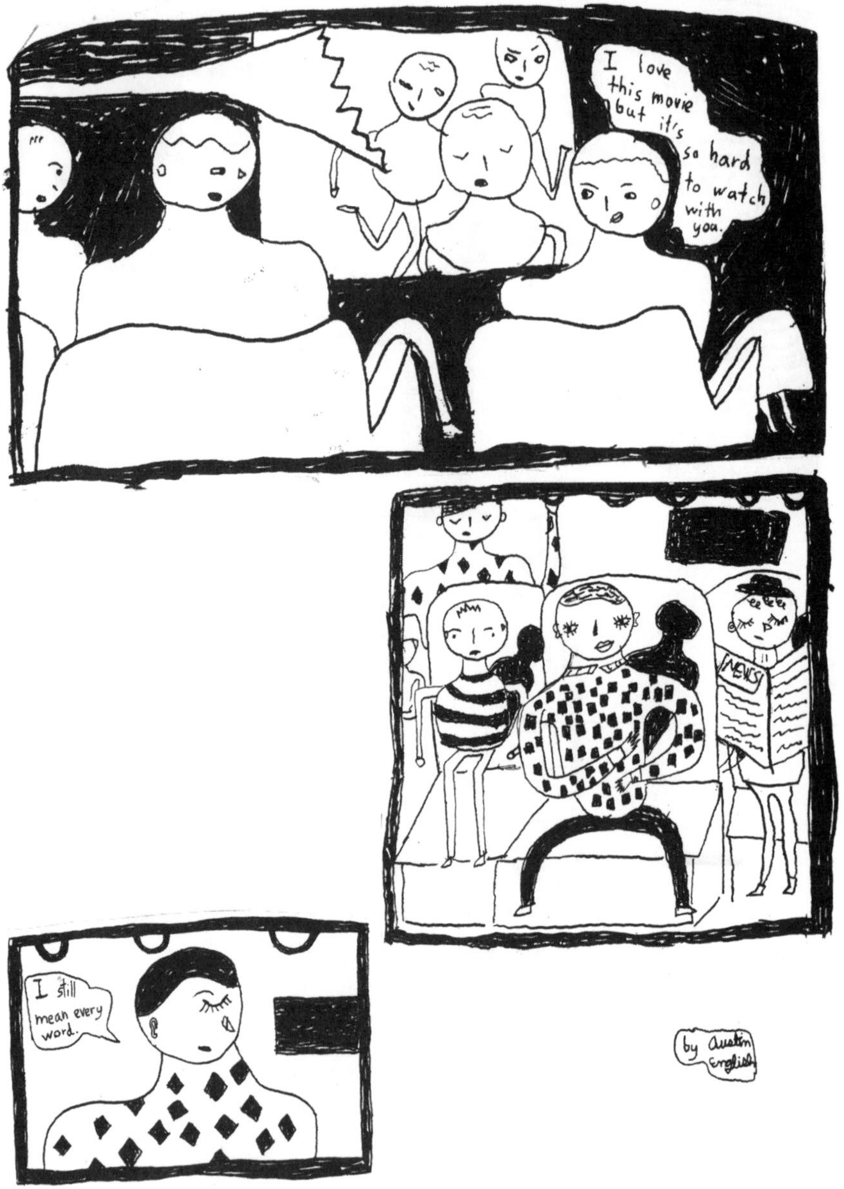
I love this movie but it's so hard to watch with you.
NEWS!
I still mean every word.
by Austin English

W4M: HOCKEY HAIR...

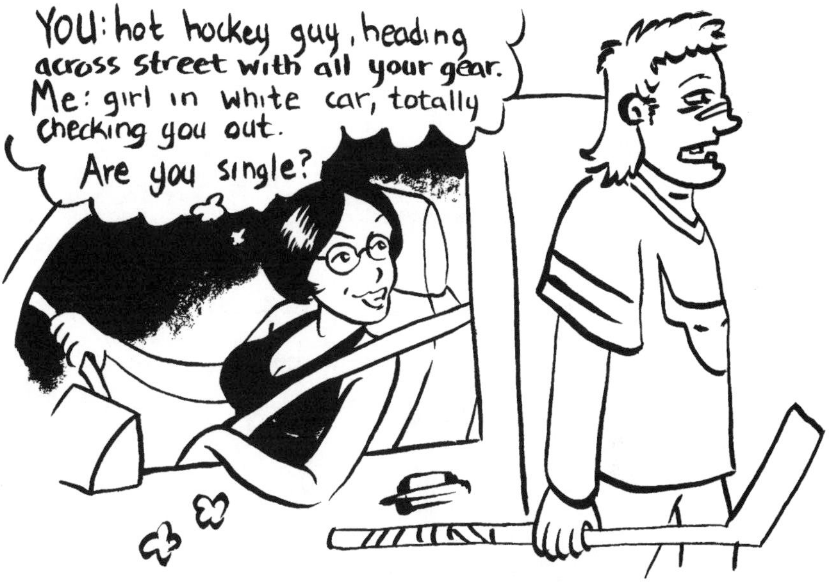
YOU: hot hockey guy, heading across street with all your gear. Me: girl in white car, totally checking you out.
Are you single?

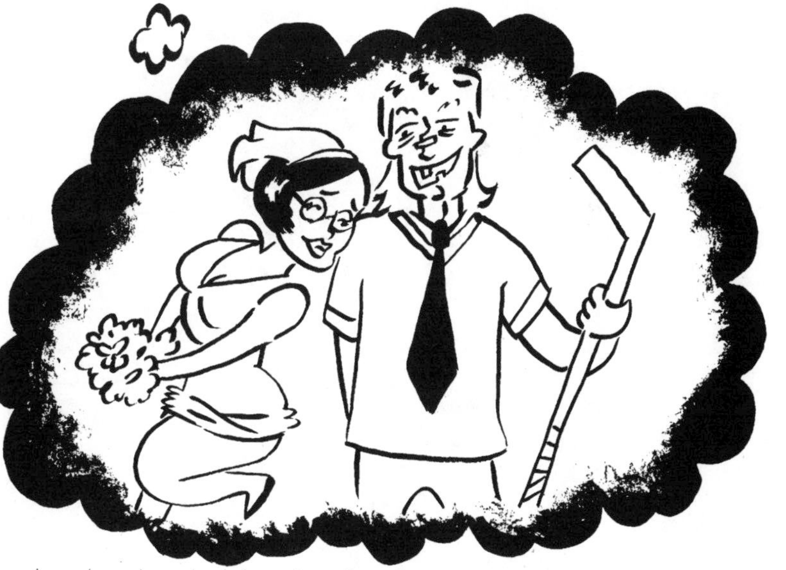

by **Colleen Frakes**

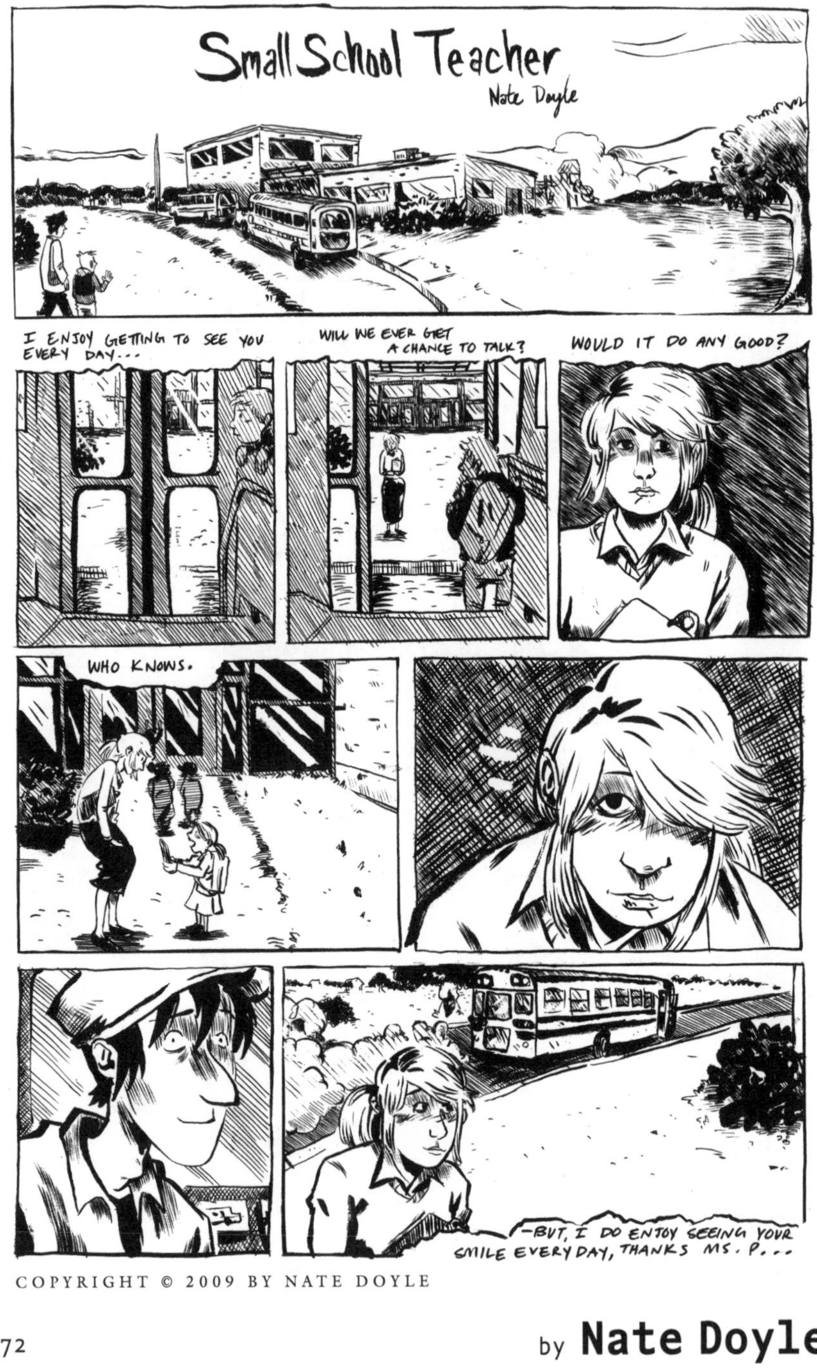
Small School Teacher
Nate Doyle
I ENJOY GETTING TO SEE YOU EVERY DAY...
WILL WE EVER GET A CHANCE TO TALK?
WOULD IT DO ANY GOOD?
WHO KNOWS.
—BUT, I DO ENJOY SEEING YOUR SMILE EVERYDAY, THANKS MS. P...

by **Nate Doyle**

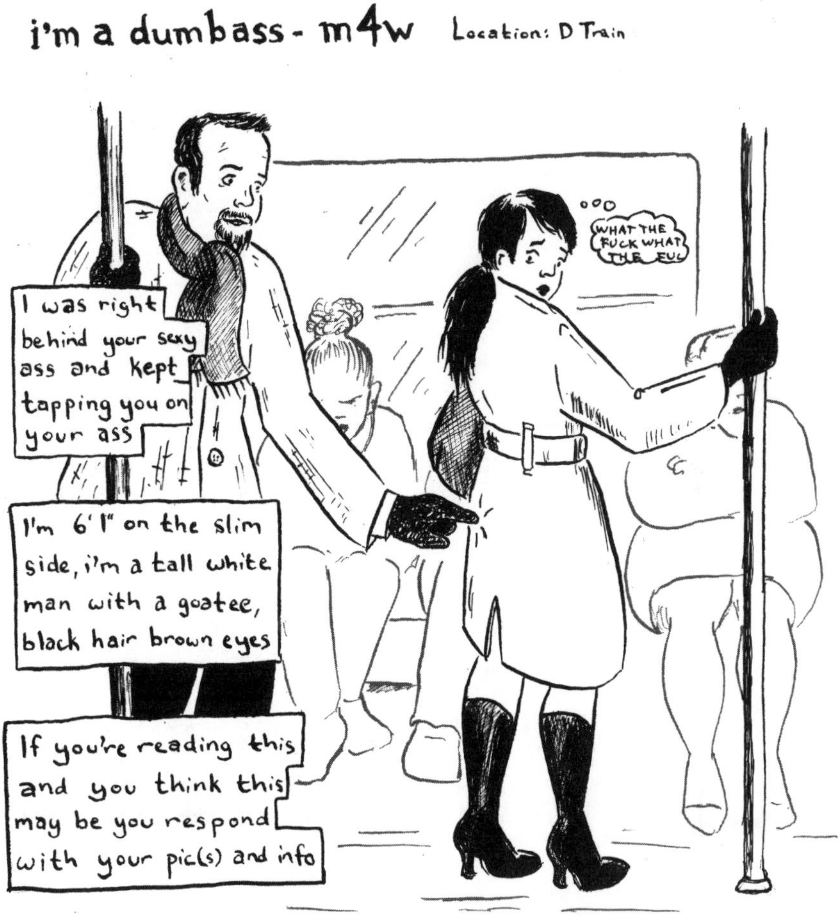
i'm a dumbass - m4w Location: D Train
I was right behind your sexy ass and kept tapping you on your ass
WHAT THE FUCK WHAT THE FU
I'm 6'1" on the slim side, i'm a tall white man with a goatee, black hair brown eyes
If you're reading this and you think this may be you respond with your pic(s) and info

by **Emily Flake**

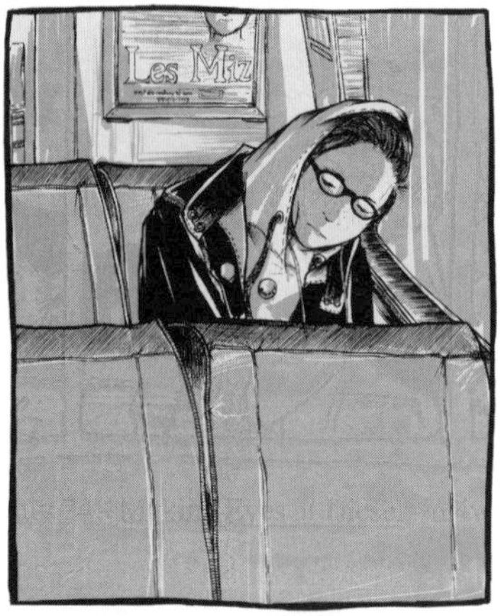
Les Miz

I watched you napping on BART... - m4w

and you opened your eyes and caught me. i guess i couldn't look away fast enough. i wanted to keep looking at you, but i didn't want to be a creep. can i look at you some more? maybe at a closer proximity?

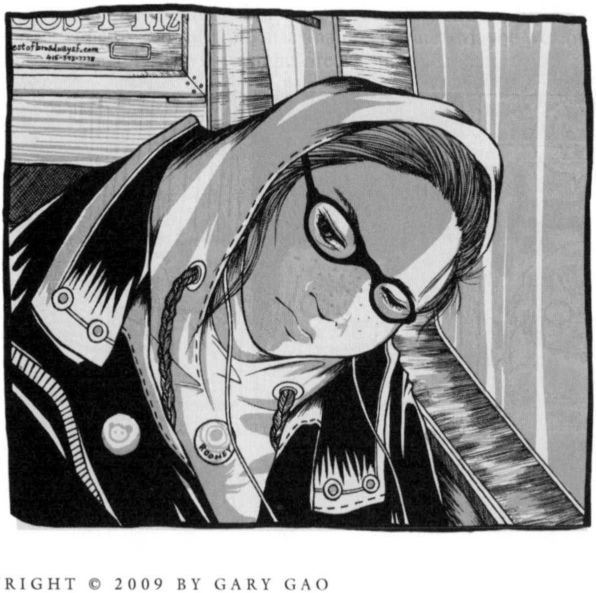

by **Gary Gao**

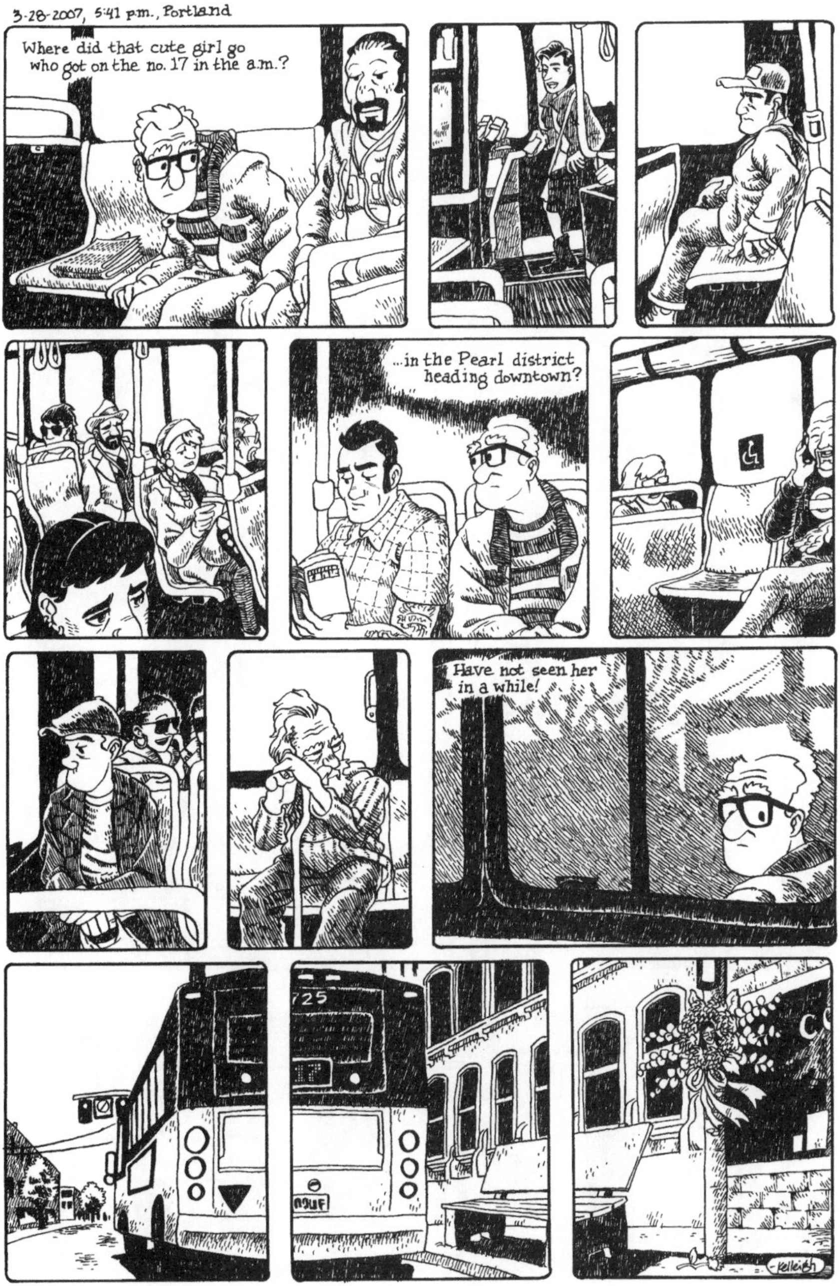
3-28-2007, 5:41 p.m., Portland
Where did that cute girl go who got on the no. 17 in the a.m.?
...in the Pearl district heading downtown?
Have not seen her in a while!
-Kelleigh

by **Indigo Kelleigh**

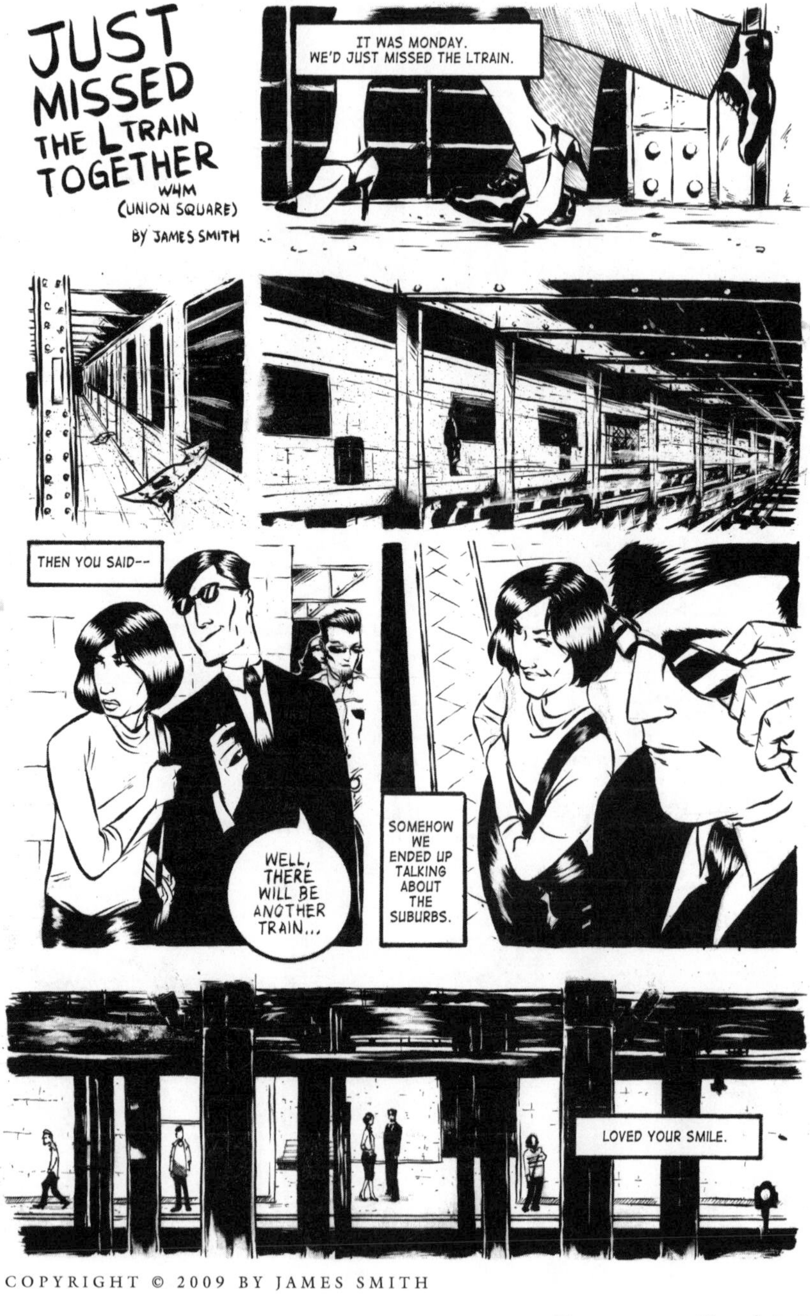
JUST MISSED THE L TRAIN TOGETHER
W4M
(UNION SQUARE)
BY JAMES SMITH
IT WAS MONDAY. WE'D JUST MISSED THE LTRAIN.
THEN YOU SAID--
WELL, THERE WILL BE ANOTHER TRAIN...
SOMEHOW WE ENDED UP TALKING ABOUT THE SUBURBS.
LOVED YOUR SMILE.

by **James Smith**

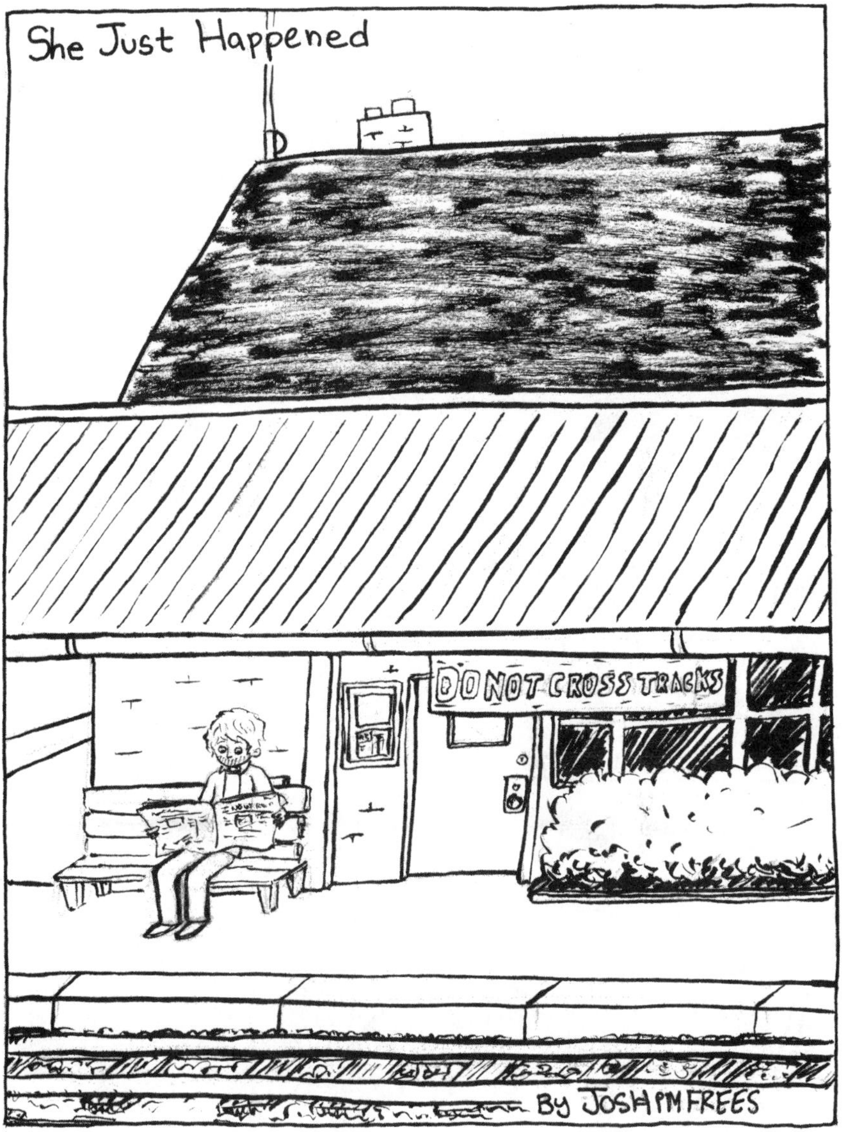
She Just Happened
DO NOT CROSS TRACKS
By JOSH PM FREES

by **Josh Frees**

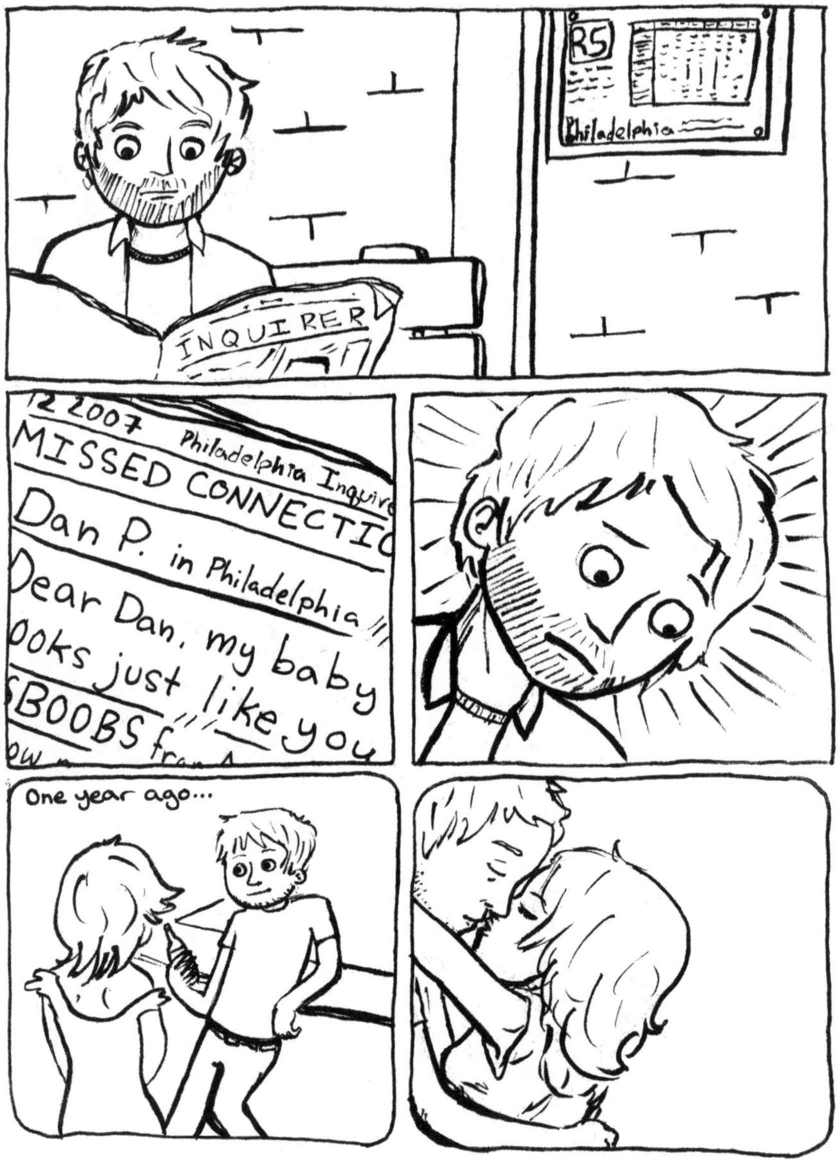
INQUIRER
RS
Philadelphia
12 2007
Philadelphia Inquire
MISSED CONNECTIO
Dan P. in Philadelphia
Dear Dan, my baby
ooks just like you
SBOOBS
One year ago...

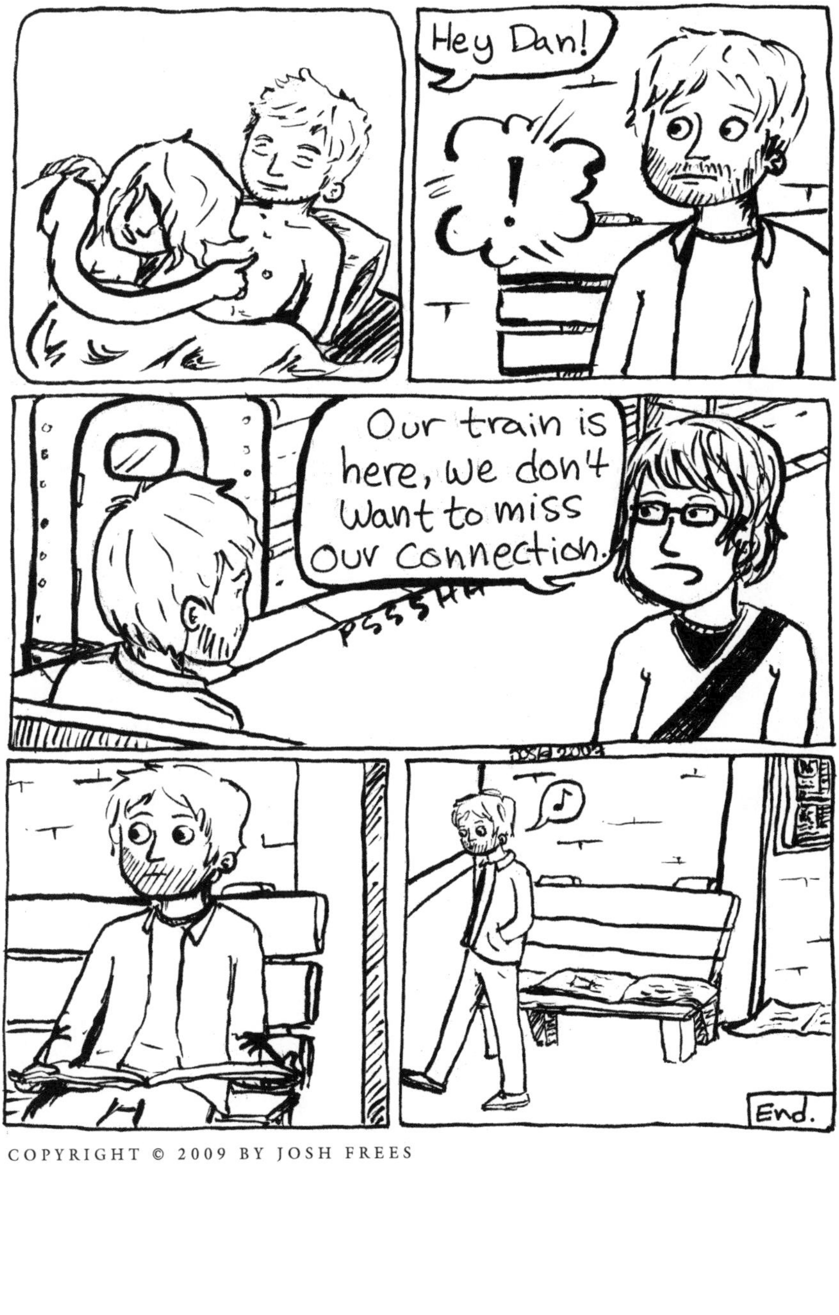
Hey Dan!
!
Our train is here, we don't Want to miss our connection.
End.

Vomit and beautiful women on the Redline. m4w-32

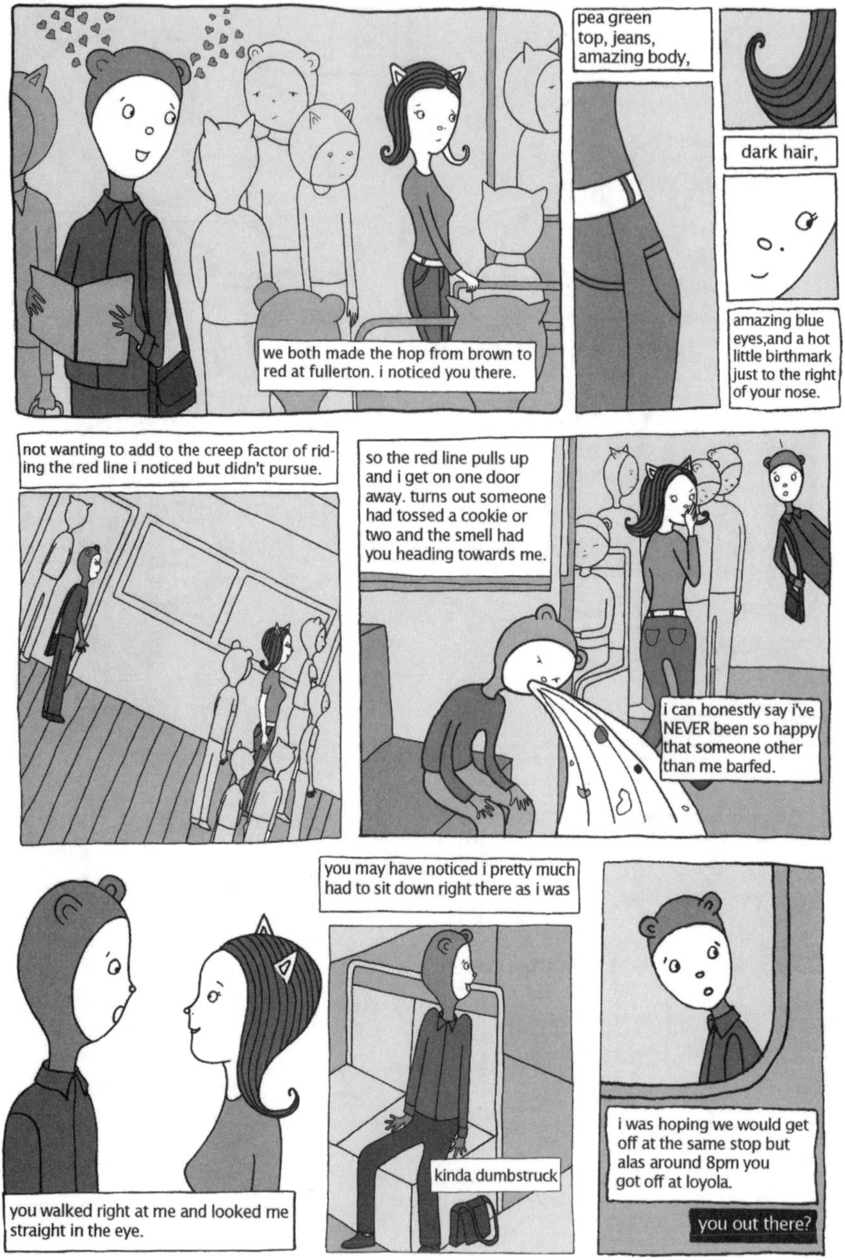

we both made the hop from brown to red at fullerton. i noticed you there.
pea green top, jeans, amazing body,
dark hair,
amazing blue eyes,and a hot little birthmark just to the right of your nose.
not wanting to add to the creep factor of riding the red line i noticed but didn't pursue.
so the red line pulls up and i get on one door away. turns out someone had tossed a cookie or two and the smell had you heading towards me.
i can honestly say i've NEVER been so happy that someone other than me barfed.
you walked right at me and looked me straight in the eye.
you may have noticed i pretty much had to sit down right there as i was
kinda dumbstruck
i was hoping we would get off at the same stop but alas around 8pm you got off at loyola.
you out there?

by **Kate O'Leary**

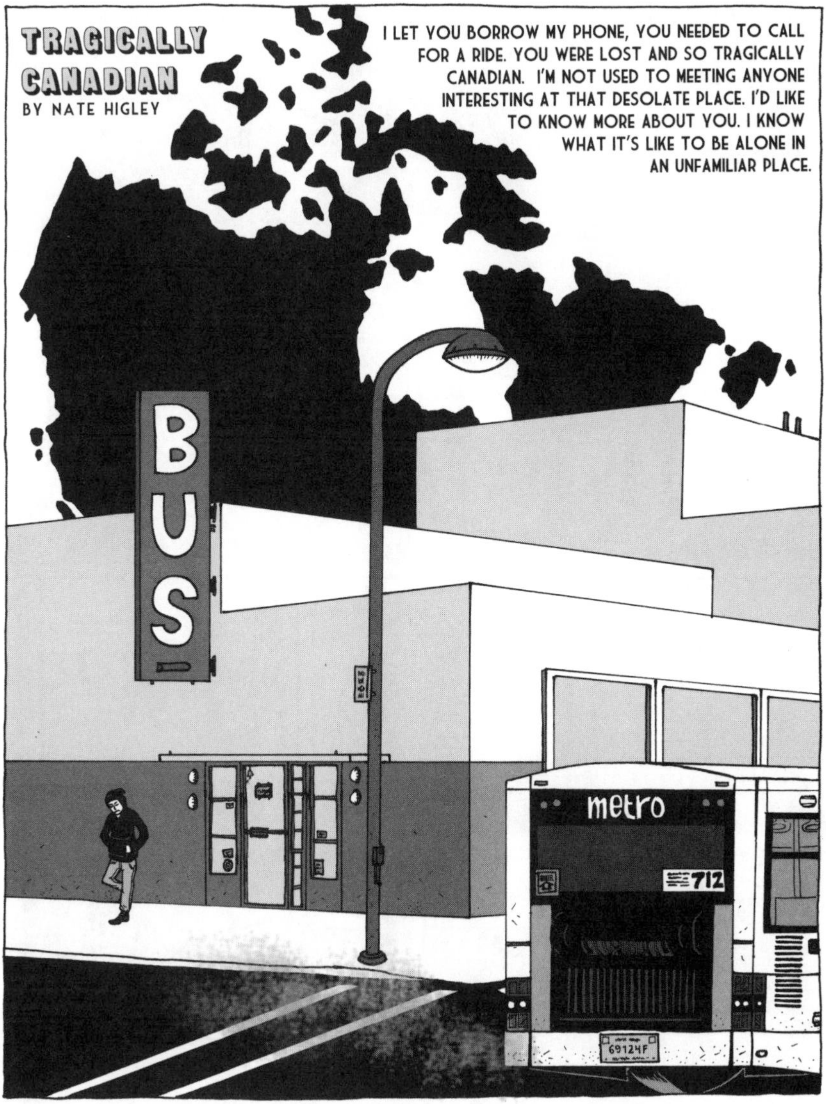
TRAGICALLY CANADIAN
BY NATE HIGLEY
I LET YOU BORROW MY PHONE, YOU NEEDED TO CALL FOR A RIDE. YOU WERE LOST AND SO TRAGICALLY CANADIAN. I'M NOT USED TO MEETING ANYONE INTERESTING AT THAT DESOLATE PLACE. I'D LIKE TO KNOW MORE ABOUT YOU. I KNOW WHAT IT'S LIKE TO BE ALONE IN AN UNFAMILIAR PLACE.
BUS
metro
712
69124F

by **Nate Higley**

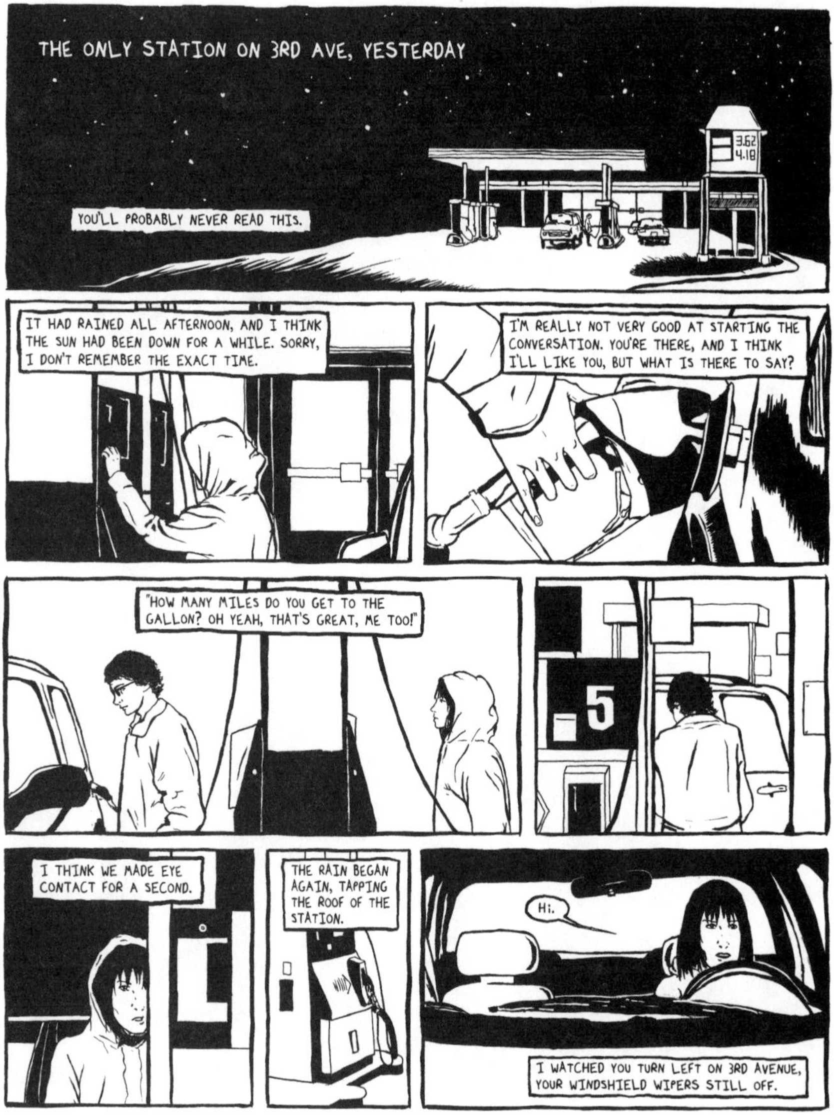
THE ONLY STATION ON 3RD AVE, YESTERDAY
3.62
4.18
YOU'LL PROBABLY NEVER READ THIS.
IT HAD RAINED ALL AFTERNOON, AND I THINK THE SUN HAD BEEN DOWN FOR A WHILE. SORRY, I DON'T REMEMBER THE EXACT TIME.
I'M REALLY NOT VERY GOOD AT STARTING THE CONVERSATION. YOU'RE THERE, AND I THINK I'LL LIKE YOU, BUT WHAT IS THERE TO SAY?
"HOW MANY MILES DO YOU GET TO THE GALLON? OH YEAH, THAT'S GREAT, ME TOO!"
5
I THINK WE MADE EYE CONTACT FOR A SECOND.
THE RAIN BEGAN AGAIN, TAPPING THE ROOF OF THE STATION.
Hi.
I WATCHED YOU TURN LEFT ON 3RD AVENUE, YOUR WINDSHIELD WIPERS STILL OFF.

by **Zachary Garrett**

PART 3.

COFFEE-SHOP CRUSHES

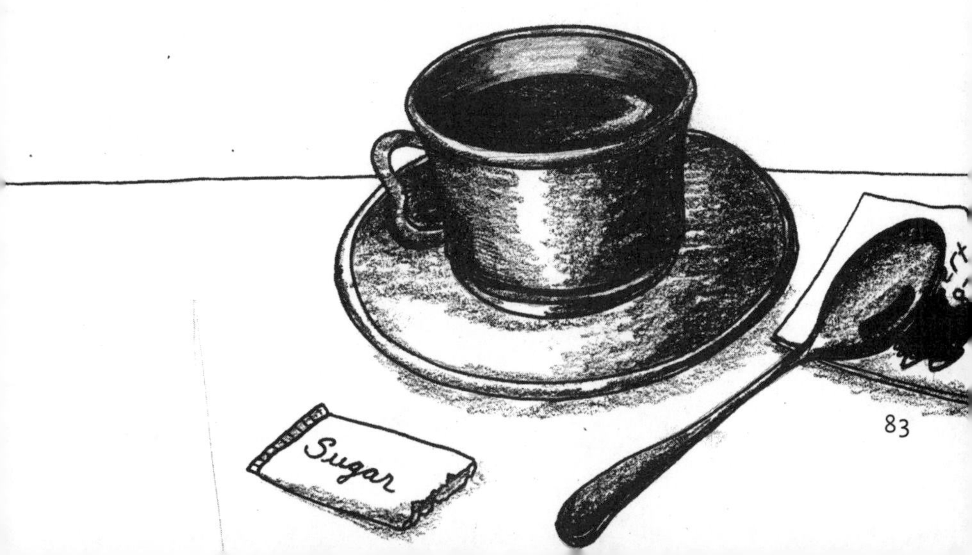
Sugar

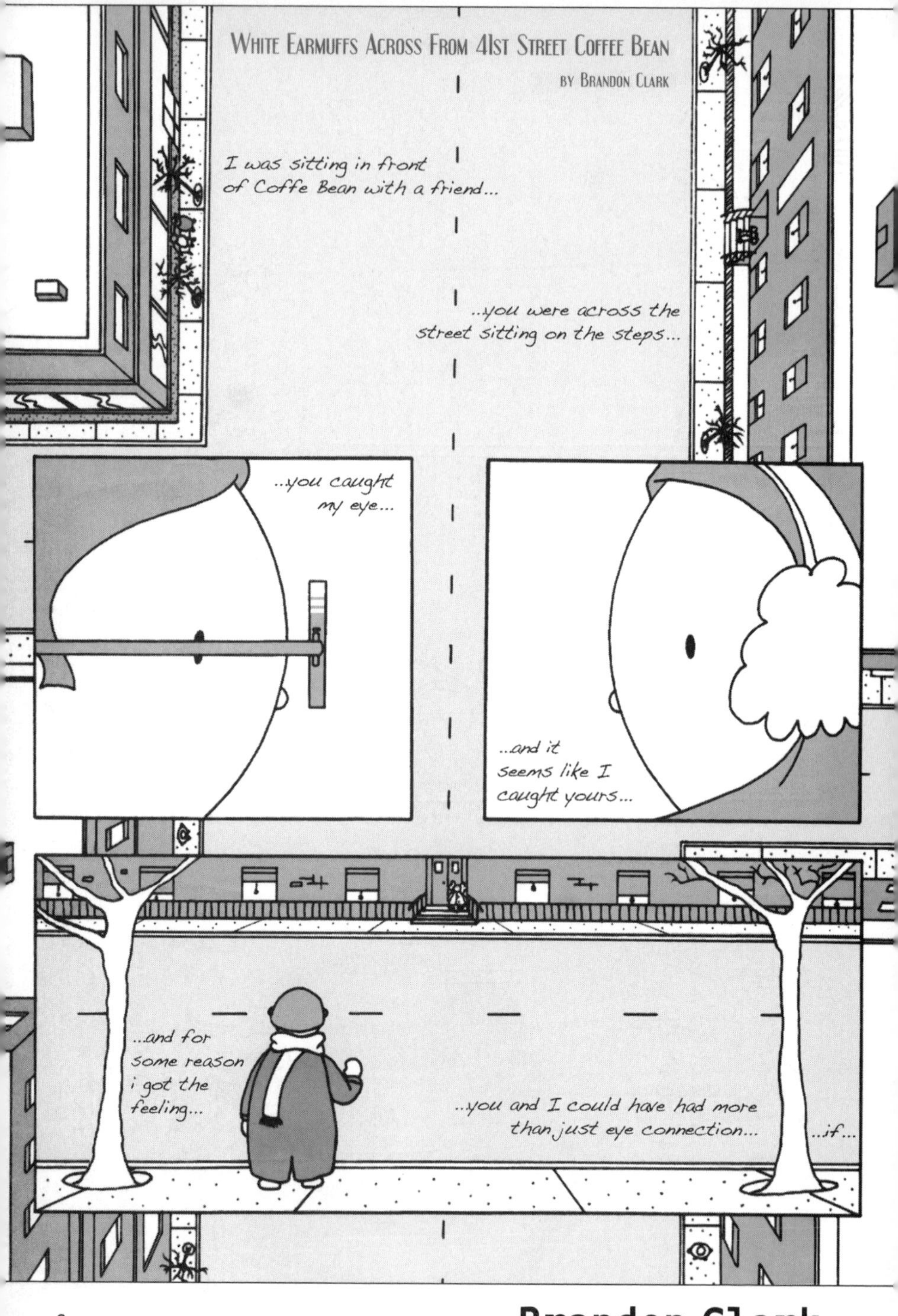
White Earmuffs Across From 41st Street Coffee Bean
by Brandon Clark
I was sitting in front of Coffe Bean with a friend...
...you were across the street sitting on the steps...
...you caught my eye...
...and it seems like I caught yours...
...and for some reason i got the feeling...
...you and I could have had more than just eye connection...
...if...

by **Brandon Clark**

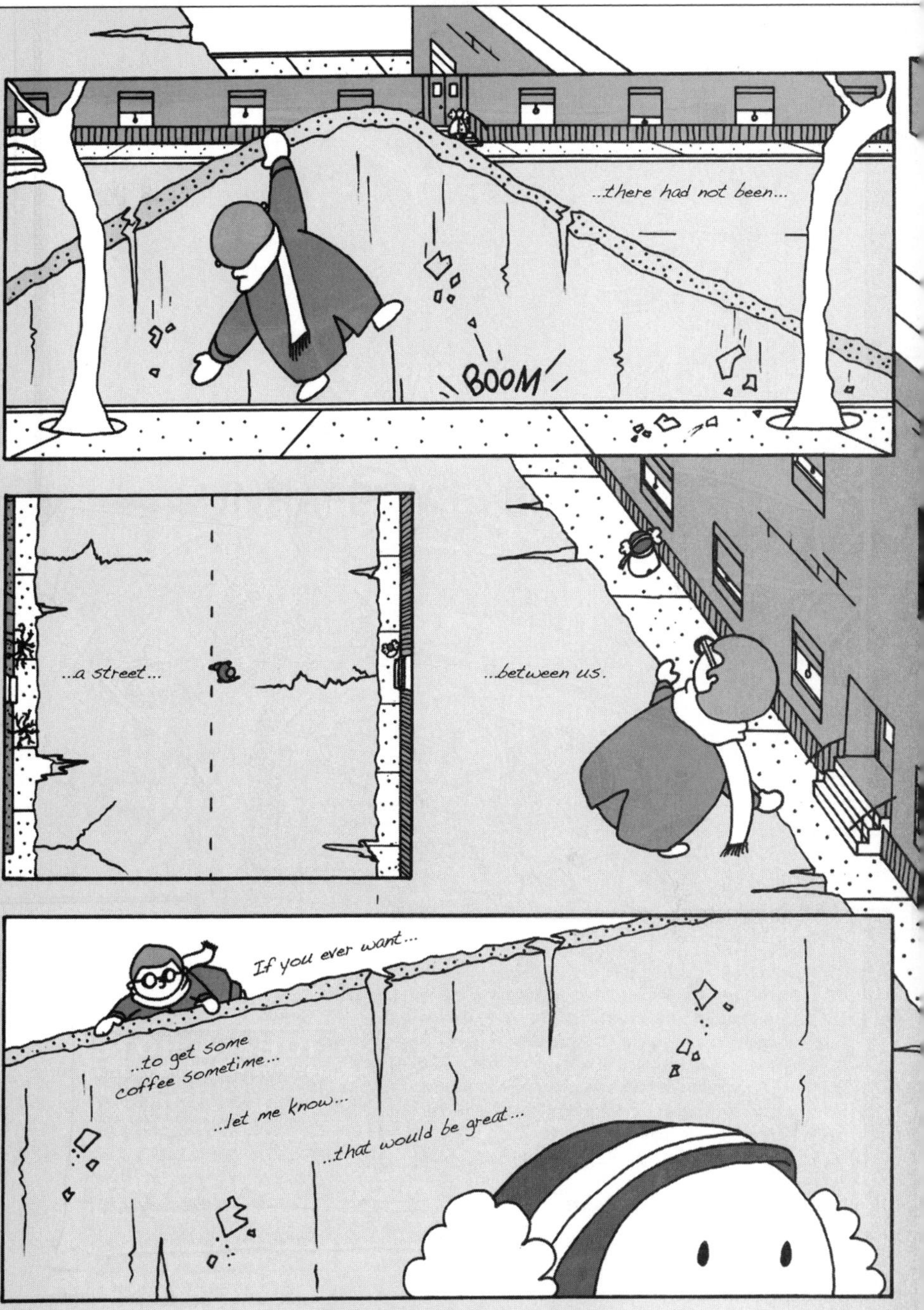
...there had not been...
BOOM
...a street...
...between us.
If you ever want...
...to get some coffee sometime...
...let me know...
...that would be great...

Reply to:pers-3508171972@craigslist.org
Date: 2008-05-20 10:08PDT

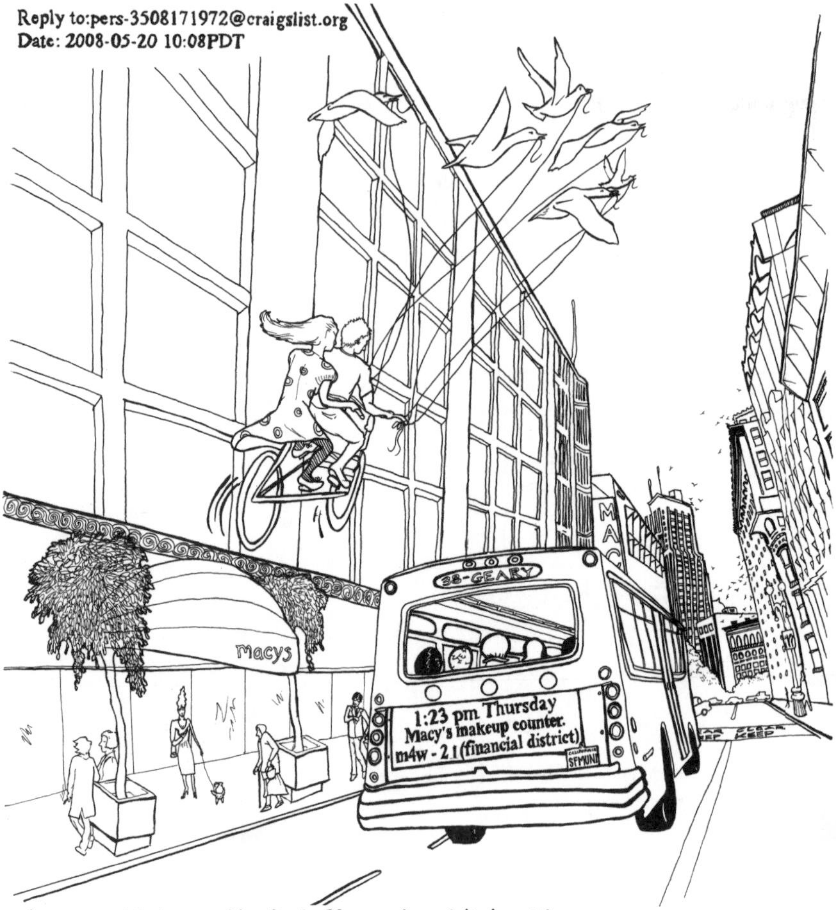
38-GEARY
macys
1:23 pm Thursday
Macy's makeup counter.
m4w - 21 (financial district)
SFMUNI

i saw you while i was waiting for the 38 geary. i was loitering at the bus stop, peering into the vastness of macy's. i saw you at the cosmetics counter applying makeup to some matronly lady, you were dazzlingly beautiful. i wanted to ask you out but my bus came & i was late to work...maybe i'll work up the courage sometime and we can go out on a date, go dancing, watch a film, feed the pigeons in the park, take a tandem bicycle ride, whatever you want...

1:23 pm Thursday
Macy's m4w - 21 (financial district)

by **Fiona Taylor**

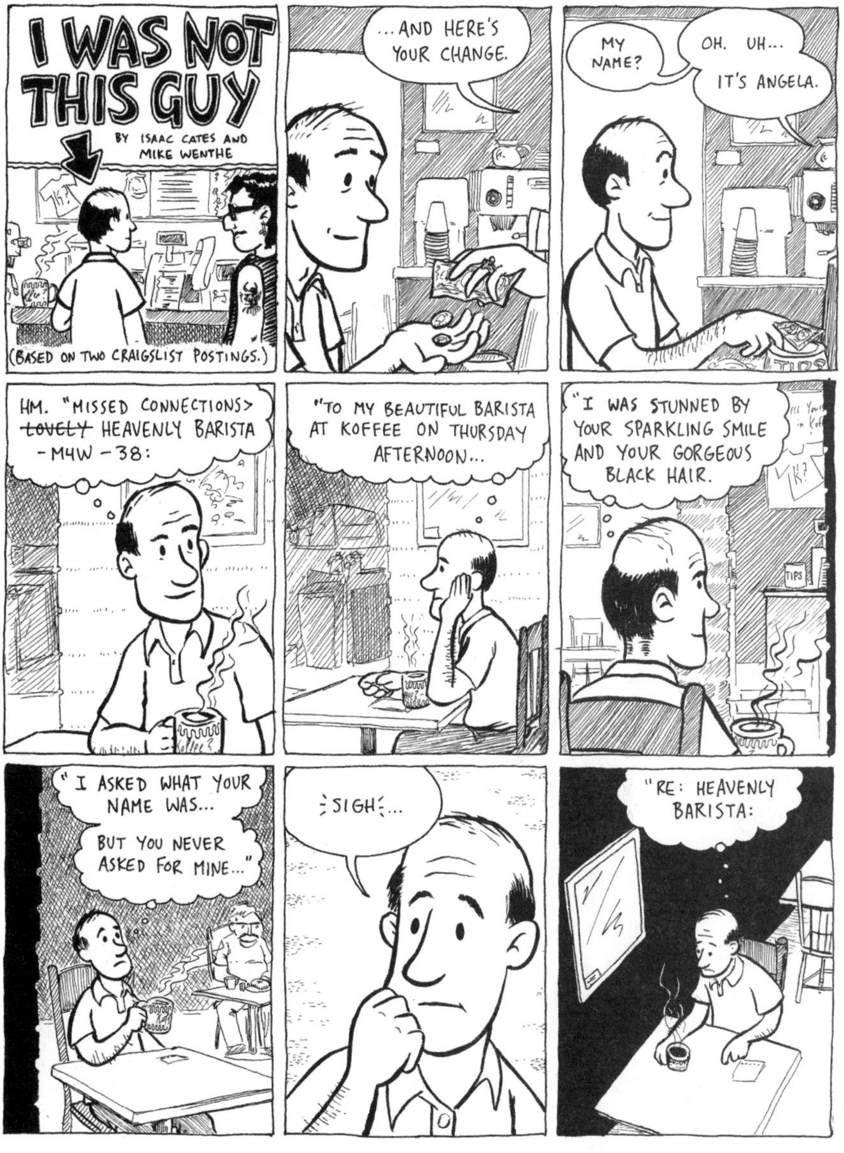
I WAS NOT THIS GUY
BY ISAAC CATES AND MIKE WENTHE
(BASED ON TWO CRAIGSLIST POSTINGS.)
...AND HERE'S YOUR CHANGE.
MY NAME?
OH. UH...
IT'S ANGELA.
HM. "MISSED CONNECTIONS> ~~LOVELY~~ HEAVENLY BARISTA -M4W -38:
"TO MY BEAUTIFUL BARISTA AT KOFFEE ON THURSDAY AFTERNOON...
"I WAS STUNNED BY YOUR SPARKLING SMILE AND YOUR GORGEOUS BLACK HAIR.
"I ASKED WHAT YOUR NAME WAS...
BUT YOU NEVER ASKED FOR MINE..."
SIGH...
"RE: HEAVENLY BARISTA:

by **Isaac Cates and Mike Wenthe**

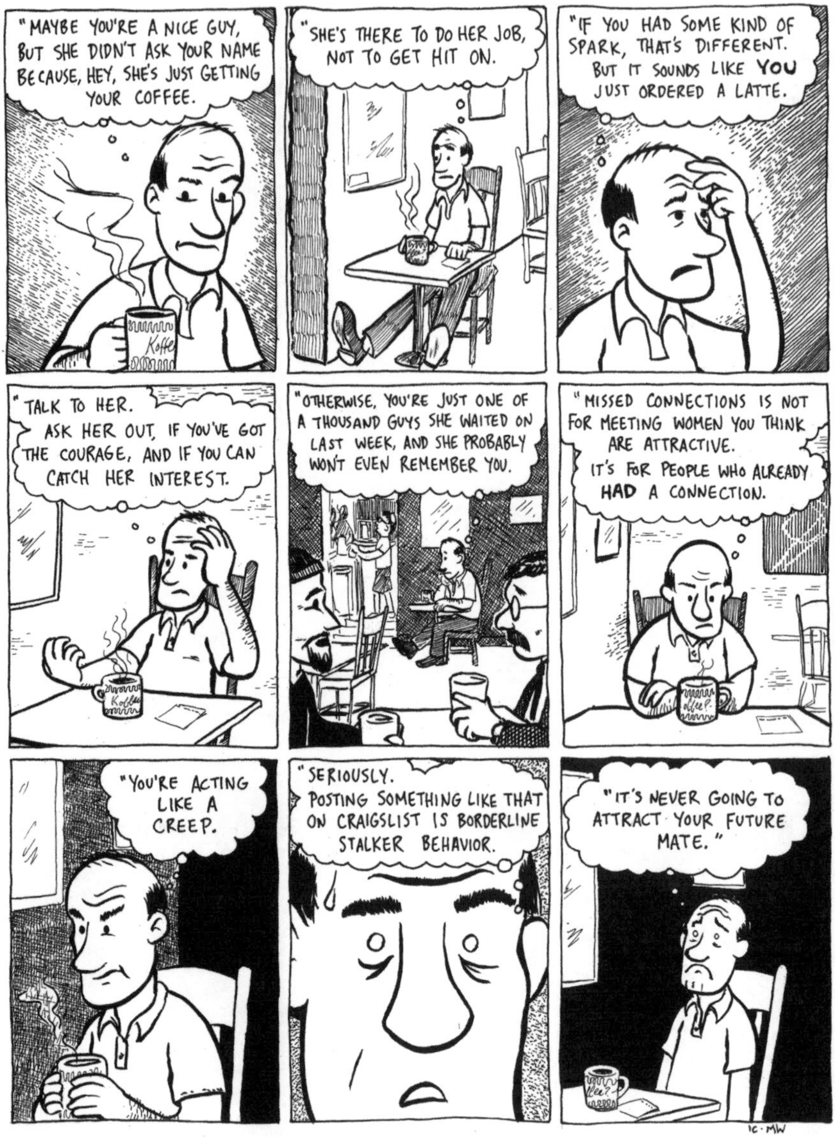
"MAYBE YOU'RE A NICE GUY, BUT SHE DIDN'T ASK YOUR NAME BECAUSE, HEY, SHE'S JUST GETTING YOUR COFFEE.
"SHE'S THERE TO DO HER JOB, NOT TO GET HIT ON.
"IF YOU HAD SOME KIND OF SPARK, THAT'S DIFFERENT. BUT IT SOUNDS LIKE YOU JUST ORDERED A LATTE.
"TALK TO HER. ASK HER OUT, IF YOU'VE GOT THE COURAGE, AND IF YOU CAN CATCH HER INTEREST.
"OTHERWISE, YOU'RE JUST ONE OF A THOUSAND GUYS SHE WAITED ON LAST WEEK, AND SHE PROBABLY WON'T EVEN REMEMBER YOU.
"MISSED CONNECTIONS IS NOT FOR MEETING WOMEN YOU THINK ARE ATTRACTIVE. IT'S FOR PEOPLE WHO ALREADY HAD A CONNECTION.
"YOU'RE ACTING LIKE A CREEP.
"SERIOUSLY. POSTING SOMETHING LIKE THAT ON CRAIGSLIST IS BORDERLINE STALKER BEHAVIOR.
"IT'S NEVER GOING TO ATTRACT YOUR FUTURE MATE."
IC · MW

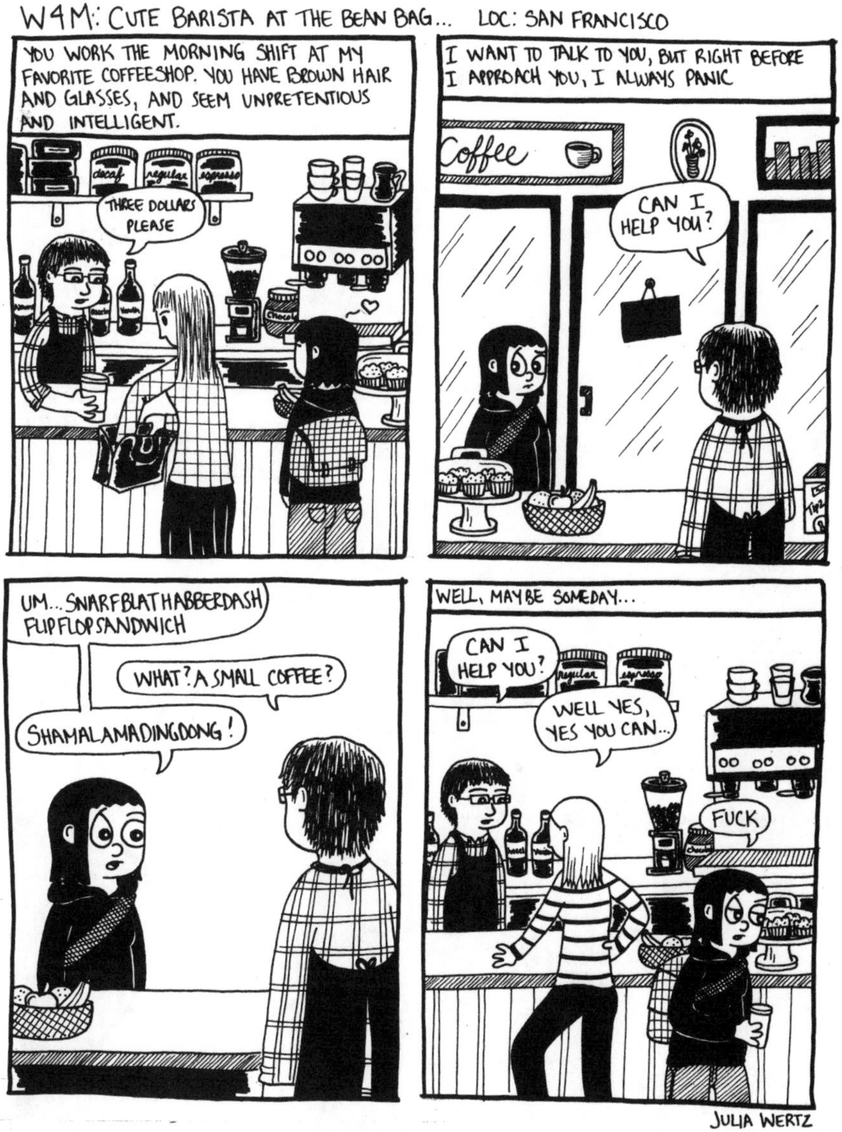
W4M: CUTE BARISTA AT THE BEAN BAG... LOC: SAN FRANCISCO
YOU WORK THE MORNING SHIFT AT MY FAVORITE COFFEESHOP. YOU HAVE BROWN HAIR AND GLASSES, AND SEEM UNPRETENTIOUS AND INTELLIGENT.
THREE DOLLARS PLEASE
I WANT TO TALK TO YOU, BUT RIGHT BEFORE I APPROACH YOU, I ALWAYS PANIC
Coffee
CAN I HELP YOU?
UM... SNARFBLATHABBERDASH FLIPFLOPSANDWICH
WHAT? A SMALL COFFEE?
SHAMALAMADINGDONG!
WELL, MAYBE SOMEDAY...
CAN I HELP YOU?
WELL YES, YES YOU CAN...
FUCK
JULIA WERTZ

by **Julia Wertz**

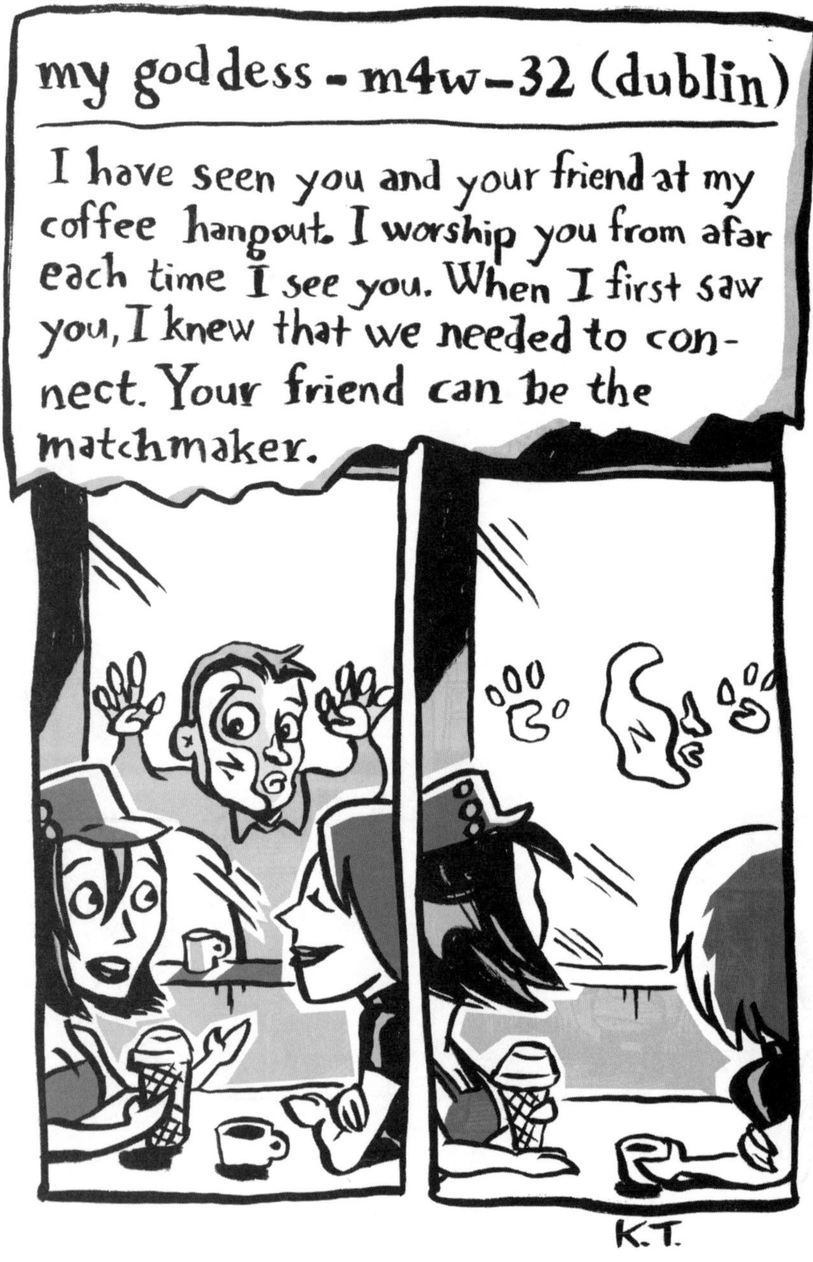
my goddess - m4w-32 (dublin)
I have seen you and your friend at my coffee hangout. I worship you from afar each time I see you. When I first saw you, I knew that we needed to connect. Your friend can be the matchmaker.
K.T.

by **Kelly Tindall**

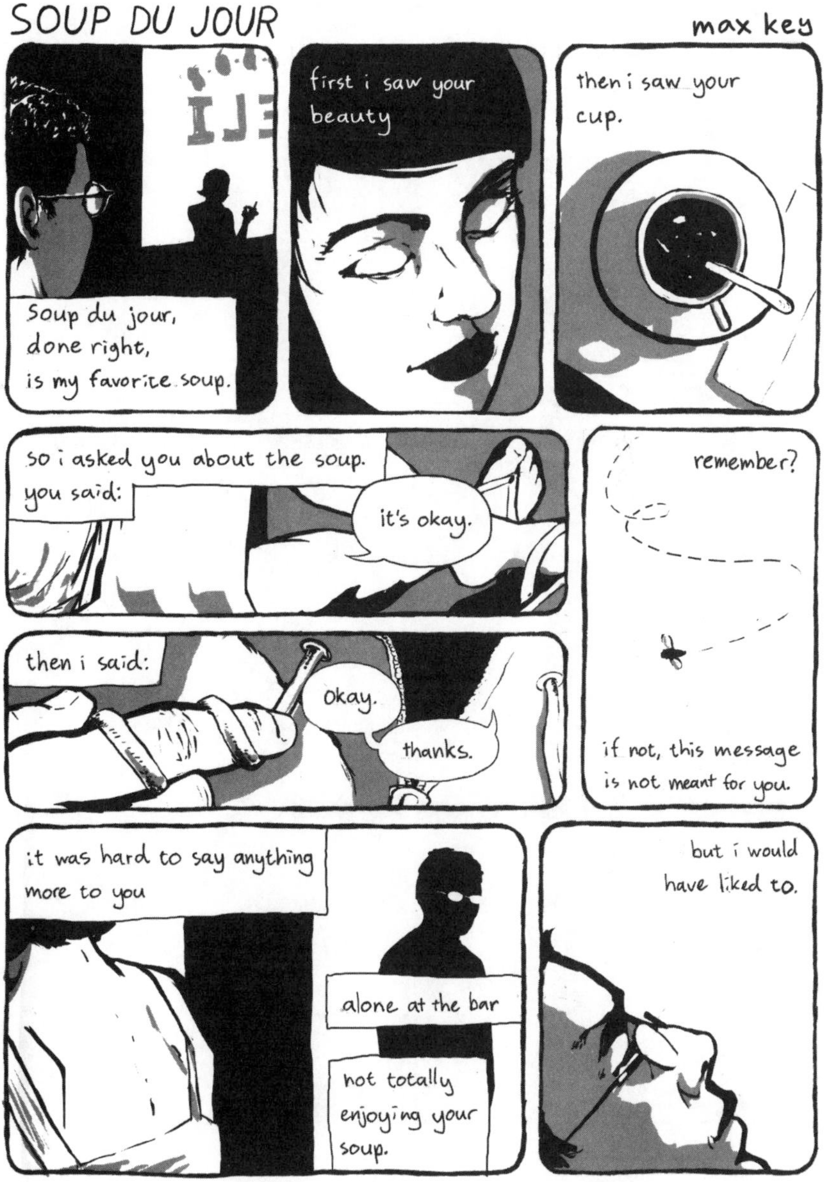
SOUP DU JOUR
max key
Soup du jour,
done right,
is my favorite soup.
first i saw your
beauty
then i saw your
cup.
so i asked you about the soup.
you said:
it's okay.
remember?
then i said:
okay.
thanks.
if not, this message
is not meant for you.
it was hard to say anything
more to you
alone at the bar
not totally
enjoying your
soup.
but i would
have liked to.

by **Max Karl Key**

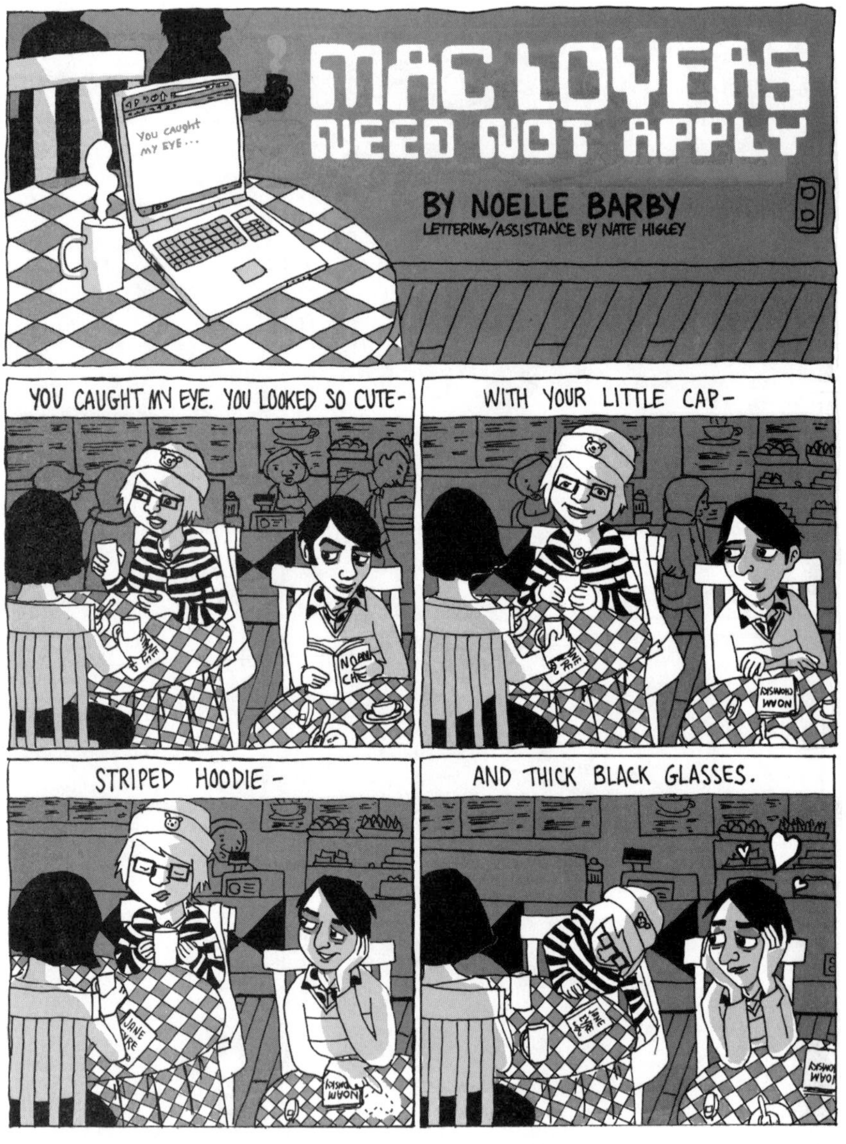
MAC LOVERS
NEED NOT APPLY
You caught my EYE...
BY NOELLE BARBY
LETTERING/ASSISTANCE BY NATE HIGLEY
YOU CAUGHT MY EYE. YOU LOOKED SO CUTE-
WITH YOUR LITTLE CAP-
STRIPED HOODIE -
AND THICK BLACK GLASSES.

 by **Noelle Barby and Nate Higley**

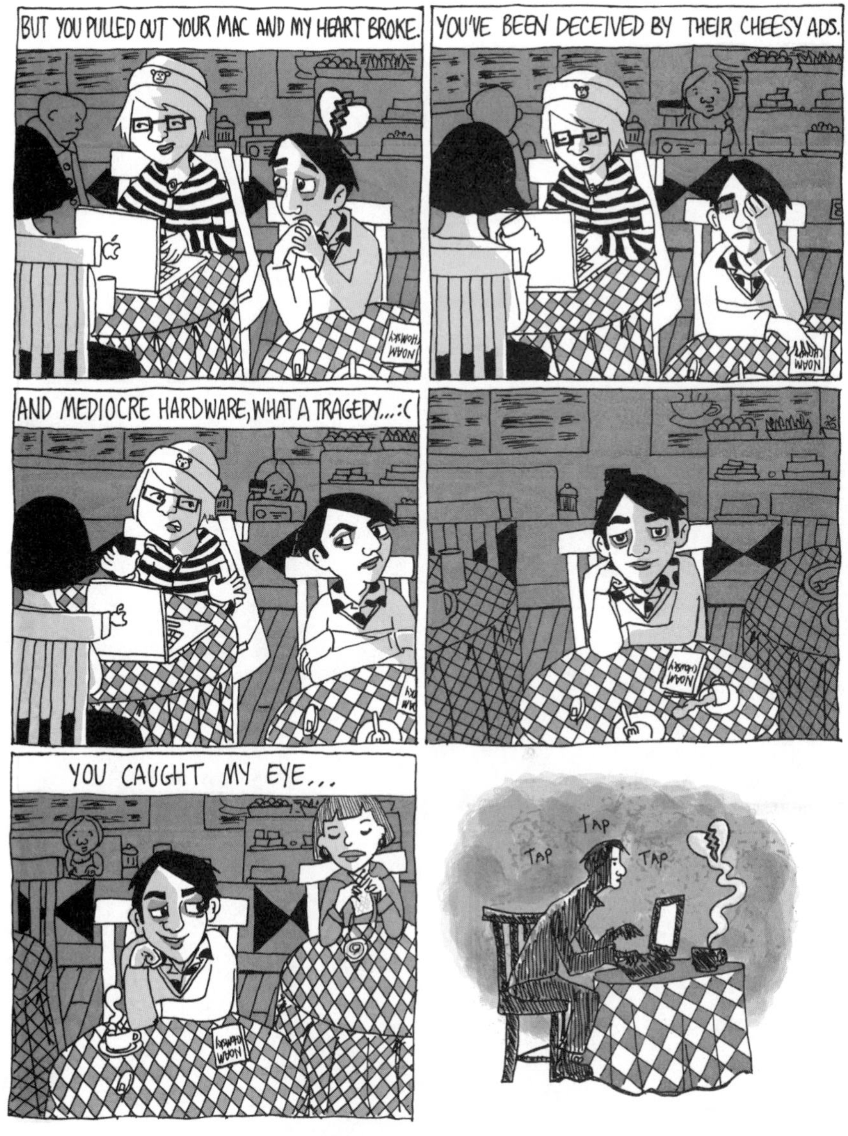
BUT YOU PULLED OUT YOUR MAC AND MY HEART BROKE.
YOU'VE BEEN DECEIVED BY THEIR CHEESY ADS.
AND MEDIOCRE HARDWARE, WHAT A TRAGEDY...:(
YOU CAUGHT MY EYE...
TAP
TAP
TAP

Missed Connections

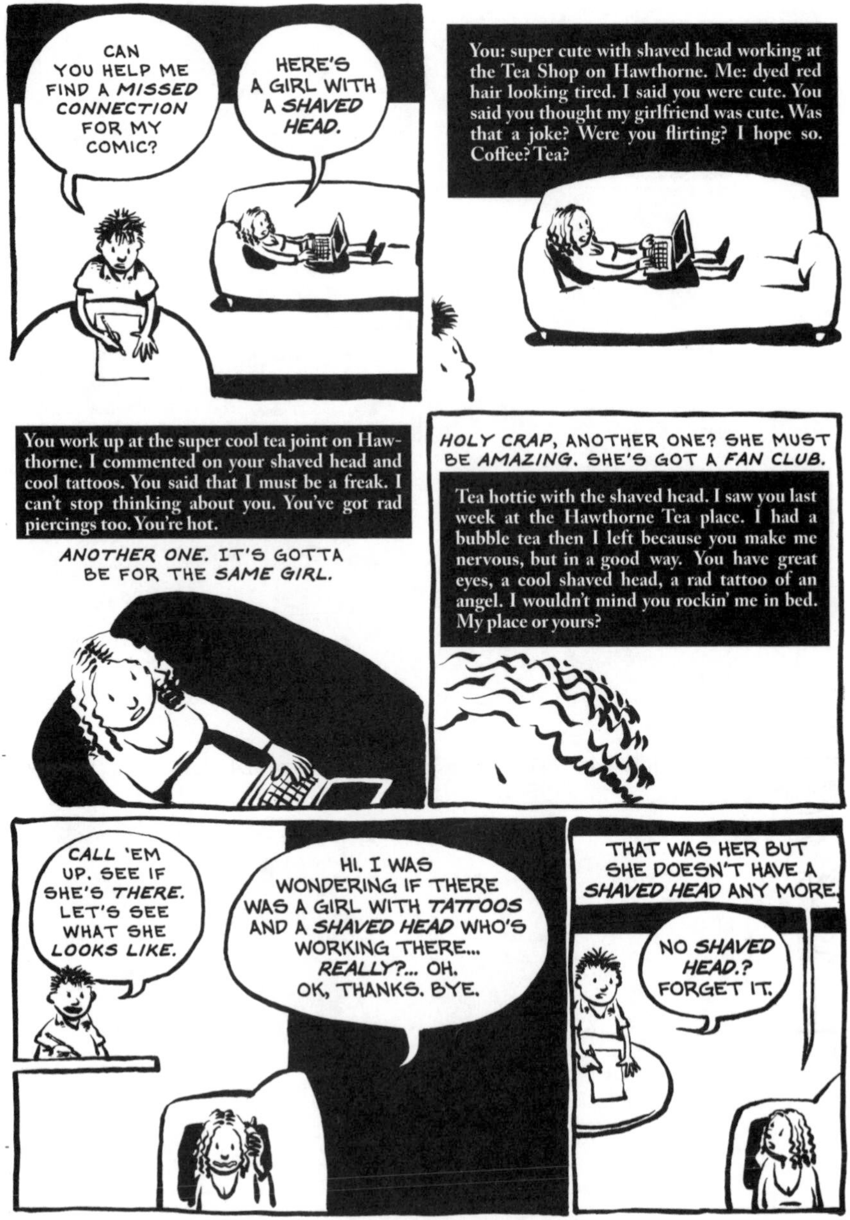

CAN YOU HELP ME FIND A *MISSED CONNECTION* FOR MY COMIC?
HERE'S A GIRL WITH A *SHAVED HEAD.*
You: super cute with shaved head working at the Tea Shop on Hawthorne. Me: dyed red hair looking tired. I said you were cute. You said you thought my girlfriend was cute. Was that a joke? Were you flirting? I hope so. Coffee? Tea?
You work up at the super cool tea joint on Hawthorne. I commented on your shaved head and cool tattoos. You said that I must be a freak. I can't stop thinking about you. You've got rad piercings too. You're hot.
ANOTHER ONE. IT'S GOTTA BE FOR THE *SAME GIRL.*
HOLY CRAP, ANOTHER ONE? SHE MUST BE *AMAZING*. SHE'S GOT A *FAN CLUB.*
Tea hottie with the shaved head. I saw you last week at the Hawthorne Tea place. I had a bubble tea then I left because you make me nervous, but in a good way. You have great eyes, a cool shaved head, a rad tattoo of an angel. I wouldn't mind you rockin' me in bed. My place or yours?
CALL 'EM UP. SEE IF SHE'S *THERE.* LET'S SEE WHAT SHE *LOOKS LIKE.*
HI. I WAS WONDERING IF THERE WAS A GIRL WITH *TATTOOS* AND A *SHAVED HEAD* WHO'S WORKING THERE... *REALLY?*... OH. OK, THANKS. BYE.
THAT WAS HER BUT SHE DOESN'T HAVE A *SHAVED HEAD* ANY MORE.
NO *SHAVED HEAD.?* FORGET IT.

by **Shannon Wheeler**

PART 4.

MORE (OR LESS) THAN A MISSED CONNECTION

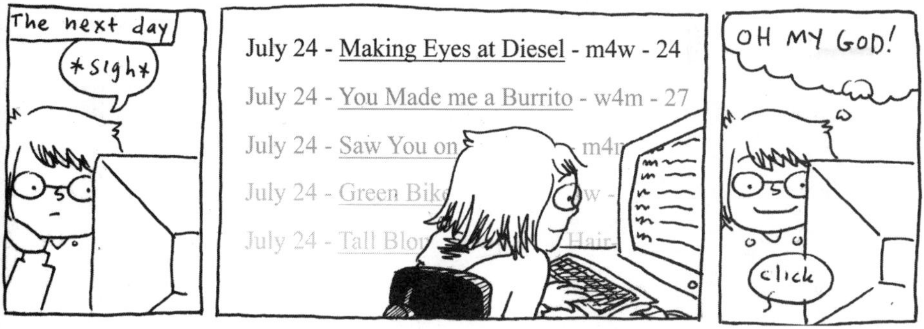

The next day
sigh
July 24 - Making Eyes at Diesel - m4w - 24
July 24 - You Made me a Burrito - w4m - 27
OH MY GOD!
click

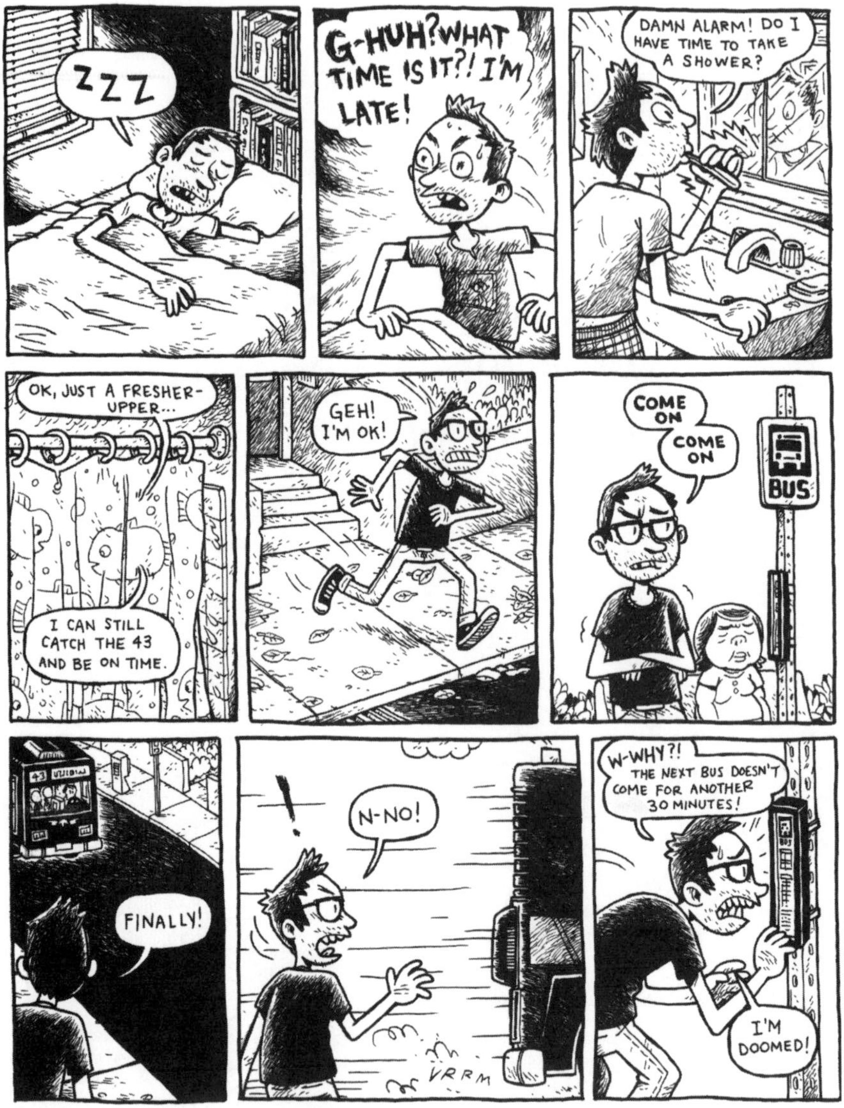
ZZZ
G-HUH? WHAT TIME IS IT?! I'M LATE!
DAMN ALARM! DO I HAVE TIME TO TAKE A SHOWER?
OK, JUST A FRESHER-UPPER...
I CAN STILL CATCH THE 43 AND BE ON TIME.
GEH! I'M OK!
COME ON
COME ON
BUS
FINALLY!
!
N-NO!
VRRM
W-WHY?! THE NEXT BUS DOESN'T COME FOR ANOTHER 30 MINUTES!
I'M DOOMED!

by **Kazimir Strzepek**

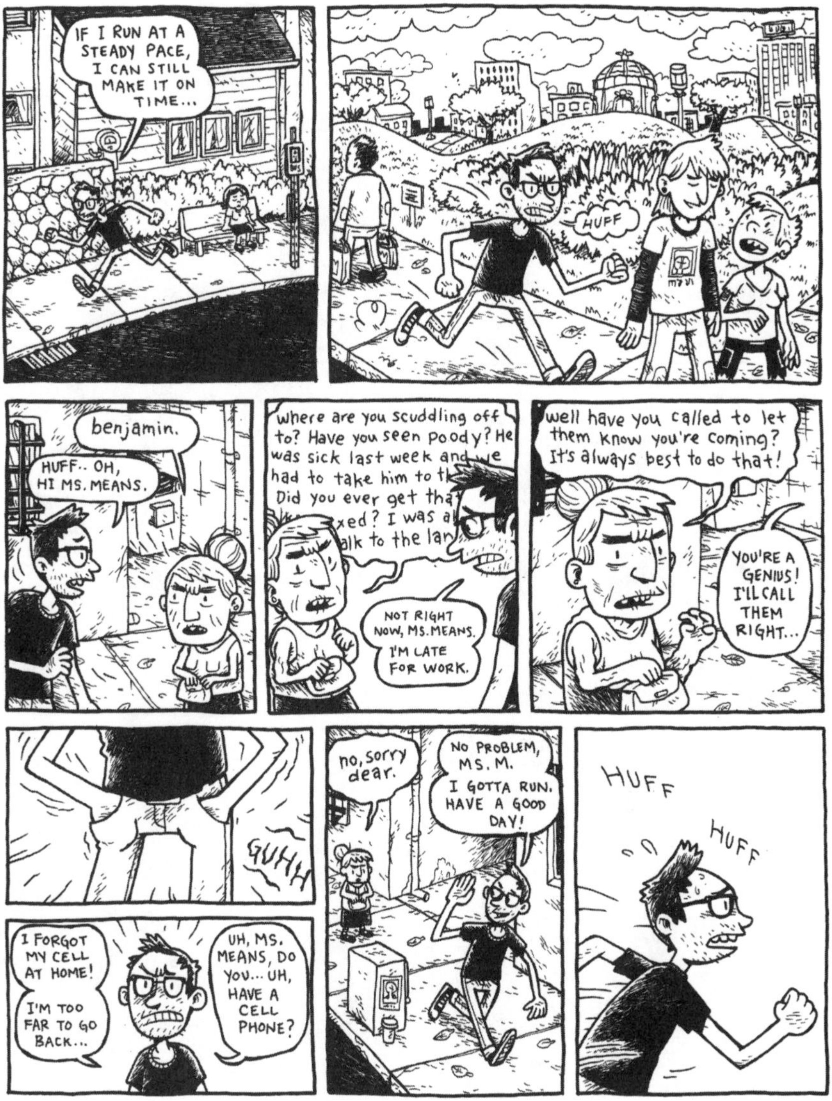
IF I RUN AT A STEADY PACE, I CAN STILL MAKE IT ON TIME...
HUFF
benjamin.
HUFF.. OH, HI MS. MEANS.
where are you scuddling off to? Have you seen poody? He was sick last week and we had to take him to th
Did you ever get tha
xed? I was a
alk to the lan
NOT RIGHT NOW, MS. MEANS.
I'M LATE FOR WORK.
well have you called to let them know you're coming? It's always best to do that!
YOU'RE A GENIUS! I'LL CALL THEM RIGHT...
GUHH
I FORGOT MY CELL AT HOME!
I'M TOO FAR TO GO BACK...
UH, MS. MEANS, DO YOU... UH, HAVE A CELL PHONE?
no, sorry dear.
NO PROBLEM, MS. M.
I GOTTA RUN. HAVE A GOOD DAY!
HUFF
HUFF

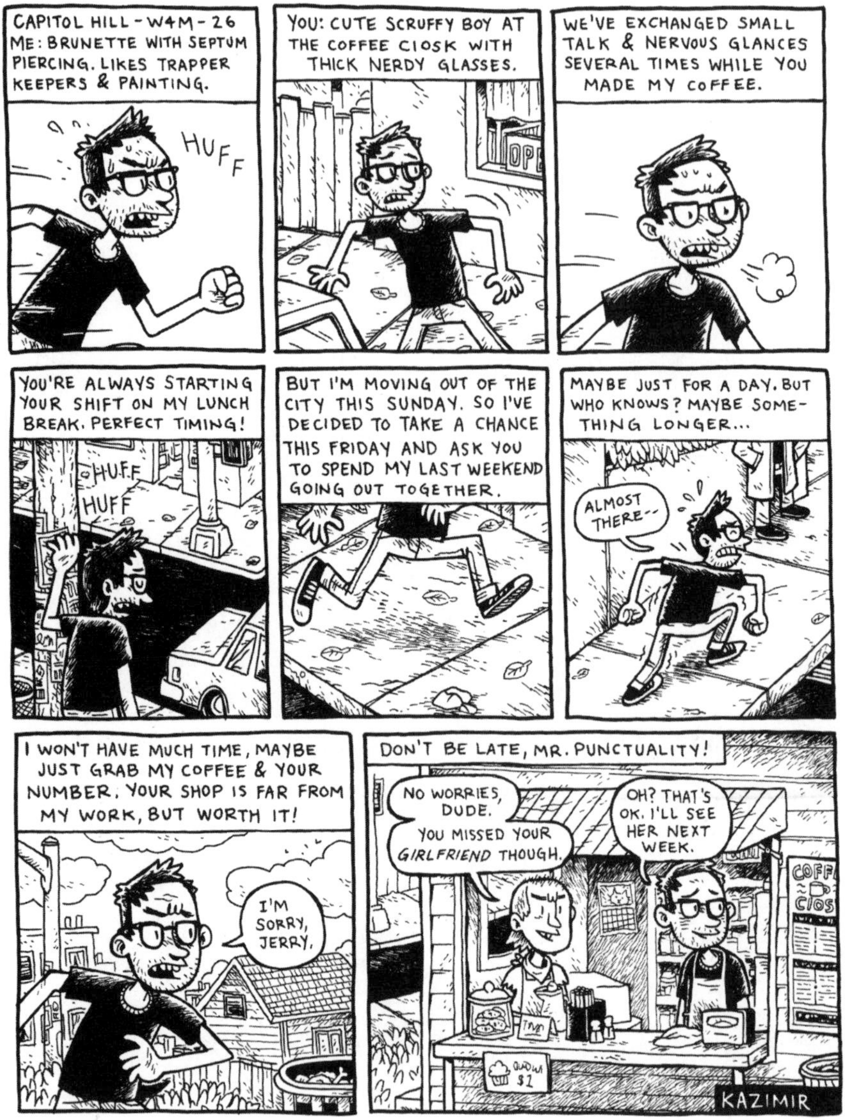
CAPITOL HILL - W4M - 26
ME: BRUNETTE WITH SEPTUM PIERCING. LIKES TRAPPER KEEPERS & PAINTING.
HUFF
YOU: CUTE SCRUFFY BOY AT THE COFFEE CIOSK WITH THICK NERDY GLASSES.
WE'VE EXCHANGED SMALL TALK & NERVOUS GLANCES SEVERAL TIMES WHILE YOU MADE MY COFFEE.
YOU'RE ALWAYS STARTING YOUR SHIFT ON MY LUNCH BREAK. PERFECT TIMING!
HUFF
HUFF
BUT I'M MOVING OUT OF THE CITY THIS SUNDAY. SO I'VE DECIDED TO TAKE A CHANCE THIS FRIDAY AND ASK YOU TO SPEND MY LAST WEEKEND GOING OUT TOGETHER.
MAYBE JUST FOR A DAY. BUT WHO KNOWS? MAYBE SOME-THING LONGER...
ALMOST THERE--
I WON'T HAVE MUCH TIME, MAYBE JUST GRAB MY COFFEE & YOUR NUMBER. YOUR SHOP IS FAR FROM MY WORK, BUT WORTH IT!
I'M SORRY, JERRY.
DON'T BE LATE, MR. PUNCTUALITY!
NO WORRIES, DUDE. YOU MISSED YOUR *GIRLFRIEND* THOUGH.
OH? THAT'S OK. I'LL SEE HER NEXT WEEK.
KAZIMIR

Missing Out by Marinaomi

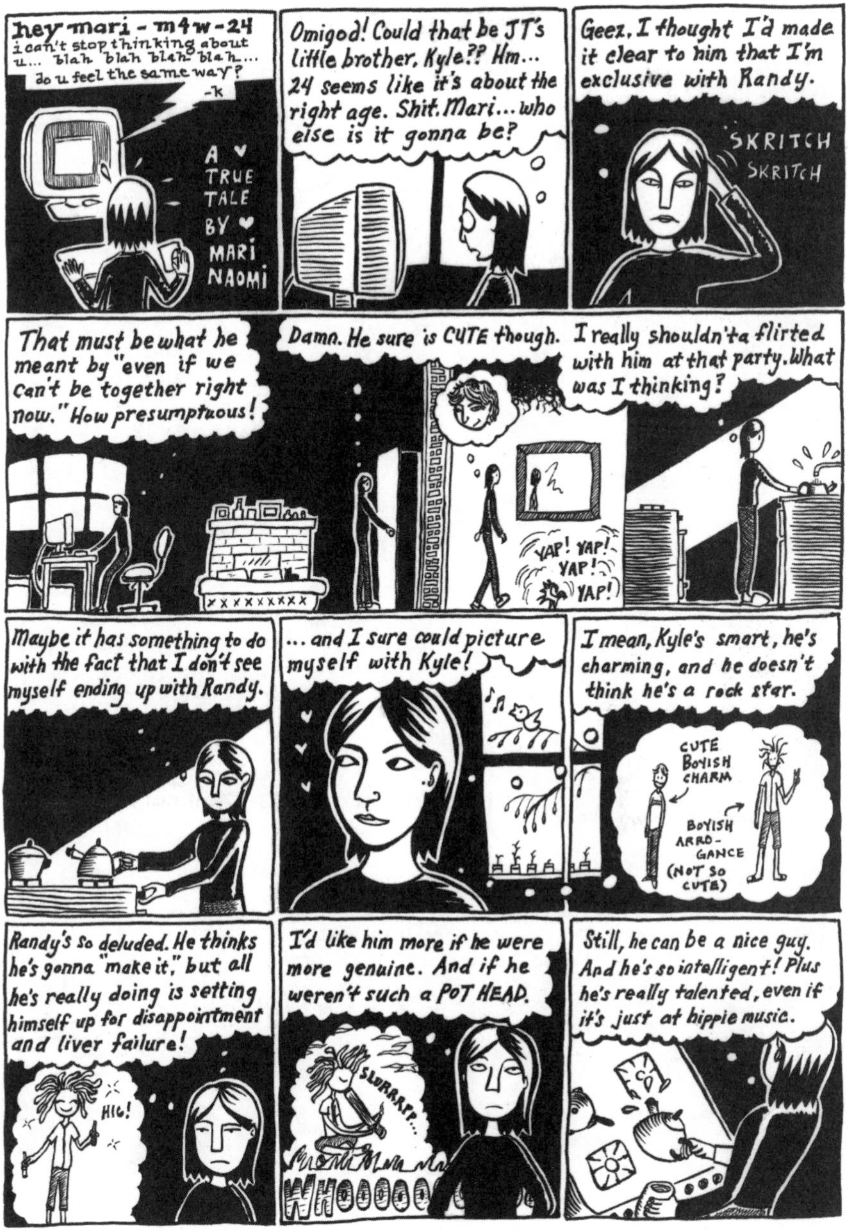

hey mari - m4w - 24
i can't stop thinking about u... blah blah blah blah... do u feel the same way? -k
A TRUE TALE BY MARI NAOMI
Omigod! Could that be JT's little brother, Kyle?? Hm... 24 seems like it's about the right age. Shit. Mari... who else is it gonna be?
Geez, I thought I'd made it clear to him that I'm exclusive with Randy.
SKRITCH
SKRITCH
That must be what he meant by "even if we can't be together right now." How presumptuous!
Damn. He sure is CUTE though.
I really shouldn't'a flirted with him at that party. What was I thinking?
YAP! YAP! YAP! YAP!
Maybe it has something to do with the fact that I don't see myself ending up with Randy.
... and I sure could picture myself with Kyle!
I mean, Kyle's smart, he's charming, and he doesn't think he's a rock star.
CUTE BOYISH CHARM
BOYISH ARRO-GANCE (NOT SO CUTE)
Randy's so deluded. He thinks he's gonna "make it," but all he's really doing is setting himself up for disappointment and liver failure!
HIC!
I'd like him more if he were more genuine. And if he weren't such a POT HEAD.
SLURRRP...
WHOOOOO
Still, he can be a nice guy. And he's so intelligent! Plus he's really talented, even if it's just at hippie music.

by **Mari Naomi**

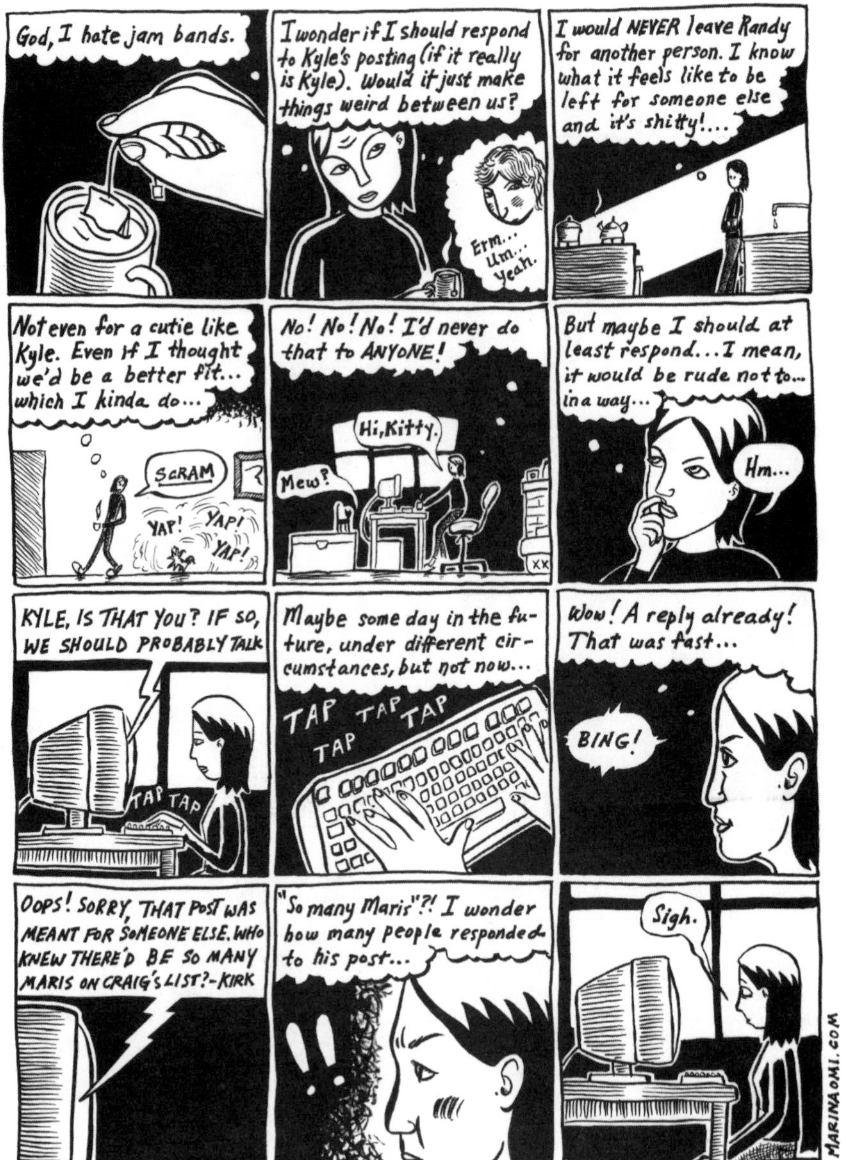
God, I hate jam bands.
I wonder if I should respond to Kyle's posting (if it really is Kyle). Would it just make things weird between us?
Erm... Um... Yeah.
I would NEVER leave Randy for another person. I know what it feels like to be left for someone else and it's shitty!...
Not even for a cutie like Kyle. Even if I thought we'd be a better fit... which I kinda do...
SCRAM
YAP! YAP! YAP!
No! No! No! I'd never do that to ANYONE!
Hi, Kitty.
Mew?
But maybe I should at least respond... I mean, it would be rude not to... in a way...
Hm...
KYLE, IS THAT YOU? IF SO, WE SHOULD PROBABLY TALK
TAP TAP
Maybe some day in the future, under different circumstances, but not now...
TAP TAP TAP TAP
Wow! A reply already! That was fast...
BING!
OOPS! SORRY, THAT POST WAS MEANT FOR SOMEONE ELSE. WHO KNEW THERE'D BE SO MANY MARIS ON CRAIG'S LIST?-KIRK
"So many Maris"?! I wonder how many people responded to his post...
Sigh.
MARINAOMI.COM

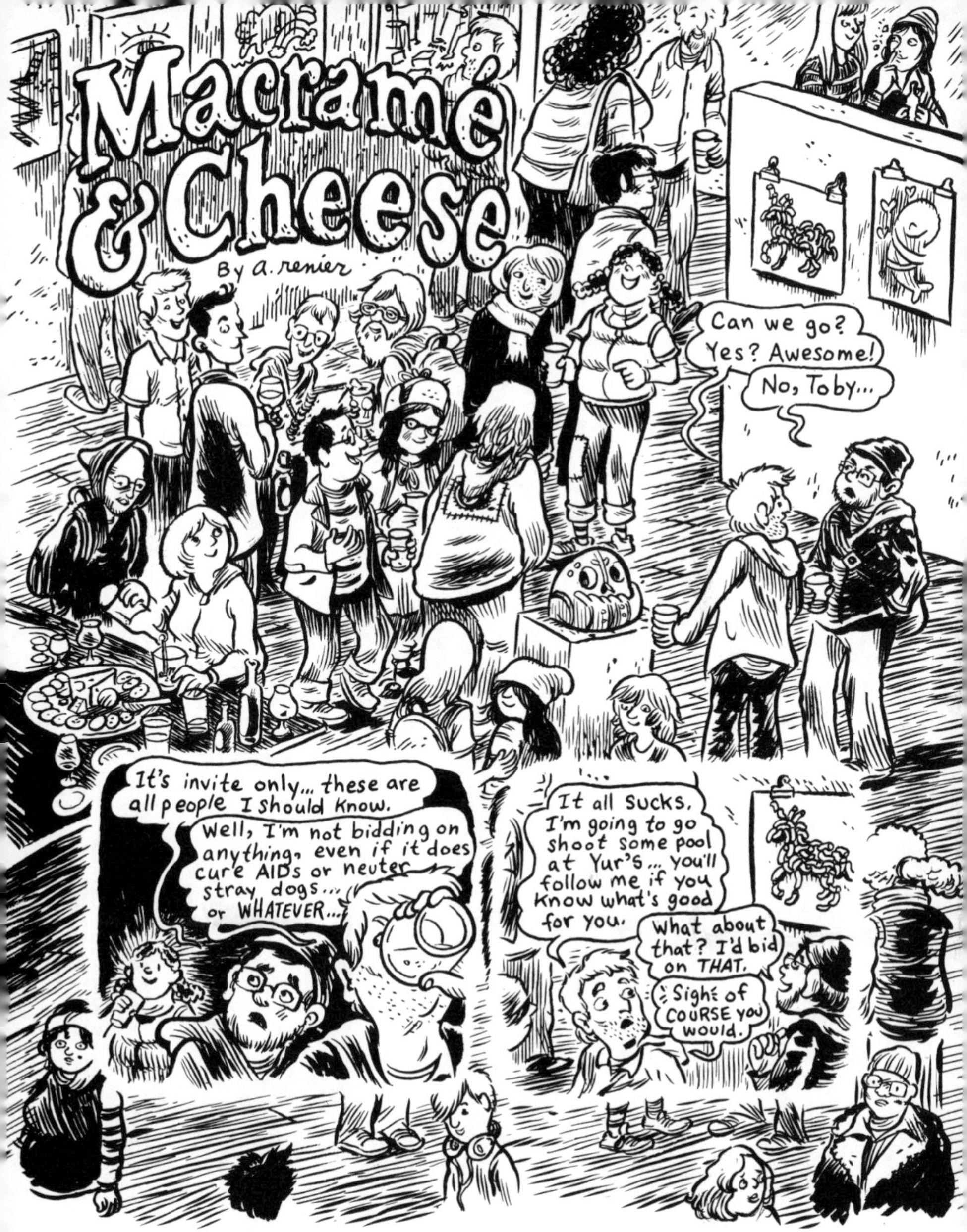
Macramé & Cheese
By a. renier
Can we go? Yes? Awesome!
No, Toby...
It's invite only... these are all people I should know.
Well, I'm not bidding on anything, even if it does cure AIDs or neuter stray dogs... or WHATEVER...
It all sucks, I'm going to go shoot some pool at Yur's... you'll follow me if you know what's good for you.
What about that? I'd bid on THAT.
Sigh: of COURSE you would.

by **Aaron Renier**

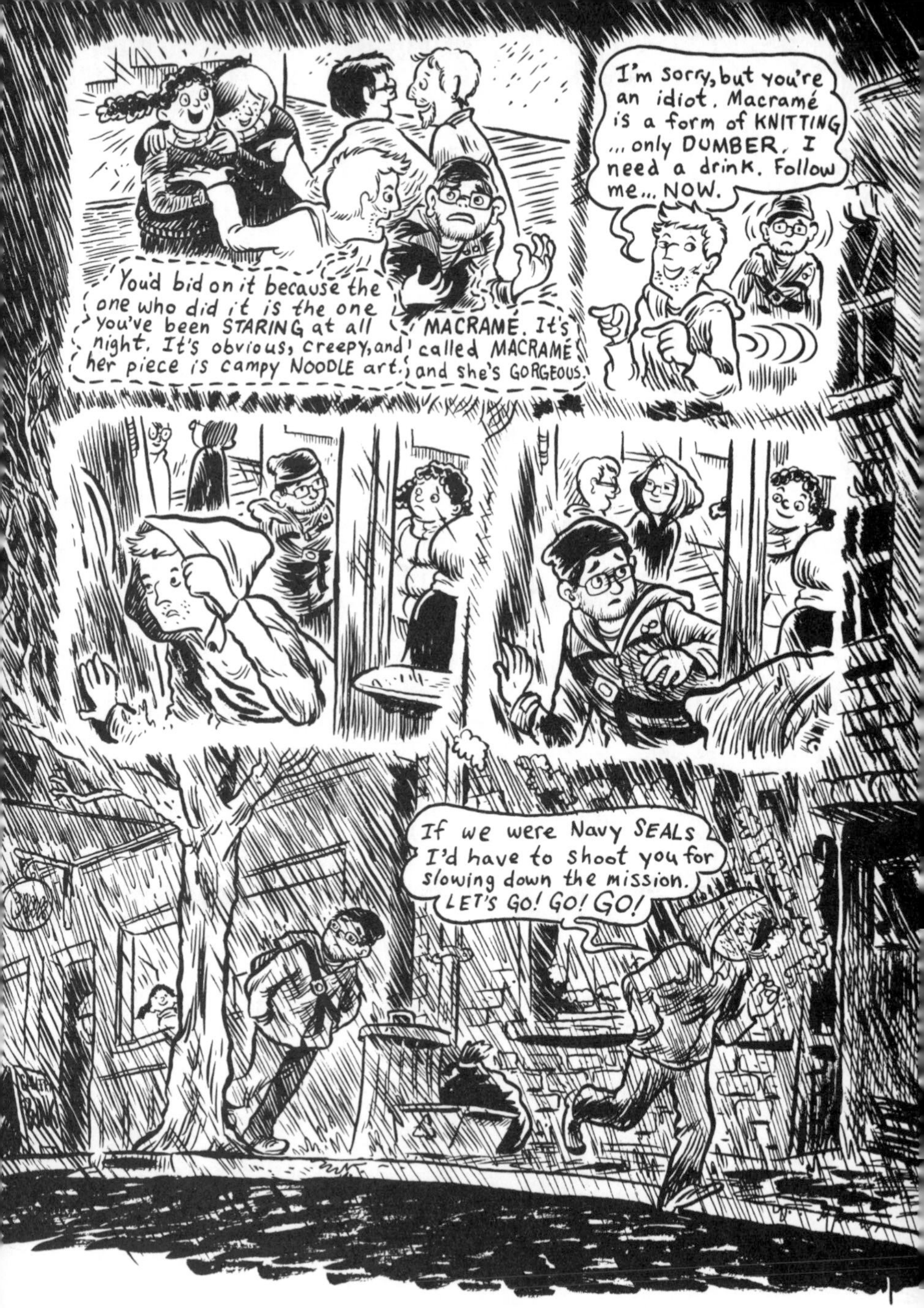
You'd bid on it because the one who did it is the one you've been STARING at all night. It's obvious, creepy, and her piece is campy NOODLE art.
MACRAMÉ. It's called MACRAMÉ and she's GORGEOUS.
I'm sorry, but you're an idiot. Macramé is a form of KNITTING ... only DUMBER. I need a drink. Follow me... NOW.
If we were Navy SEALS I'd have to shoot you for slowing down the mission. LET'S GO! GO! GO!

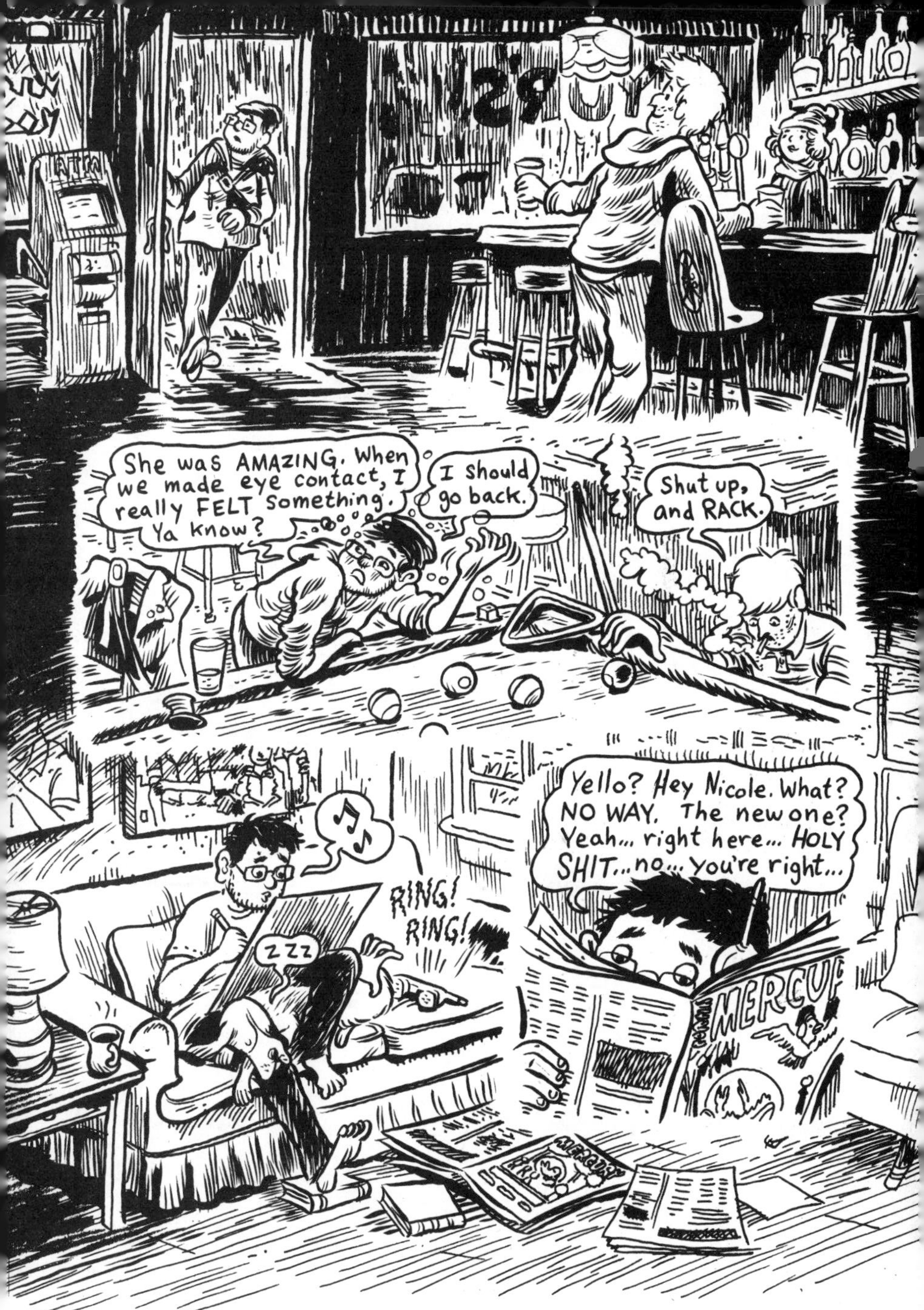
She was AMAZING. When we made eye contact, I really FELT something. Ya know?
I should go back.
Shut up, and RACK.
RING! RING!
ZZZ
Yello? Hey Nicole. What? NO WAY. The new one? Yeah... right here... HOLY SHIT... no... You're right...

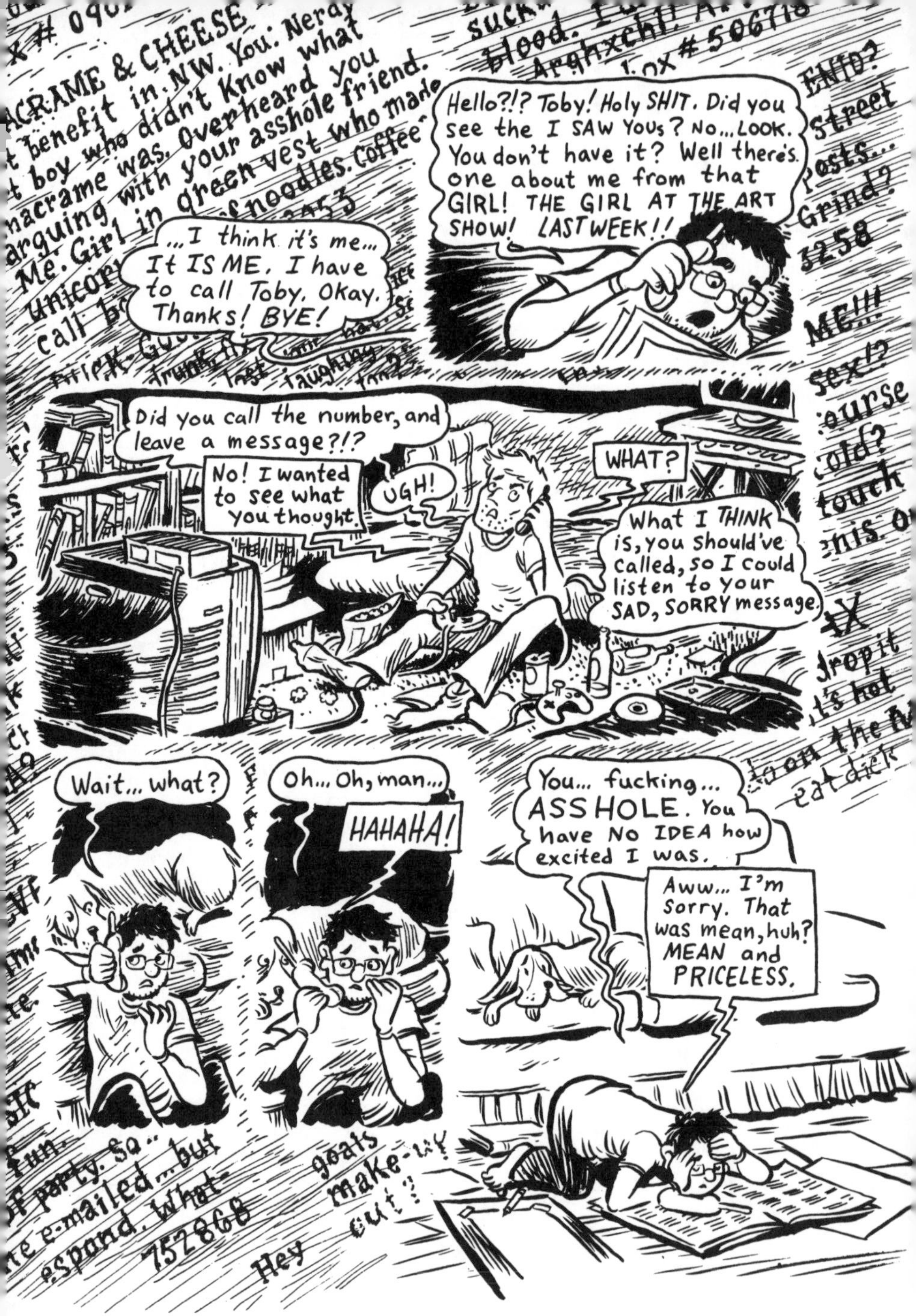
...I think it's me... It IS ME. I have to call Toby. Okay. Thanks! BYE!
Hello?!? Toby! Holy SHIT. Did you see the I SAW YOUs? No... LOOK. You don't have it? Well there's one about me from that GIRL! THE GIRL AT THE ART SHOW! LAST WEEK!!
Did you call the number, and leave a message?!?
No! I wanted to see what you thought.
UGH!
WHAT?
What I THINK is, you should've called, so I could listen to your SAD, SORRY message.
Wait... what?
Oh... Oh, man...
HAHAHA!
You... fucking... ASSHOLE. You have NO IDEA how excited I was.
Aww... I'm sorry. That was mean, huh? MEAN and PRICELESS.

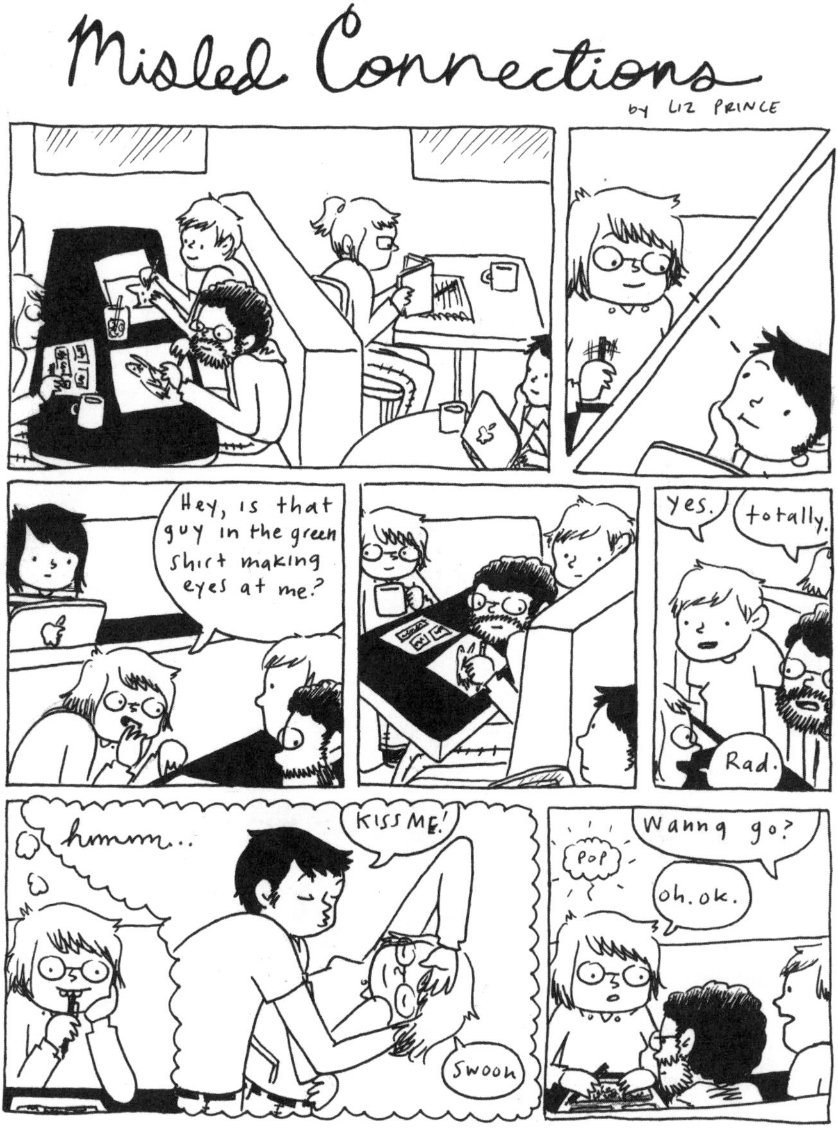
Misled Connections
by LIZ PRINCE
Hey, is that guy in the green shirt making eyes at me?
yes.
totally.
Rad.
hmmm..
KISS ME!
Swoon
Wanna go?
Pop
oh. ok.

by **Liz Prince**

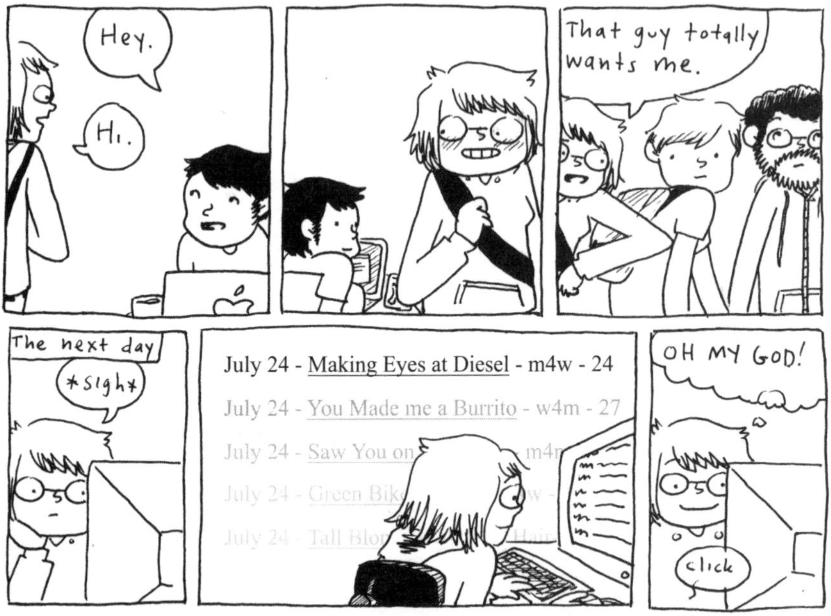
Hey.
Hi.
That guy totally wants me.
The next day
sigh
July 24 - Making Eyes at Diesel - m4w - 24
July 24 - You Made me a Burrito - w4m - 27
July 24 - Saw You on
OH MY GOD!
click

Making Eyes at Diesel - m4w - 24
Reply to: pers-867530919@craigslist.org
Date: 2007-7-24, 11:42PM EST

Saw you doing work at Diesel earlier tonight, you walked by and said hi as you were leaving. I thought your striped shirt and black hair were cute. Maybe we could meet there on purpose. Sincerely, The Guy in the Green Shirt

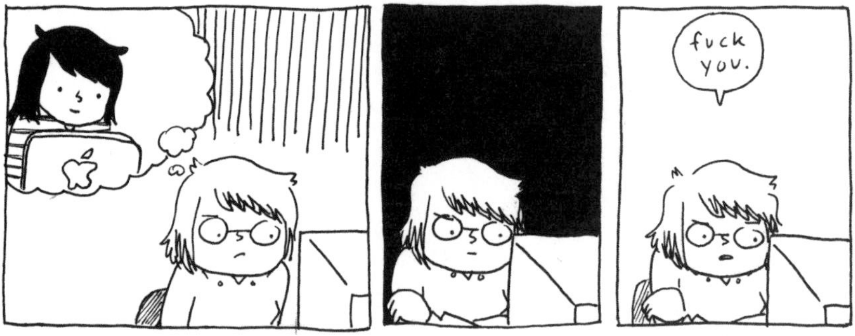
fuck you.

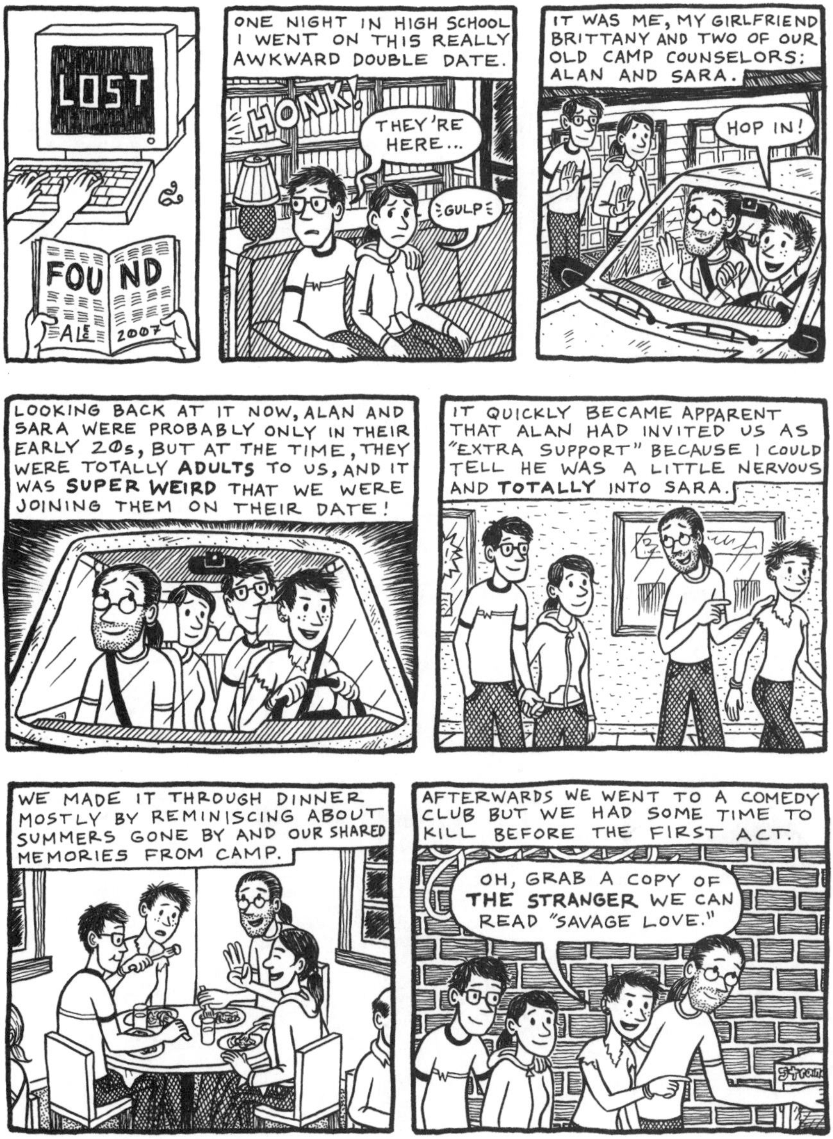
LOST
FOUND
ALE 2007
ONE NIGHT IN HIGH SCHOOL I WENT ON THIS REALLY AWKWARD DOUBLE DATE.
HONK!
THEY'RE HERE...
GULP
IT WAS ME, MY GIRLFRIEND BRITTANY AND TWO OF OUR OLD CAMP COUNSELORS: ALAN AND SARA.
HOP IN!
LOOKING BACK AT IT NOW, ALAN AND SARA WERE PROBABLY ONLY IN THEIR EARLY 20s, BUT AT THE TIME, THEY WERE TOTALLY **ADULTS** TO US, AND IT WAS **SUPER WEIRD** THAT WE WERE JOINING THEM ON THEIR DATE!
IT QUICKLY BECAME APPARENT THAT ALAN HAD INVITED US AS "EXTRA SUPPORT" BECAUSE I COULD TELL HE WAS A LITTLE NERVOUS AND **TOTALLY** INTO SARA.
WE MADE IT THROUGH DINNER MOSTLY BY REMINISCING ABOUT SUMMERS GONE BY AND OUR SHARED MEMORIES FROM CAMP.
AFTERWARDS WE WENT TO A COMEDY CLUB BUT WE HAD SOME TIME TO KILL BEFORE THE FIRST ACT.
OH, GRAB A COPY OF **THE STRANGER** WE CAN READ "SAVAGE LOVE."

by **Alec Longstreth**

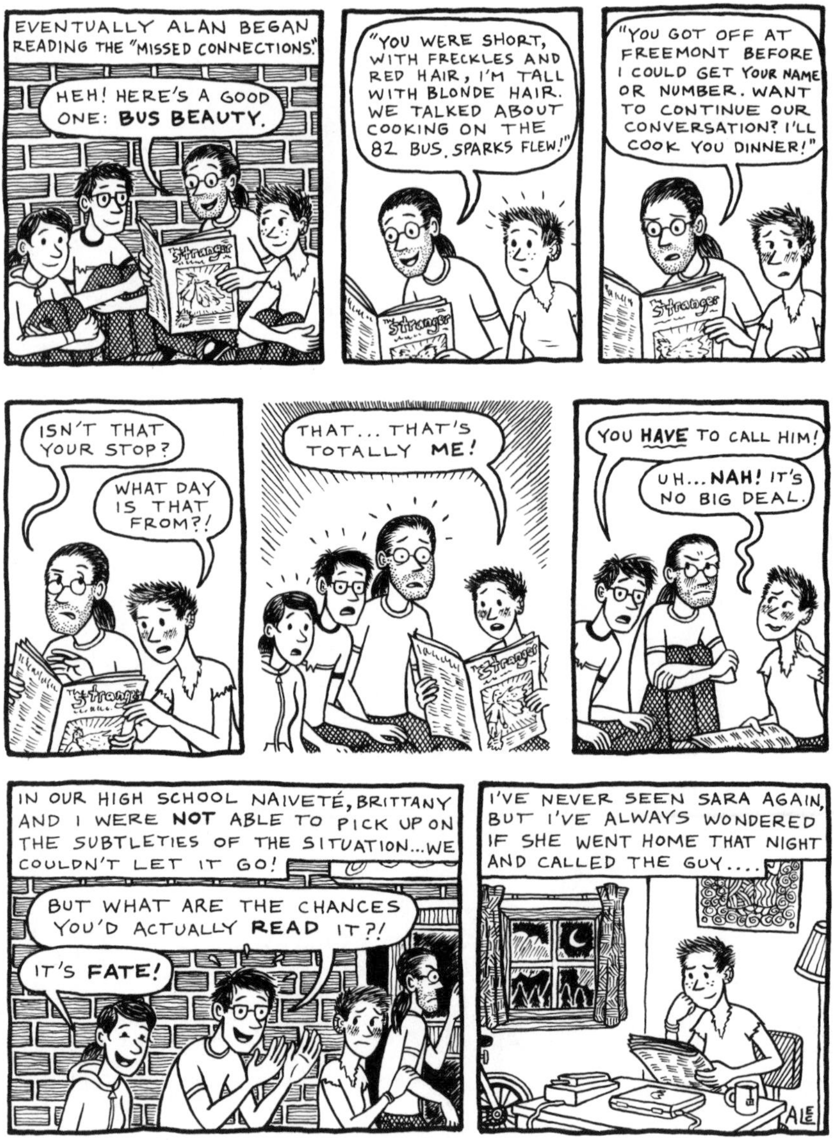
EVENTUALLY ALAN BEGAN READING THE "MISSED CONNECTIONS."
HEH! HERE'S A GOOD ONE: BUS BEAUTY.
"YOU WERE SHORT, WITH FRECKLES AND RED HAIR, I'M TALL WITH BLONDE HAIR. WE TALKED ABOUT COOKING ON THE 82 BUS. SPARKS FLEW!"
"YOU GOT OFF AT FREEMONT BEFORE I COULD GET YOUR NAME OR NUMBER. WANT TO CONTINUE OUR CONVERSATION? I'LL COOK YOU DINNER!"
ISN'T THAT YOUR STOP?
WHAT DAY IS THAT FROM?!
THAT... THAT'S TOTALLY ME!
YOU HAVE TO CALL HIM!
UH... NAH! IT'S NO BIG DEAL.
IN OUR HIGH SCHOOL NAIVETÉ, BRITTANY AND I WERE NOT ABLE TO PICK UP ON THE SUBTLETIES OF THE SITUATION... WE COULDN'T LET IT GO!
BUT WHAT ARE THE CHANCES YOU'D ACTUALLY READ IT?!
IT'S FATE!
I'VE NEVER SEEN SARA AGAIN, BUT I'VE ALWAYS WONDERED IF SHE WENT HOME THAT NIGHT AND CALLED THE GUY....
ALE

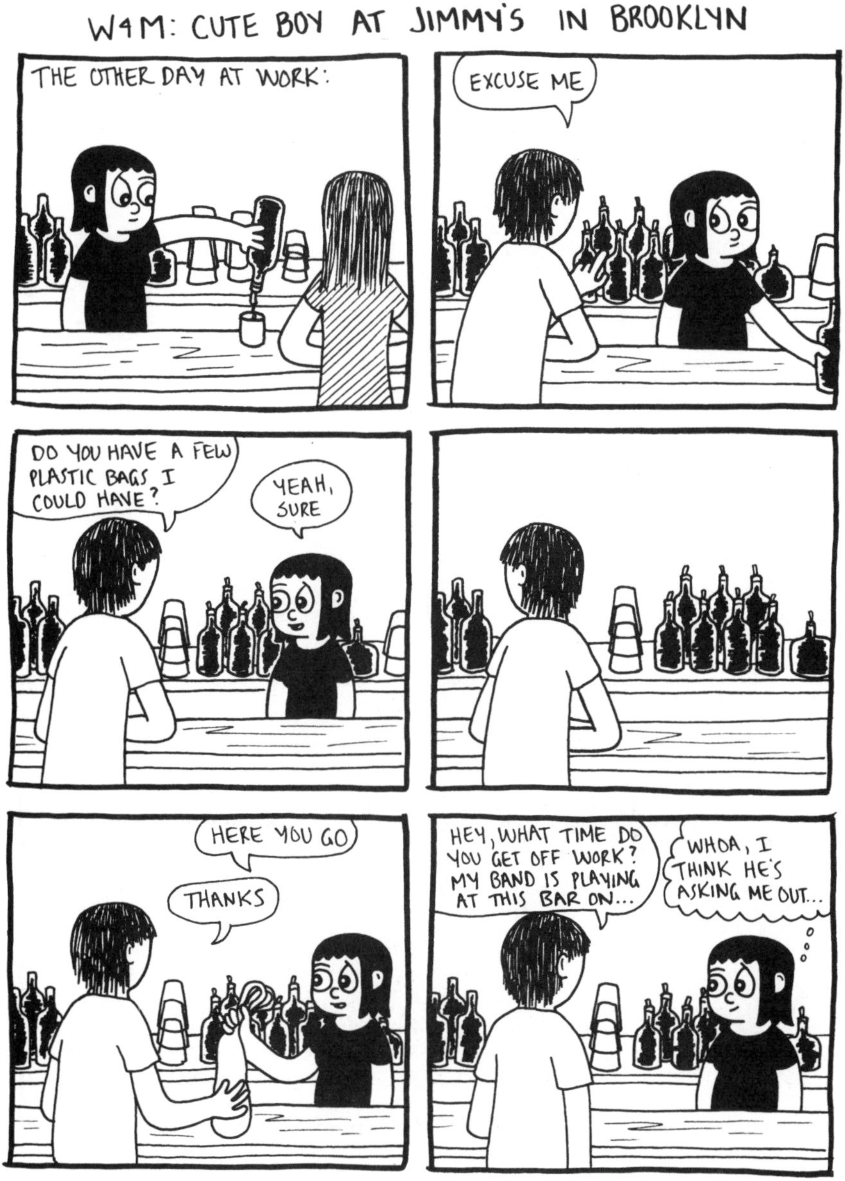
W4M: CUTE BOY AT JIMMY'S IN BROOKLYN
THE OTHER DAY AT WORK:
EXCUSE ME
DO YOU HAVE A FEW PLASTIC BAGS I COULD HAVE?
YEAH, SURE
HERE YOU GO
THANKS
HEY, WHAT TIME DO YOU GET OFF WORK? MY BAND IS PLAYING AT THIS BAR ON...
WHOA, I THINK HE'S ASKING ME OUT...

by **Julia Wertz**

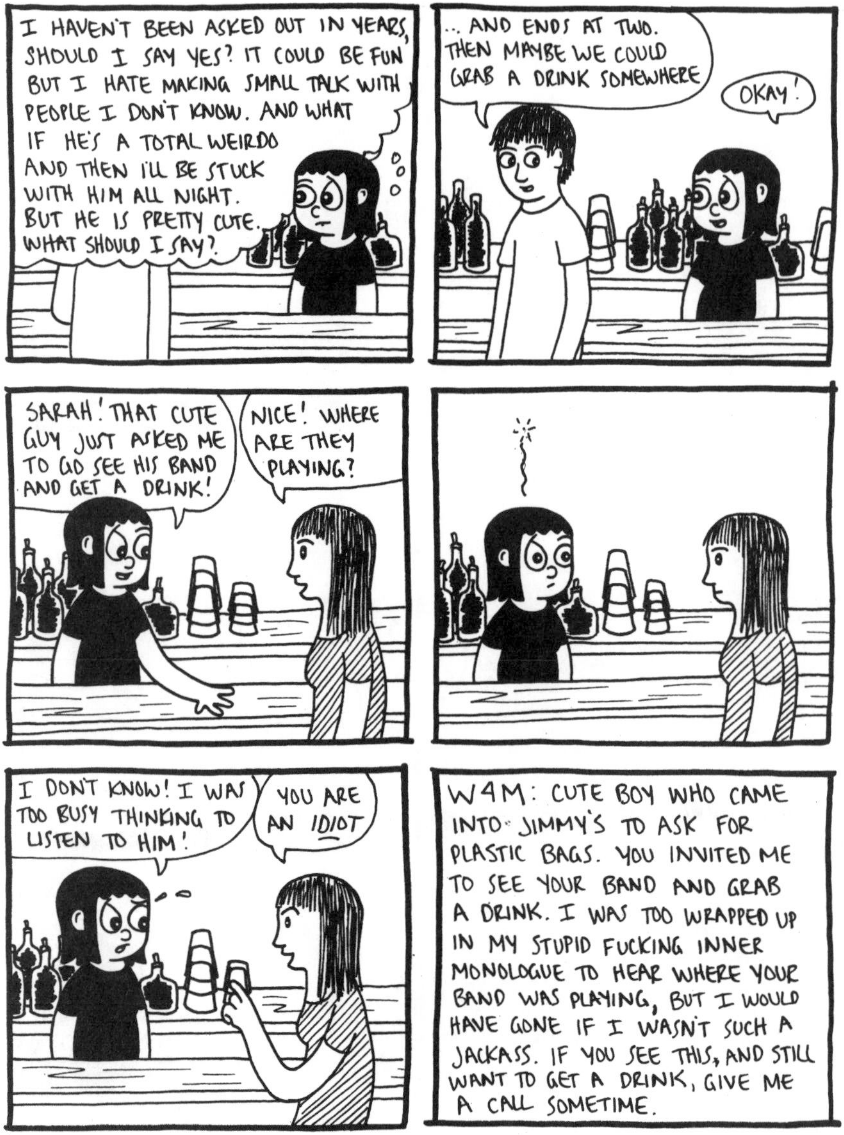
I HAVEN'T BEEN ASKED OUT IN YEARS, SHOULD I SAY YES? IT COULD BE FUN BUT I HATE MAKING SMALL TALK WITH PEOPLE I DON'T KNOW. AND WHAT IF HE'S A TOTAL WEIRDO AND THEN I'LL BE STUCK WITH HIM ALL NIGHT. BUT HE IS PRETTY CUTE. WHAT SHOULD I SAY?
... AND ENDS AT TWO. THEN MAYBE WE COULD GRAB A DRINK SOMEWHERE
OKAY!
SARAH! THAT CUTE GUY JUST ASKED ME TO GO SEE HIS BAND AND GET A DRINK!
NICE! WHERE ARE THEY PLAYING?
I DON'T KNOW! I WAS TOO BUSY THINKING TO LISTEN TO HIM!
YOU ARE AN IDIOT
W4M: CUTE BOY WHO CAME INTO JIMMY'S TO ASK FOR PLASTIC BAGS. YOU INVITED ME TO SEE YOUR BAND AND GRAB A DRINK. I WAS TOO WRAPPED UP IN MY STUPID FUCKING INNER MONOLOGUE TO HEAR WHERE YOUR BAND WAS PLAYING, BUT I WOULD HAVE GONE IF I WASN'T SUCH A JACKASS. IF YOU SEE THIS, AND STILL WANT TO GET A DRINK, GIVE ME A CALL SOMETIME.

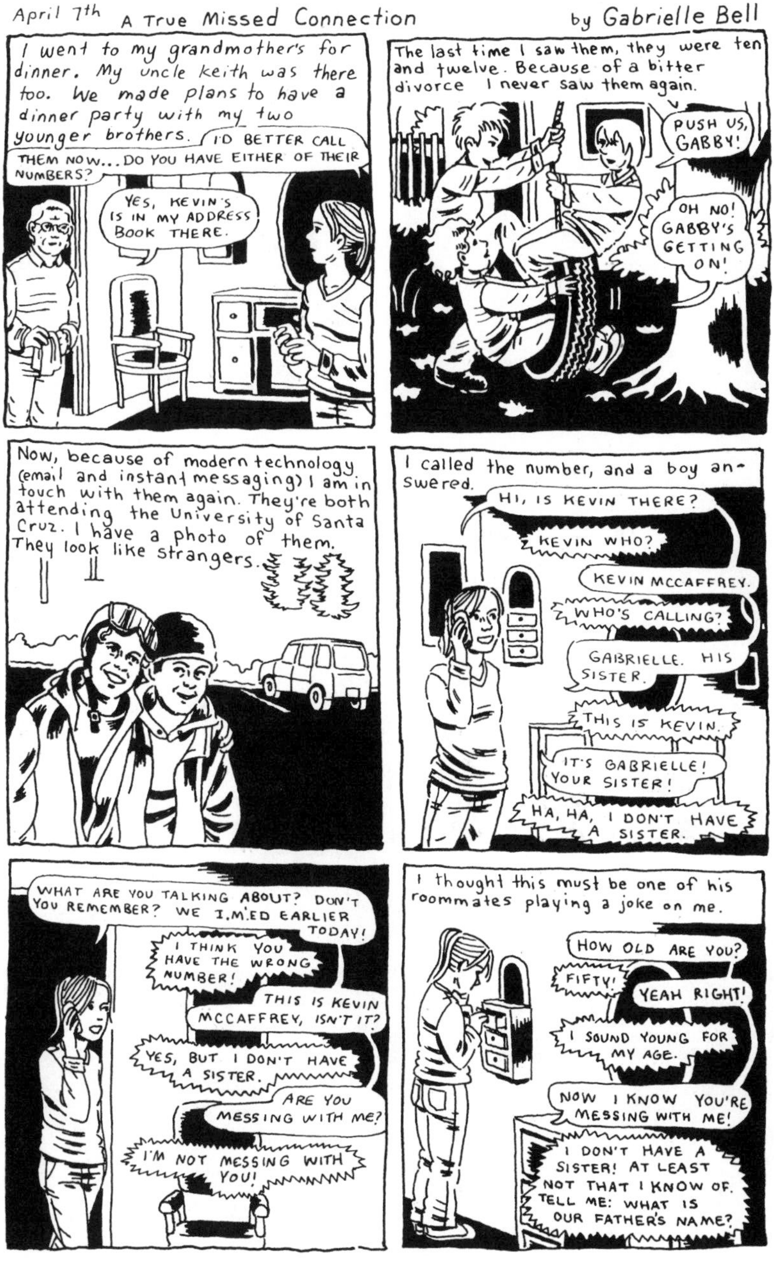
April 7th
A True Missed Connection
by Gabrielle Bell
I went to my grandmother's for dinner. My uncle keith was there too. We made plans to have a dinner party with my two younger brothers.
I'D BETTER CALL THEM NOW... DO YOU HAVE EITHER OF THEIR NUMBERS?
YES, KEVIN'S IS IN MY ADDRESS BOOK THERE.
The last time I saw them, they were ten and twelve. Because of a bitter divorce I never saw them again.
PUSH US, GABBY!
OH NO! GABBY'S GETTING ON!
Now, because of modern technology (email and instant messaging) I am in touch with them again. They're both attending the University of Santa Cruz. I have a photo of them. They look like strangers.
I called the number, and a boy answered.
HI, IS KEVIN THERE?
KEVIN WHO?
KEVIN MCCAFFREY.
WHO'S CALLING?
GABRIELLE. HIS SISTER.
THIS IS KEVIN.
IT'S GABRIELLE! YOUR SISTER!
HA, HA, I DON'T HAVE A SISTER.
WHAT ARE YOU TALKING ABOUT? DON'T YOU REMEMBER? WE I.M.'ED EARLIER TODAY!
I THINK YOU HAVE THE WRONG NUMBER!
THIS IS KEVIN MCCAFFREY, ISN'T IT?
YES, BUT I DON'T HAVE A SISTER.
ARE YOU MESSING WITH ME?
I'M NOT MESSING WITH YOU!
I thought this must be one of his roommates playing a joke on me.
HOW OLD ARE YOU?
FIFTY!
YEAH RIGHT!
I SOUND YOUNG FOR MY AGE.
NOW I KNOW YOU'RE MESSING WITH ME!
I DON'T HAVE A SISTER! AT LEAST NOT THAT I KNOW OF. TELL ME: WHAT IS OUR FATHER'S NAME?

by **Gabrielle Bell**

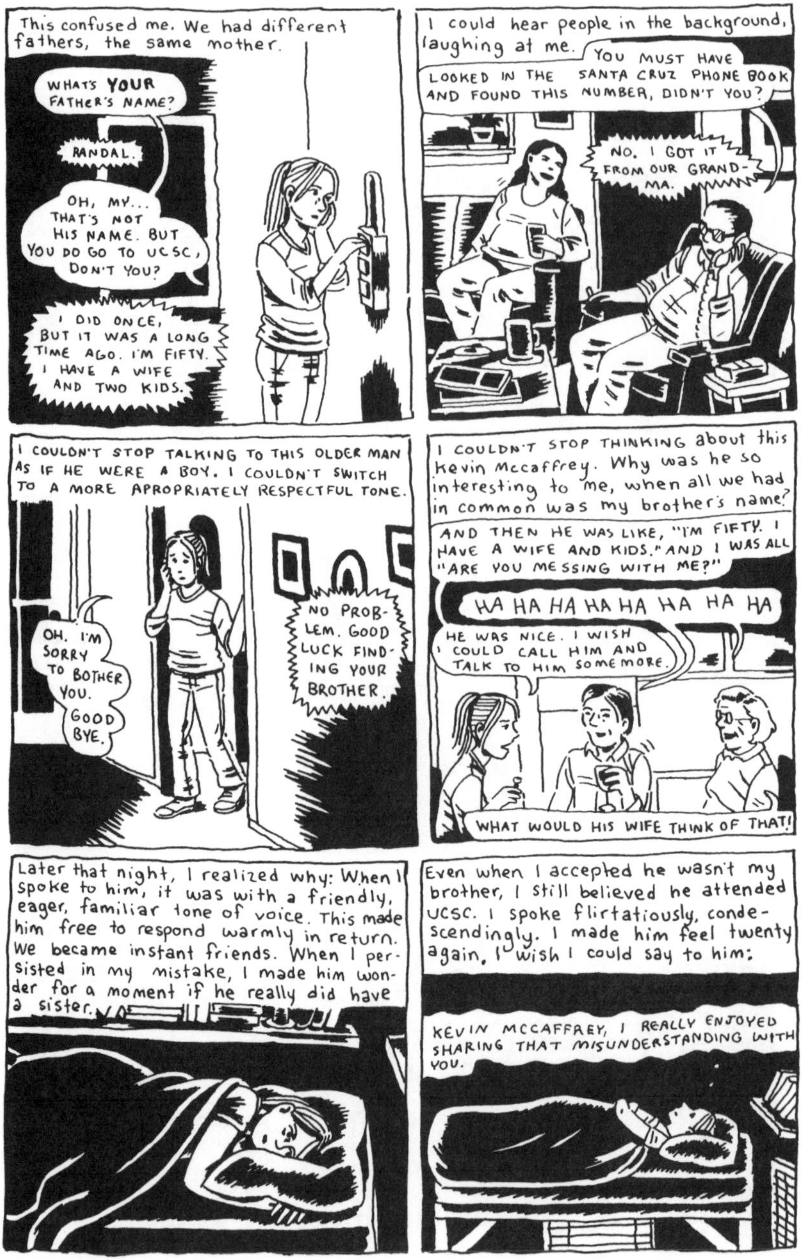
This confused me. We had different fathers, the same mother.
WHAT'S YOUR FATHER'S NAME?
RANDAL.
OH, MY... THAT'S NOT HIS NAME. BUT YOU DO GO TO UCSC, DON'T YOU?
I DID ONCE, BUT IT WAS A LONG TIME AGO. I'M FIFTY. I HAVE A WIFE AND TWO KIDS.
I could hear people in the background, laughing at me.
YOU MUST HAVE LOOKED IN THE SANTA CRUZ PHONE BOOK AND FOUND THIS NUMBER, DIDN'T YOU?
NO. I GOT IT FROM OUR GRAND-MA.
I COULDN'T STOP TALKING TO THIS OLDER MAN AS IF HE WERE A BOY. I COULDN'T SWITCH TO A MORE APROPRIATELY RESPECTFUL TONE.
OH. I'M SORRY TO BOTHER YOU.
GOOD BYE.
NO PROB-LEM. GOOD LUCK FIND-ING YOUR BROTHER.
I COULDN'T STOP THINKING about this Kevin McCaffrey. Why was he so interesting to me, when all we had in common was my brother's name?
AND THEN HE WAS LIKE, "I'M FIFTY. I HAVE A WIFE AND KIDS." AND I WAS ALL "ARE YOU MESSING WITH ME?"
HA HA HA HA HA HA HA HA
HE WAS NICE. I WISH I COULD CALL HIM AND TALK TO HIM SOME MORE.
WHAT WOULD HIS WIFE THINK OF THAT!
Later that night, I realized why: When I spoke to him, it was with a friendly, eager, familiar tone of voice. This made him free to respond warmly in return. We became instant friends. When I persisted in my mistake, I made him wonder for a moment if he really did have a sister.
Even when I accepted he wasn't my brother, I still believed he attended UCSC. I spoke flirtatiously, condescendingly. I made him feel twenty again. I wish I could say to him:
KEVIN MCCAFFREY, I REALLY ENJOYED SHARING THAT MISUNDERSTANDING WITH YOU.

So... She Married Me Anyway.

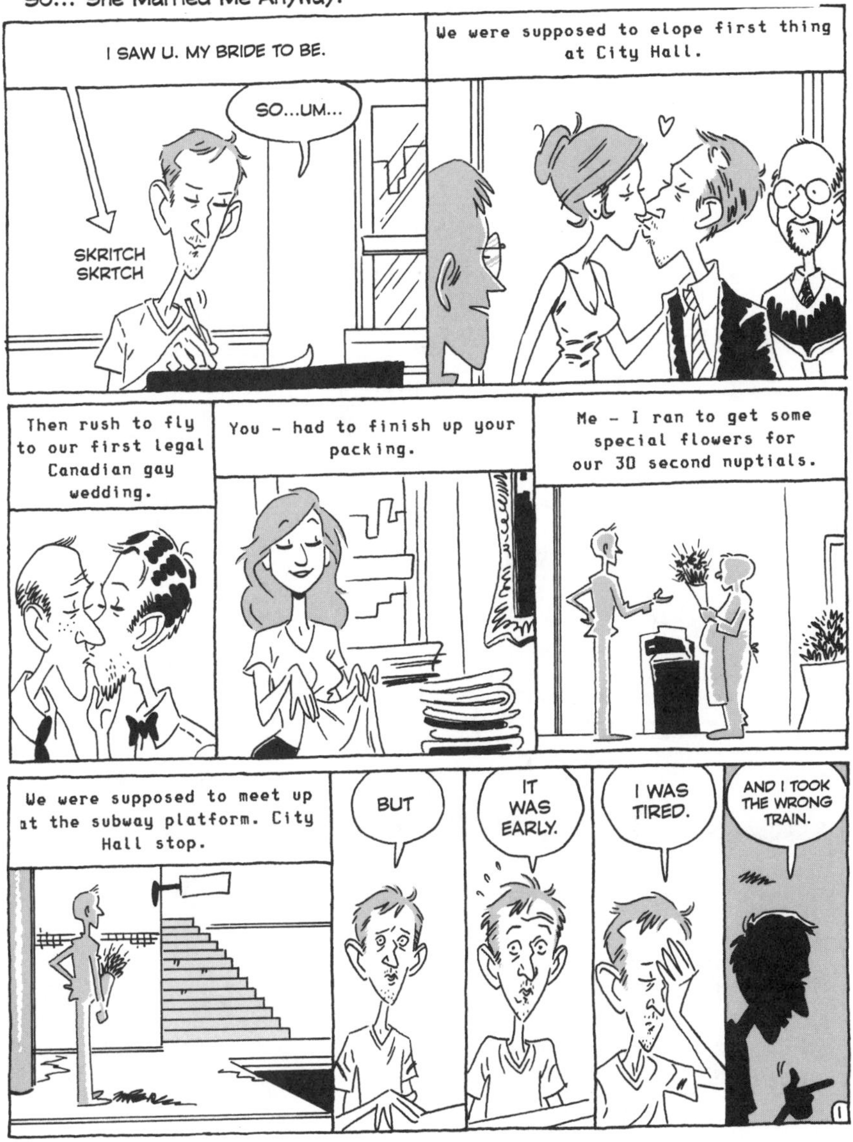
I SAW U. MY BRIDE TO BE.
SO...UM...
SKRITCH
SKRTCH
We were supposed to elope first thing at City Hall.
Then rush to fly to our first legal Canadian gay wedding.
You - had to finish up your packing.
Me - I ran to get some special flowers for our 30 second nuptials.
We were supposed to meet up at the subway platform. City Hall stop.
BUT
IT WAS EARLY.
I WAS TIRED.
AND I TOOK THE WRONG TRAIN.
1

by **Jonathan Baylis and T.J. Kirsch**

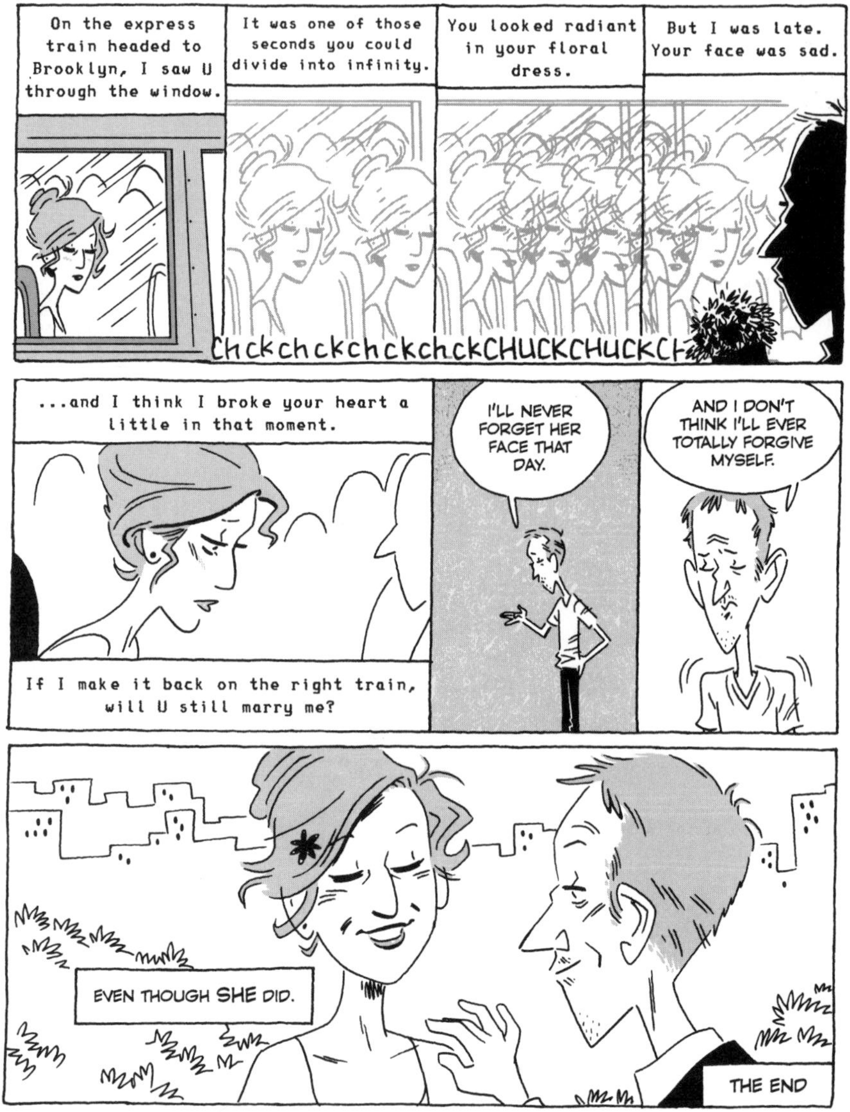
On the express train headed to Brooklyn, I saw U through the window.
It was one of those seconds you could divide into infinity.
You looked radiant in your floral dress.
But I was late. Your face was sad.
ChckchckchckchckCHUCKCHUCKCH
...and I think I broke your heart a little in that moment.
If I make it back on the right train, will U still marry me?
I'LL NEVER FORGET HER FACE THAT DAY.
AND I DON'T THINK I'LL EVER TOTALLY FORGIVE MYSELF.
EVEN THOUGH SHE DID.
THE END

written by JONATHAN BAYLIS and drawn by T.J. KIRSCH

OE + JB

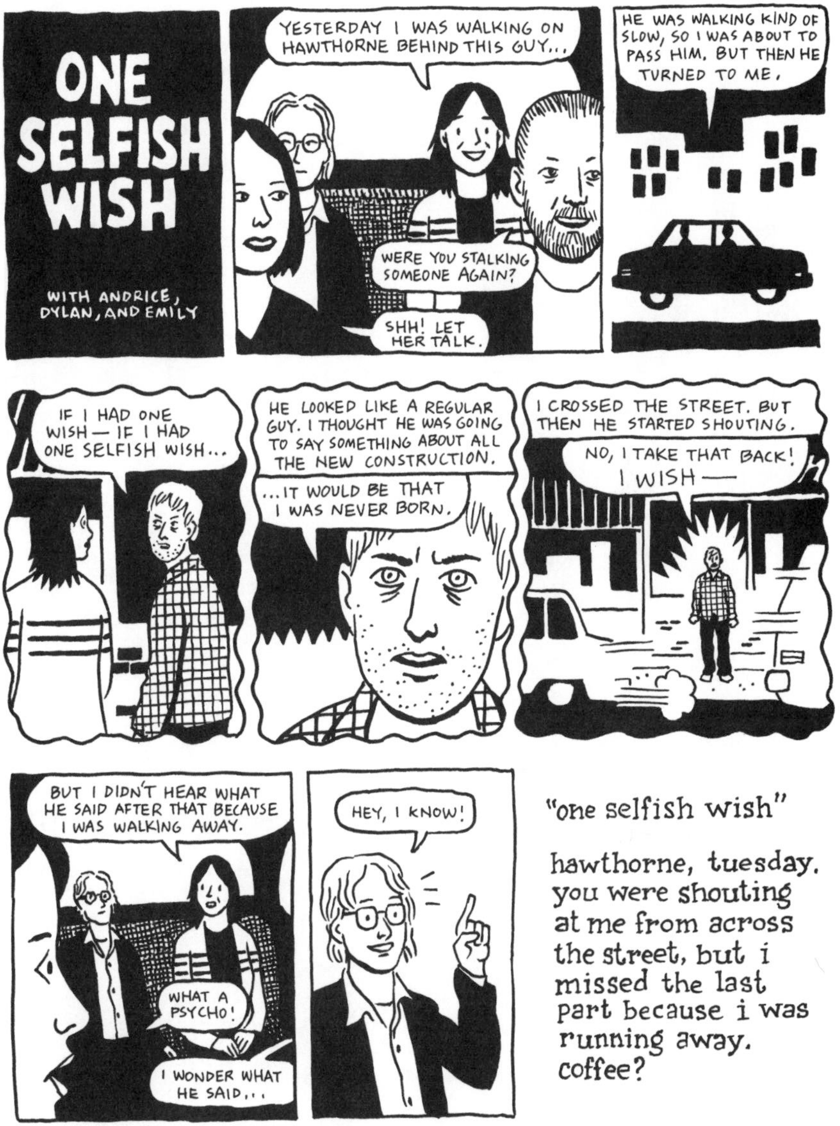
ONE SELFISH WISH
WITH ANDRICE, DYLAN, AND EMILY
YESTERDAY I WAS WALKING ON HAWTHORNE BEHIND THIS GUY...
WERE YOU STALKING SOMEONE AGAIN?
SHH! LET HER TALK.
HE WAS WALKING KIND OF SLOW, SO I WAS ABOUT TO PASS HIM. BUT THEN HE TURNED TO ME.
IF I HAD ONE WISH — IF I HAD ONE SELFISH WISH...
HE LOOKED LIKE A REGULAR GUY. I THOUGHT HE WAS GOING TO SAY SOMETHING ABOUT ALL THE NEW CONSTRUCTION.
...IT WOULD BE THAT I WAS NEVER BORN.
I CROSSED THE STREET. BUT THEN HE STARTED SHOUTING.
NO, I TAKE THAT BACK! I WISH —
BUT I DIDN'T HEAR WHAT HE SAID AFTER THAT BECAUSE I WAS WALKING AWAY.
WHAT A PSYCHO!
I WONDER WHAT HE SAID...
HEY, I KNOW!

"one selfish wish"

hawthorne, tuesday. you were shouting at me from across the street, but i missed the last part because i was running away. coffee?

by **Jesse Reklaw**

PART 5.

UNHAPPILY EVER AFTER

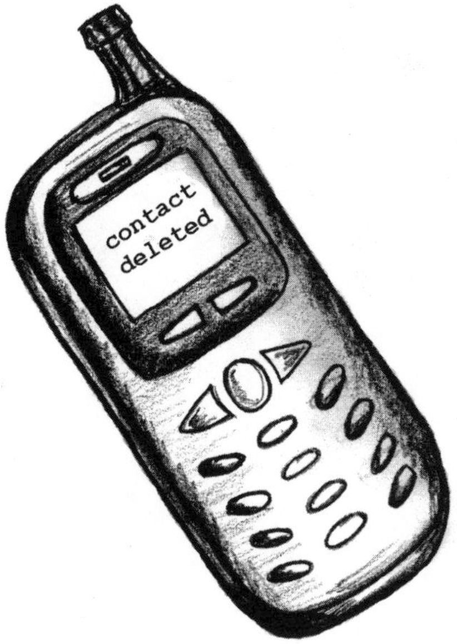
contact
deleted

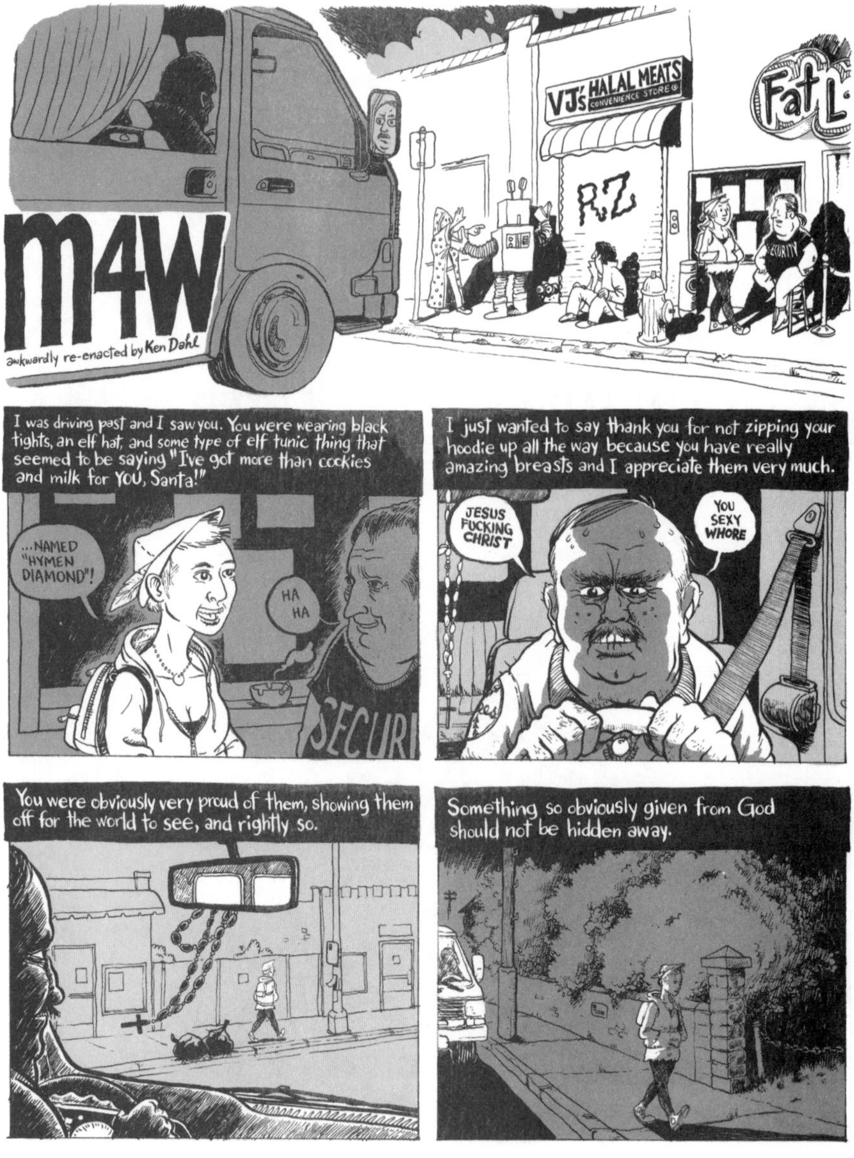
m4w
awkwardly re-enacted by Ken Dahl
VJ's HALAL MEATS
CONVENIENCE STORE
RZ
SECURITY
I was driving past and I saw you. You were wearing black tights, an elf hat, and some type of elf tunic thing that seemed to be saying "I've got more than cookies and milk for YOU, Santa!"
...NAMED "HYMEN DIAMOND"!
HA HA
SECURI
I just wanted to say thank you for not zipping your hoodie up all the way because you have really amazing breasts and I appreciate them very much.
JESUS FUCKING CHRIST
YOU SEXY WHORE
You were obviously very proud of them, showing them off for the world to see, and rightly so.
Something so obviously given from God should not be hidden away.

by **Ken Dahl**

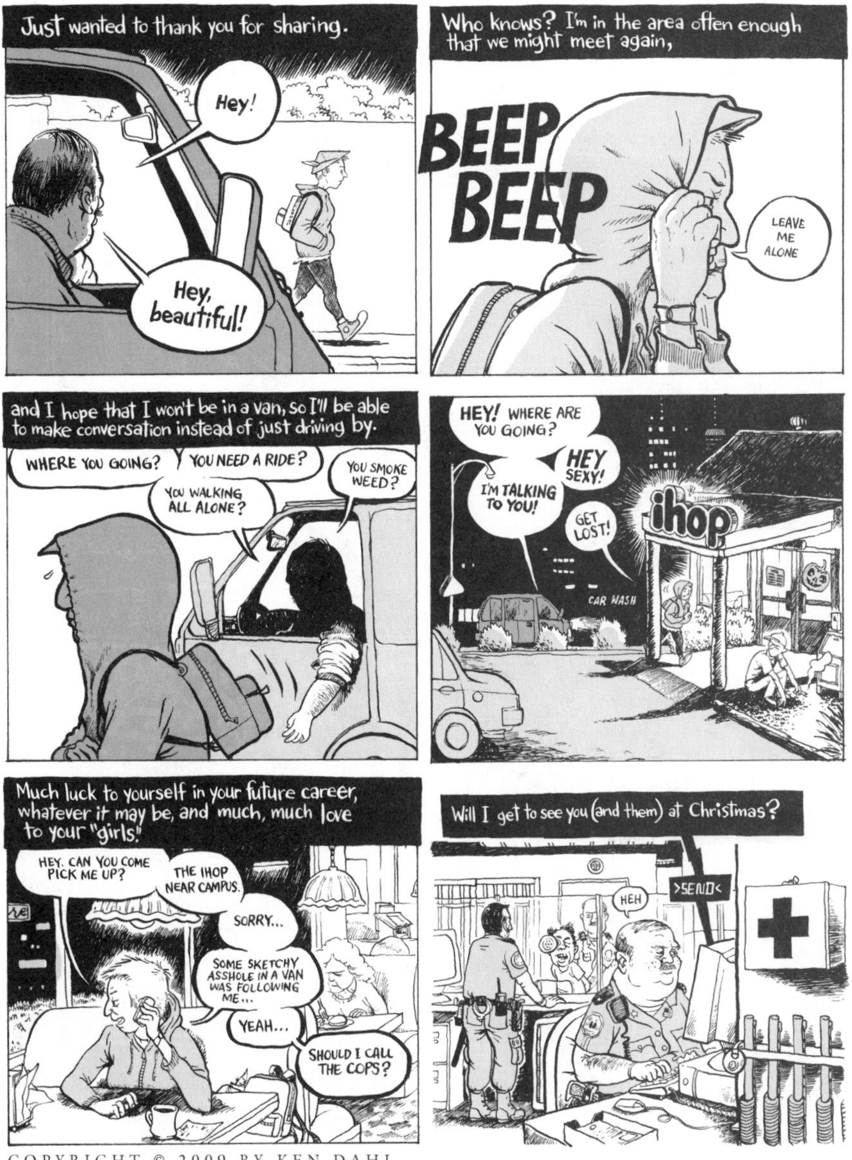
Just wanted to thank you for sharing.
Hey!
Hey, beautiful!
Who knows? I'm in the area often enough that we might meet again,
BEEP BEEP
LEAVE ME ALONE
and I hope that I won't be in a van, so I'll be able to make conversation instead of just driving by.
WHERE YOU GOING?
YOU NEED A RIDE?
YOU WALKING ALL ALONE?
YOU SMOKE WEED?
HEY! WHERE ARE YOU GOING?
HEY SEXY!
I'M TALKING TO YOU!
GET LOST!
ihop
CAR WASH
Much luck to yourself in your future career, whatever it may be, and much, much love to your "girls."
HEY. CAN YOU COME PICK ME UP?
THE IHOP NEAR CAMPUS.
SORRY...
SOME SKETCHY ASSHOLE IN A VAN WAS FOLLOWING ME...
YEAH...
SHOULD I CALL THE COPS?
Will I get to see you (and them) at Christmas?
>SEND<
HEH

I keep missing you W4M

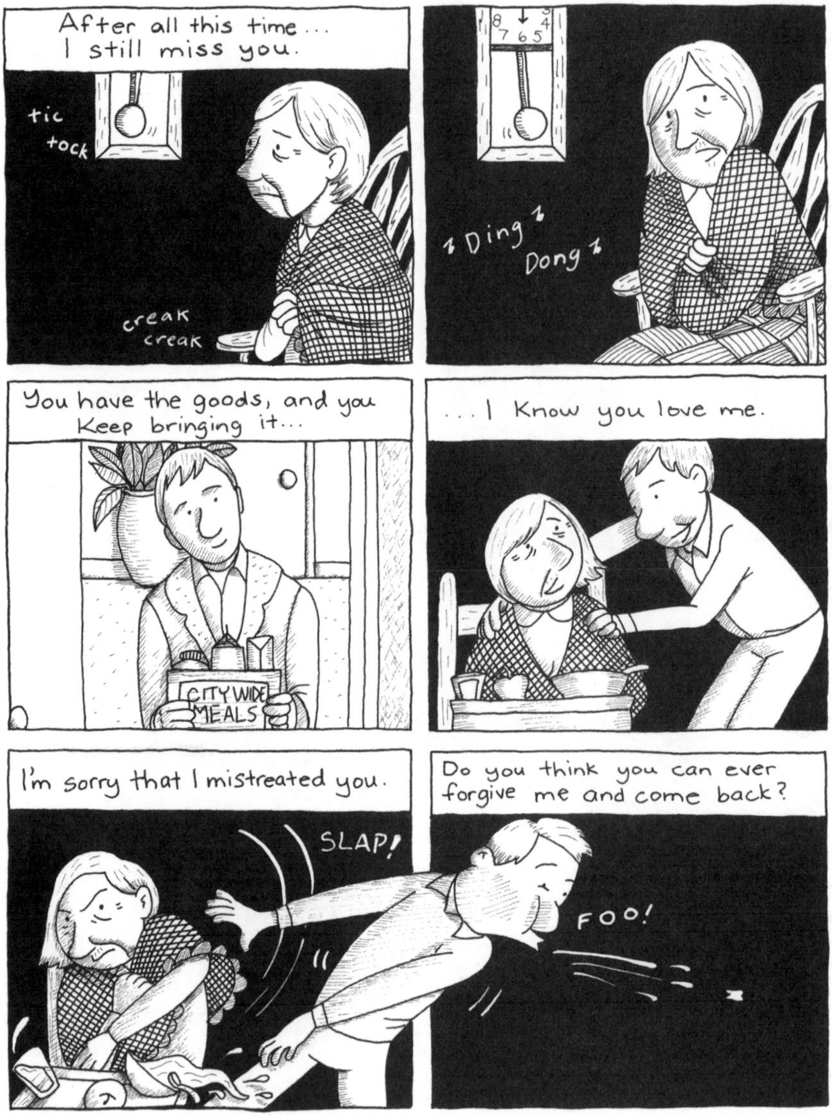
After all this time... I still miss you.
tic tock
creak creak
Ding Dong
You have the goods, and you Keep bringing it...
CITY WIDE MEALS
...I Know you love me.
I'm sorry that I mistreated you.
SLAP!
Do you think you can ever forgive me and come back?
FOO!

by **Arlene O'Leary**

happy birthday - w4m

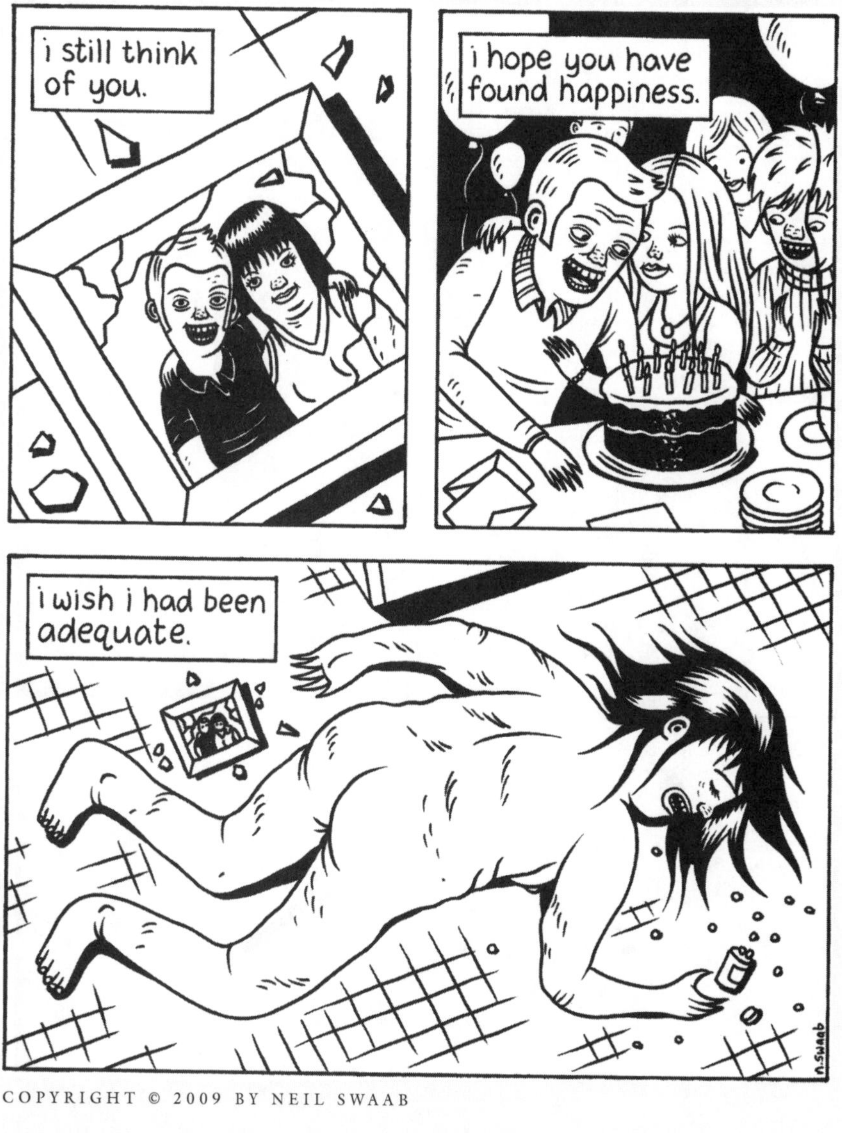
i still think of you.
i hope you have found happiness.
i wish i had been adequate.
n.swaab

by **Neil Swaab**

STANLEY'S ON FRID-AY NIGHT (HEINZ BOTTLE THROWER GIRLS) BY m4w
YOU AND YOUR FRIEND WERE SO
MEAN TO ME!
WHEN I APPROA-CHED YOU TO
INTRODUCE MYSELF...
WTF! HAVE SOME CLASS!
WHY
WERE YOU BOTH SO MEAN TO ME?!
I'M A NICE GUY
F LINCOLN PARK GIRLS!
PS
I HAVE MORE MONEY THAN GOD AND COULD BUY YOU TWO SO SUCK A FAT ONE.
IT IS NOT OK TO CONTACT THIS POSTER WITH SERVICES OR OTHER COMMERCIAL INTERESTS

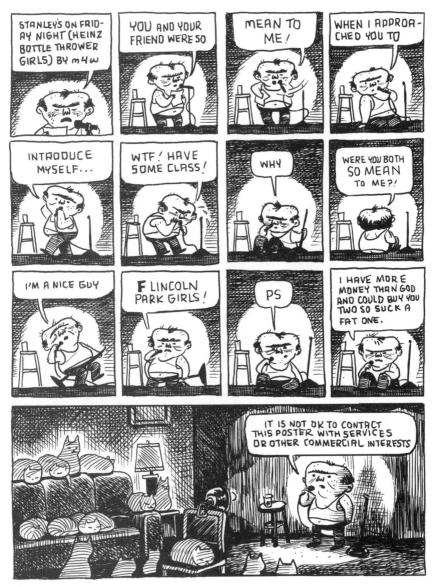

by **Laura Park**

I will miss you Steve... Can we still be friends?

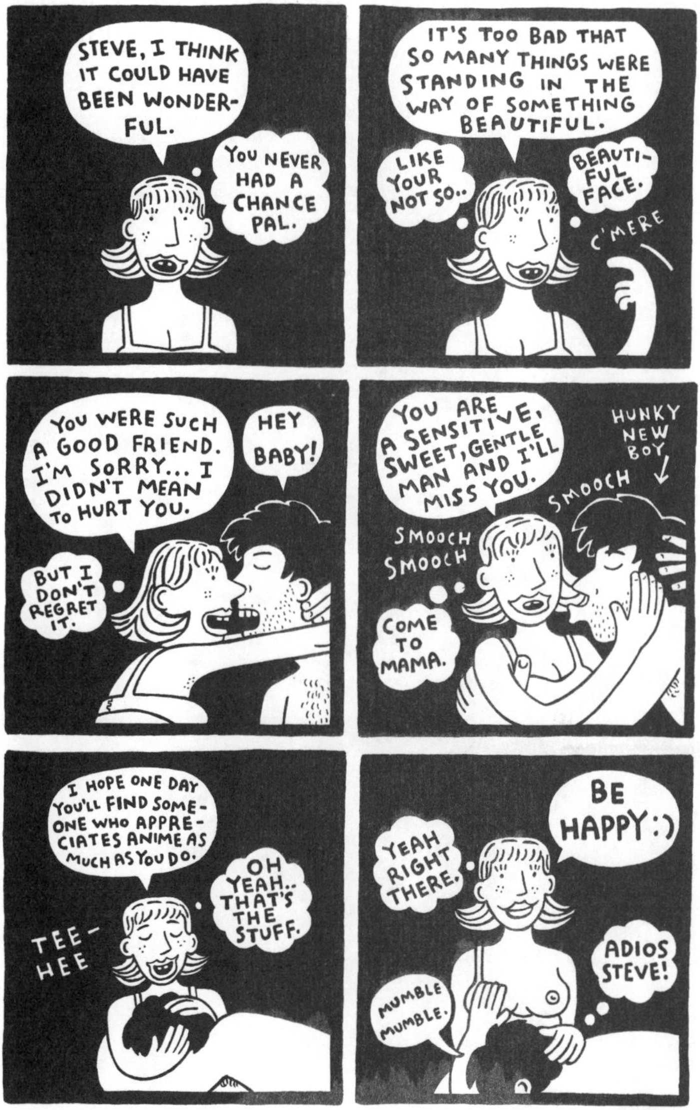
STEVE, I THINK IT COULD HAVE BEEN WONDERFUL.
YOU NEVER HAD A CHANCE PAL.
IT'S TOO BAD THAT SO MANY THINGS WERE STANDING IN THE WAY OF SOMETHING BEAUTIFUL.
LIKE YOUR NOT SO..
BEAUTIFUL FACE.
C'MERE
YOU WERE SUCH A GOOD FRIEND. I'M SORRY... I DIDN'T MEAN TO HURT YOU.
HEY BABY!
BUT I DON'T REGRET IT.
YOU ARE A SENSITIVE, SWEET, GENTLE MAN AND I'LL MISS YOU.
HUNKY NEW BOY
SMOOCH
SMOOCH SMOOCH
COME TO MAMA.
I HOPE ONE DAY YOU'LL FIND SOMEONE WHO APPRECIATES ANIME AS MUCH AS YOU DO.
OH YEAH.. THAT'S THE STUFF.
TEE-HEE
BE HAPPY :)
YEAH RIGHT THERE.
ADIOS STEVE!
MUMBLE MUMBLE.

THE END
A.N.S

by **Aron Nels Steinke**

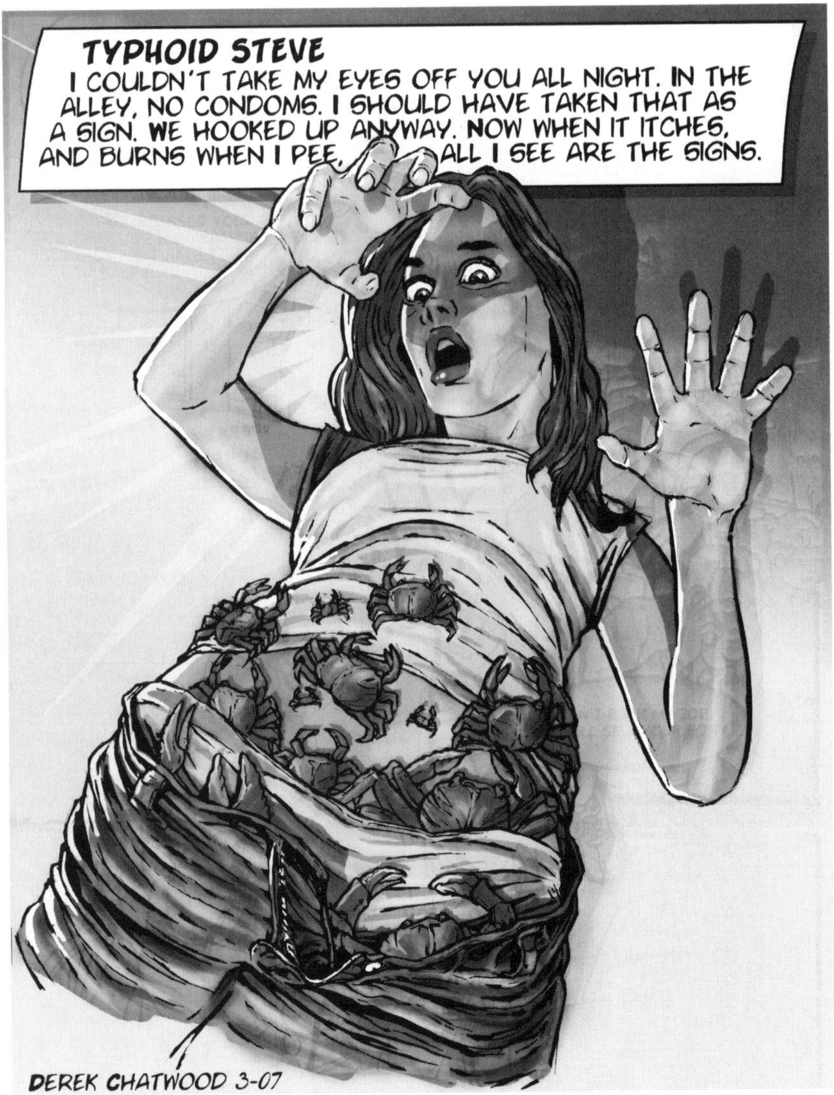
TYPHOID STEVE
I COULDN'T TAKE MY EYES OFF YOU ALL NIGHT. IN THE ALLEY, NO CONDOMS. I SHOULD HAVE TAKEN THAT AS A SIGN. WE HOOKED UP ANYWAY. NOW WHEN IT ITCHES, AND BURNS WHEN I PEE, ALL I SEE ARE THE SIGNS.
DEREK CHATWOOD 3-07

by **Derek Chatwood**

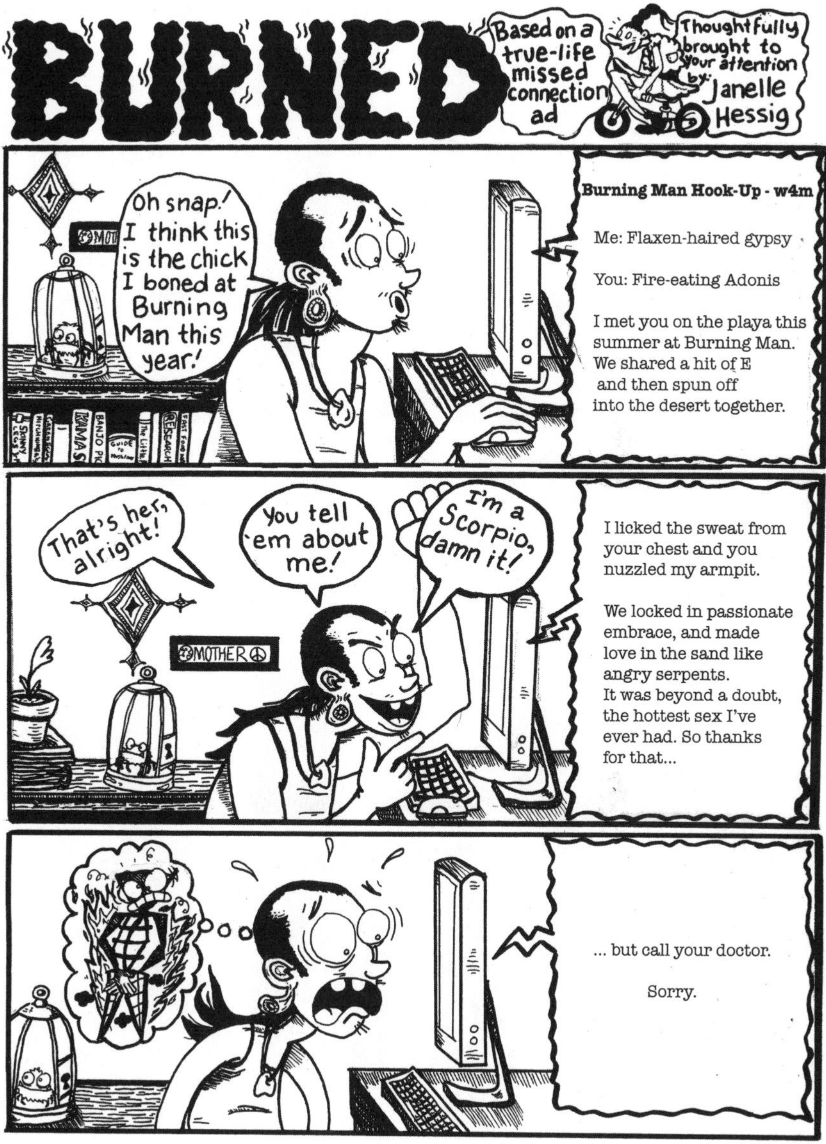
BURNED
Based on a true-life missed connection ad
Thoughtfully brought to your attention by: Janelle Hessig
Oh snap! I think this is the chick I boned at Burning Man this year!
Burning Man Hook-Up - w4m
Me: Flaxen-haired gypsy
You: Fire-eating Adonis
I met you on the playa this summer at Burning Man. We shared a hit of E and then spun off into the desert together.
That's her, alright!
You tell 'em about me!
I'm a Scorpio, damn it!
MOTHER
I licked the sweat from your chest and you nuzzled my armpit.
We locked in passionate embrace, and made love in the sand like angry serpents. It was beyond a doubt, the hottest sex I've ever had. So thanks for that...
... but call your doctor.
Sorry.

by **Janelle Hessig**

GORGEOUS WOMAN in PUEBLO SAFEWAY

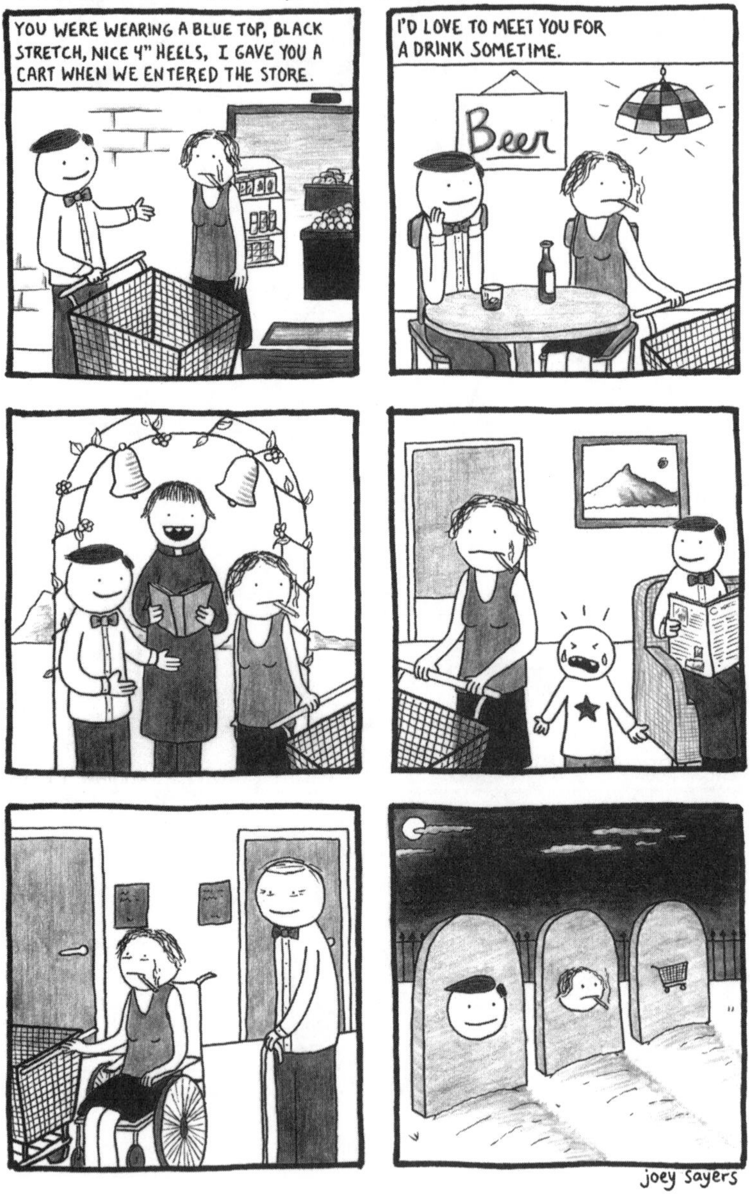
YOU WERE WEARING A BLUE TOP, BLACK STRETCH, NICE 4" HEELS, I GAVE YOU A CART WHEN WE ENTERED THE STORE.
I'D LOVE TO MEET YOU FOR A DRINK SOMETIME.
Beer
joey sayers

by **Joey Sayers**

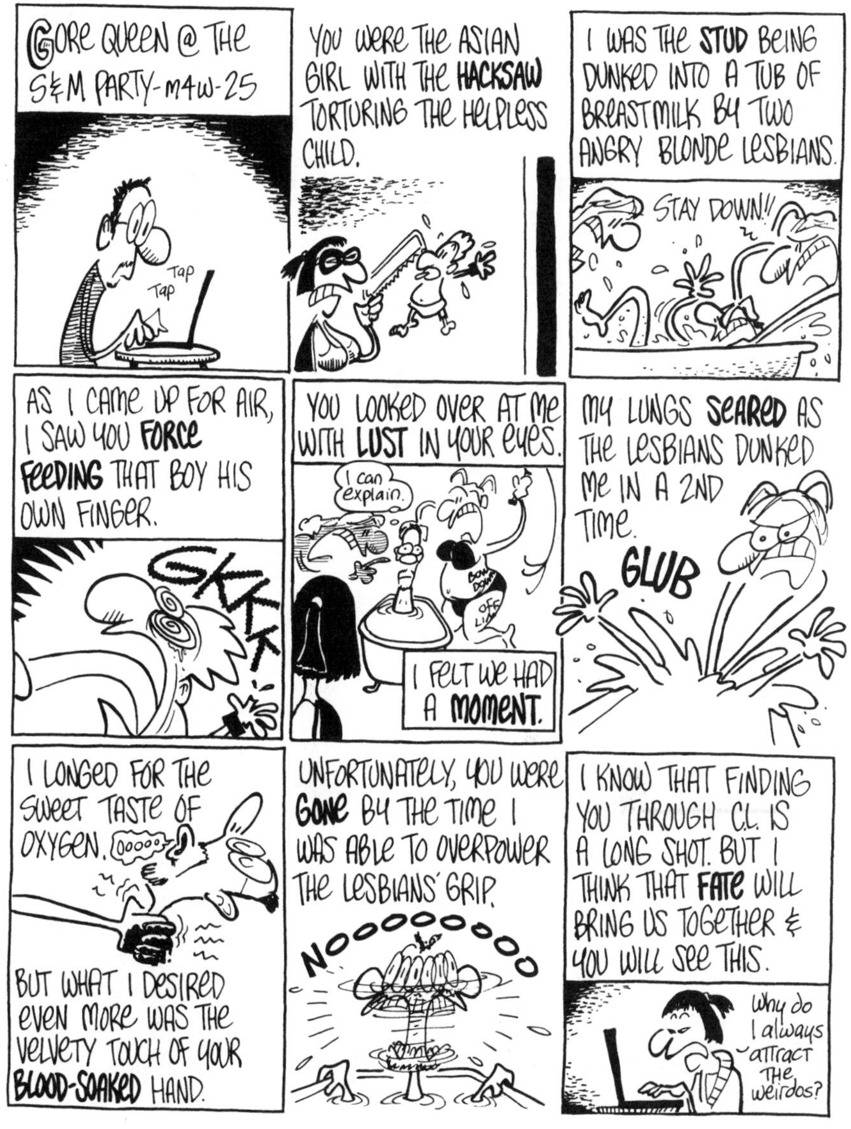
GORE QUEEN @ THE S&M PARTY-M4W-25
Tap Tap
YOU WERE THE ASIAN GIRL WITH THE HACKSAW TORTURING THE HELPLESS CHILD.
I WAS THE STUD BEING DUNKED INTO A TUB OF BREASTMILK BY TWO ANGRY BLONDE LESBIANS.
STAY DOWN!!
AS I CAME UP FOR AIR, I SAW YOU FORCE FEEDING THAT BOY HIS OWN FINGER.
GKKKK
YOU LOOKED OVER AT ME WITH LUST IN YOUR EYES.
I can explain.
I FELT WE HAD A MOMENT.
MY LUNGS SEARED AS THE LESBIANS DUNKED ME IN A 2ND TIME.
GLUB
I LONGED FOR THE SWEET TASTE OF OXYGEN.
ooooo
BUT WHAT I DESIRED EVEN MORE WAS THE VELVETY TOUCH OF YOUR BLOOD-SOAKED HAND.
UNFORTUNATELY, YOU WERE GONE BY THE TIME I WAS ABLE TO OVERPOWER THE LESBIANS' GRIP.
NOOOOOOOOOO
I KNOW THAT FINDING YOU THROUGH C.L. IS A LONG SHOT. BUT I THINK THAT FATE WILL BRING US TOGETHER & YOU WILL SEE THIS.
Why do I always attract the weirdos?

by **Keith Knight**

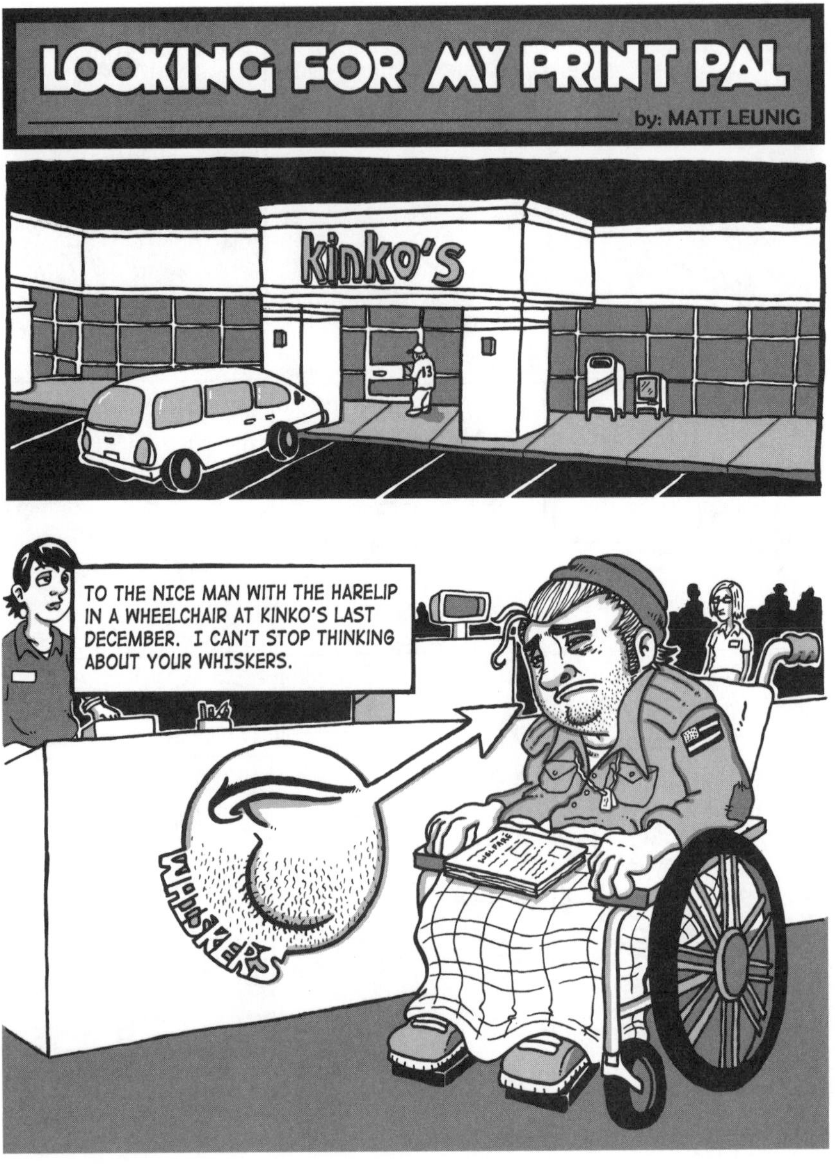
LOOKING FOR MY PRINT PAL
by: MATT LEUNIG
kinko's
TO THE NICE MAN WITH THE HARELIP IN A WHEELCHAIR AT KINKO'S LAST DECEMBER. I CAN'T STOP THINKING ABOUT YOUR WHISKERS.
WHISKERS

by **Matt Leunig**

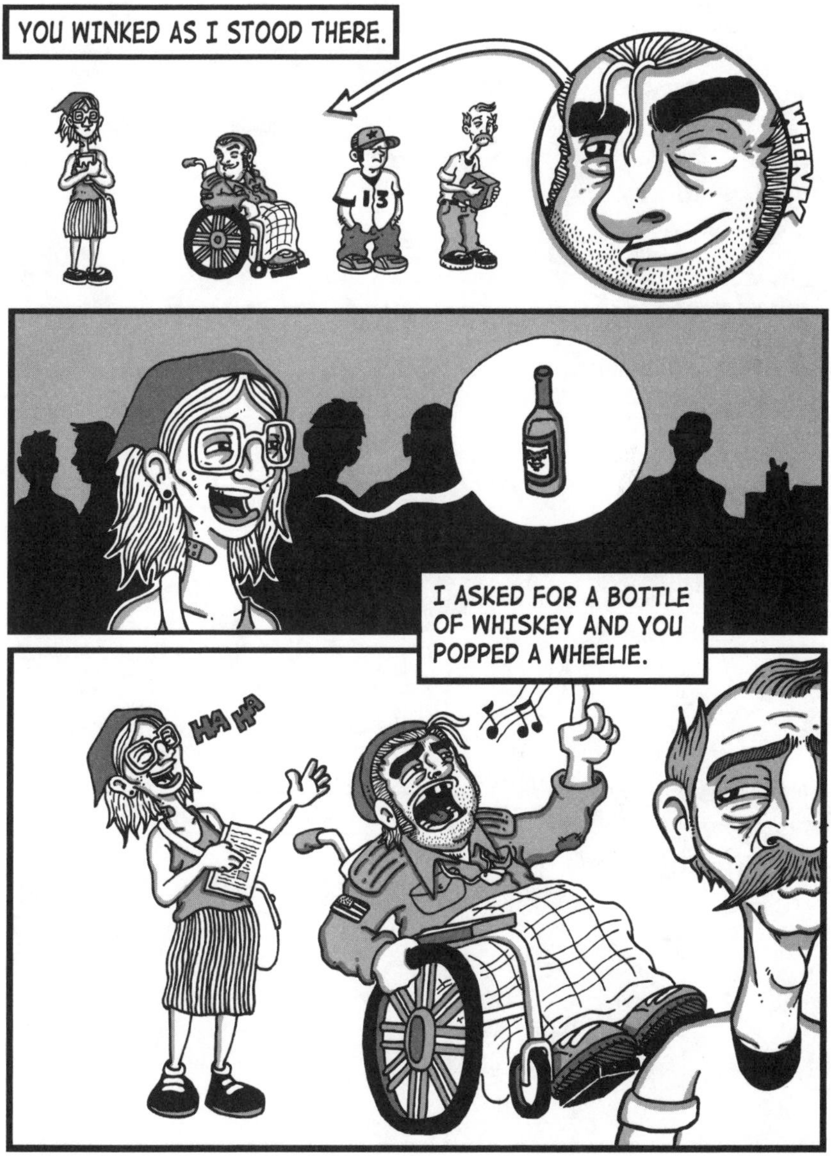
YOU WINKED AS I STOOD THERE.
WINK
I ASKED FOR A BOTTLE OF WHISKEY AND YOU POPPED A WHEELIE.
HA HA

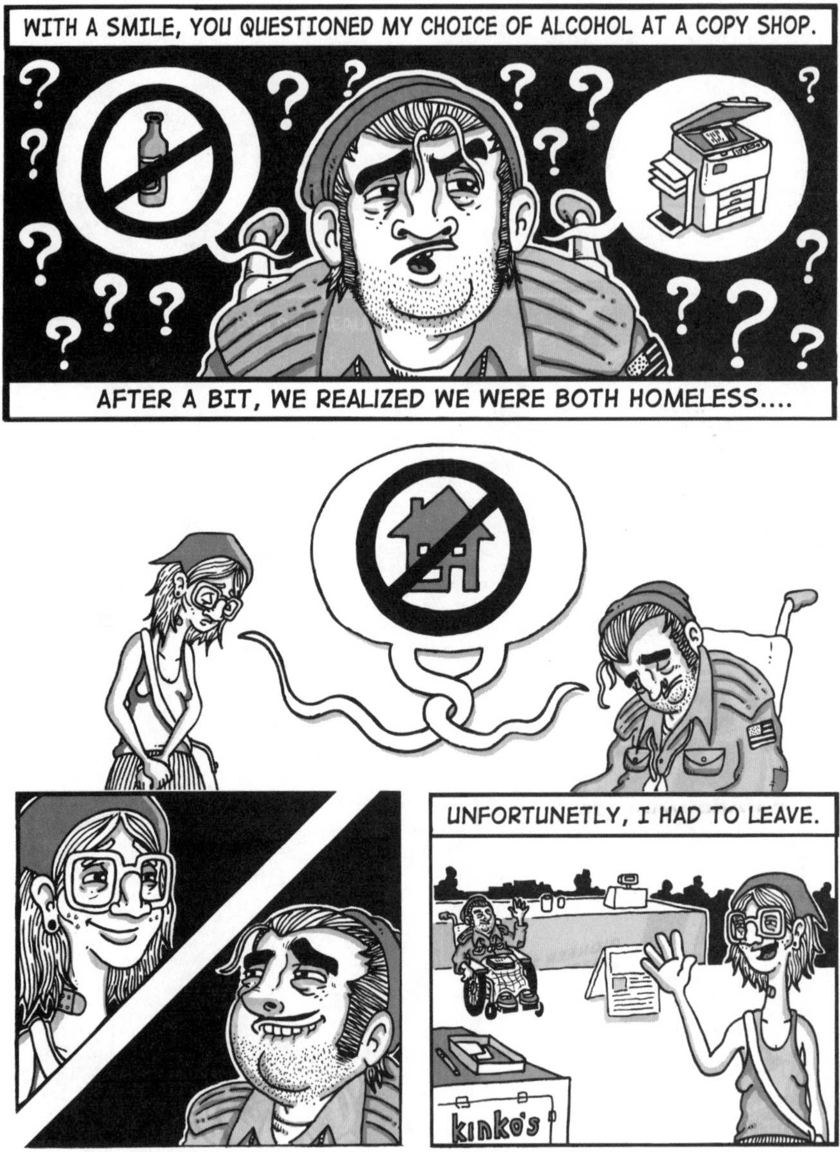
WITH A SMILE, YOU QUESTIONED MY CHOICE OF ALCOHOL AT A COPY SHOP.
AFTER A BIT, WE REALIZED WE WERE BOTH HOMELESS....
UNFORTUNETLY, I HAD TO LEAVE.
kinko's

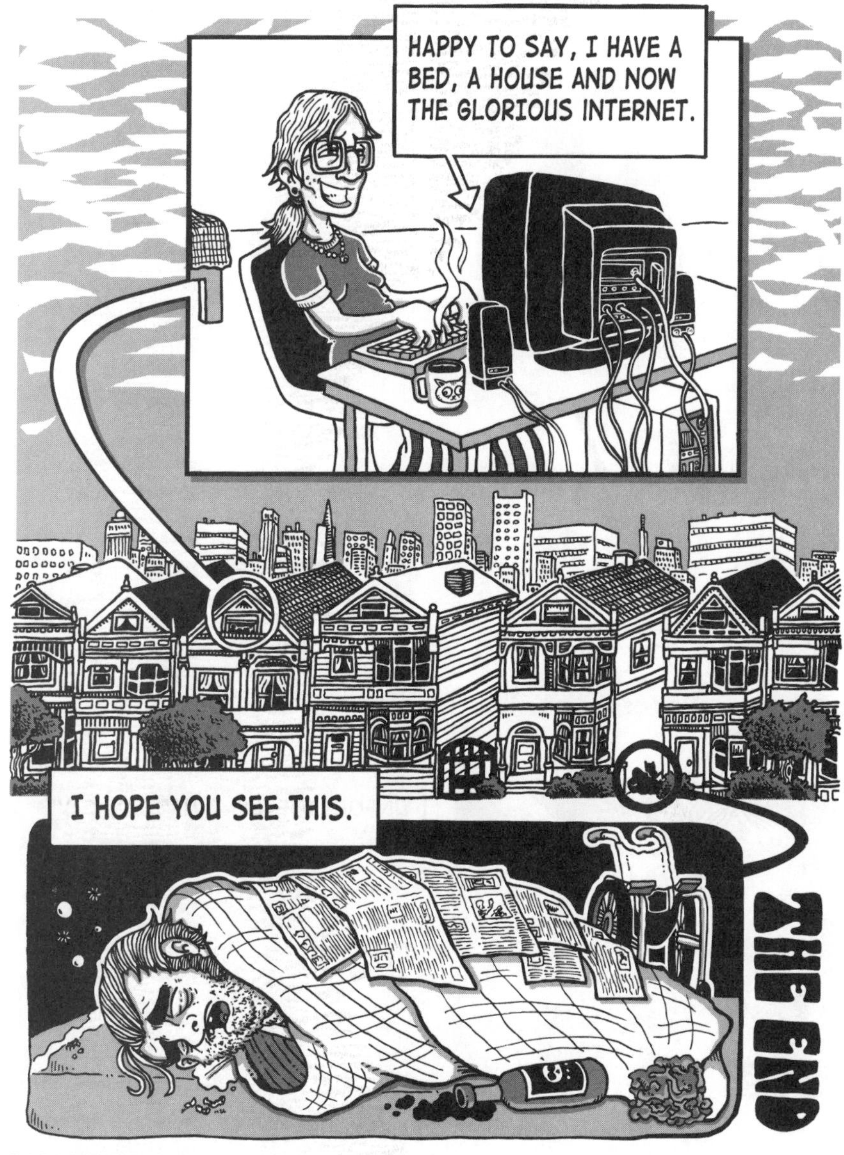
HAPPY TO SAY, I HAVE A BED, A HOUSE AND NOW THE GLORIOUS INTERNET.
I HOPE YOU SEE THIS.
THE END

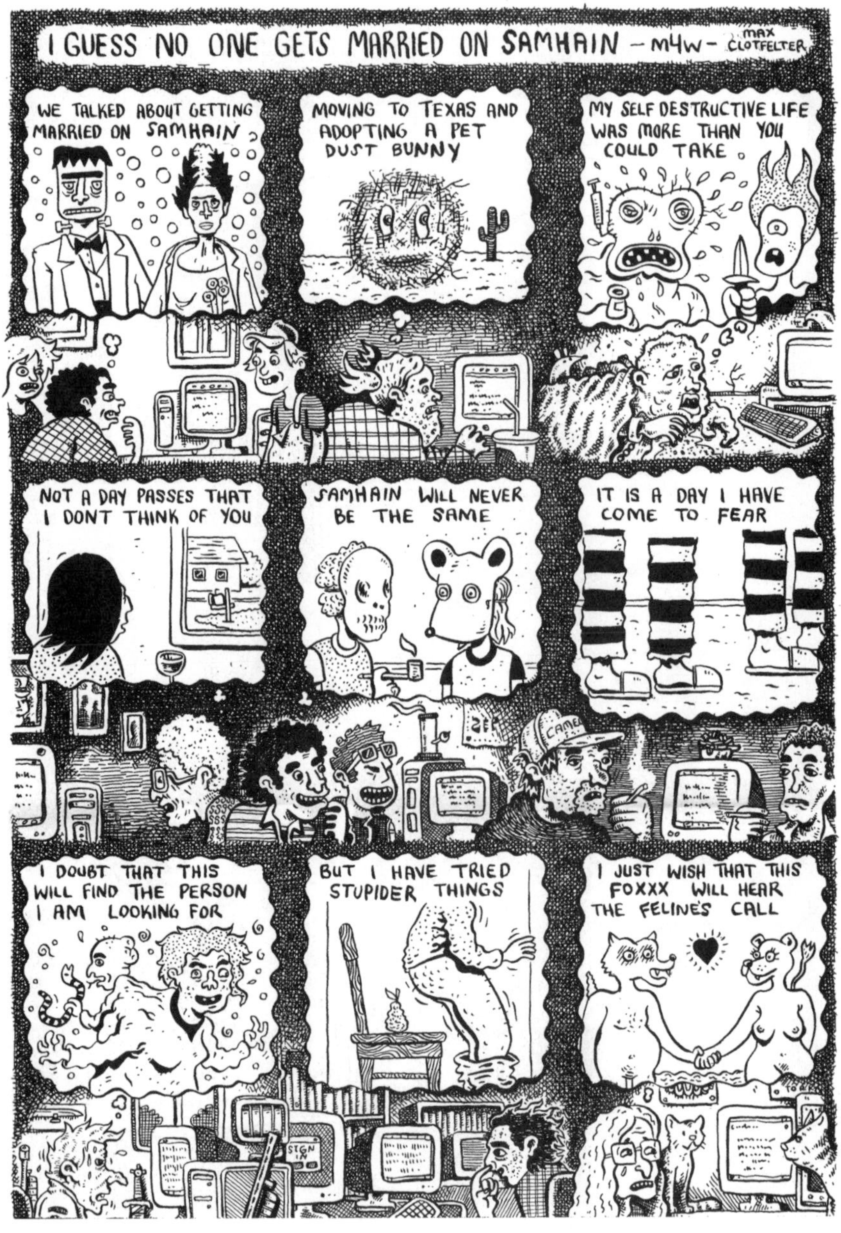

I GUESS NO ONE GETS MARRIED ON SAMHAIN - M4W - MAX CLOTFELTER
WE TALKED ABOUT GETTING MARRIED ON SAMHAIN
MOVING TO TEXAS AND ADOPTING A PET DUST BUNNY
MY SELF DESTRUCTIVE LIFE WAS MORE THAN YOU COULD TAKE
NOT A DAY PASSES THAT I DONT THINK OF YOU
SAMHAIN WILL NEVER BE THE SAME
IT IS A DAY I HAVE COME TO FEAR
I DOUBT THAT THIS WILL FIND THE PERSON I AM LOOKING FOR
BUT I HAVE TRIED STUPIDER THINGS
I JUST WISH THAT THIS FOXXX WILL HEAR THE FELINE'S CALL

by **Max Clotfelter**

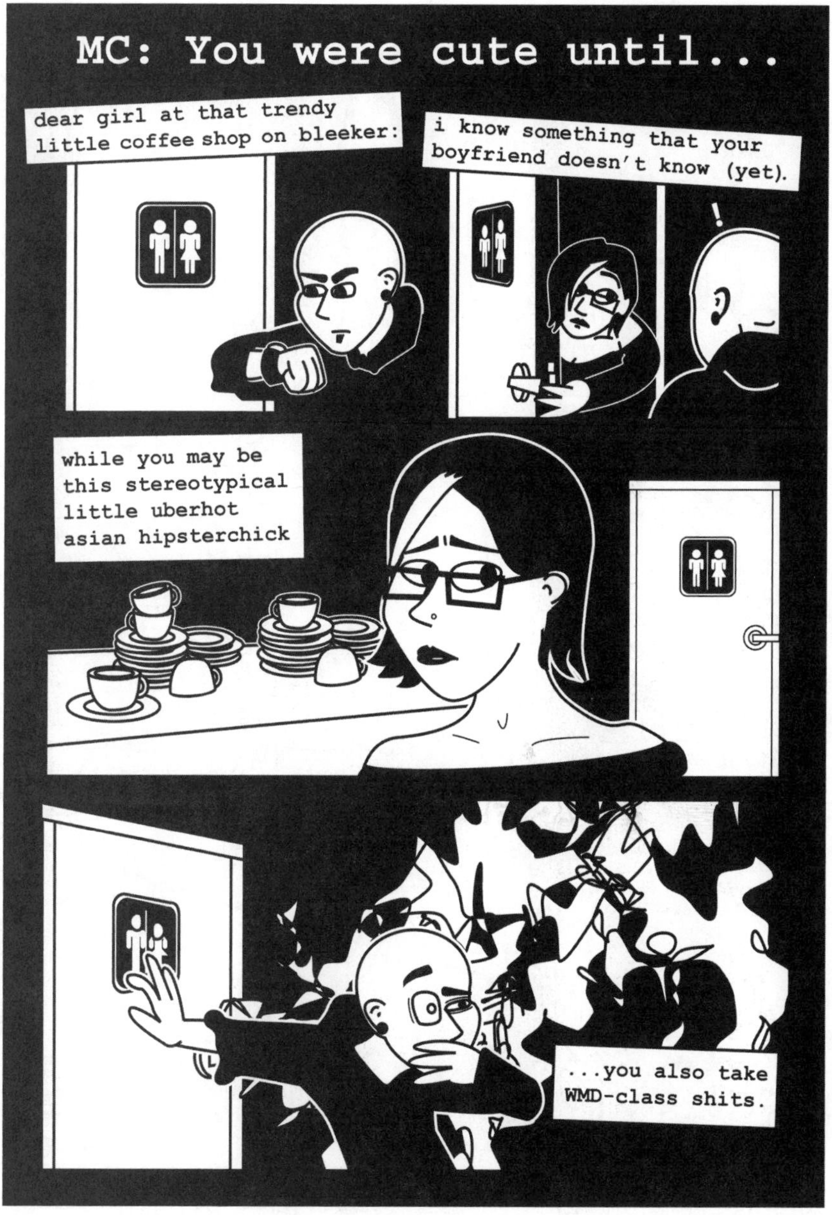
MC: You were cute until...
dear girl at that trendy little coffee shop on bleeker:
i know something that your boyfriend doesn't know (yet).
!
while you may be this stereotypical little uberhot asian hipsterchick
...you also take WMD-class shits.

by **Sam Merwin**

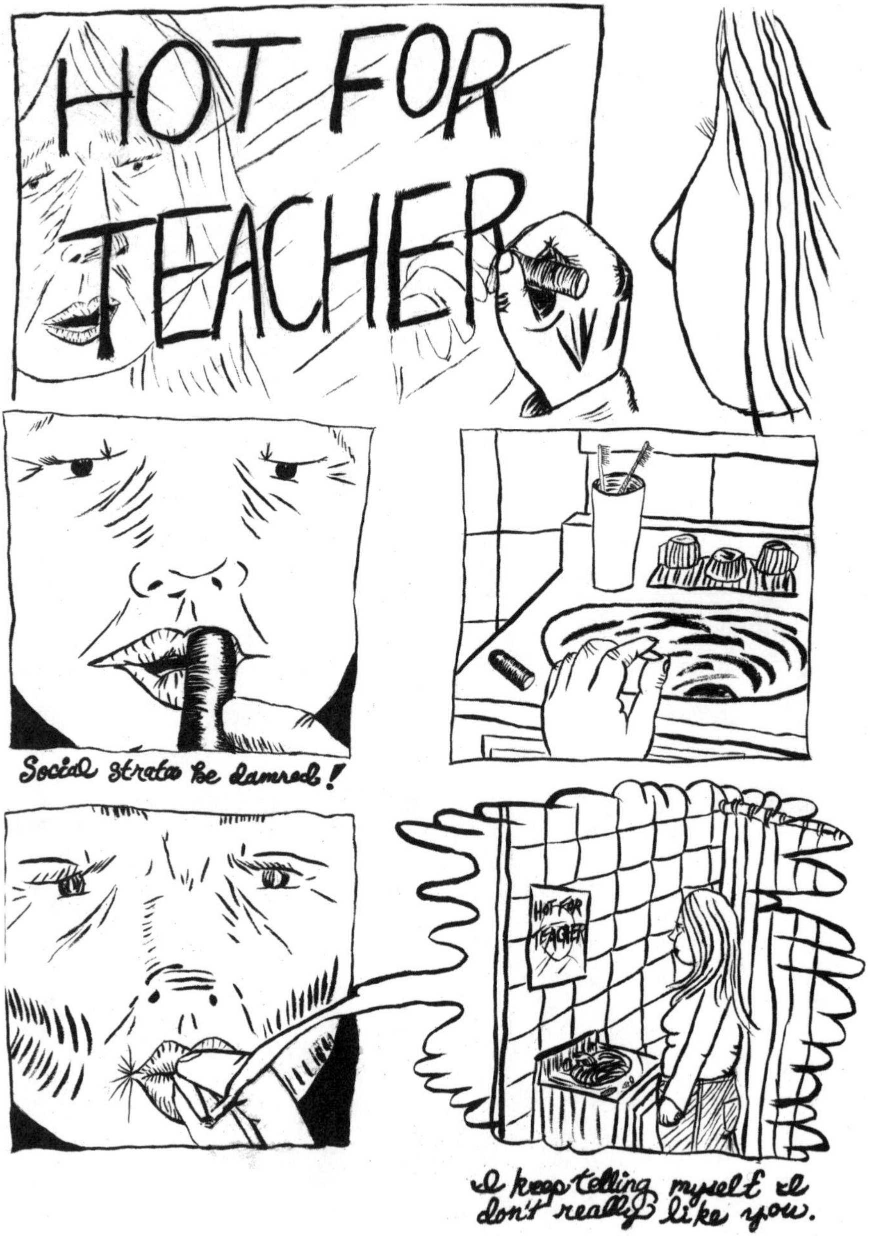
HOT FOR TEACHER
Social strata be damned!
HOT FOR TEACHER
I keep telling myself I don't really like you.

by **Shannon O'Leary**

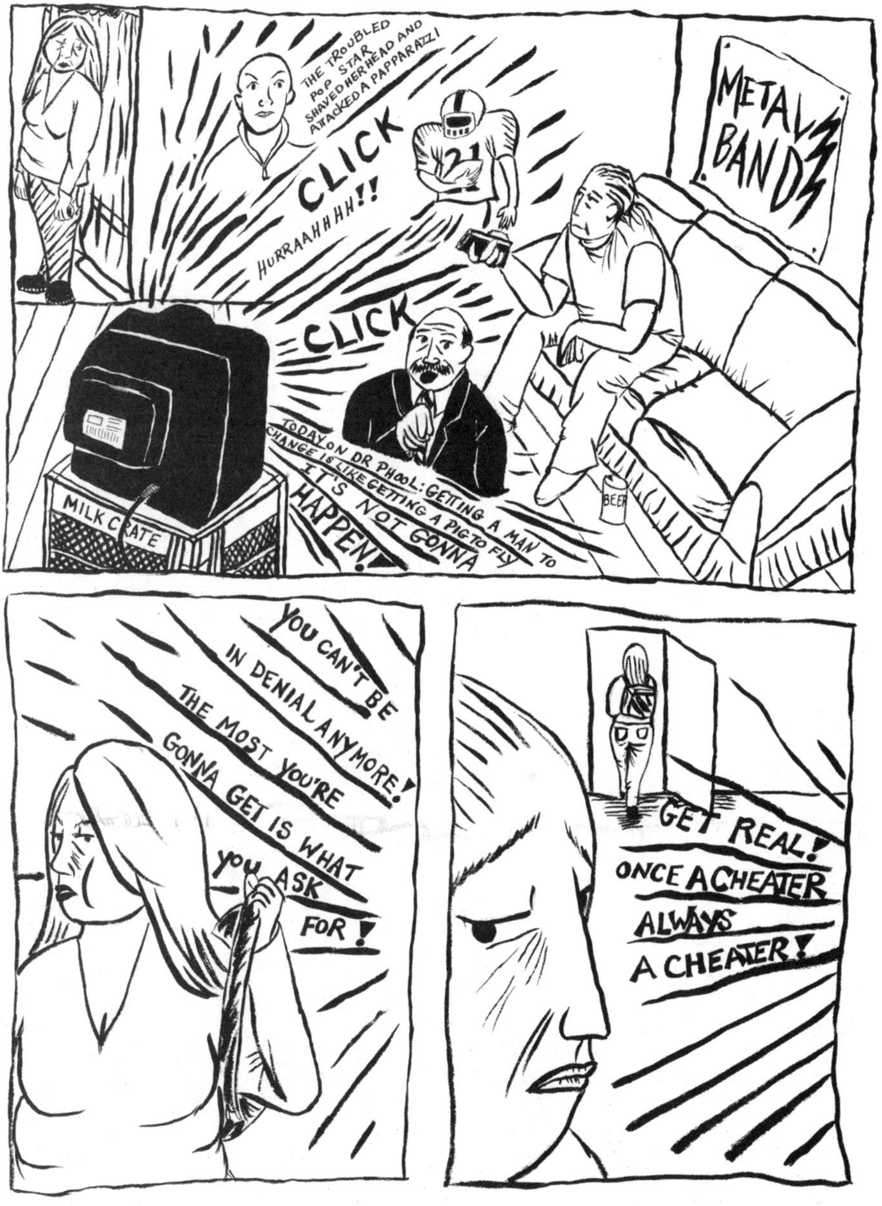
THE TROUBLED POP STAR SHAVED HER HEAD AND ATTACKED A PAPPARAZZI!
CLICK
HURRAAHHHH!!
21
METAL BANDS
CLICK
TODAY ON DR PHOOL: GETTING A MAN TO CHANGE IS LIKE GETTING A PIG TO FLY
IT'S NOT GONNA HAPPEN!
MILK CRATE
BEER
YOU CAN'T BE IN DENIAL ANYMORE!
THE MOST YOU'RE GONNA GET IS WHAT YOU ASK FOR!
GET REAL!
ONCE A CHEATER ALWAYS A CHEATER!

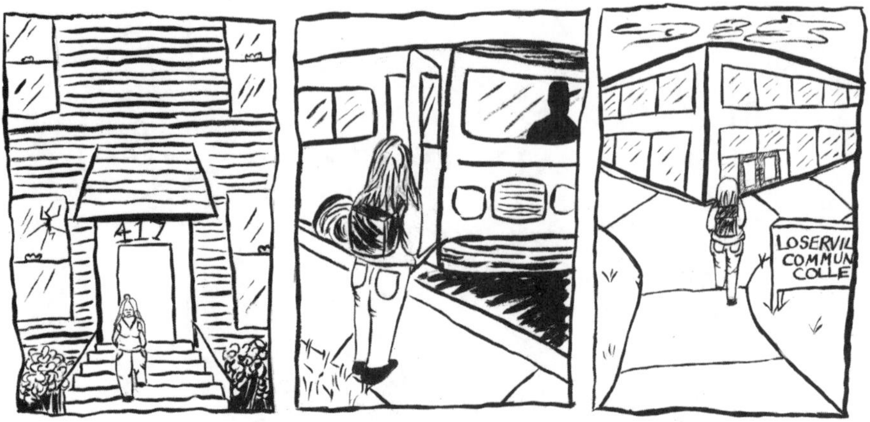
417
LOSERVIL
COMMUN
COLLE

I wallow in my lower-class life.

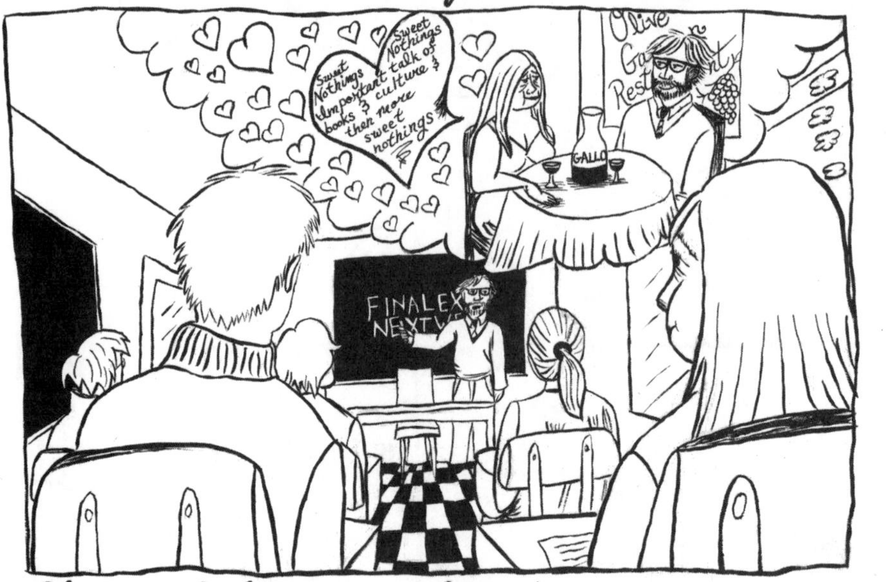
Sweet Nothings
Sweet Nothings
Important talk of books & culture & then more sweet nothings
GALLO
FINALEX
NEXTW

You are clearly out of my league but my dreams are not my own. Last night I had a pleasant one in which we spoke at length about nothing. And yet... the end is near...

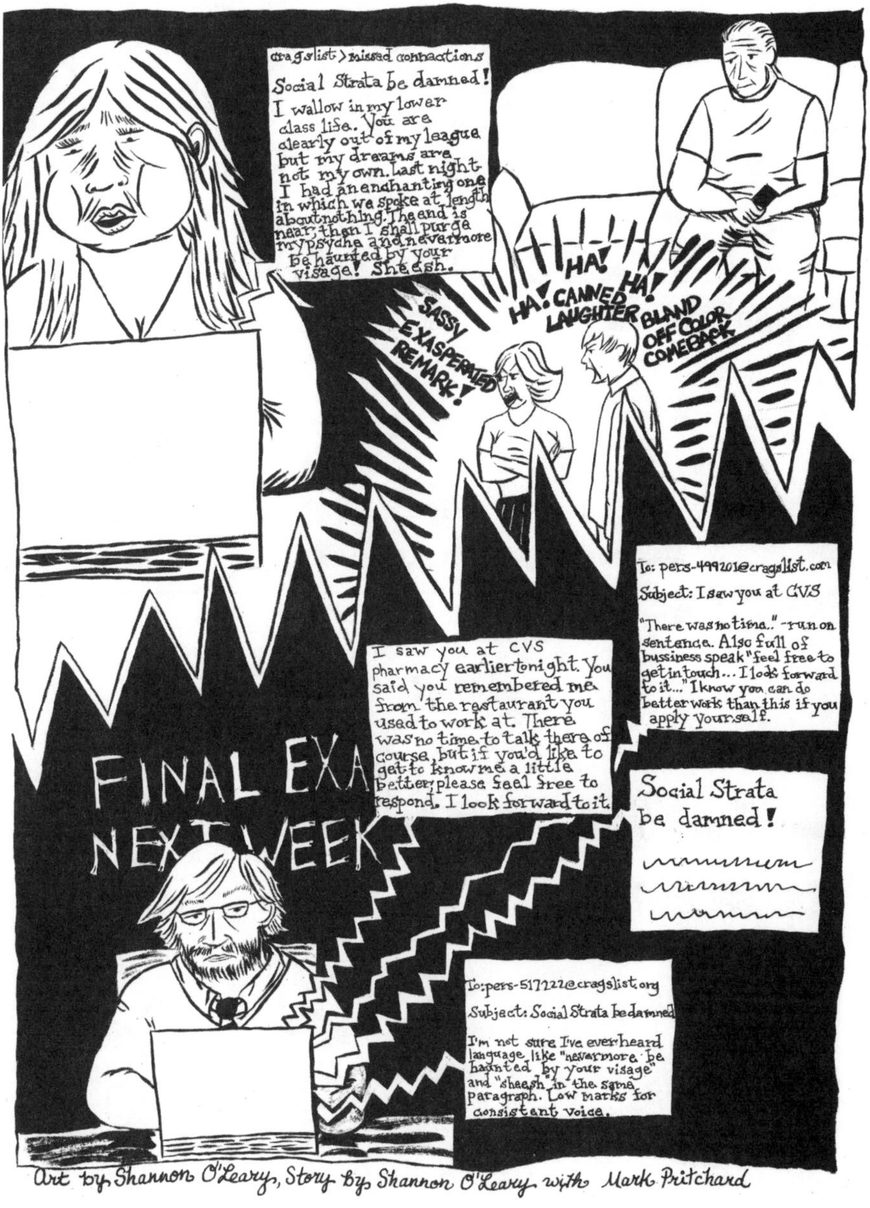
cragslist > missed connections
Social Strata be damned!
I wallow in my lower class life. You are clearly out of my league but my dreams are not my own. Last night I had an enchanting one in which we spoke at length about nothing. The end is near; then I shall purge my psyche and nevermore be haunted by your visage! Sheesh.
SASSY EXASPERATED REMARK!
HA! HA! HA!
CANNED LAUGHTER
BLAND OFF COLOR COMEBACK
To: pers-499201@cragslist.com
Subject: I saw you at CVS
"There was no time.." -run on sentence. Also full of bussiness speak "feel free to get in touch... I look forward to it..." I know you can do better work than this if you apply yourself.
I saw you at CVS pharmacy earlier tonight. You said you remembered me from the restaurant you used to work at. There was no time to talk there of course, but if you'd like to get to know me a little better, please feel free to respond. I look forward to it.
FINAL EXA
NEXT WEEK
Social Strata be damned!
To: pers-517222@cragslist.org
Subject: Social Strata be damned
I'm not sure I've ever heard language like "nevermore be haunted by your visage" and "sheesh" in the same paragraph. Low marks for consistent voice.

Art by Shannon O'Leary, Story by Shannon O'Leary with Mark Pritchard

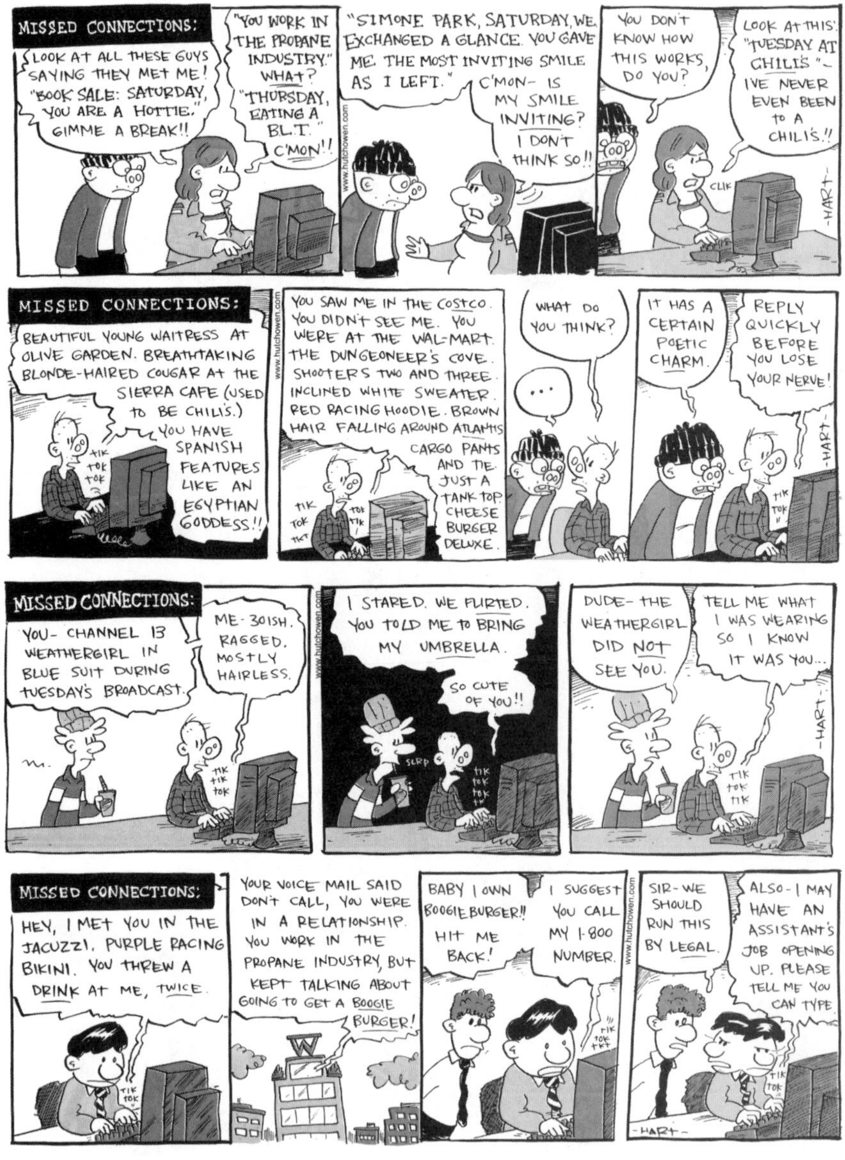
MISSED CONNECTIONS:
LOOK AT ALL THESE GUYS SAYING THEY MET ME! "BOOK SALE: SATURDAY, YOU ARE A HOTTIE." GIMME A BREAK!!
"YOU WORK IN THE PROPANE INDUSTRY." WHAT? "THURSDAY, EATING A B.L.T." C'MON!!
"SIMONE PARK, SATURDAY, WE EXCHANGED A GLANCE. YOU GAVE ME THE MOST INVITING SMILE AS I LEFT."
C'MON– IS MY SMILE INVITING? I DON'T THINK SO!!
www.hutchowen.com
YOU DON'T KNOW HOW THIS WORKS, DO YOU?
LOOK AT THIS: "TUESDAY AT CHILI'S" – I'VE NEVER EVEN BEEN TO A CHILI'S!!
CLIK
-HART-
MISSED CONNECTIONS:
BEAUTIFUL YOUNG WAITRESS AT OLIVE GARDEN. BREATHTAKING BLONDE-HAIRED COUGAR AT THE SIERRA CAFE (USED TO BE CHILI'S.) YOU HAVE SPANISH FEATURES LIKE AN EGYPTIAN GODDESS!!
TIK TOK TOK
www.hutchowen.com
YOU SAW ME IN THE COSTCO. YOU DIDN'T SEE ME. YOU WERE AT THE WAL-MART. THE DUNGEONEER'S COVE. SHOOTERS TWO AND THREE. INCLINED WHITE SWEATER. RED RACING HOODIE. BROWN HAIR FALLING AROUND ATLANTIS CARGO PANTS AND TIE. JUST A TANK TOP. CHEESE BURGER DELUXE.
TIK TOK TKT
TOK TIK
WHAT DO YOU THINK?
...
IT HAS A CERTAIN POETIC CHARM.
REPLY QUICKLY BEFORE YOU LOSE YOUR NERVE!
TIK TOK
-HART-
MISSED CONNECTIONS:
YOU– CHANNEL 13 WEATHERGIRL IN BLUE SUIT DURING TUESDAY'S BROADCAST.
ME– 30ISH. RAGGED. MOSTLY HAIRLESS.
TIK TIK TOK
www.hutchowen.com
I STARED. WE FLIRTED. YOU TOLD ME TO BRING MY UMBRELLA.
SO CUTE OF YOU!!
SLRP
TIK TOK TOK TK
DUDE– THE WEATHERGIRL DID NOT SEE YOU.
TELL ME WHAT I WAS WEARING SO I KNOW IT WAS YOU...
TIK TOK TIK
-HART-
MISSED CONNECTIONS:
HEY, I MET YOU IN THE JACUZZI. PURPLE RACING BIKINI. YOU THREW A DRINK AT ME, TWICE.
TIK TOK
YOUR VOICE MAIL SAID DON'T CALL, YOU WERE IN A RELATIONSHIP. YOU WORK IN THE PROPANE INDUSTRY, BUT KEPT TALKING ABOUT GOING TO GET A BOOGIE BURGER!
BABY I OWN BOOGIE BURGER!! HIT ME BACK!
I SUGGEST YOU CALL MY 1-800 NUMBER.
TIK TOK TKT
www.hutchowen.com
SIR– WE SHOULD RUN THIS BY LEGAL.
ALSO– I MAY HAVE AN ASSISTANT'S JOB OPENING UP. PLEASE TELL ME YOU CAN TYPE.
TIK TOK
-HART-

by **Tom Hart**

PART 6.

FINDING LOVE IN UNEXPECTED PLACES

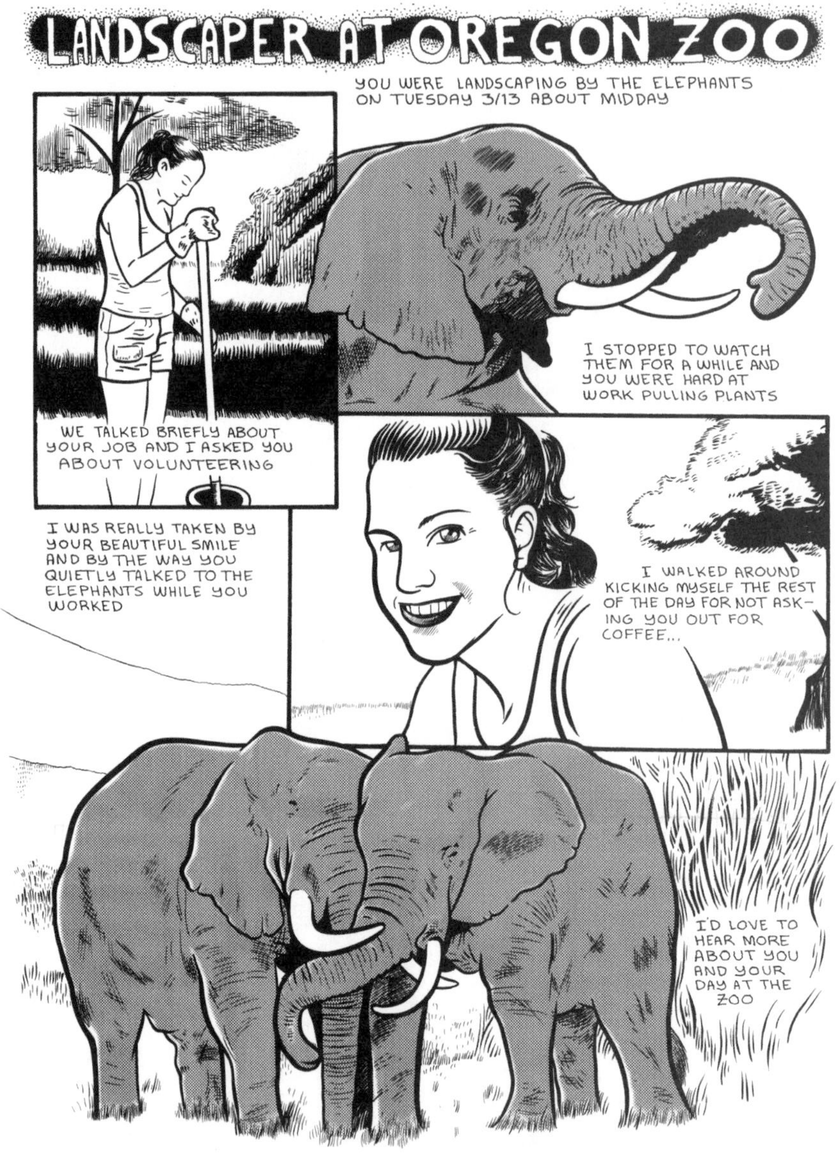
LANDSCAPER AT OREGON ZOO
YOU WERE LANDSCAPING BY THE ELEPHANTS ON TUESDAY 3/13 ABOUT MIDDAY
I STOPPED TO WATCH THEM FOR A WHILE AND YOU WERE HARD AT WORK PULLING PLANTS
WE TALKED BRIEFLY ABOUT YOUR JOB AND I ASKED YOU ABOUT VOLUNTEERING
I WAS REALLY TAKEN BY YOUR BEAUTIFUL SMILE AND BY THE WAY YOU QUIETLY TALKED TO THE ELEPHANTS WHILE YOU WORKED
I WALKED AROUND KICKING MYSELF THE REST OF THE DAY FOR NOT ASKING YOU OUT FOR COFFEE...
I'D LOVE TO HEAR MORE ABOUT YOU AND YOUR DAY AT THE ZOO

by **Elijah J. Brubaker**

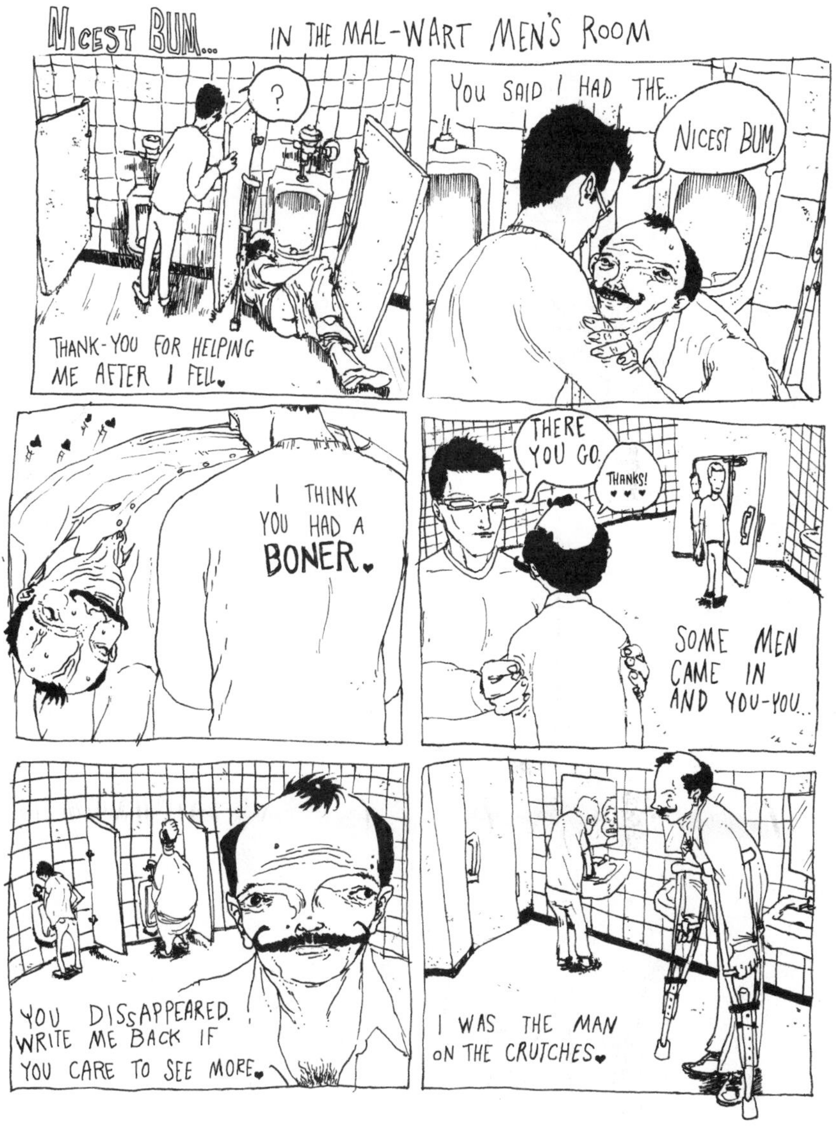
NICEST BUM... IN THE MAL-WART MEN'S ROOM
?
THANK-YOU FOR HELPING ME AFTER I FELL.
YOU SAID I HAD THE...
NICEST BUM.
I THINK YOU HAD A BONER.
THERE YOU GO.
THANKS!
SOME MEN CAME IN AND YOU-YOU...
YOU DISSAPPEARED. WRITE ME BACK IF YOU CARE TO SEE MORE.
I WAS THE MAN ON THE CRUTCHES.

by **David Bessent**

Same Ol' Saturday Night...

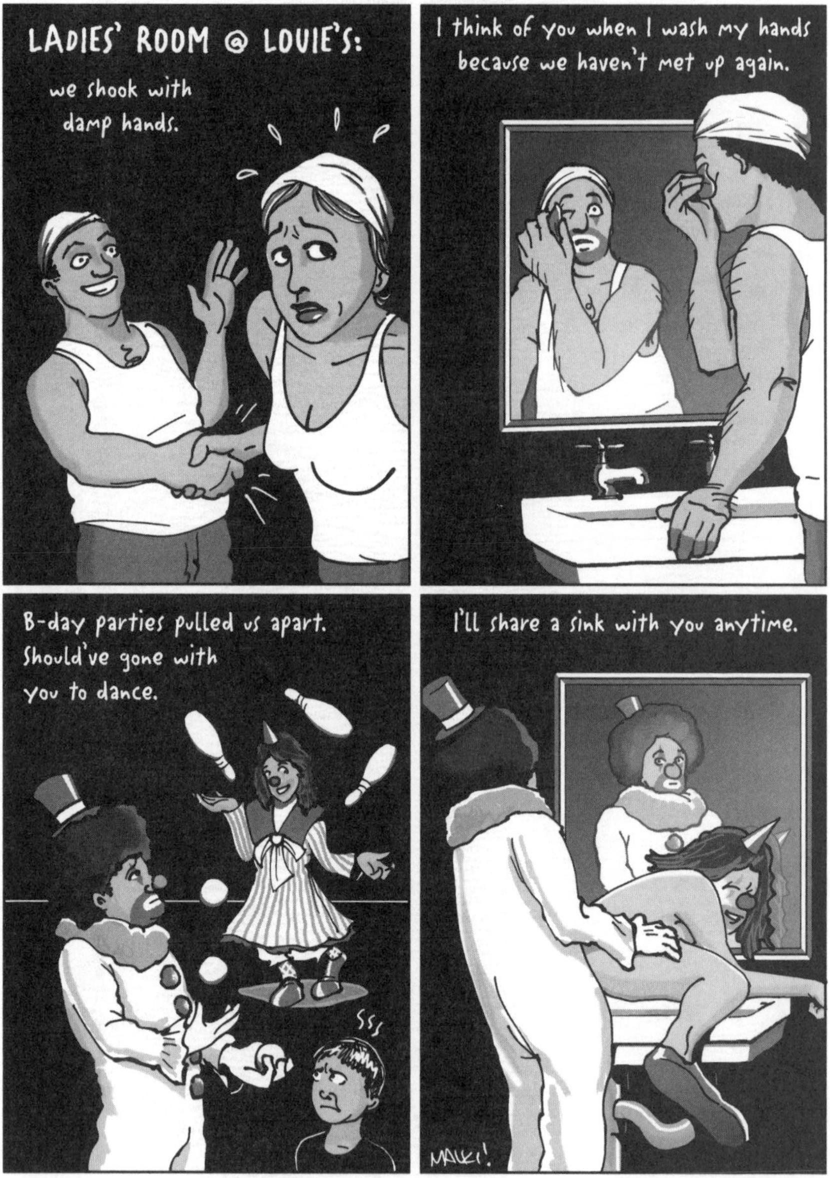
LADIES' ROOM @ LOUIE'S:
we shook with damp hands.
I think of you when I wash my hands because we haven't met up again.
B-day parties pulled us apart. Should've gone with you to dance.
SSS
I'll share a sink with you anytime.
MALKI!

by **David Malki**

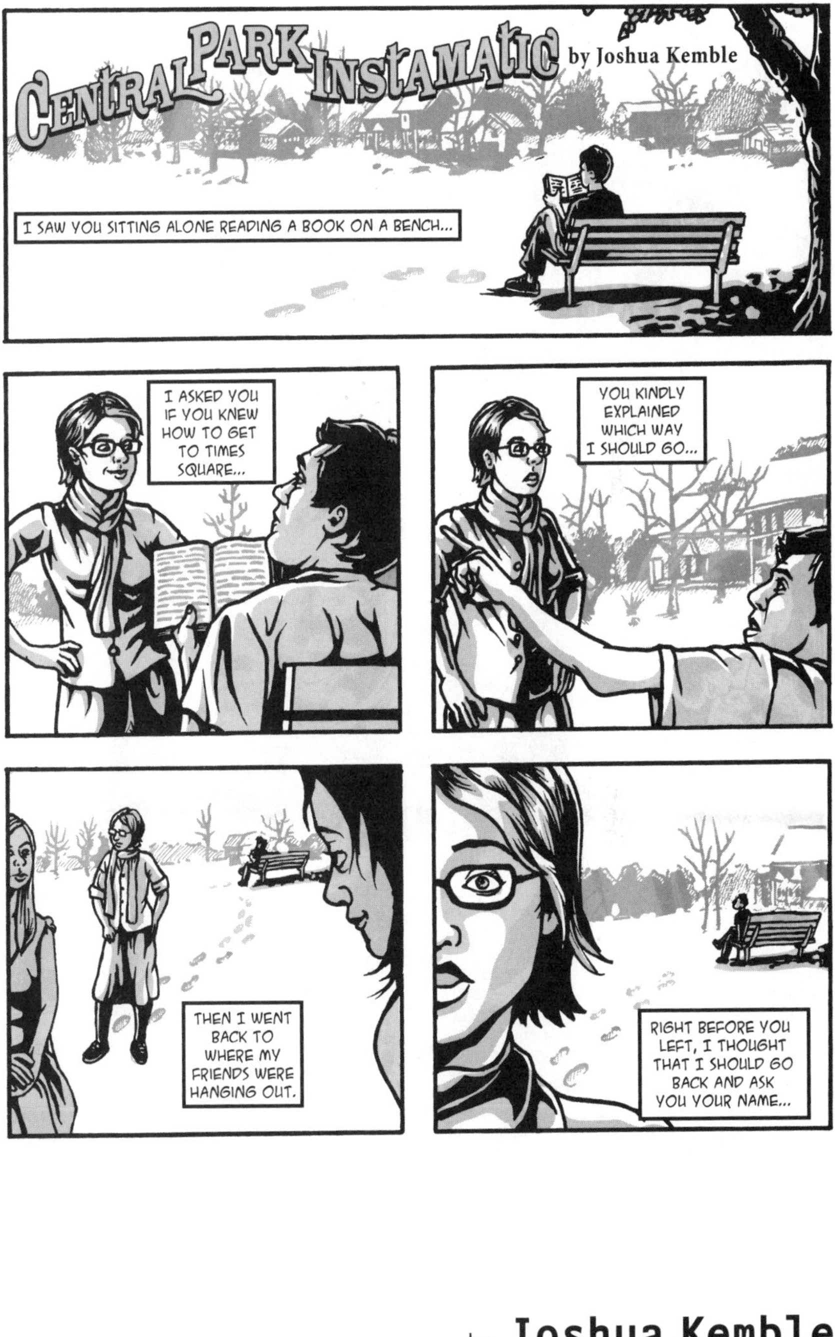
CENTRAL PARK INSTAMATIC
by Joshua Kemble
I SAW YOU SITTING ALONE READING A BOOK ON A BENCH...
I ASKED YOU IF YOU KNEW HOW TO GET TO TIMES SQUARE...
YOU KINDLY EXPLAINED WHICH WAY I SHOULD GO...
THEN I WENT BACK TO WHERE MY FRIENDS WERE HANGING OUT.
RIGHT BEFORE YOU LEFT, I THOUGHT THAT I SHOULD GO BACK AND ASK YOU YOUR NAME...

by **Joshua Kemble**

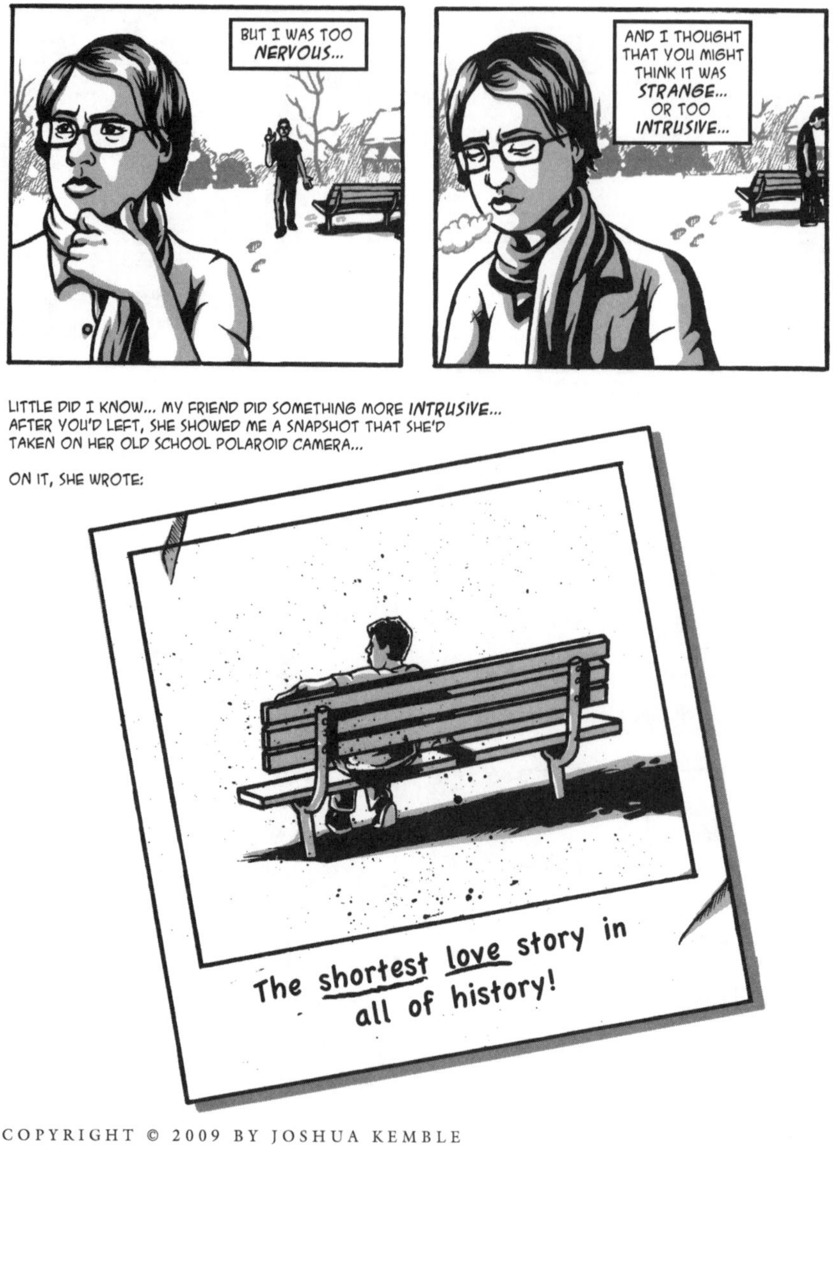
BUT I WAS TOO NERVOUS...
AND I THOUGHT THAT YOU MIGHT THINK IT WAS STRANGE... OR TOO INTRUSIVE...
LITTLE DID I KNOW... MY FRIEND DID SOMETHING MORE INTRUSIVE... AFTER YOU'D LEFT, SHE SHOWED ME A SNAPSHOT THAT SHE'D TAKEN ON HER OLD SCHOOL POLAROID CAMERA...
ON IT, SHE WROTE:
The shortest love story in all of history!

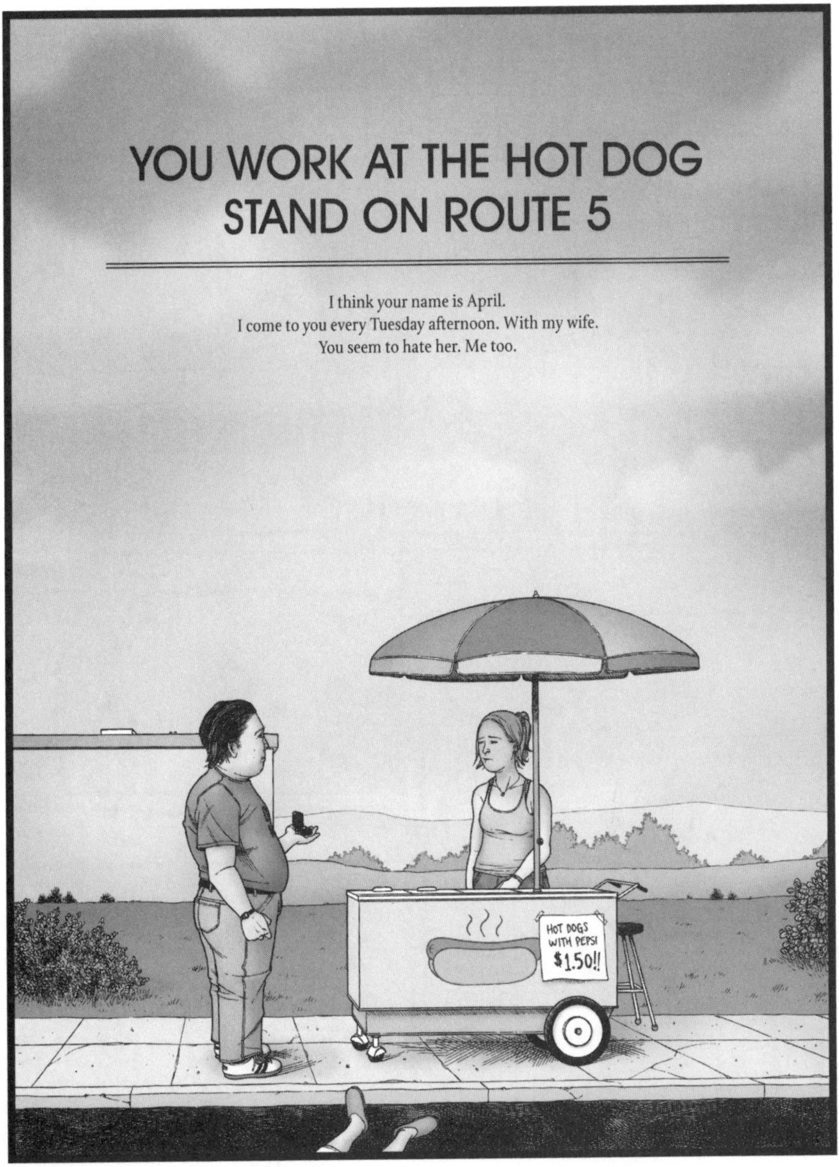
YOU WORK AT THE HOT DOG STAND ON ROUTE 5
I think your name is April.
I come to you every Tuesday afternoon. With my wife.
You seem to hate her. Me too.
HOT DOGS WITH PEPSI $1.50!!

by **Jon Adams**

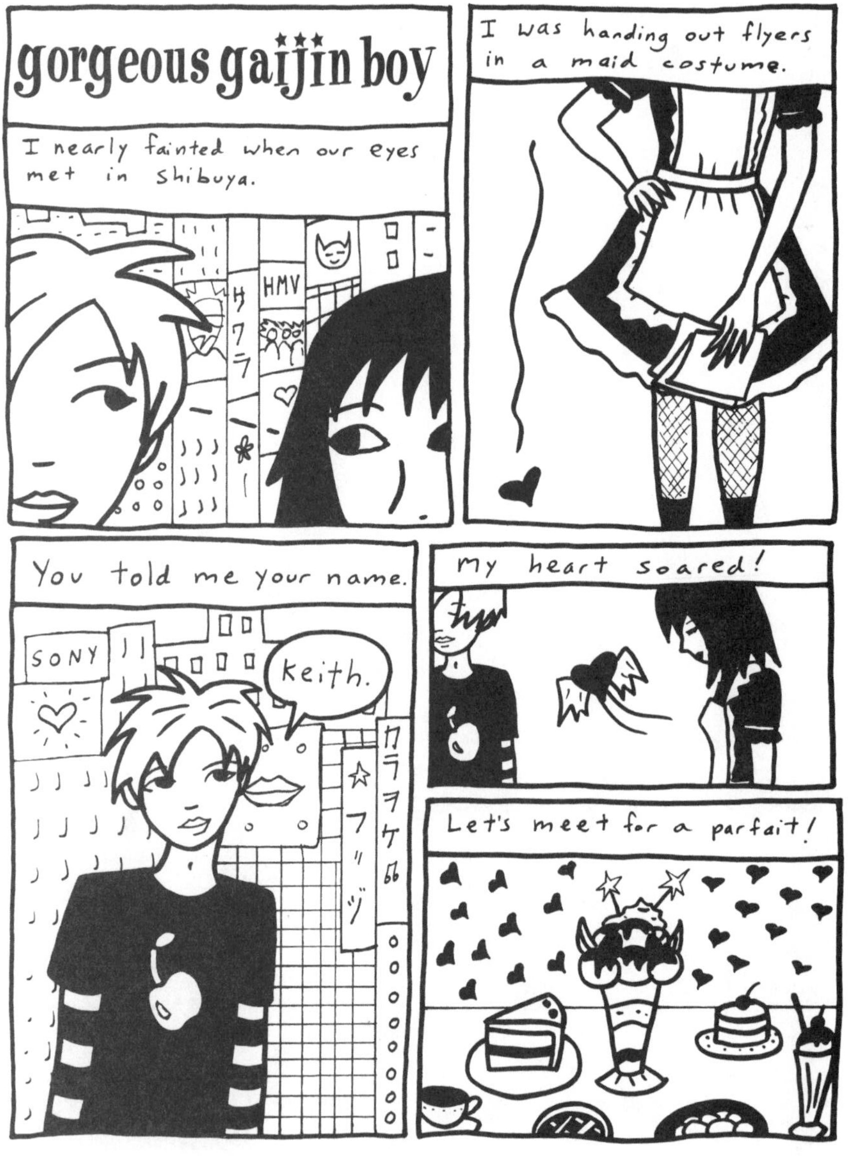
gorgeous gaijin boy
I nearly fainted when our eyes met in Shibuya.
HMV
I was handing out flyers in a maid costume.
You told me your name.
SONY
keith.
my heart soared!
Let's meet for a parfait!

by **Abby Denson**

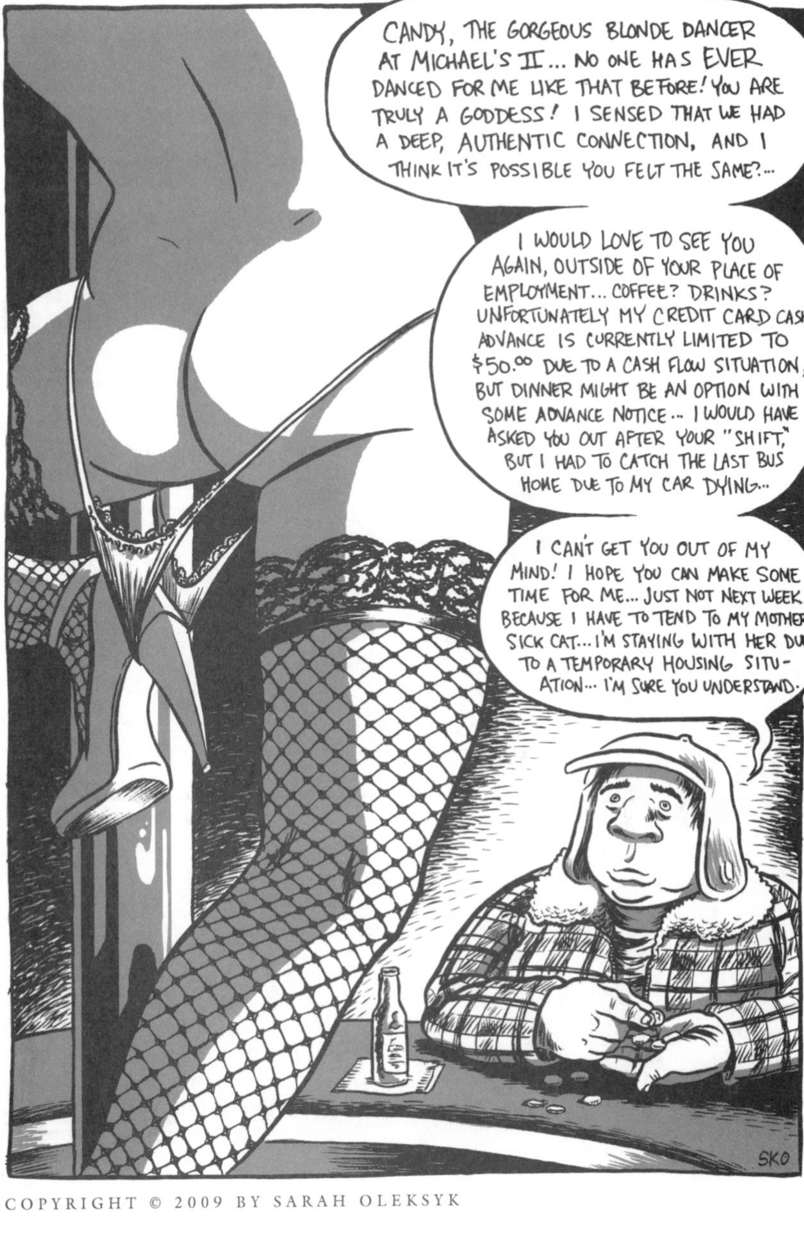
CANDY, THE GORGEOUS BLONDE DANCER AT MICHAEL'S II... NO ONE HAS EVER DANCED FOR ME LIKE THAT BEFORE! YOU ARE TRULY A GODDESS! I SENSED THAT WE HAD A DEEP, AUTHENTIC CONNECTION, AND I THINK IT'S POSSIBLE YOU FELT THE SAME?...
I WOULD LOVE TO SEE YOU AGAIN, OUTSIDE OF YOUR PLACE OF EMPLOYMENT... COFFEE? DRINKS? UNFORTUNATELY MY CREDIT CARD CASH ADVANCE IS CURRENTLY LIMITED TO $50.00 DUE TO A CASH FLOW SITUATION, BUT DINNER MIGHT BE AN OPTION WITH SOME ADVANCE NOTICE... I WOULD HAVE ASKED YOU OUT AFTER YOUR "SHIFT," BUT I HAD TO CATCH THE LAST BUS HOME DUE TO MY CAR DYING...
I CAN'T GET YOU OUT OF MY MIND! I HOPE YOU CAN MAKE SOME TIME FOR ME... JUST NOT NEXT WEEK, BECAUSE I HAVE TO TEND TO MY MOTHER'S SICK CAT... I'M STAYING WITH HER DUE TO A TEMPORARY HOUSING SITU-ATION... I'M SURE YOU UNDERSTAND.
SKO

by **Sarah Oleksyk**

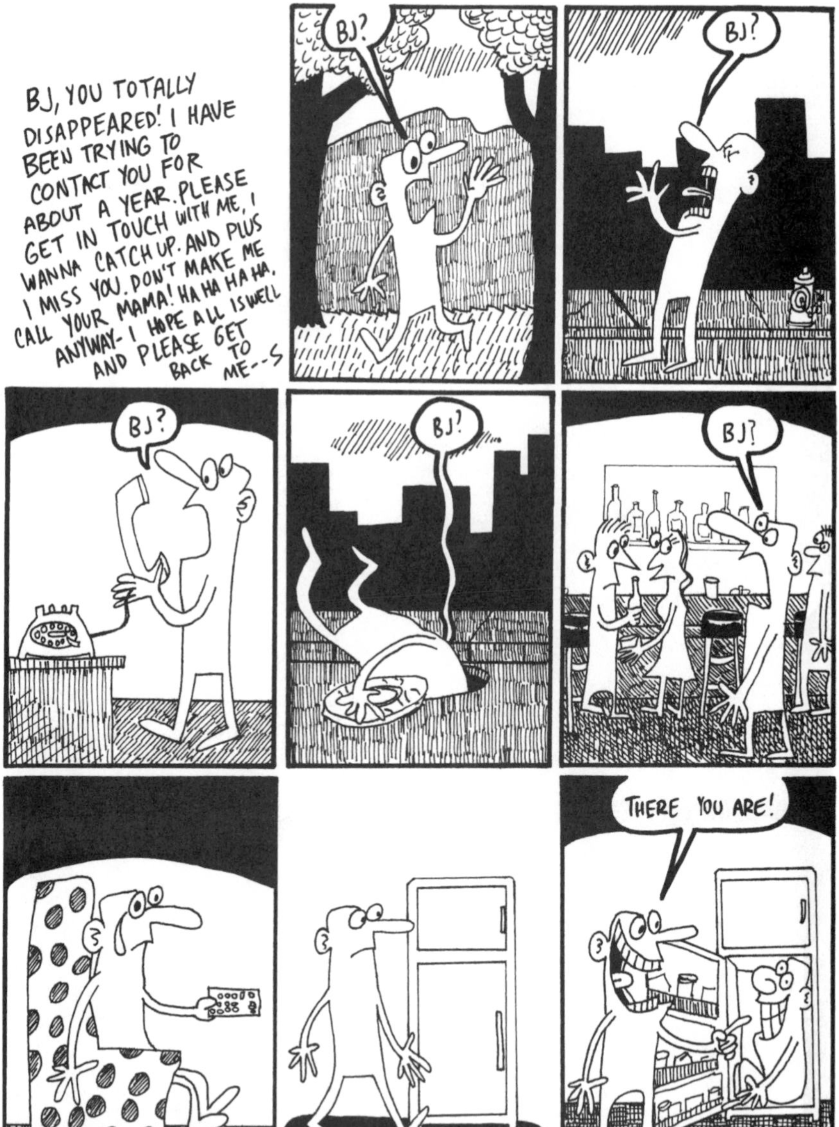
BJ, YOU TOTALLY DISAPPEARED! I HAVE BEEN TRYING TO CONTACT YOU FOR ABOUT A YEAR. PLEASE GET IN TOUCH WITH ME, I WANNA CATCH UP. AND PLUS I MISS YOU. DON'T MAKE ME CALL YOUR MAMA! HA HA HA HA. ANYWAY- I HOPE ALL IS WELL AND PLEASE GET BACK TO ME--S
BJ?
BJ?
BJ?
BJ?
BJ?
THERE YOU ARE!

by **Sam Henderson**

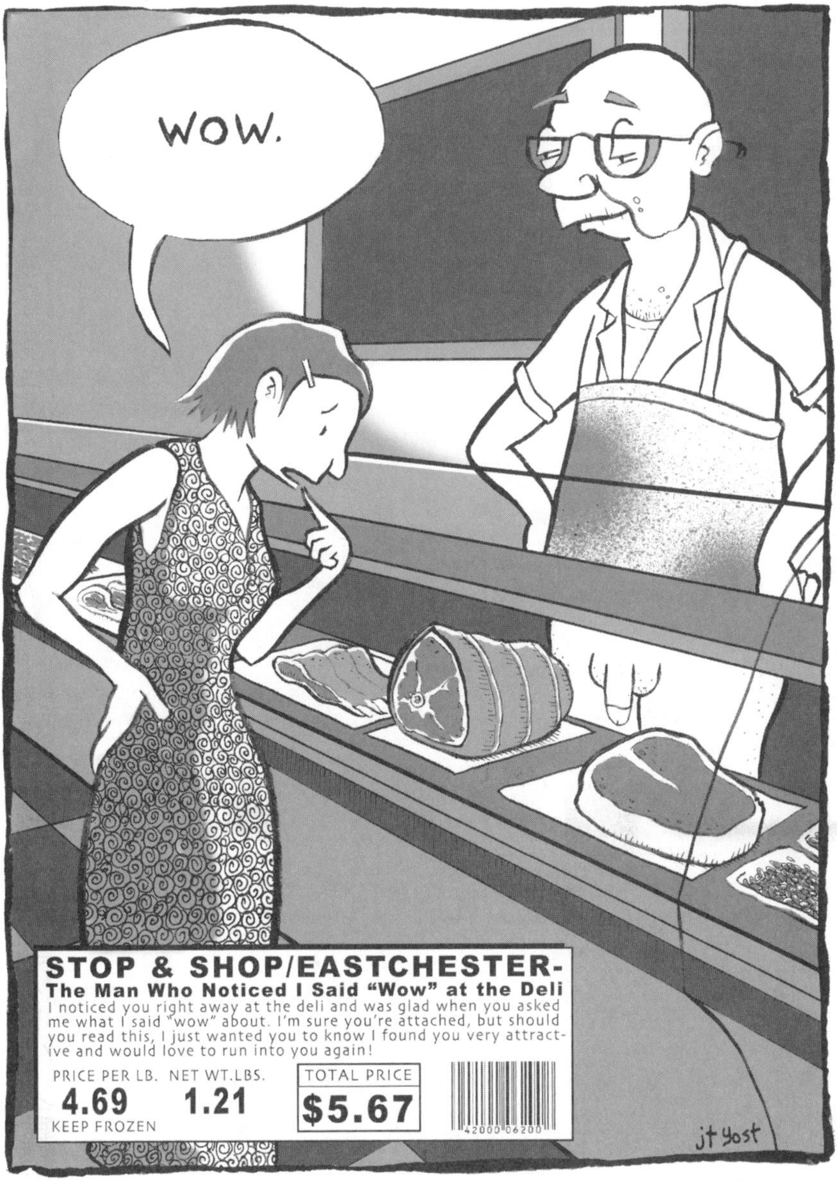
WOW.
STOP & SHOP/EASTCHESTER-
The Man Who Noticed I Said "Wow" at the Deli
I noticed you right away at the deli and was glad when you asked me what I said "wow" about. I'm sure you're attached, but should you read this, I just wanted you to know I found you very attractive and would love to run into you again!
PRICE PER LB. 4.69
NET WT.LBS. 1.21
KEEP FROZEN
TOTAL PRICE $5.67
jt yost

by **J.T. Yost**

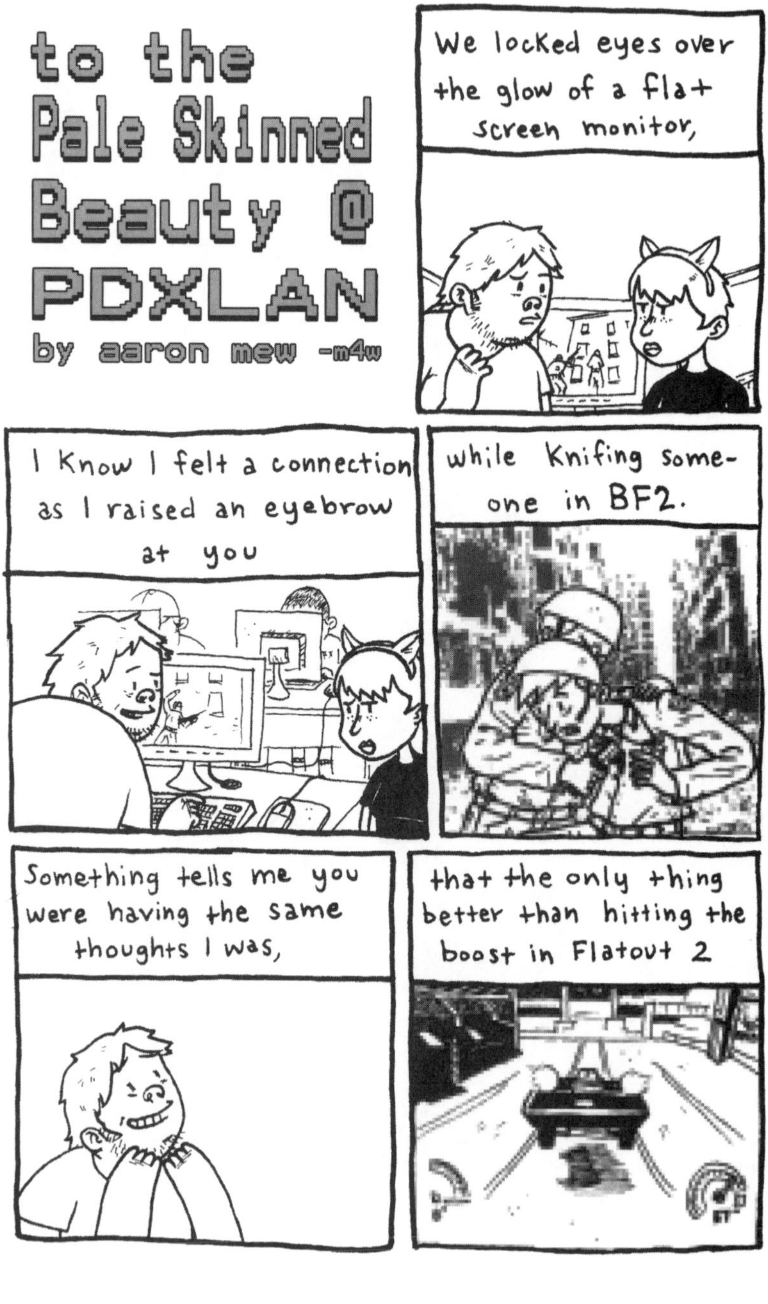
to the Pale Skinned Beauty @ PDXLAN
by aaron mew -m4w
We locked eyes over the glow of a flat screen monitor,
I know I felt a connection as I raised an eyebrow at you
while knifing some-one in BF2.
Something tells me you were having the same thoughts I was,
that the only thing better than hitting the boost in Flatout 2

by **Aaron Mew**

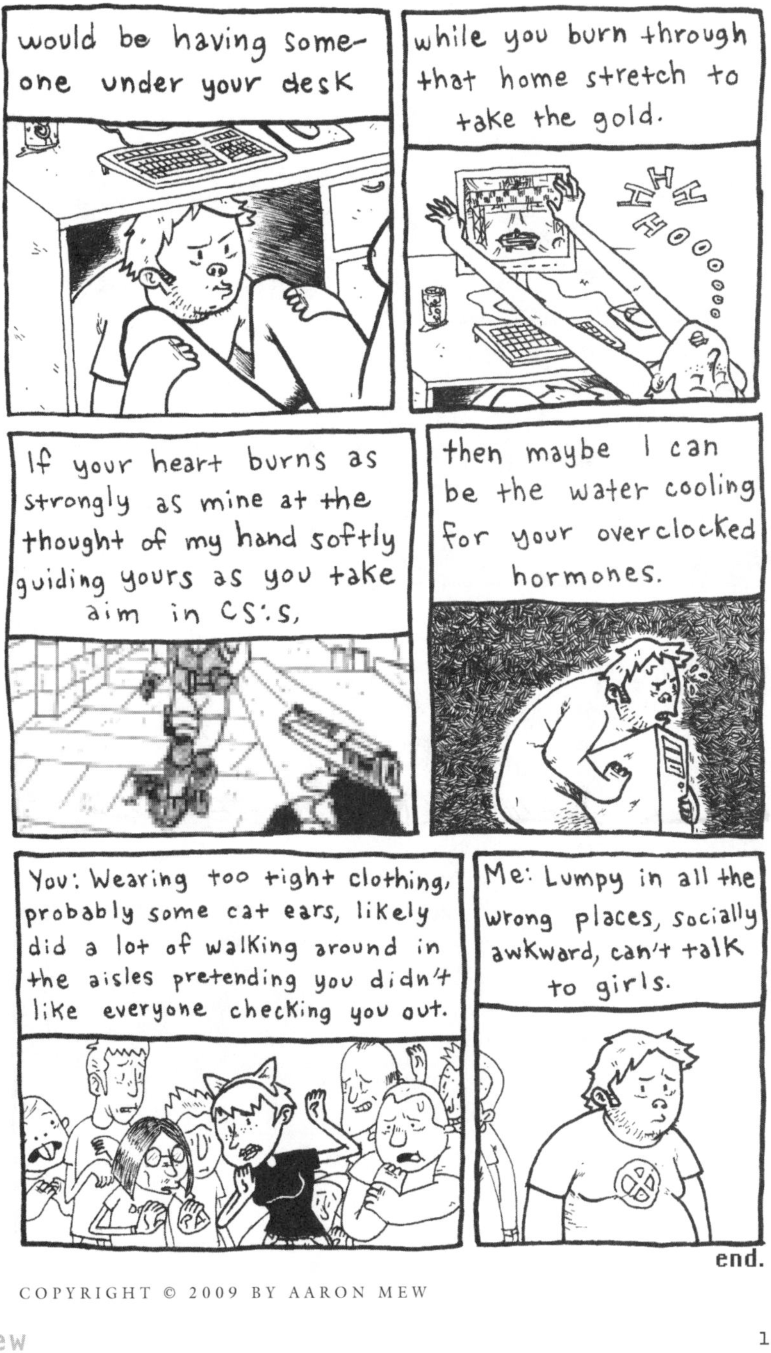
would be having some-one under your desk
while you burn through that home stretch to take the gold.
HHHHOOOooooo
If your heart burns as strongly as mine at the thought of my hand softly guiding yours as you take aim in CS:S,
then maybe I can be the water cooling for your overclocked hormones.
You: Wearing too tight clothing, probably some cat ears, likely did a lot of walking around in the aisles pretending you didn't like everyone checking you out.
Me: Lumpy in all the wrong places, socially awkward, can't talk to girls.
end.

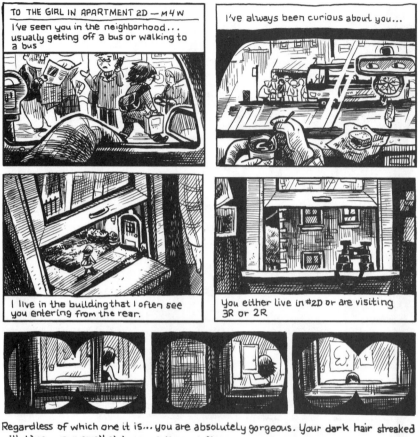

TO THE GIRL IN APARTMENT 2D — M4W
I've seen you in the neighborhood... usually getting off a bus or walking to a bus
I've always been curious about you...
I live in the building that I often see you entering from the rear.
You either live in #2D or are visiting 3R or 2R
Regardless of which one it is... you are absolutely gorgeous. Your dark hair streaked with blue...your small stature and those clothes you wear...WOW.
I wish I could talk to you, maybe even wash your hair. If you DO live in 2D I know we'd get along. I always hear good music coming from 2D.

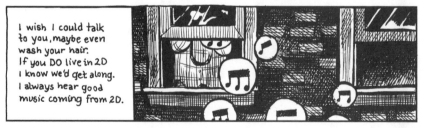

by **Laura Park**

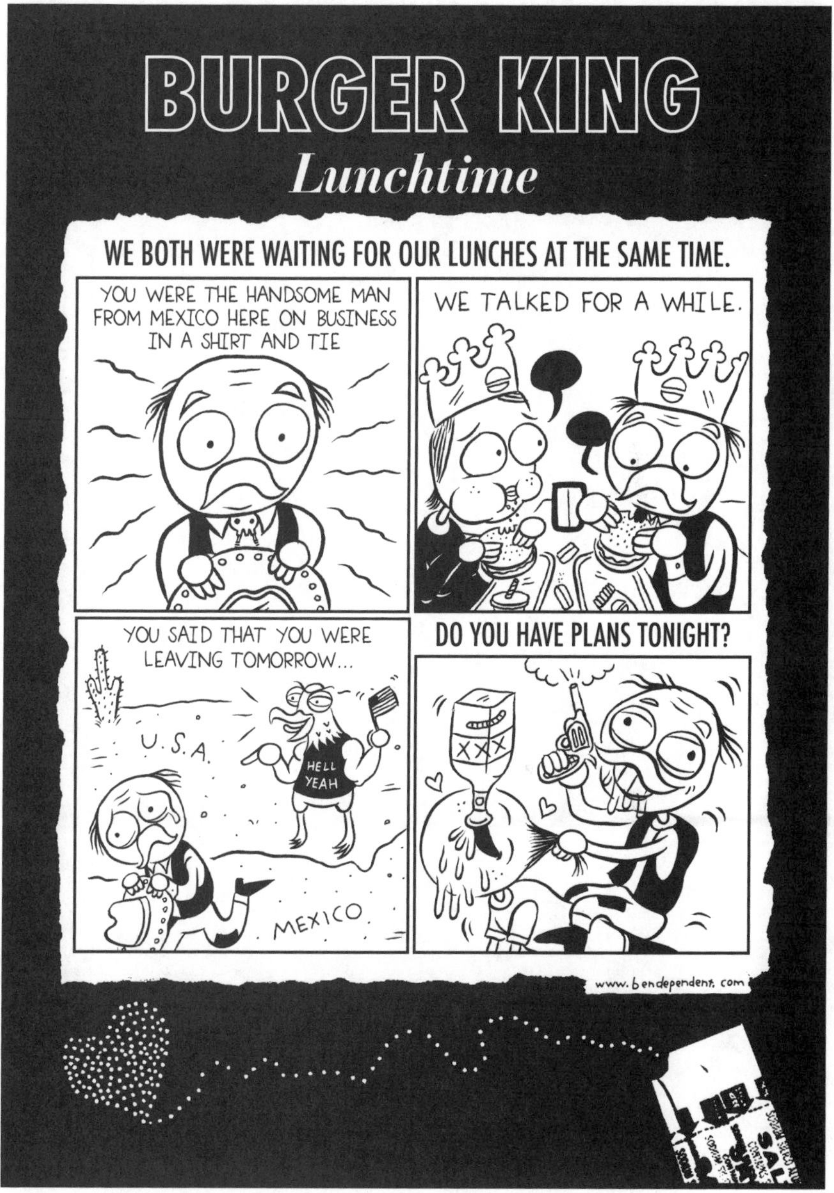
BURGER KING
Lunchtime
WE BOTH WERE WAITING FOR OUR LUNCHES AT THE SAME TIME.
YOU WERE THE HANDSOME MAN FROM MEXICO HERE ON BUSINESS IN A SHIRT AND TIE
WE TALKED FOR A WHILE.
YOU SAID THAT YOU WERE LEAVING TOMORROW...
U.S.A.
HELL YEAH
MEXICO
DO YOU HAVE PLANS TONIGHT?
XXX
www.bendependent.com

by **Ben Claassen III**

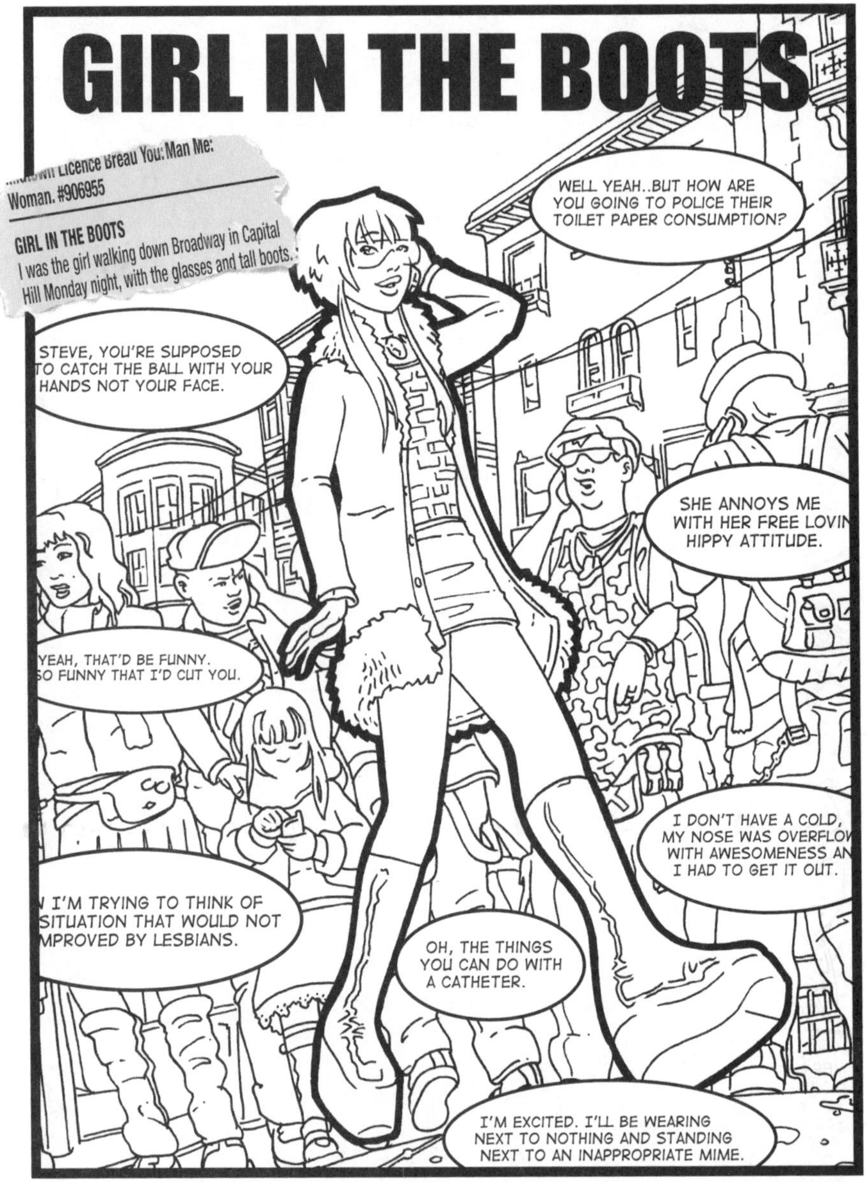
GIRL IN THE BOOTS
Licence Breau You: Man Me:
Woman. #906955
GIRL IN THE BOOTS
I was the girl walking down Broadway in Capital
Hill Monday night, with the glasses and tall boots.
WELL YEAH..BUT HOW ARE YOU GOING TO POLICE THEIR TOILET PAPER CONSUMPTION?
STEVE, YOU'RE SUPPOSED TO CATCH THE BALL WITH YOUR HANDS NOT YOUR FACE.
SHE ANNOYS ME WITH HER FREE LOVIN HIPPY ATTITUDE.
YEAH, THAT'D BE FUNNY. SO FUNNY THAT I'D CUT YOU.
I DON'T HAVE A COLD, MY NOSE WAS OVERFLOW WITH AWESOMENESS AN I HAD TO GET IT OUT.
I'M TRYING TO THINK OF SITUATION THAT WOULD NOT MPROVED BY LESBIANS.
OH, THE THINGS YOU CAN DO WITH A CATHETER.
I'M EXCITED. I'LL BE WEARING NEXT TO NOTHING AND STANDING NEXT TO AN INAPPROPRIATE MIME.

by **The Ink Lab**

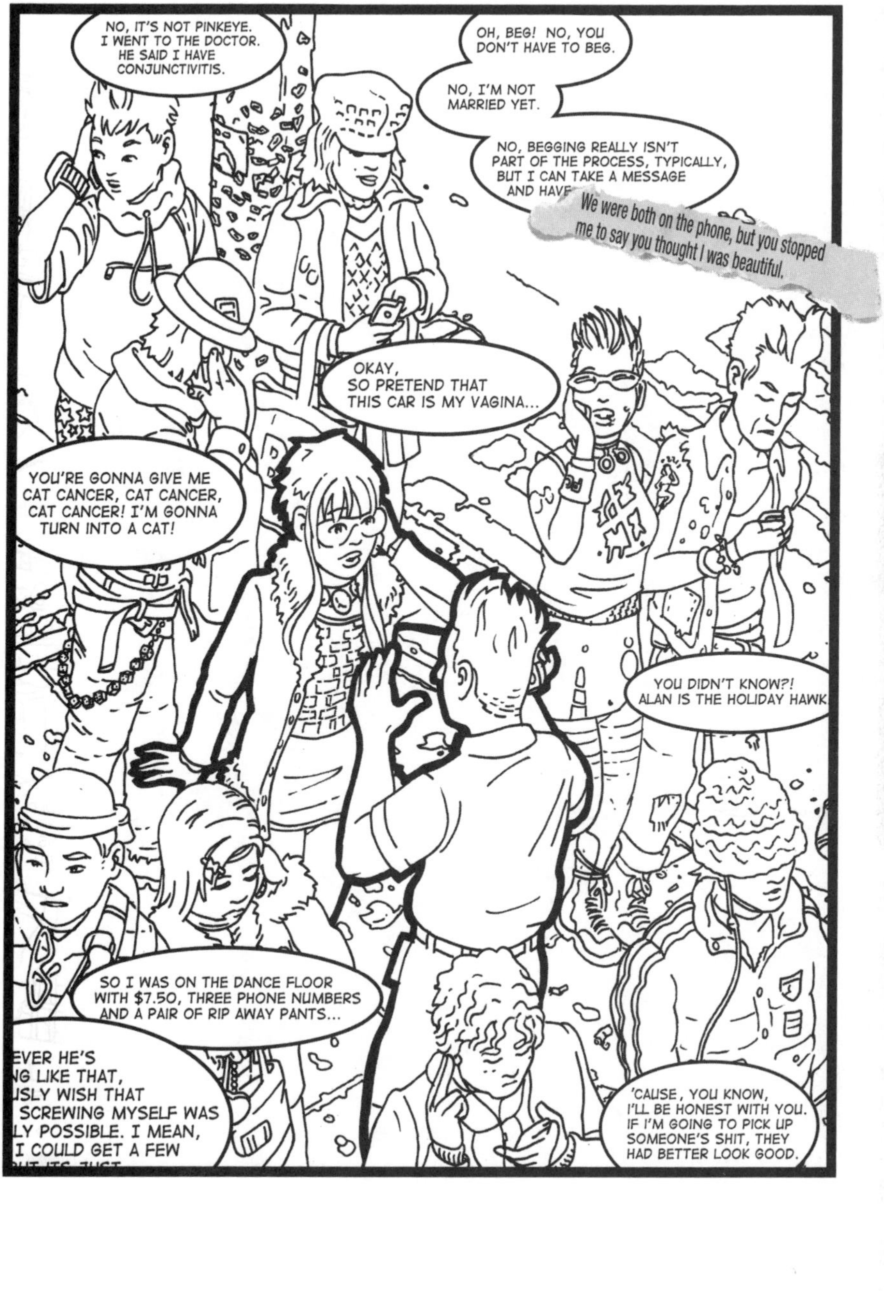
NO, IT'S NOT PINKEYE. I WENT TO THE DOCTOR. HE SAID I HAVE CONJUNCTIVITIS.
OH, BEG! NO, YOU DON'T HAVE TO BEG.
NO, I'M NOT MARRIED YET.
NO, BEGGING REALLY ISN'T PART OF THE PROCESS, TYPICALLY, BUT I CAN TAKE A MESSAGE AND HAVE
We were both on the phone, but you stopped me to say you thought I was beautiful.
OKAY, SO PRETEND THAT THIS CAR IS MY VAGINA...
YOU'RE GONNA GIVE ME CAT CANCER, CAT CANCER, CAT CANCER! I'M GONNA TURN INTO A CAT!
YOU DIDN'T KNOW?! ALAN IS THE HOLIDAY HAWK
SO I WAS ON THE DANCE FLOOR WITH $7.50, THREE PHONE NUMBERS AND A PAIR OF RIP AWAY PANTS...
EVER HE'S
NG LIKE THAT,
USLY WISH THAT
SCREWING MYSELF WAS
LY POSSIBLE. I MEAN,
I COULD GET A FEW
'CAUSE, YOU KNOW, I'LL BE HONEST WITH YOU. IF I'M GOING TO PICK UP SOMEONE'S SHIT, THEY HAD BETTER LOOK GOOD.

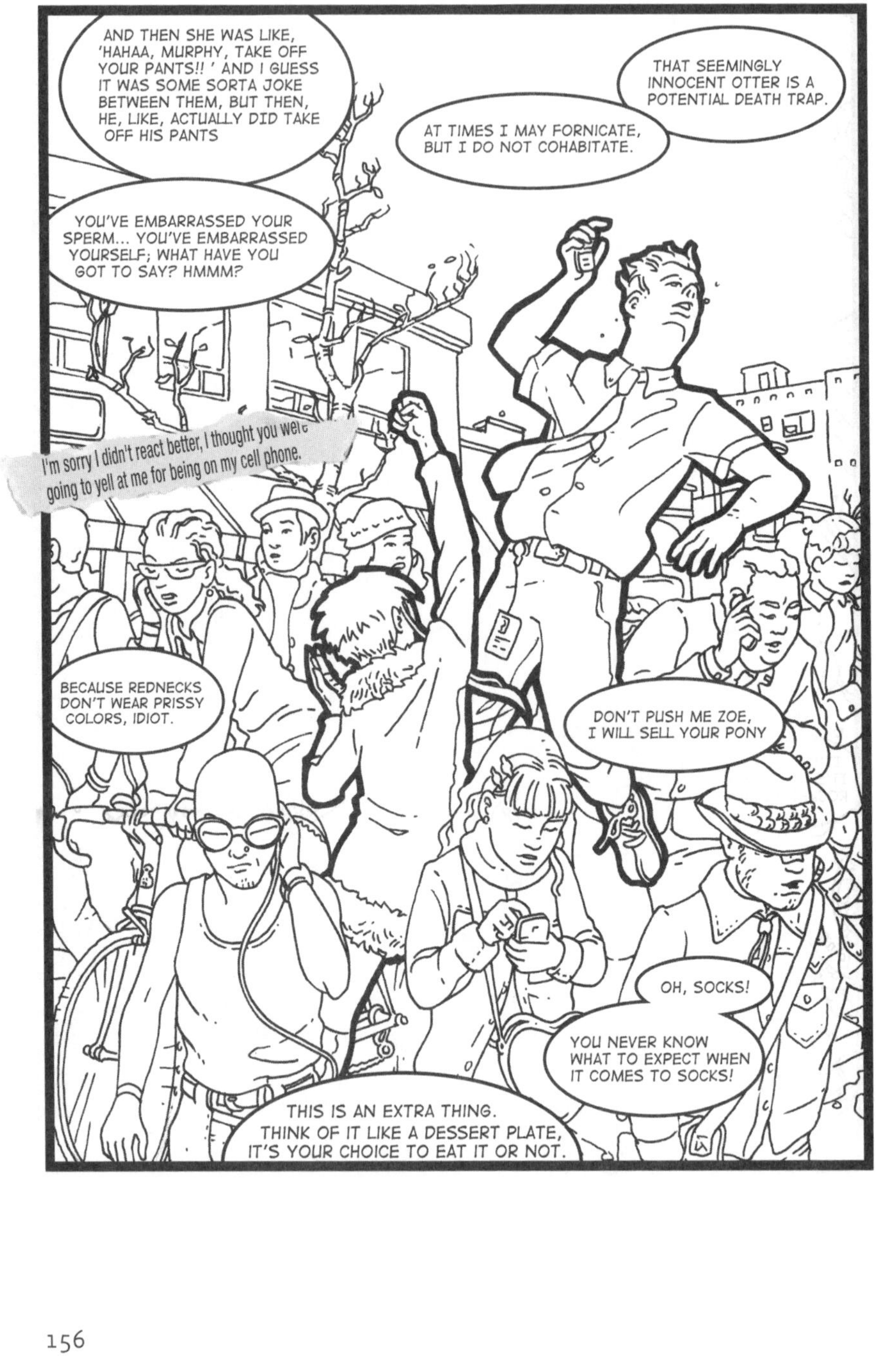
AND THEN SHE WAS LIKE, 'HAHAA, MURPHY, TAKE OFF YOUR PANTS!! ' AND I GUESS IT WAS SOME SORTA JOKE BETWEEN THEM, BUT THEN, HE, LIKE, ACTUALLY DID TAKE OFF HIS PANTS
THAT SEEMINGLY INNOCENT OTTER IS A POTENTIAL DEATH TRAP.
AT TIMES I MAY FORNICATE, BUT I DO NOT COHABITATE.
YOU'VE EMBARRASSED YOUR SPERM... YOU'VE EMBARRASSED YOURSELF; WHAT HAVE YOU GOT TO SAY? HMMM?
I'm sorry I didn't react better, I thought you were going to yell at me for being on my cell phone.
BECAUSE REDNECKS DON'T WEAR PRISSY COLORS, IDIOT.
DON'T PUSH ME ZOE, I WILL SELL YOUR PONY
OH, SOCKS!
YOU NEVER KNOW WHAT TO EXPECT WHEN IT COMES TO SOCKS!
THIS IS AN EXTRA THING. THINK OF IT LIKE A DESSERT PLATE, IT'S YOUR CHOICE TO EAT IT OR NOT.

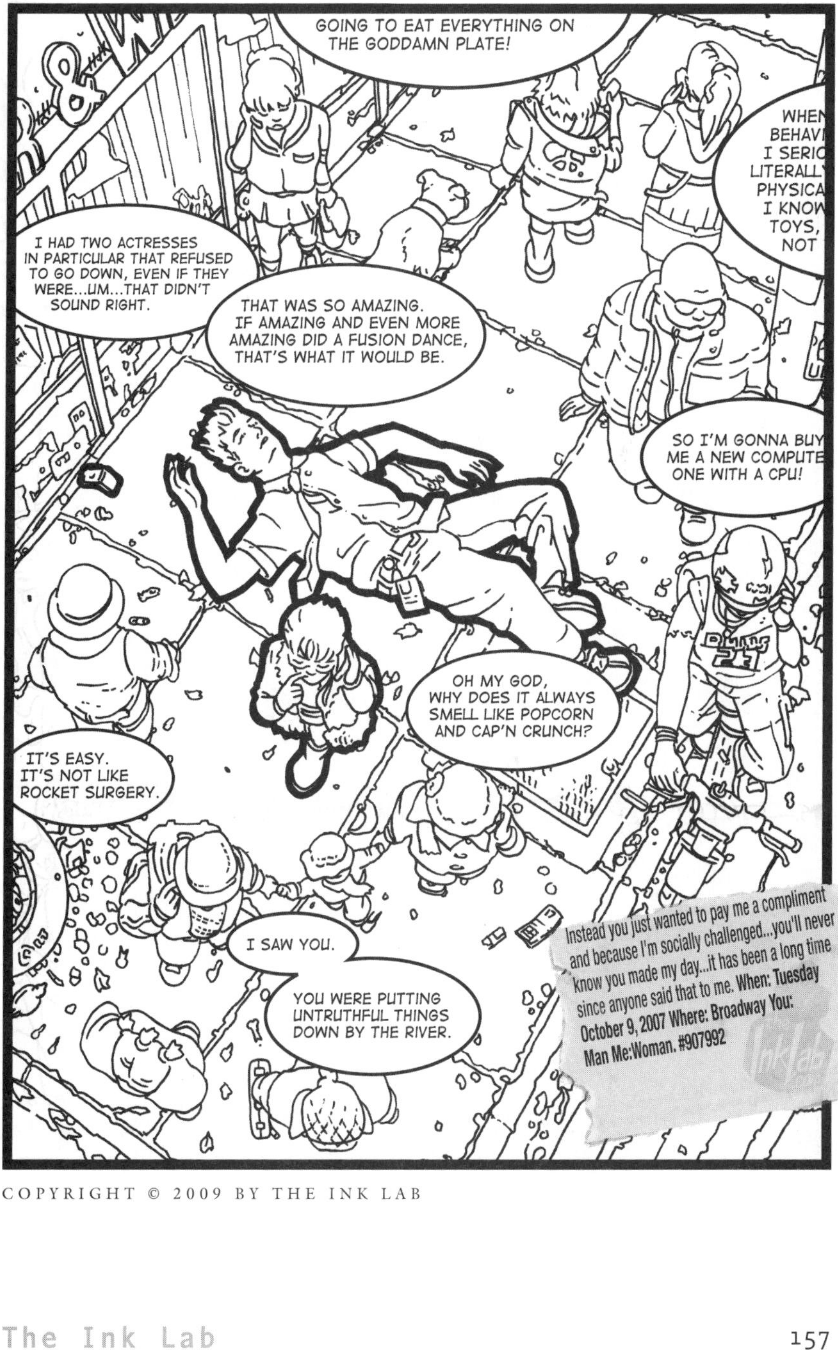
GOING TO EAT EVERYTHING ON
THE GODDAMN PLATE!
WHEN
BEHAV
I SERI
LITERALL
PHYSIC
I KNO
TOYS,
NOT
I HAD TWO ACTRESSES IN PARTICULAR THAT REFUSED TO GO DOWN, EVEN IF THEY WERE...UM...THAT DIDN'T SOUND RIGHT.
THAT WAS SO AMAZING. IF AMAZING AND EVEN MORE AMAZING DID A FUSION DANCE, THAT'S WHAT IT WOULD BE.
SO I'M GONNA BUY ME A NEW COMPUTE ONE WITH A CPU!
OH MY GOD, WHY DOES IT ALWAYS SMELL LIKE POPCORN AND CAP'N CRUNCH?
IT'S EASY. IT'S NOT LIKE ROCKET SURGERY.
I SAW YOU.
YOU WERE PUTTING UNTRUTHFUL THINGS DOWN BY THE RIVER.
Instead you just wanted to pay me a compliment and because I'm socially challenged...you'll never know you made my day...it has been a long time since anyone said that to me. When: Tuesday October 9, 2007 Where: Broadway You: Man Me:Woman. #907992

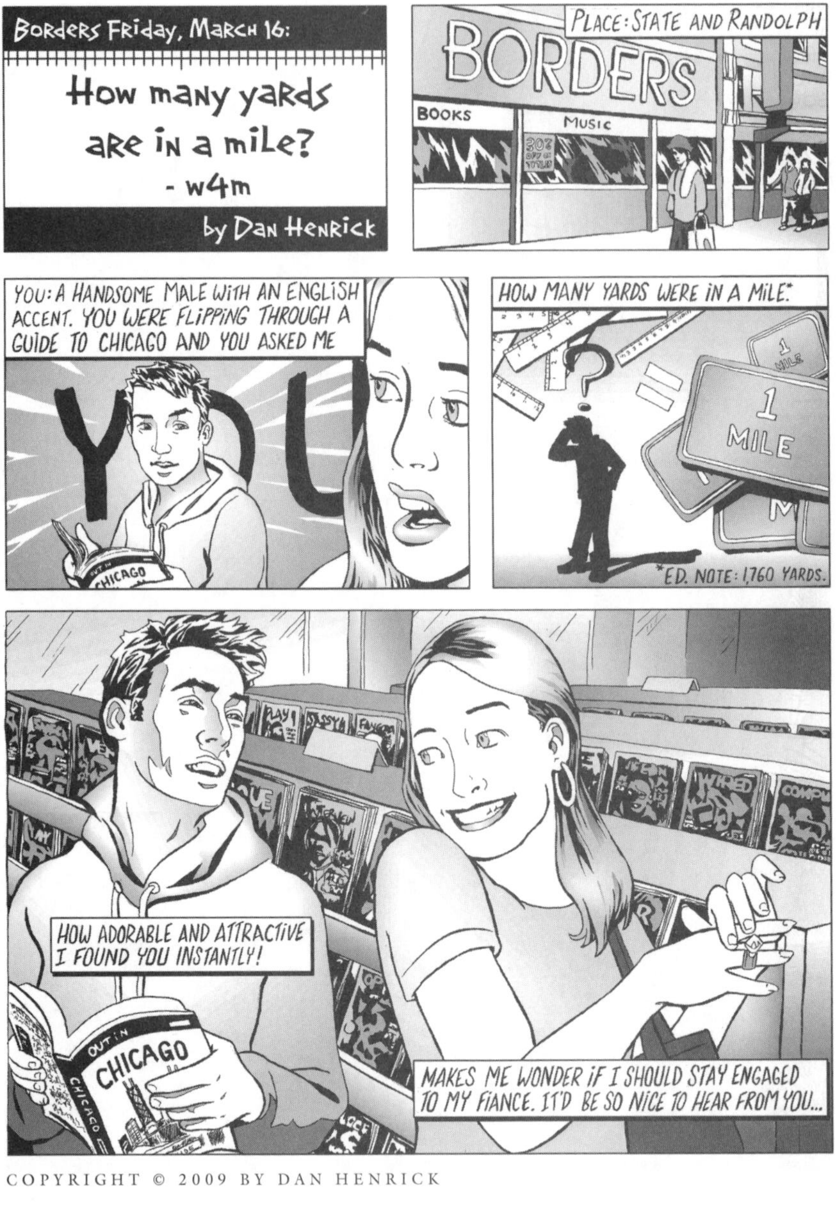
Borders Friday, March 16:
How many yards are in a mile? - w4m
by Dan Henrick
PLACE: STATE AND RANDOLPH
BORDERS
BOOKS
MUSIC
YOU: A HANDSOME MALE WITH AN ENGLISH ACCENT. YOU WERE FLIPPING THROUGH A GUIDE TO CHICAGO AND YOU ASKED ME
YOU
HOW MANY YARDS WERE IN A MILE.*
1 MILE
*ED. NOTE: 1,760 YARDS.
HOW ADORABLE AND ATTRACTIVE I FOUND YOU INSTANTLY!
OUT IN CHICAGO
MAKES ME WONDER IF I SHOULD STAY ENGAGED TO MY FIANCE. IT'D BE SO NICE TO HEAR FROM YOU...

by **Dan Henrick**

John Philip Sousa Gravesite - m4m

by Dan Mazur

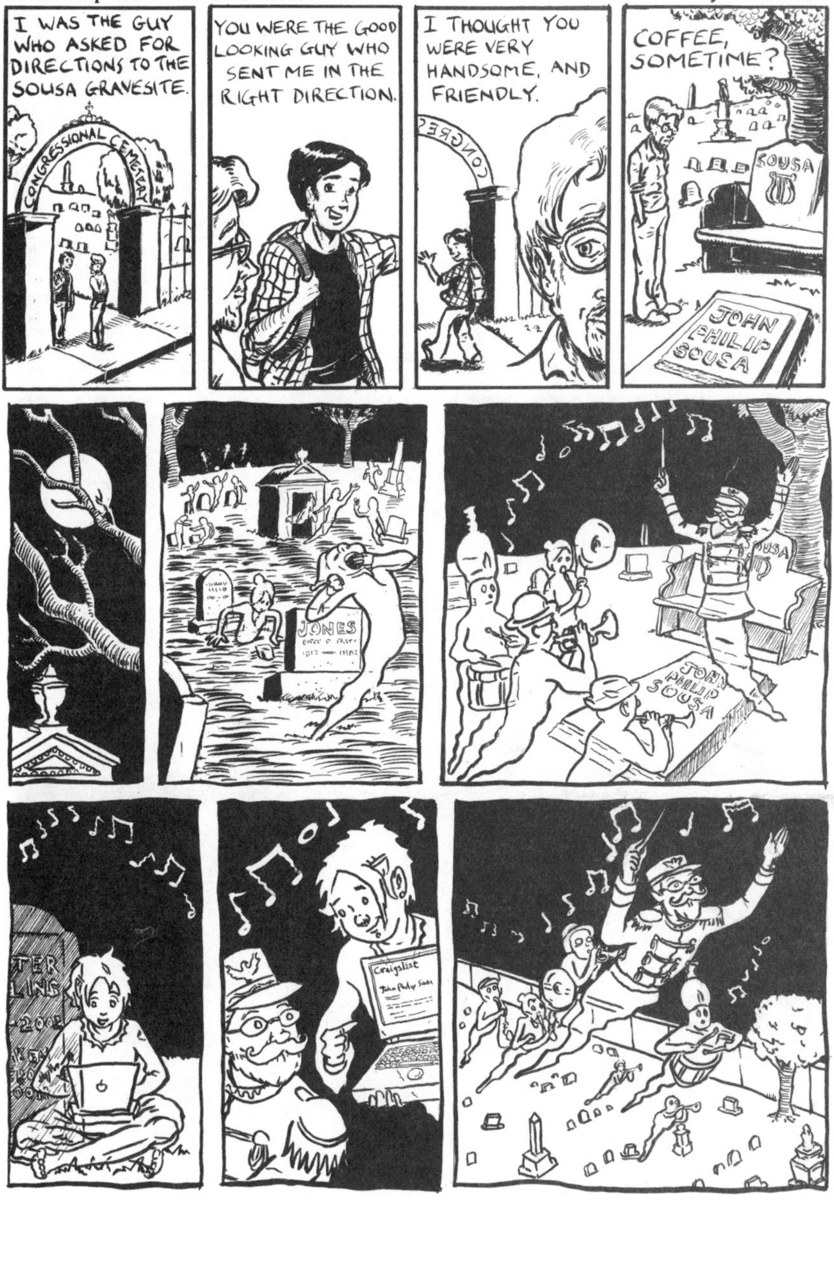
I WAS THE GUY WHO ASKED FOR DIRECTIONS TO THE SOUSA GRAVESITE.
CONGRESSIONAL CEMETERY
YOU WERE THE GOOD LOOKING GUY WHO SENT ME IN THE RIGHT DIRECTION.
I THOUGHT YOU WERE VERY HANDSOME, AND FRIENDLY.
COFFEE, SOMETIME?
SOUSA
JOHN PHILIP SOUSA
JONES
JOHN PHILIP SOUSA
Craigslist

by **Dan Mazur**

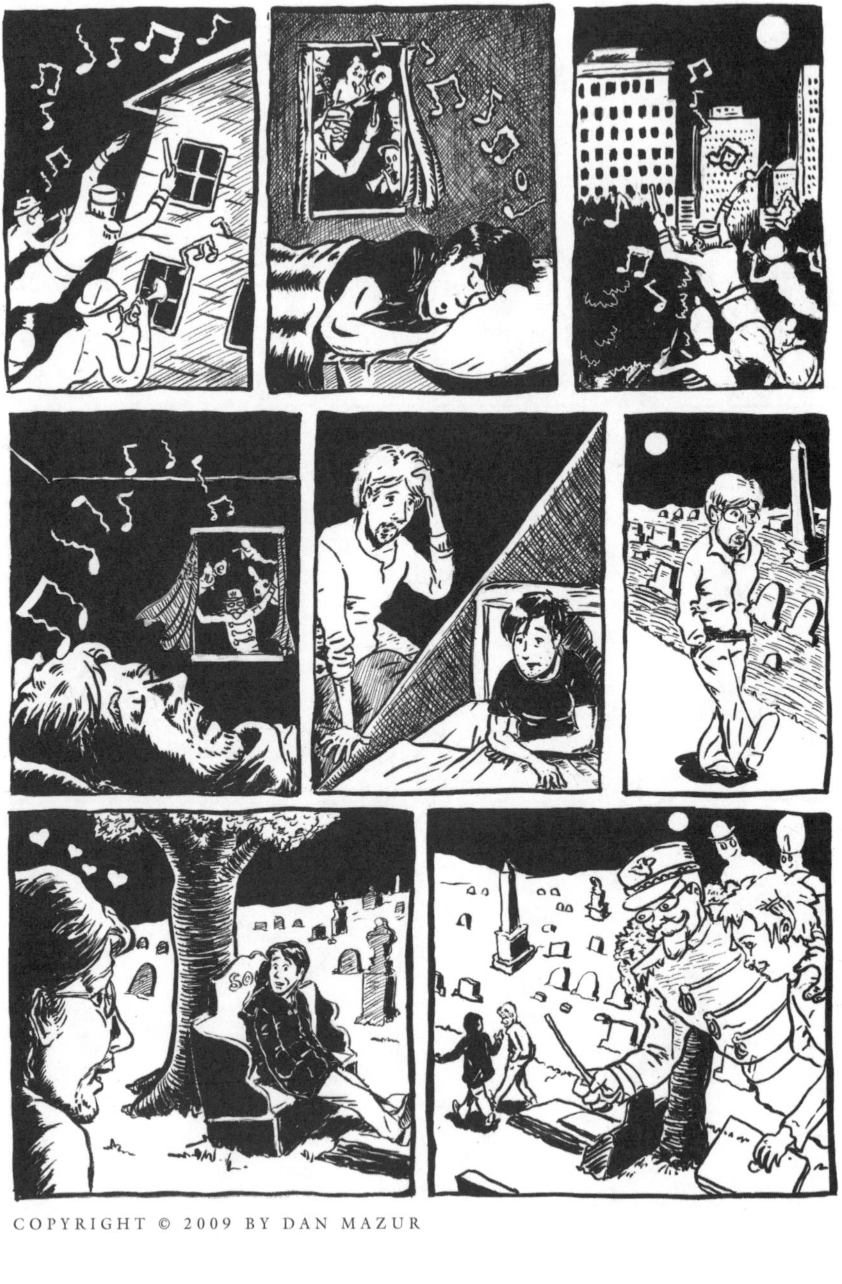

PORK PIE HAT

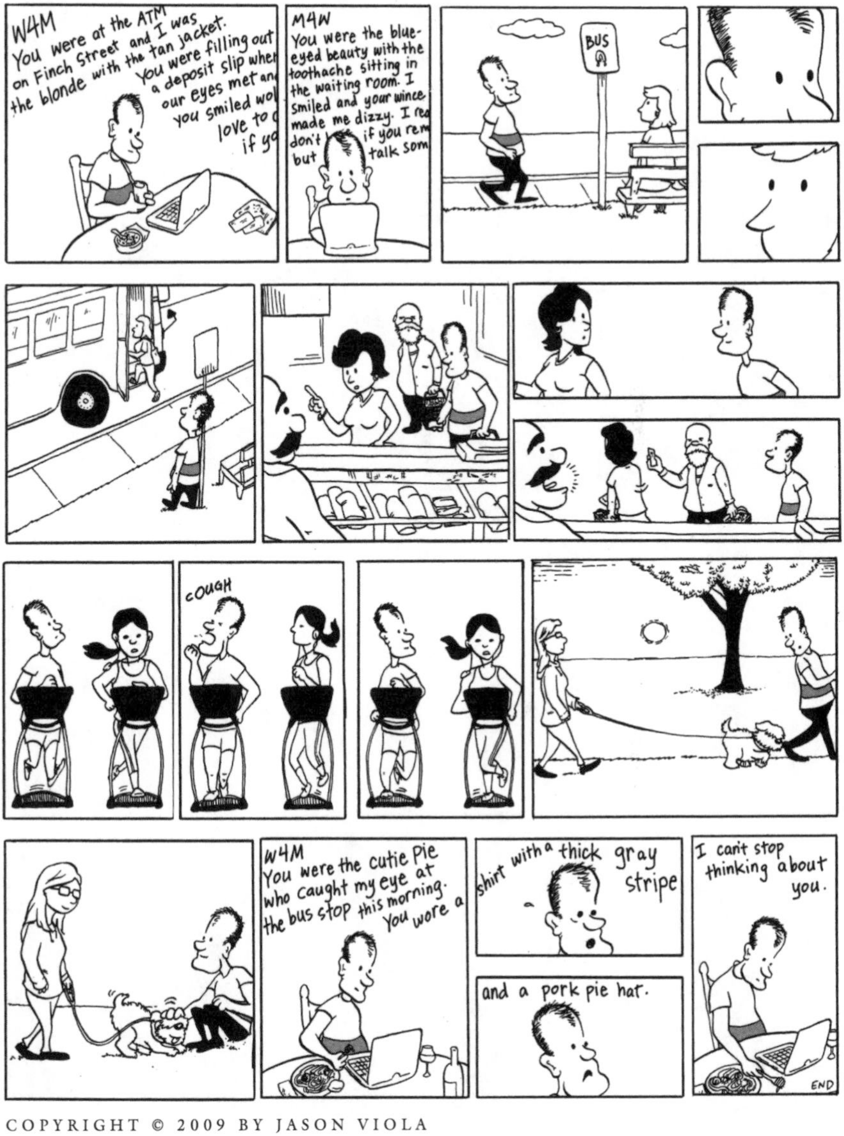
W4M
You were at the ATM on Finch Street and I was the blonde with the tan jacket. You were filling out a deposit slip when our eyes met and you smiled
M4W
You were the blue-eyed beauty with the toothache sitting in the waiting room. I smiled and your wince made me dizzy.
BUS
COUGH
W4M
You were the cutie Pie who caught my eye at the bus stop this morning. You wore a
shirt with a thick gray stripe
and a pork pie hat.
I can't stop thinking about you.
END

by **Jason Viola**

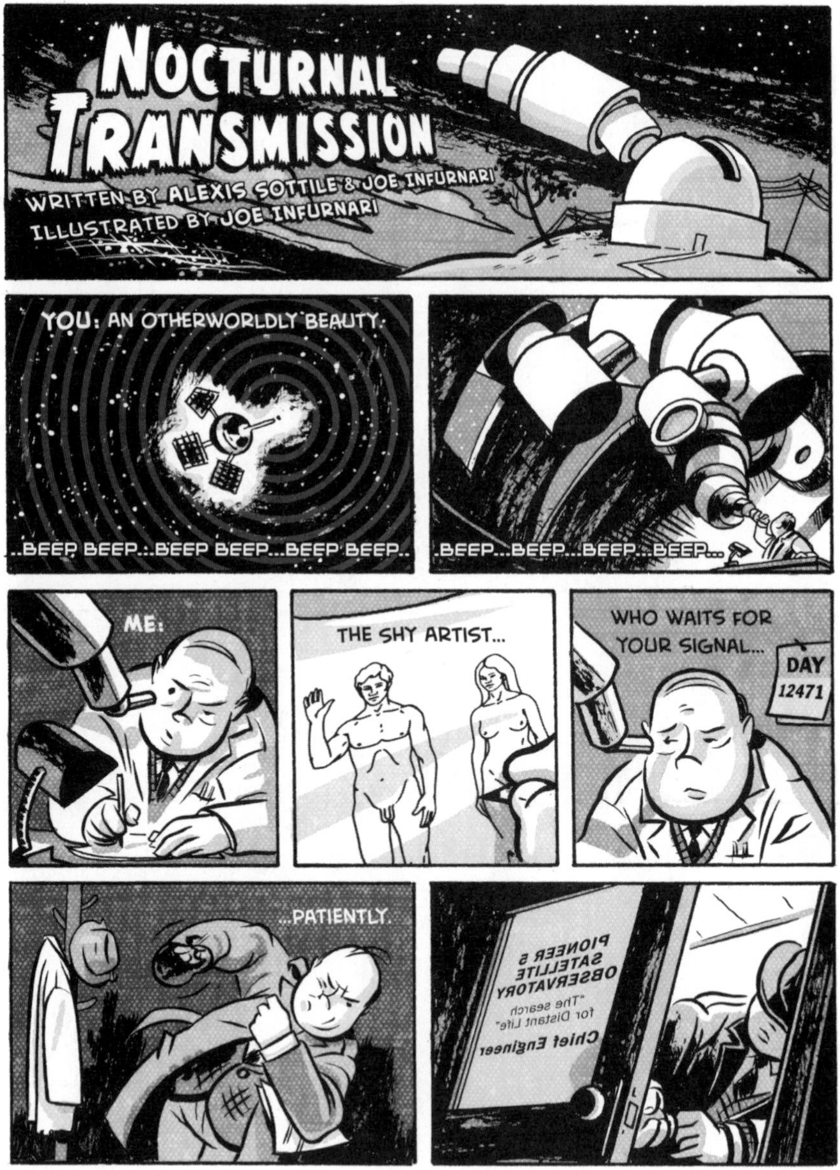
NOCTURNAL TRANSMISSION
WRITTEN BY ALEXIS SOTTILE & JOE INFURNARI
ILLUSTRATED BY JOE INFURNARI
YOU: AN OTHERWORLDLY BEAUTY.
..BEEP BEEP...BEEP BEEP...BEEP BEEP..
.BEEP...BEEP...BEEP...BEEP...
ME:
THE SHY ARTIST...
WHO WAITS FOR YOUR SIGNAL...
DAY
12471
...PATIENTLY.
PIONEER 5
SATELLITE
OBSERVATORY
"The search
for Distant Life"
Chief Engineer

by **Joe Infurnari and Alexis Sottile**

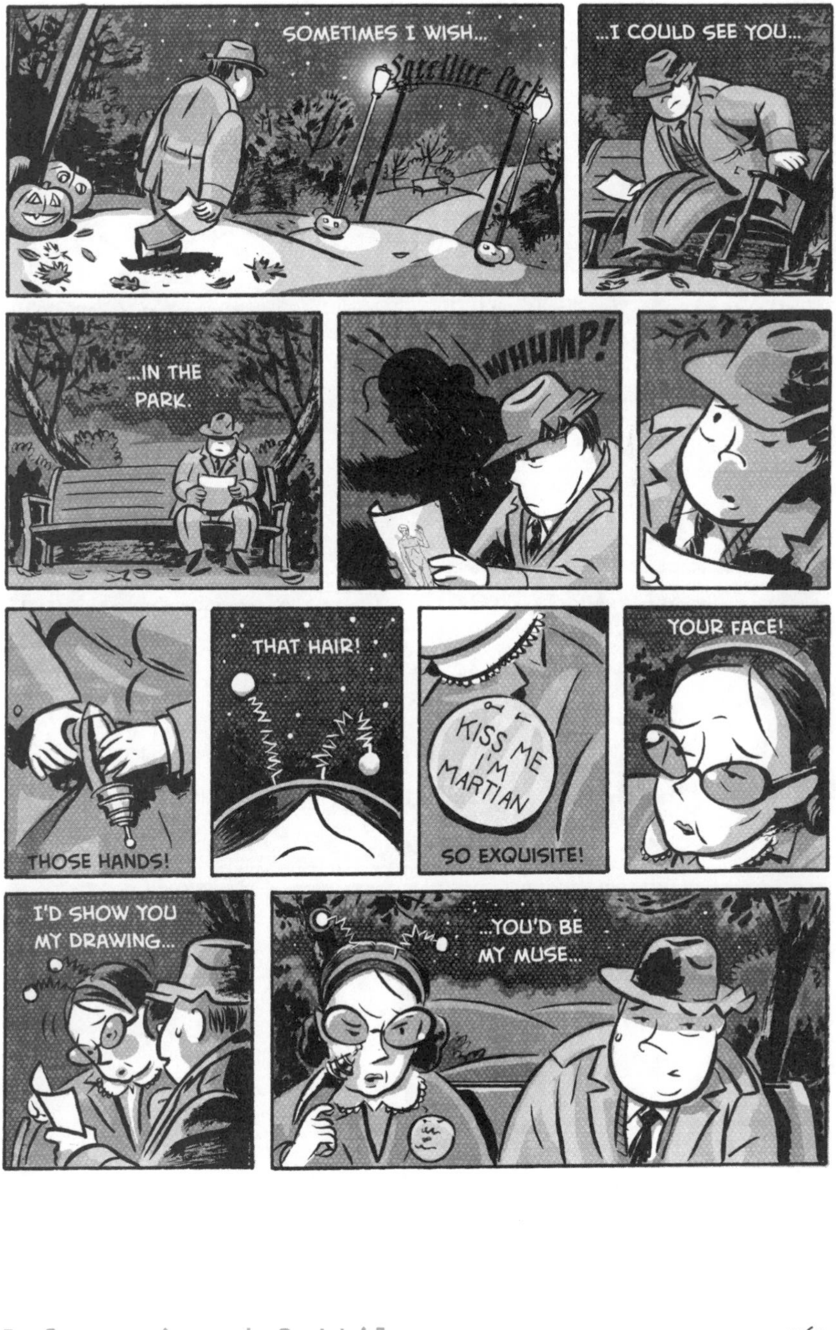
SOMETIMES I WISH...
Satellite Park
...I COULD SEE YOU...
...IN THE PARK.
WHUMP!
THOSE HANDS!
THAT HAIR!
KISS ME I'M MARTIAN
SO EXQUISITE!
YOUR FACE!
I'D SHOW YOU MY DRAWING...
...YOU'D BE MY MUSE...

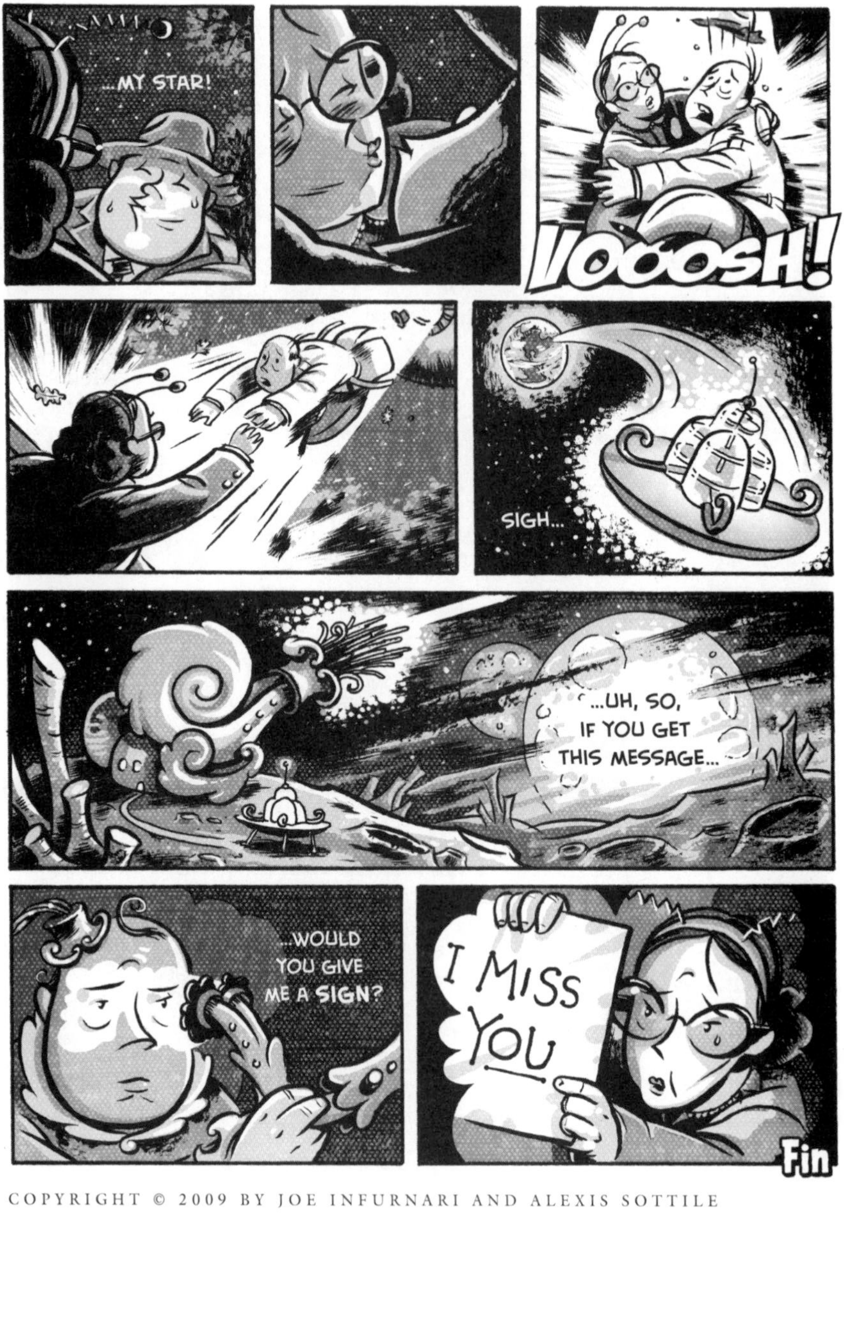
...MY STAR!
VOOOSH!
SIGH...
...UH, SO,
IF YOU GET
THIS MESSAGE...
...WOULD
YOU GIVE
ME A SIGN?
I MISS
YOU
Fin

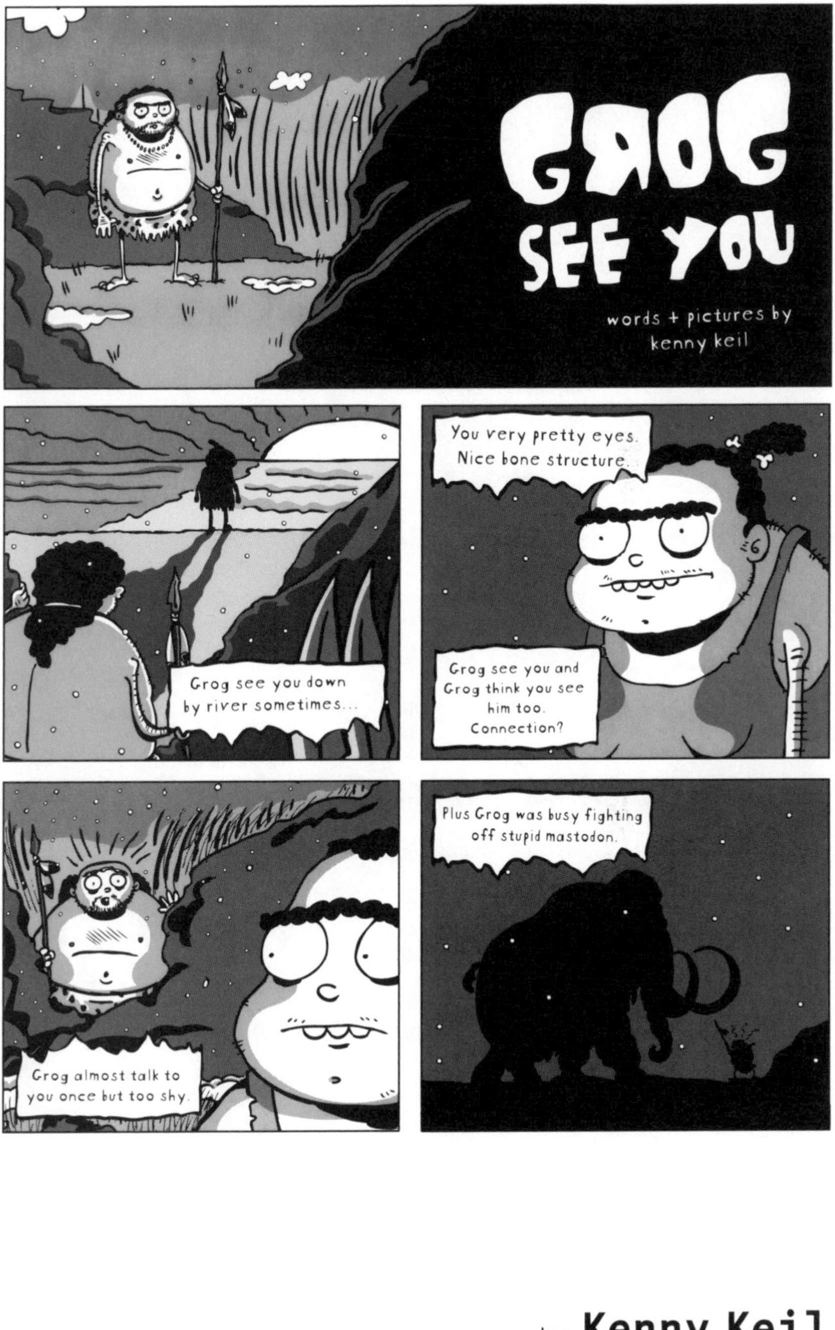
GROG SEE YOU
words + pictures by
kenny keil
Grog see you down by river sometimes...
You very pretty eyes. Nice bone structure.
Grog see you and Grog think you see him too. Connection?
Grog almost talk to you once but too shy.
Plus Grog was busy fighting off stupid mastodon.

by **Kenny Keil**

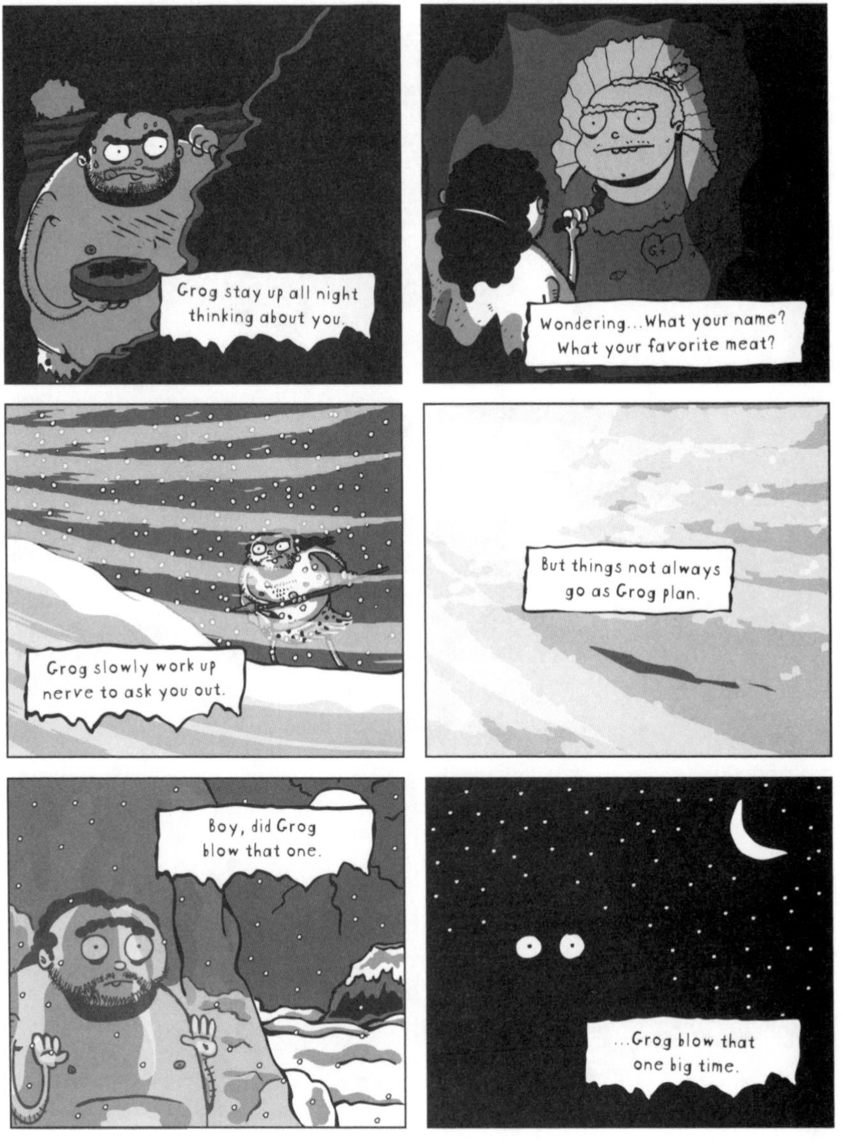
Grog stay up all night
thinking about you.
Wondering... What your name?
What your favorite meat?
Grog slowly work up
nerve to ask you out.
But things not always
go as Grog plan.
Boy, did Grog
blow that one.
...Grog blow that
one big time.

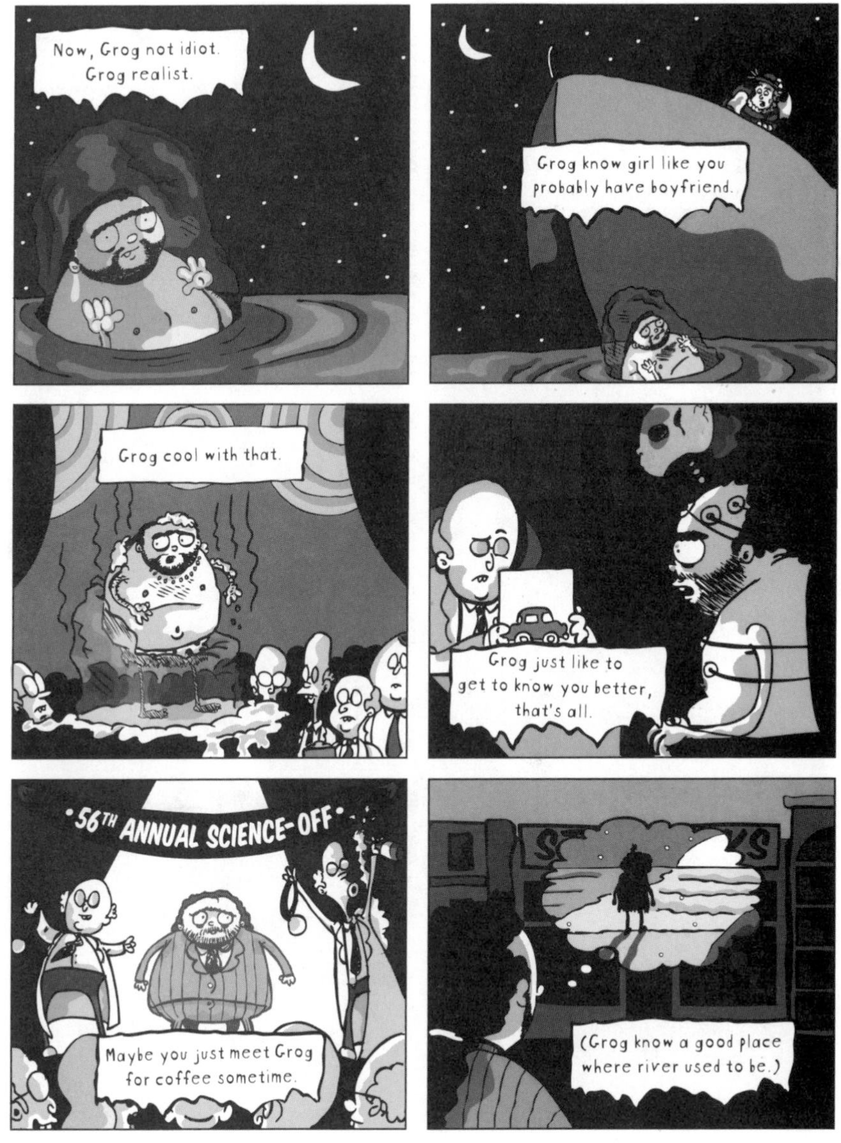
Now, Grog not idiot. Grog realist.
Grog know girl like you probably have boyfriend.
Grog cool with that.
Grog just like to get to know you better, that's all.
56TH ANNUAL SCIENCE-OFF
Maybe you just meet Grog for coffee sometime.
(Grog know a good place where river used to be.)

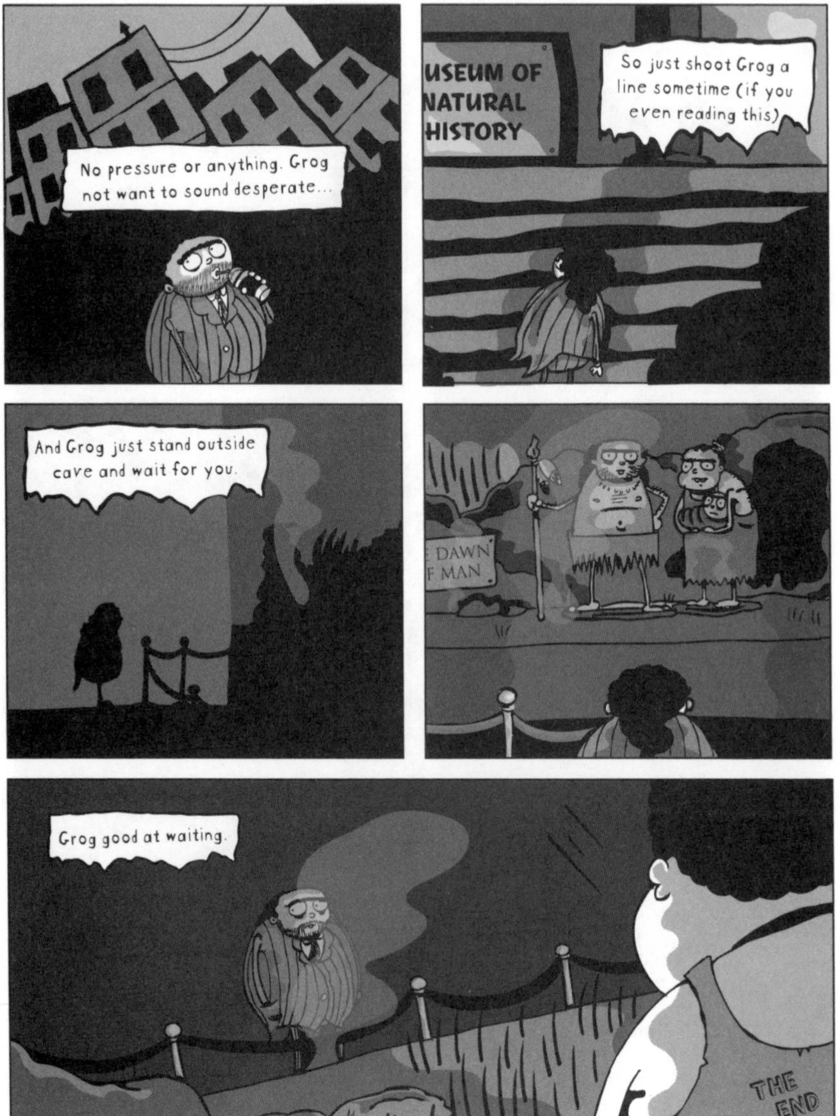
No pressure or anything. Grog not want to sound desperate...
USEUM OF NATURAL HISTORY
So just shoot Grog a line sometime (if you even reading this)
And Grog just stand outside cave and wait for you.
E DAWN F MAN
Grog good at waiting.
THE END

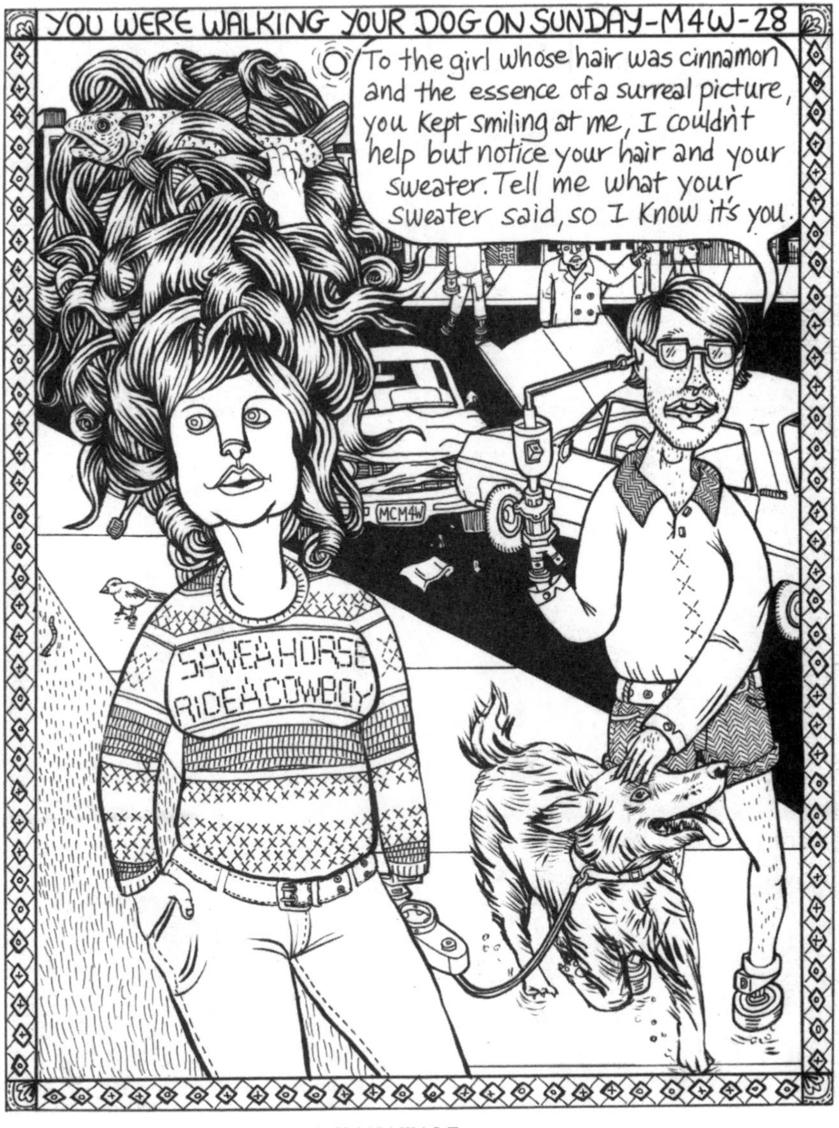
YOU WERE WALKING YOUR DOG ON SUNDAY-M4W-28
To the girl whose hair was cinnamon and the essence of a surreal picture, you kept smiling at me, I couldn't help but notice your hair and your sweater. Tell me what your sweater said, so I know it's you.
MCM4W
SAVE A HORSE RIDE A COWBOY

by **Lisa Hanawalt**

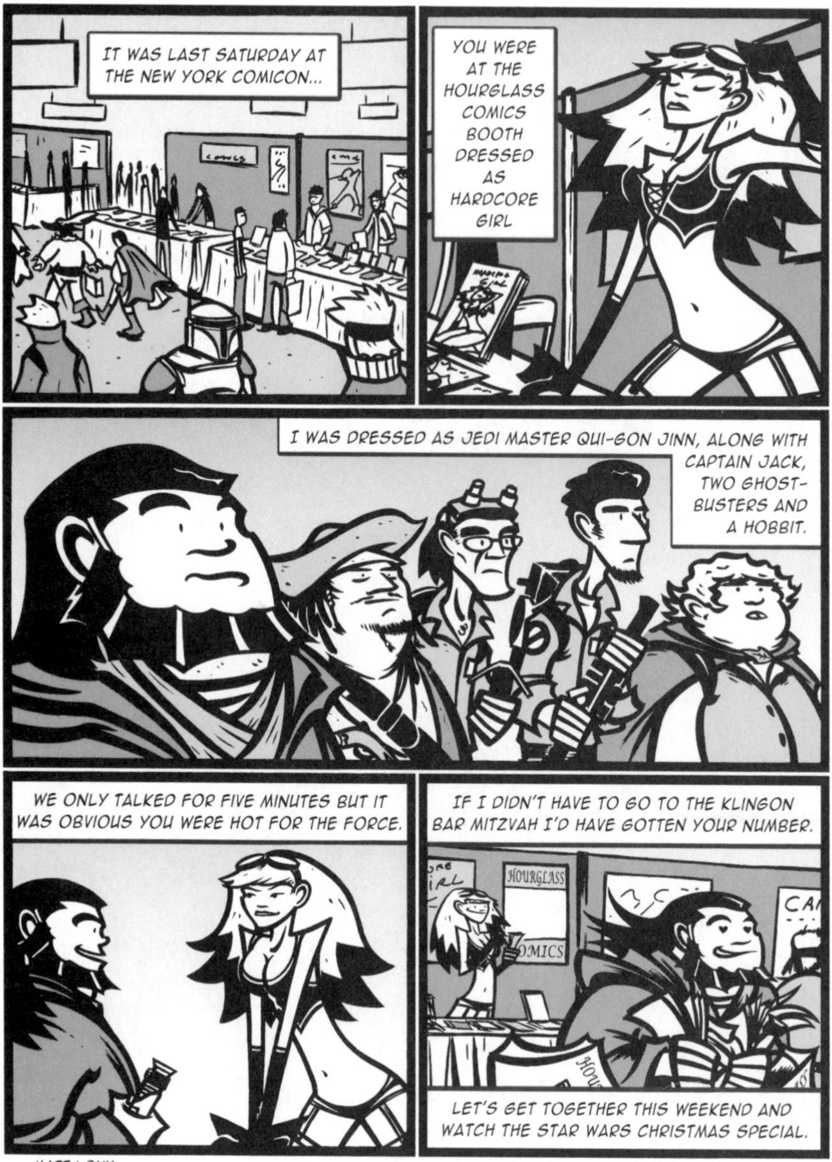
IT WAS LAST SATURDAY AT THE NEW YORK COMICON...
YOU WERE AT THE HOURGLASS COMICS BOOTH DRESSED AS HARDCORE GIRL
I WAS DRESSED AS JEDI MASTER QUI-GON JINN, ALONG WITH CAPTAIN JACK, TWO GHOST-BUSTERS AND A HOBBIT.
WE ONLY TALKED FOR FIVE MINUTES BUT IT WAS OBVIOUS YOU WERE HOT FOR THE FORCE.
IF I DIDN'T HAVE TO GO TO THE KLINGON BAR MITZVAH I'D HAVE GOTTEN YOUR NUMBER.
HOURGLASS
COMICS
LET'S GET TOGETHER THIS WEEKEND AND WATCH THE STAR WARS CHRISTMAS SPECIAL.

MATT LOUX

by **Matthew Loux**

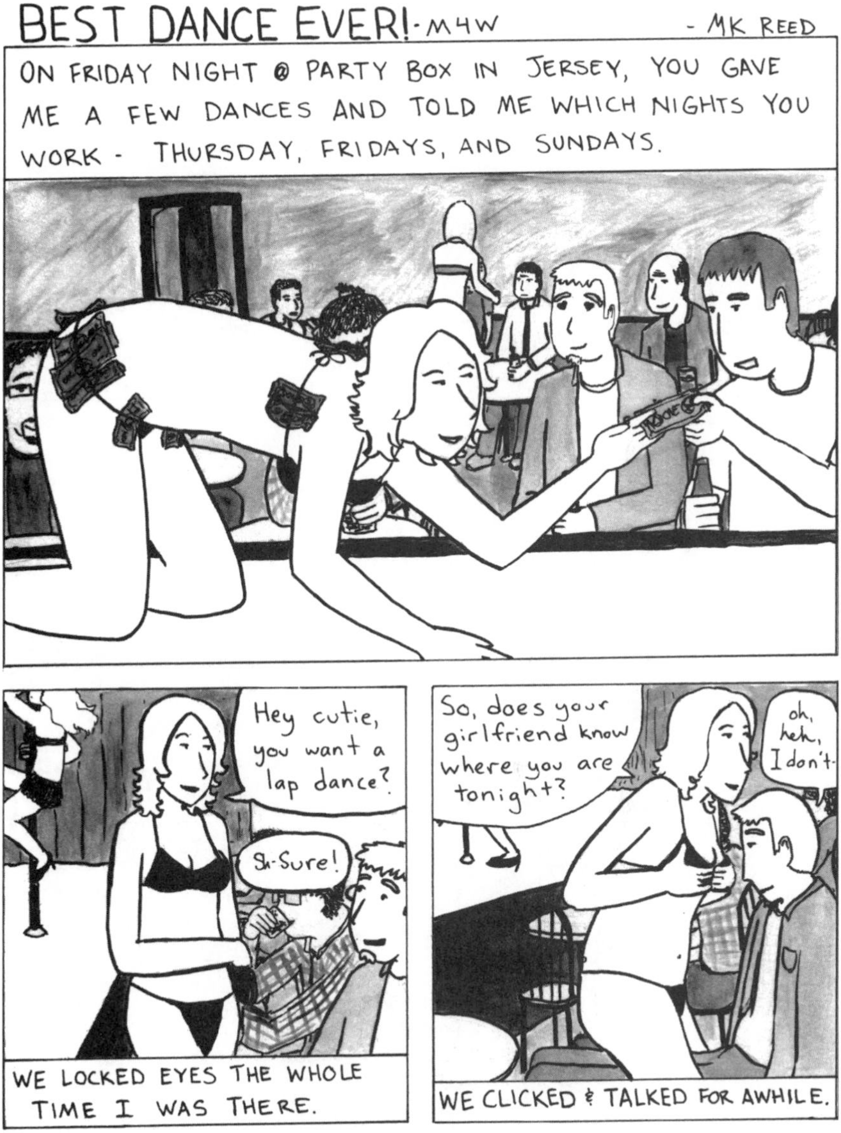
BEST DANCE EVER! - M4W
- MK REED
ON FRIDAY NIGHT @ PARTY BOX IN JERSEY, YOU GAVE ME A FEW DANCES AND TOLD ME WHICH NIGHTS YOU WORK - THURSDAY, FRIDAYS, AND SUNDAYS.
Hey cutie, you want a lap dance?
Sh-Sure!
WE LOCKED EYES THE WHOLE TIME I WAS THERE.
So, does your girlfriend know where you are tonight?
oh, heh, I don't-
WE CLICKED & TALKED FOR AWHILE.

by **MK Reed**

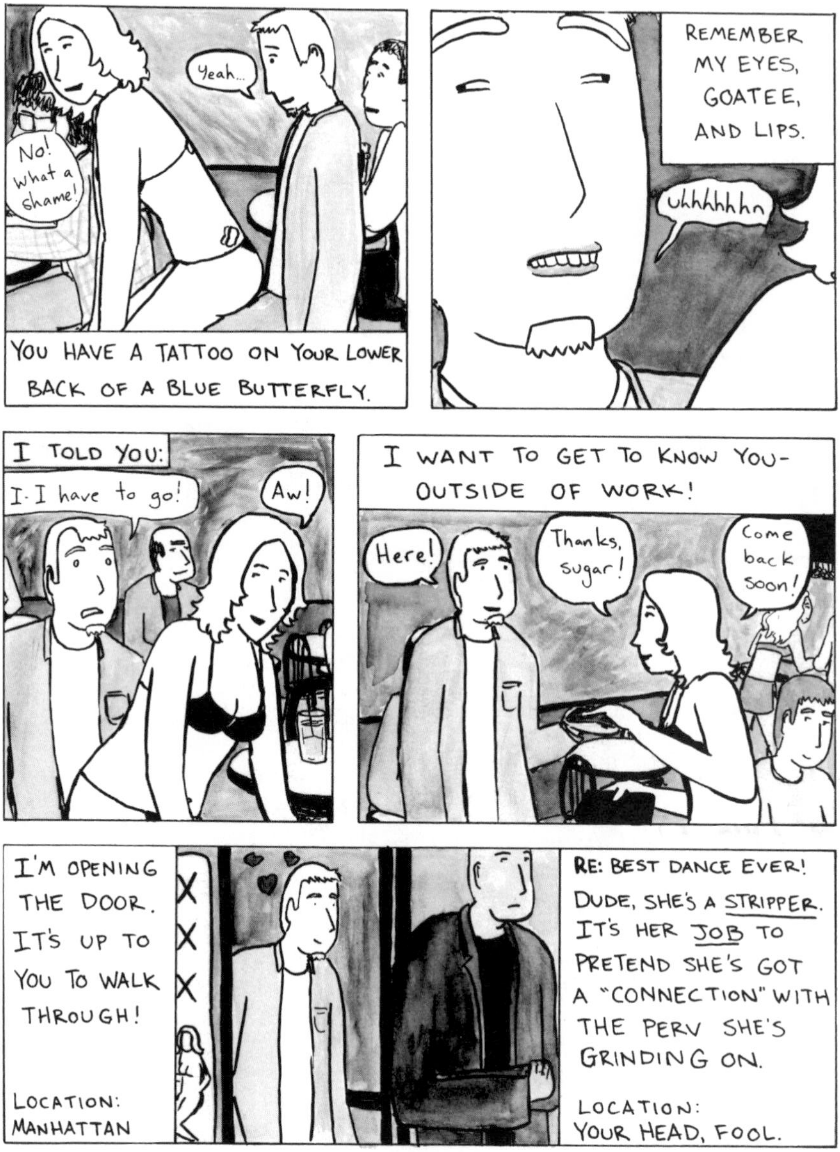
Yeah...
No! what a shame!
YOU HAVE A TATTOO ON YOUR LOWER BACK OF A BLUE BUTTERFLY.
REMEMBER MY EYES, GOATEE, AND LIPS.
uhhhhhhn
I TOLD YOU:
I-I have to go!
Aw!
I WANT TO GET TO KNOW YOU- OUTSIDE OF WORK!
Here!
Thanks, sugar!
Come back soon!
I'M OPENING THE DOOR. IT'S UP TO YOU TO WALK THROUGH!
LOCATION: MANHATTAN
XXX
RE: BEST DANCE EVER!
DUDE, SHE'S A STRIPPER. IT'S HER JOB TO PRETEND SHE'S GOT A "CONNECTION" WITH THE PERV SHE'S GRINDING ON.
LOCATION: YOUR HEAD, FOOL.

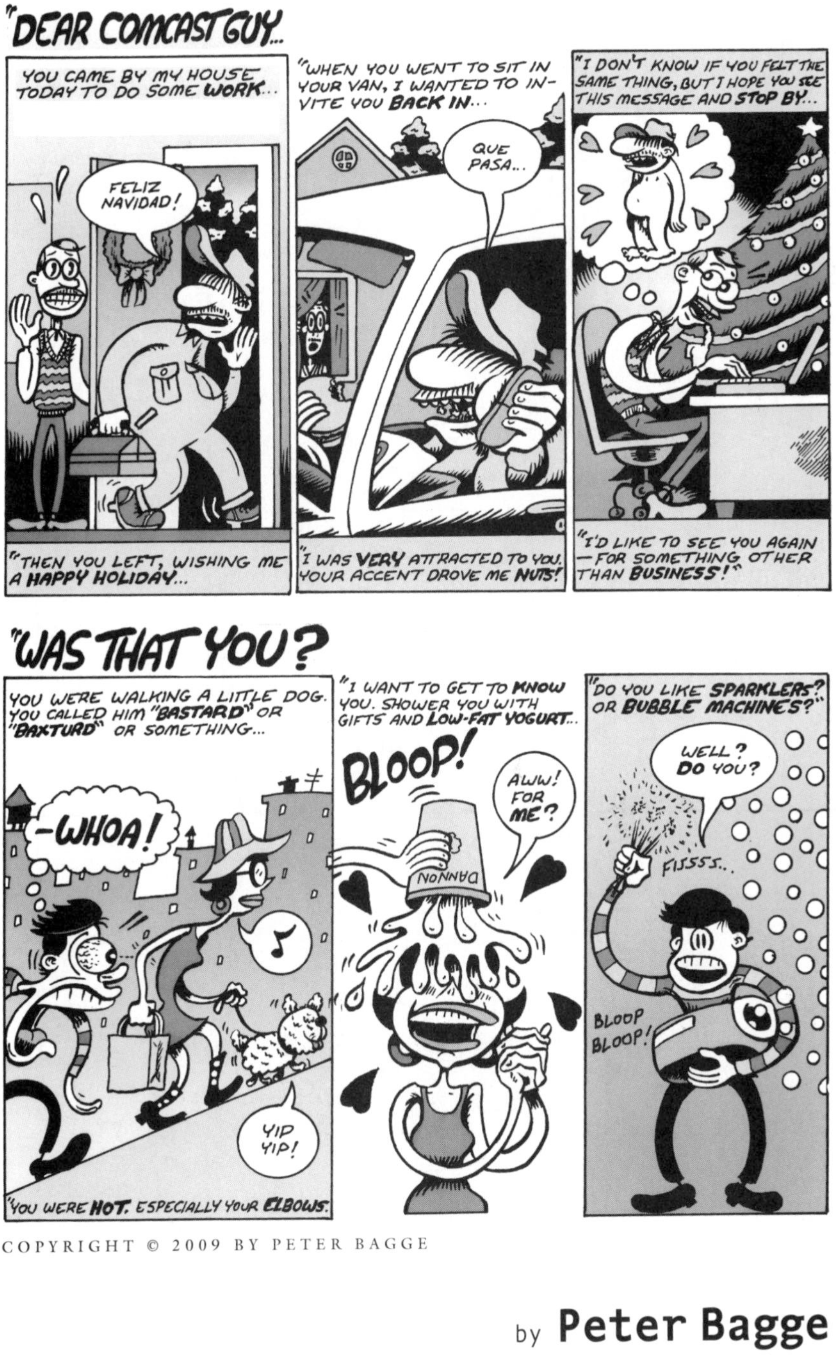
"DEAR COMCAST GUY...
YOU CAME BY MY HOUSE TODAY TO DO SOME WORK...
FELIZ NAVIDAD!
"THEN YOU LEFT, WISHING ME A HAPPY HOLIDAY...
"WHEN YOU WENT TO SIT IN YOUR VAN, I WANTED TO IN-VITE YOU BACK IN...
QUE PASA...
"I WAS VERY ATTRACTED TO YOU. YOUR ACCENT DROVE ME NUTS!
"I DON'T KNOW IF YOU FELT THE SAME THING, BUT I HOPE YOU SEE THIS MESSAGE AND STOP BY...
"I'D LIKE TO SEE YOU AGAIN —FOR SOMETHING OTHER THAN BUSINESS!"
"WAS THAT YOU?
YOU WERE WALKING A LITTLE DOG. YOU CALLED HIM "BASTARD" OR "BAXTURD" OR SOMETHING...
-WHOA!
YIP YIP!
"YOU WERE HOT. ESPECIALLY YOUR ELBOWS.
"I WANT TO GET TO KNOW YOU. SHOWER YOU WITH GIFTS AND LOW-FAT YOGURT...
BLOOP!
AWW! FOR ME?
DANNON
"DO YOU LIKE SPARKLERS? OR BUBBLE MACHINES?"
WELL? DO YOU?
FISSSS...
BLOOP BLOOP!

by **Peter Bagge**

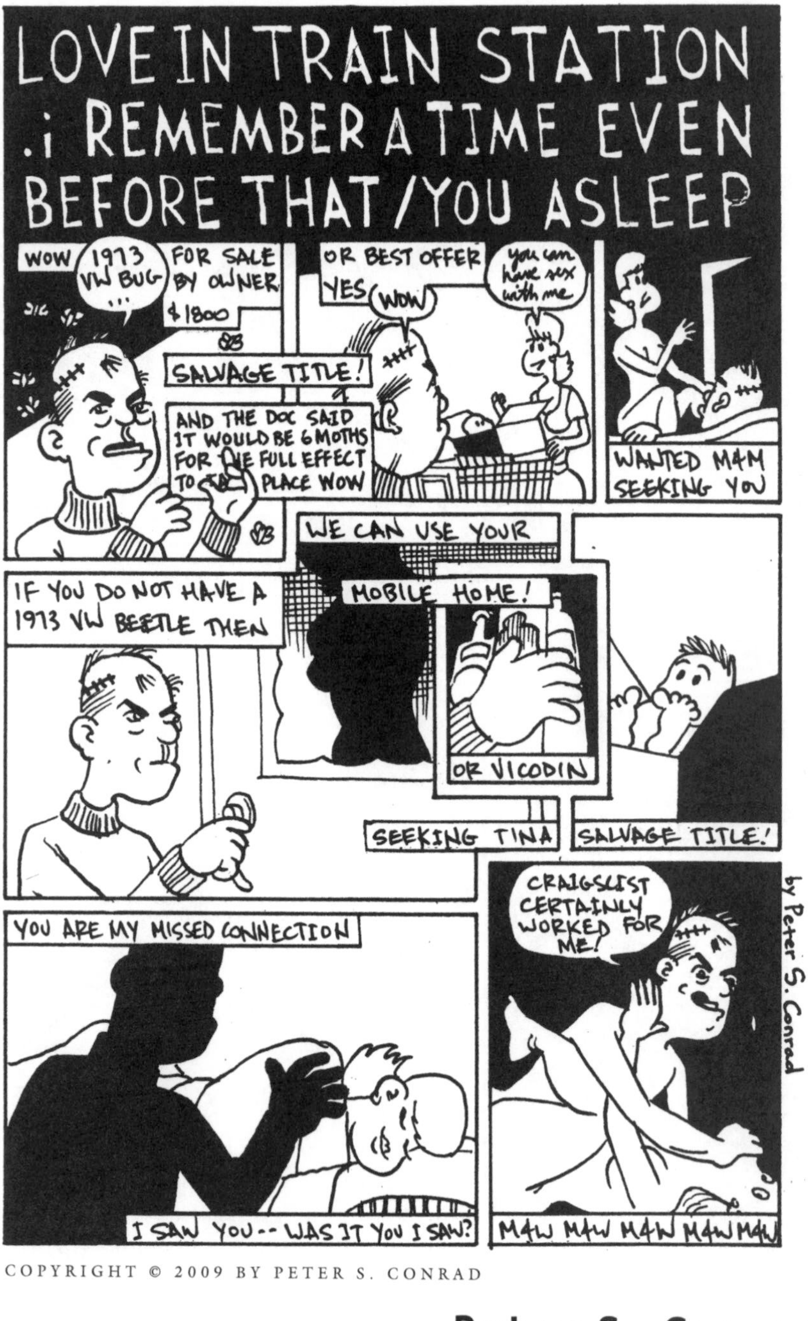
LOVE IN TRAIN STATION .i REMEMBER A TIME EVEN BEFORE THAT / YOU ASLEEP
WOW
1973 VW BUG ...
FOR SALE BY OWNER
$1800
SALVAGE TITLE!
AND THE DOC SAID IT WOULD BE 6 MOTHS FOR E FULL EFFECT TO PLACE WOW
OR BEST OFFER
YES
WOW
you can have sex with me
WANTED M4M SEEKING YOU
IF YOU DO NOT HAVE A 1973 VW BEETLE THEN
WE CAN USE YOUR
MOBILE HOME!
OR VICODIN
SEEKING TINA
SALVAGE TITLE!
YOU ARE MY MISSED CONNECTION
I SAW YOU -- WAS IT YOU I SAW?
CRAIGSLIST CERTAINLY WORKED FOR ME!
M4W M4W M4W M4W M4W
by Peter S. Conrad

by **Peter S. Conrad**

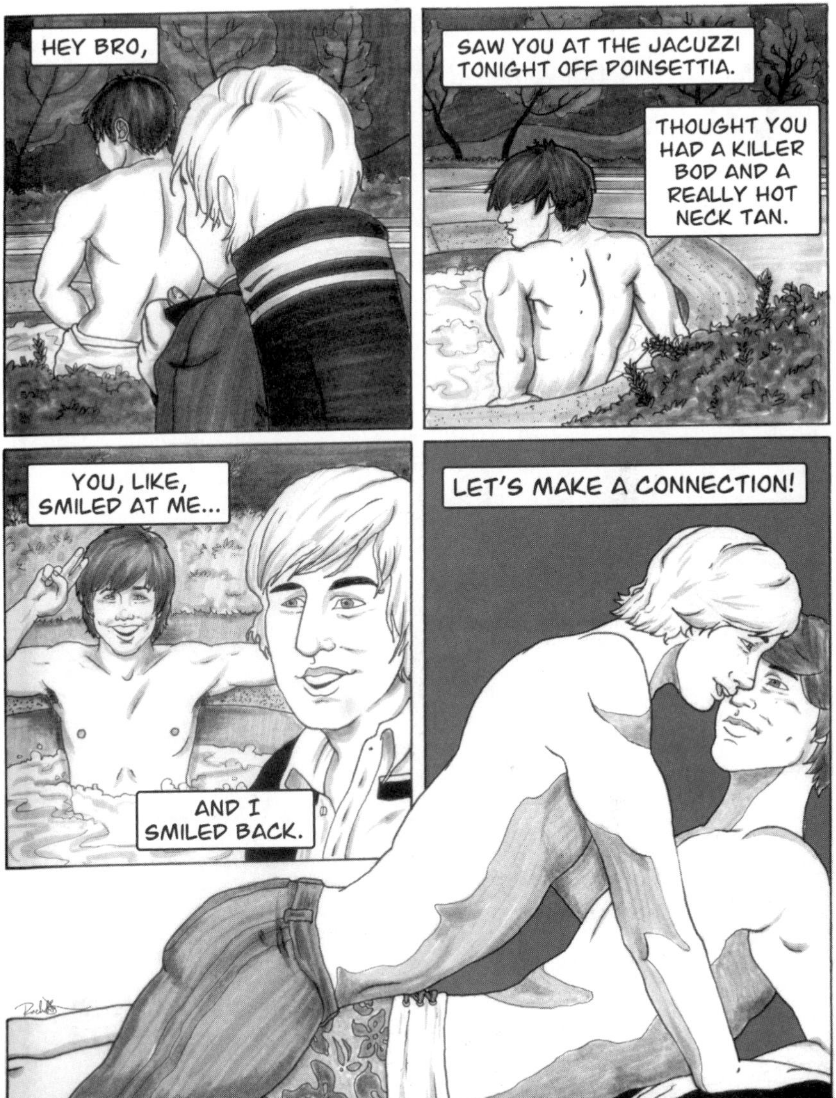
HEY BRO,
SAW YOU AT THE JACUZZI TONIGHT OFF POINSETTIA.
THOUGHT YOU HAD A KILLER BOD AND A REALLY HOT NECK TAN.
YOU, LIKE, SMILED AT ME...
AND I SMILED BACK.
LET'S MAKE A CONNECTION!

by **Rachel Dukes**

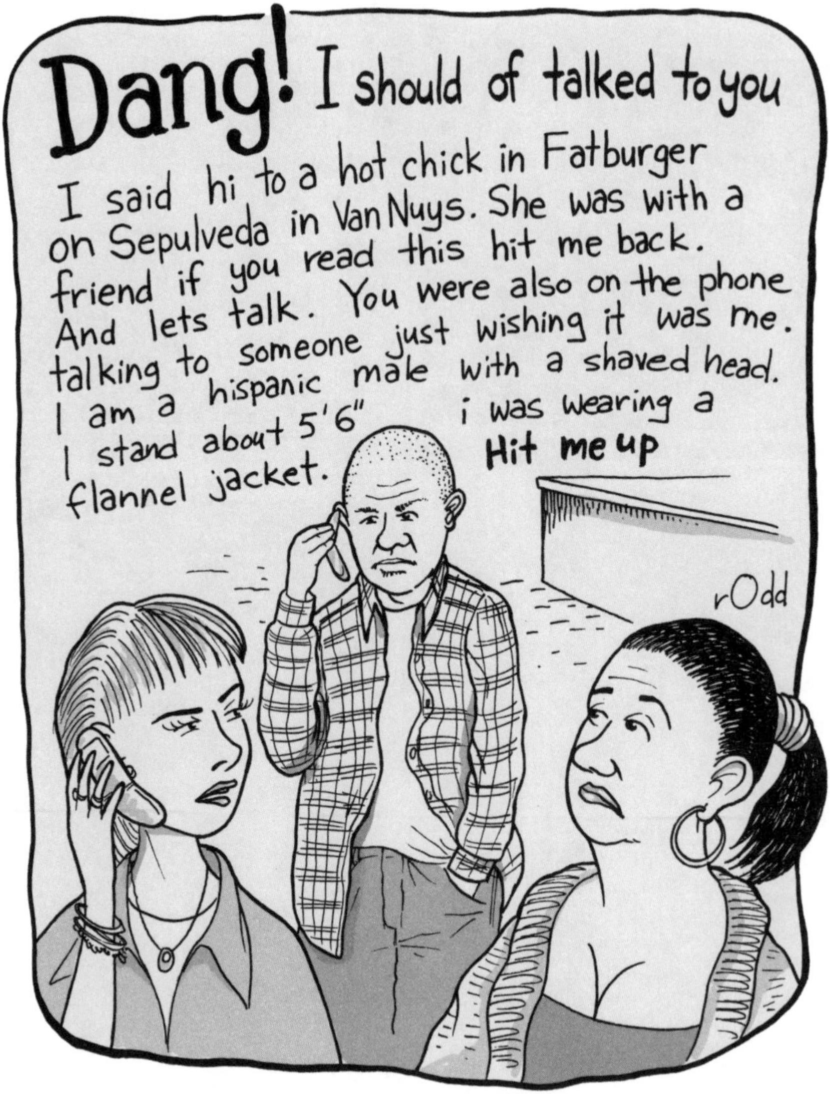
Dang! I should of talked to you
I said hi to a hot chick in Fatburger
on Sepulveda in Van Nuys. She was with a
friend if you read this hit me back.
And lets talk. You were also on the phone
talking to someone just wishing it was me.
I am a hispanic male with a shaved head.
I stand about 5'6"
i was wearing a
flannel jacket.
Hit me up
rOdd

by **Rodd Perry**

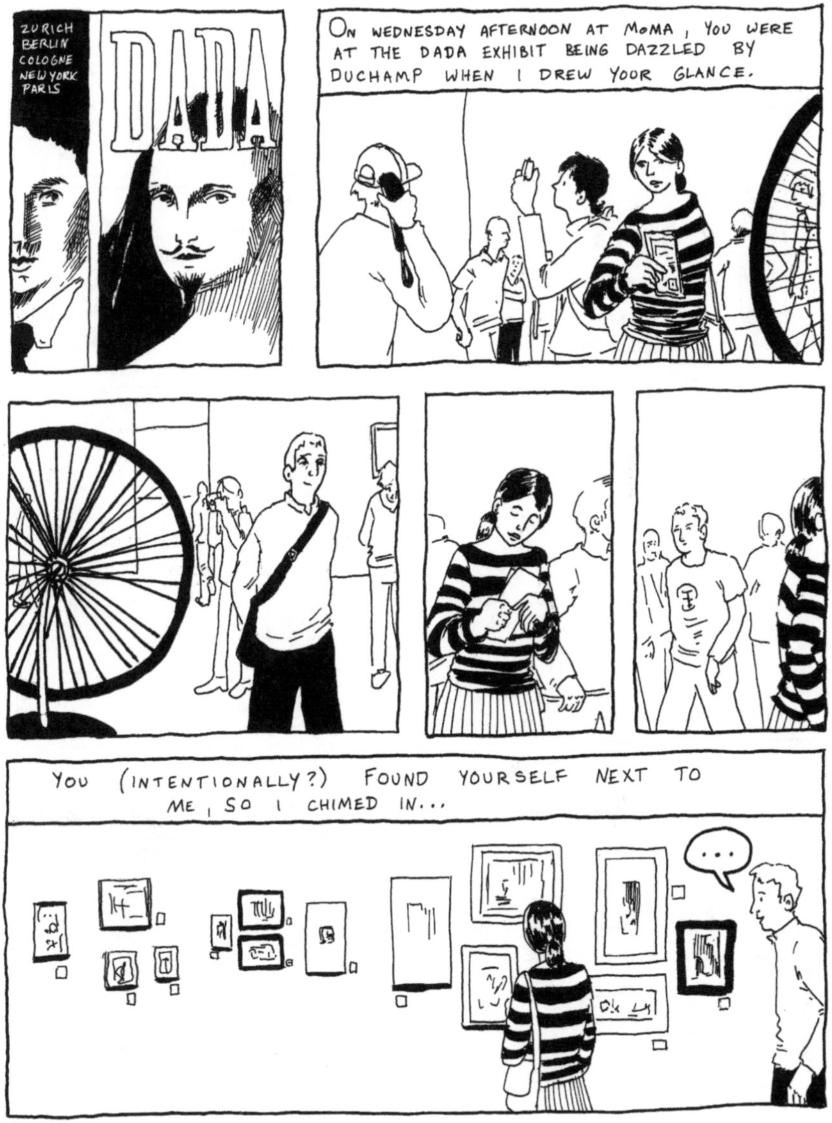
ZURICH
BERLIN
COLOGNE
NEW YORK
PARIS
DADA
ON WEDNESDAY AFTERNOON AT MOMA, YOU WERE AT THE DADA EXHIBIT BEING DAZZLED BY DUCHAMP WHEN I DREW YOUR GLANCE.
YOU (INTENTIONALLY?) FOUND YOURSELF NEXT TO ME, SO I CHIMED IN...
...

by **Sarah Glidden**

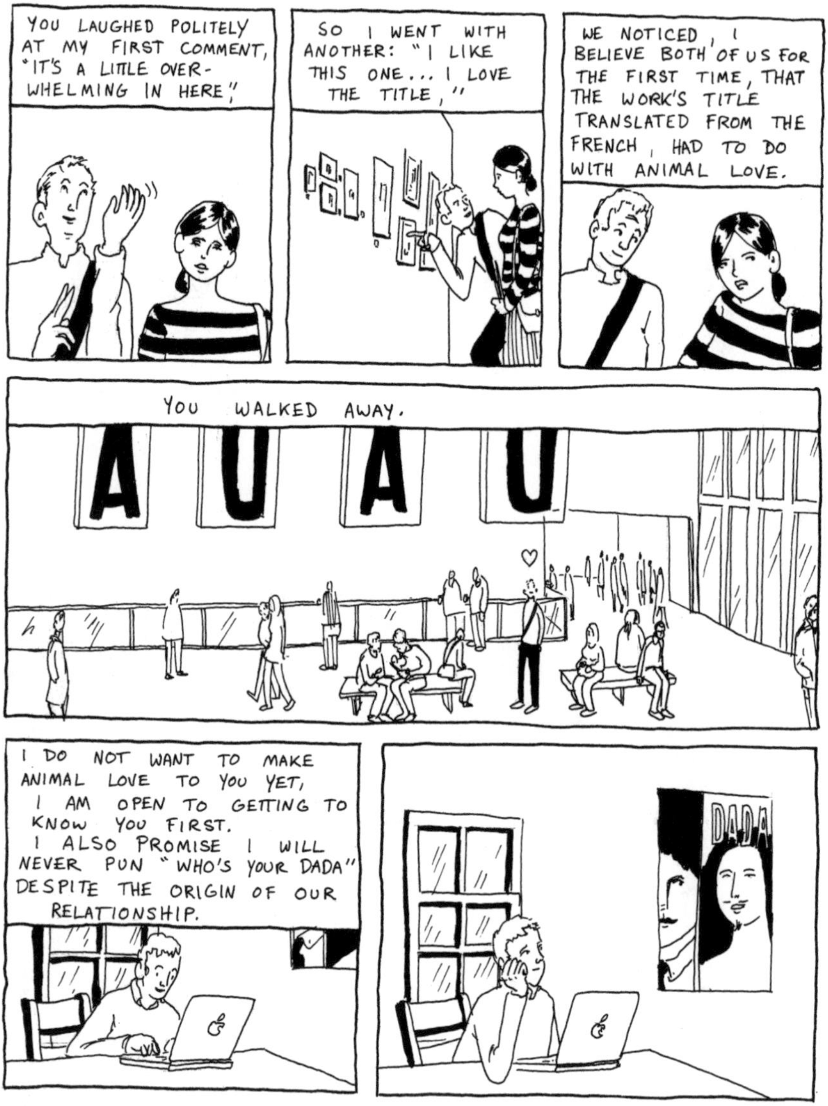
YOU LAUGHED POLITELY AT MY FIRST COMMENT, "IT'S A LITTLE OVER-WHELMING IN HERE."
SO I WENT WITH ANOTHER: "I LIKE THIS ONE... I LOVE THE TITLE."
WE NOTICED, I BELIEVE BOTH OF US FOR THE FIRST TIME, THAT THE WORK'S TITLE TRANSLATED FROM THE FRENCH, HAD TO DO WITH ANIMAL LOVE.
YOU WALKED AWAY.
I DO NOT WANT TO MAKE ANIMAL LOVE TO YOU YET,
I AM OPEN TO GETTING TO KNOW YOU FIRST.
I ALSO PROMISE I WILL NEVER PUN "WHO'S YOUR DADA" DESPITE THE ORIGIN OF OUR RELATIONSHIP.
DADA

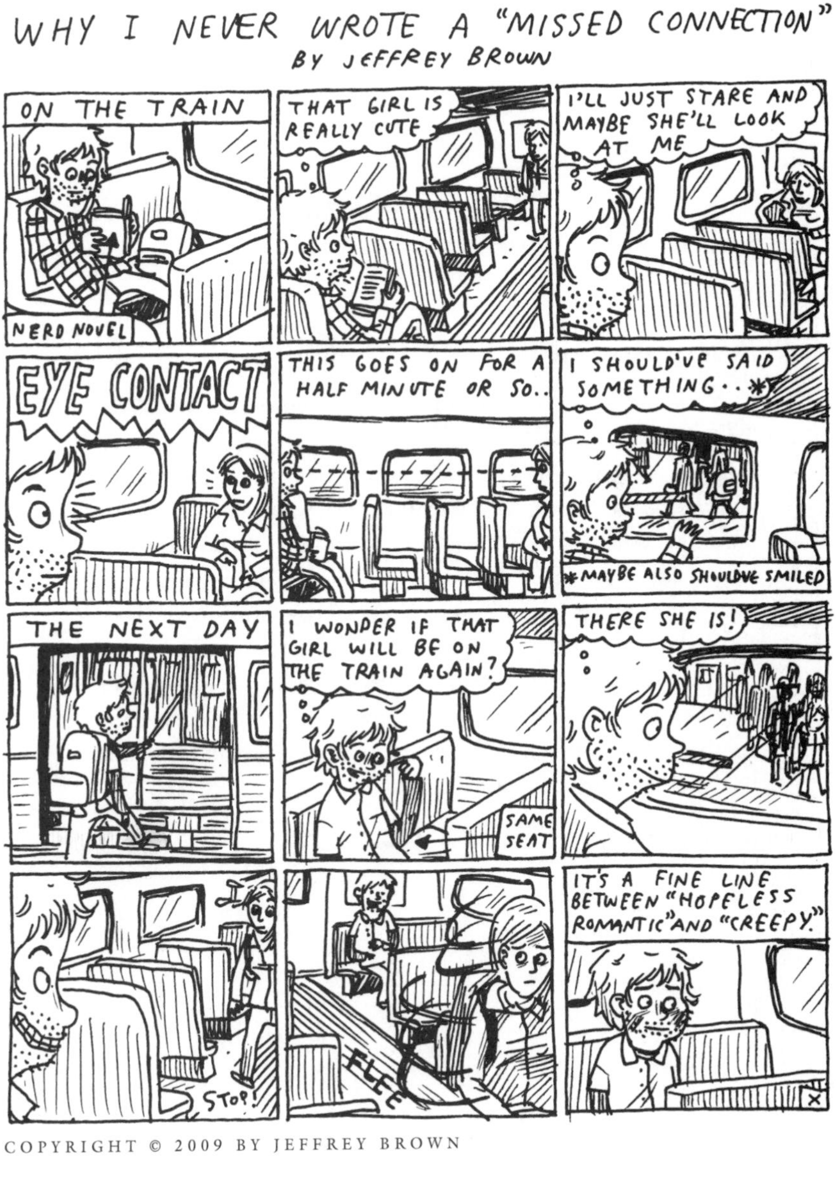
WHY I NEVER WROTE A "MISSED CONNECTION"
BY JEFFREY BROWN
ON THE TRAIN
NERD NOVEL
THAT GIRL IS REALLY CUTE
I'LL JUST STARE AND MAYBE SHE'LL LOOK AT ME
EYE CONTACT
THIS GOES ON FOR A HALF MINUTE OR SO..
I SHOULD'VE SAID SOMETHING..*
*MAYBE ALSO SHOULD'VE SMILED
THE NEXT DAY
I WONDER IF THAT GIRL WILL BE ON THE TRAIN AGAIN?
SAME SEAT
THERE SHE IS!
STOP!
FLEE
IT'S A FINE LINE BETWEEN "HOPELESS ROMANTIC" AND "CREEPY."

by **Jeffrey Brown**

ACKNOWLEDGMENTS

MANY THANKS TO:

Everyone who contributed to this project, especially Laura Park. To Sarah Glidden, without whom this project would have never made it out of my "ideas" notebook and onto real paper. To my family for their support, especially my mom, who still continues to e-mail me articles about "real" careers. To Michelle Brower, who took charge and rescued this book from languishing in obscurity in the stack of papers on my desk, and to Lindsay Orman and Three Rivers Press for giving it a chance. And, of course, thank you to everyone who ever fell instantly in love, was fooled by friends, had a bad encounter, or wanted the last word and went looking for another chance through missed connection ads. Without them, this book never would have existed at all.

CONTRIBUTORS

AARON MEW,
www.scubotch.com
You: girl with Aeropostal t-shirt and
Gucci bag
Me: not interested

AARON RENIER,
aaronrenier.com
You: Like the mailbox in the classic film
the Lake House, this ad was written in
the future for you, yes YOU, the girl of
my dreams.
Me: Inconveniently I live twenty years
in the future, and . . . I am old. BUT
my present self would LOVE if you
contacted him. This is not a joke.

ABBY DENSON,
www.abbycomix.com
You: cute rocker boy with shaggy hair
Me: crazed rock 'n' roll art girl

ADAM KIDDER,
adamkidder.com
You: girl with stroller standing in the
road outside the Waffle House
Me: guy with half-eaten Grilled Bacon
Texas Cheesesteak™ Melt Plate

ALEC LONGSTRETH,
www.alec-longstreth.com

ALEXIS SOTTILE,
alexisperplexus@yahoo.com
You: earthman cartographer with a sex-
tant to my dreams
Me: space wayfarer looking for clan-
destine nocturnal exchanges of alien
technology

ARLENE O'LEARY,
oharlene.livejournal.com
Me: nerdy artsy chick from Brooklyn,
New York
You: my nerdy wet dream come true

ARON NELS STEINKE,
www.aronnelssteinke.com
You: enjoy wearing dresses and eating
vegetables
Me: tall guy with tight pants

AUSTIN ENGLISH,
austin.robertson.english@gmail.com
You: girl with gigantic hoop earrings
Me: sponging up your emotions

Ben Claassen III,
www.bendependent.com
You: funny
Me: laughing

Brandon Clark,
clarkillustrationanddesign.blogspot.
com
You: tall, skinny, wearing red sweater
Me: muscular, anchor tattoo, wearing
sailor suit

Calvin Wong,
calwong@gmail.com
You: chubby bespectacled Asian in blue
hoodie and chin-length hair, listening
intently to your iPod on Montgomery
Street BART
Me: same, but sporting disfiguring facial
scar and a bionic hand; I was going to
warn you about a future calamity that
would destroy mankind as we know it,
but you got off at Embarcadero

Cathy Leamy,
www.metrokitty.com
You: hipster geek buying a *Doctor Who*
boxed set
Me: jumpy redhead with Dunkin' Do-
nuts coffee

Colleen Frakes,
www.cowboyorange.com
25 y/o DDF SWF in WRJ
ISO comic to call my own

Corinne Mucha,
corinne.nicole.mucha@gmail.com
You: messy hair, possibly nearsighted
Me: lime green sweatshirt, strange hat

Damien Jay,
www.damienjay.com
You: on your pillow making piggy
sounds waiting to go for a walk
Me: let me finish this one thing and
then I'll be ready

Damon Brown aka The Ink Lab
You: look great in that shirt
Me: Damon of theinklab.com

Dan Archer,
www.archburger.blogspot.com
You: a rambunctious blonde looking
pensive in P&C
Me: the muscled myope who winked at
you in the red meat aisle

Daniel Barlow,
barlowdaniel@gmail.com,
www.vermontcomics.com
You: redhead with glitter makeup and
fancy frames, busting out of your bond-
age gear
Me: wide-eyed and lost writer often
mistaken for Harry Potter or Dan
Rather

Dan Henrick,
www.danhenrick.com

DAVID BESSENT,
www.flickr.com/davidbessent
You: cute black girl, SMILED, touched
your hair, neck, and shoulder after you
almost hit me with your car on 16th
St./Camelback
Me: on bicycle, white, lanky, bearded,
dark blue jacket with orange stripes on
sleeves and safe, but maybe I should
have sacrificed femur to meet you

DAN MAZUR,
danmazur.livejournal.com
Me: curly hair, glasses, slovenly attire
You: my mind

DAVID MALKI,
www.wondermark.com
You were the time traveler in the green
scarf.
I was the dude you stranded in 1885.

DEREK CHATWOOD,
www.poprelics.com

ELIJAH J. BRUBAKER,
www.elijahbrubaker.com
You: large throng of squealing half-
naked beauties
Me: intensely handsome stud with tons
of self-esteem

EMILY FLAKE,
www.eflakeagogo.com
Me: fat old chick, intermittently weep-
ing and glaring, hunched up drunk in
the corner
You: laughing at me with all your

friends before you snuck over and took
me to the alley for some rough stuff

FIONA TAYLOR,
msfionataylor@gmail.com

GABRIELLE BELL,
www.drawnandquarterly.com

GARY GAO,
angrytoast@gmail.com

GREG MEANS,
www.tugboatpress.com
You: most beautiful woman in the world
Me: great personality

INDIGO KELLEIGH,
www.lunarbistro.com
You: tall, bespectacled brunette with
amazonian physique and thigh-highs
Me: emotionally stunted manchild,
nursing a stout by the pool table

ISAAC CATES,
www.satisfactorycomics.blogspot.com
You: interested in experiments and for-
mal constraints
Me: cranky college professor–type who
collaborates well

J.T. YOST,
www.jtyost.com
You: special lady at the Waffle House
Me: scattered and smothered, but not
covered

JAMES SMITH,
www.jamesmith.org
You: bookstore security guard
Me: skinny guy dancing to Wu Tang/
Patsy Cline mix in the magazine section

JANELLE HESSIG,
www.gimmieaction.com

JASON MARTIN,
myspace.com/laterbornzine
You: fan of poignant autobiographical
comics
Me: drawer of said comics

JASON VIOLA,
jviola@thebulletpoints.com
You: the alien in the silver spaceship
with flashing blue lights
Me: in my backyard wondering why you
keep passing me by

JEFFREY BROWN,
www.jeffreybrowncomics.com
You: open-minded reader with good
sense of humor and tolerance for unin-
tentional self pity
Me: professional cartoonist, father of
one

JESSE REKLAW,
www.slowwave.com
You: politely ignoring me
Me: 37 y.o. former dungeonmaster into
comics, kitty cats, and a good cry

JOAN REILLY,
illustration@joanreilly.com
You: smart, sensitive reader with a soft
spot for sad stories
Me: sad girl trapped in a happy girl's
body

JOE INFURNARI,
joe@joeinfurnari.com,
www.joeinfurnari.com,
www.theprocesscomic.com
You: intergalactic space traveler with a
celestial body and a cosmic imagination
Me: ufologist transmitting images into
the galaxy in search of an otherworldly
exchange

JOEY SAYERS,
www.jsayers.com
You: a giant ball of rock, circling a distant star
Me: a single electron in the middle of a
pumpkin pie

JOHN ISAACSON,
www.unlay.com
You: small-time crook
Me: empty cash drawer

JON ADAMS,
www.hisportfolio.com,
citycyclops.com
You: woman who looks just like my
dead wife, walking down the street
Me: man curled up in bushes, alter-
nately laughing and crying to himself

JONATHAN BAYLIS,
www.sobuttons.com
You: Canadian-born, stand-up comic,
red lipstick wearing, Joni Mitchell lover
Me: Bronx-born, glee club baritone,
goatee sporting, bagel eater

JONATHAN HILL,
www.oneofthejohns.com
You: beatso
Me: Lego-muncher

JOSH FREES,
joshpm.livejournal.com
You: the best dancer in the show
Me: the short guy in the front singing
along and trying to catch your eye

JOSHUA KEMBLE,
www.sidewithus.com/joshkemble
You: engaged, half-Japanese indy children's book author
Me: engaged ugly skinny nerd illustra-
tor with ugly fat pug . . . oh shit, we're
already engaged!

JULIA WERTZ,
www.fartparty.org
You: trucker, fucker, corn-shucker
Me: hiding in the girls' bathroom during milk break

JULIE BEHN,
Julie.Behn@gmail.com
Cute and loving comic-book contessa
sipping tea and looking for lifelong
travel experience.

KATE O'LEARY,
www.kateoleary.com,
kate@kateoleary.com

KAZIMIR STRZEPEK,
www.scubotch.com
You: nurd with good comic tastes,
reading my bio
Me: nurd with good comic tastes,
drawing fucked up shit

KEITH KNIGHT,
www.kchronicles.com

KELLY TINDALL,
www.kellytindall.com
You: a nattily attired vixen boasting
high heels and low standards
Me: a bigfoot-obsessed misanthrope
with tiny feet and love to spare

KEN DAHL,
fantods@gmail.com
You: cranky pizza-faced nearsighted
bum with greasy hair and nine fingers
Me: smitten

KENNY KEIL,
kwkeil@gmail.com,
www.talestosuffice.com
Me: my back against the record machine, I ain't the worst that you've seen
You: might as well jump Go ahead,
jump

LAURA PARK
You: semitransparent specter whistling
down the alley
Me: slouchy gawker

LISA HANAWALT,
lobsterrags@yahoo.com,
www.lobsterrags.com
You: glistening vixen with BBQ fixin's
Me: doodling conquistadors, car
crashes, and complicated clothing in the
corner

LIZ PRINCE,
lizprincepower@hotmail.com
You: bearded
Me: totally into bearded dudes

LUCY KNISLEY,
www.StopPayingAttention.com
You: mustachioed ice-cream vendor
with a cart full of delicious ice-cream!
Me: Pippi Longstocking–type, with ink-
stained hands. I was chasing you down
the street. Why didn't you stop?

MARIA SEQUEIRA,
www.mariasequeira.com

MARI NAOMI,
www.marinaomi.com
You: skinny hipster with bed head
Me: amerasian gal with bed head on the
brain

MARLENE KRYZA,
www.kryza.biz,
www.marlenekryza.com

MATT LEUNIG,
www.scrapedknee.com
Me: red-bearded, ink drinking, Bigfoot
lover
You: beautiful, talented, gracious,
comic-reading public

MATTHEW BERNIER,
www.Matthew-Bernier.com
You: a lady possessed of the charms of
experience and maturity
Me: an appreciator of soft gray drapes
and antique knockers

MATTHEW LOUX,
www.actionmatt.com
You: adoring literature fan hungry for
the blood of sequential art
Me: comics artist by day, demon slayer
by night, holding a Winsor Newton
brush in one hand and the sword of jus-
tice in the other

MAX CLOTFELTER,
www.scubotch.com
You: homeless woman with spider tat-
tooed on face
Me: trying to hide boner

MAX KARL KEY,
www.oddcircumstance.com
You: flawless specimen on the park lawn
Me: gaunt fellow avoiding sidewalk
cracks; be the east coast to my west?

MEGAN BAEHR,
www.friedwontons.com
You: just right for me
Me: just right for you

MIKE WENTHE,
www.satisfactorycomics.blogspot.com
You: tolerant of puns; fond of reading
and travel
Me: Reed Richards–type: skinny, gray-
ing, prone to overthinking

MINTY LEWIS,
www.pscomics.com
You: the one with the big butt and the
Snickers bar
Me: the other one with the big butt and
the Snickers bar, but i am saving half
for later

MK REED,
www.mkreed.com
You: chubby myopic dork, on second
Ten Sack of evening
Me: dashing brunette in corner, deli-
cately rendering your harelip

NATE DOYLE,
www.ndcrookedteeth.blogspot.com
You: should have been looking where
you were going . . .
Me: I was the kid on the bike you ran
over.

NATE HIGLEY,
www.natehigley.com
You: red jumpsuit, cold-blooded, digs
relavish . . .
Me: hates red dust, looking for something sirius . . .

NEIL SWAAB,
www.mrwiggleslovesyou.com,
www.neilswaab.com

NOELLE BARBY,
www.noellebarby.com
You: Lookin' for a Daddy?
Me: I'm it.

PETER BAGGE,
www.peterbagge.com
You: Mitzi Gaynor lookalike
Me: Wayne Newton wannabe

PETER S. CONRAD,
www.paperdummy.com
Saw you reading me but was too shy to
make a move. Come back for another
look!

RACHEL DUKES,
www.poseurink.com

RAMA HUGHES,
www.ramahughes.com
Me: teacher, artist, blockhead
You: love it!

ROBIN ENRICO,
www.robinenrico.com
You: zaftig, opinionated, culture vulture
Me: skinny, book-slut, clotheshorse

RODD PERRY,
www.guyandrodd.com

SAM HENDERSON,
www.magicwhistle.com
You: nonsmoking, right-handed, blue-
eyed, blonde-haired, introverted, epileptic
atheist cartoonist with glasses who is
160 lbs. and 6'0" and yearns to leave this
syphilitic gloryhole and come back to the
city
Me: nonsmoking, right-handed, blue-
eyed, blonde-haired, introverted, epileptic
atheist cartoonist with glasses who is
160 lbs. and 6'0" and yearns to leave this
syphilitic gloryhole and come back to the
city

SAM MERWIN,
www.smerwin.com,
smerwin@gmail.com
You: cute meat-eating hippie girl in Car-
hartts at the coffee shop
Me: underemployed graphic designer,
scruffy, cleans up nice

SARA PECHEREK,
www.awkwardplanet.com,
www.icgenesis.com

SARAH GLIDDEN,
www.smallnoises.com
You: completing the New York Times
crossword puzzle on the Q train to
Brooklyn
Me: Wondering what you got for 36
down. How am I supposed to know who
won the bronze medal for Nordic skiing
in the 1956 Olympics?

SARAH MOREAN,
www.smorean.com
You: dapper gent
Me: modest dame

SARAH OLEKSYK,
www.saraholeksyk.com
You: stunning, slurring, in the wrong
bathroom
Me: Charm, wit, and beauty wrapped in
a thin shell of humbleness. I held your
merkin. Coffee?

SHAENON K. GARRITY,
www.shaenon.com
You: person not named Shaenon
Me: person named Shaenon

SHANNON O'LEARY,
www.fortunesbitch.com,
www.petnoir.com
You: It's not you, it's me.
Me: It's not me, it's you.

SHANNON SHAW,
shannoncshaw@gmail.com
You: flirtatious hobo with a heart o' gold
Me: enormous gap-toothed sasquatchious
quasi-babe

SHANNON WHEELER,
www.tmcm.com
You: demanding too much, giving too
little
Me: stressed-out on deadlines writing
another opera, and cartooning for The
Onion and various alt weeklies

SINA GRACE,
conosina@yahoo.com,
www.sinagrace.com
You: brooding lockjaw
Me: skinny, dark-haired dandy, with a
shit-eating grin

TESSA BRUNTON,
www.tessasbraces.blogspot.com
You: Level Five Dungeon Master read-
ing *Heavy Metal*
Me: mostly naked viking princess from
Middle-earth with battle-axe

T.J. KIRSCH,
www.tjkirsch.com,
thomasjohn811@aol.com
You: imaginary friend of mine—
dismissive of all things comics,
"low" art
Me: insistent, flipping you off with
both hands, then running away

TOM HART,
www.hutchowen.com
You: hairy, alert, alive with pleasure
Me: cartoonist, teacher, Shropshire
slasher

WILLIAM SCHAFF,
www.williamschaff.com
You: probably my dream come true and
my worst nightmare
Me: probably your dream come true
and your worst nightmare

ZACHARY GARRETT,
www.zacharygarrett.com
You: offering a worn, plastic wallet,
giggling
Me: digging through my pockets,
oblivious

ABOUT THE AUTHOR

JULIA WERTZ is the creator of the humorous autobiographical comic books *The Fart Party* from Atomic Book Co. They have nothing to do with farts. Born in 1982 in the San Francisco Bay area, Julia's backwoods upbringing still causes her to use words like "dude" and "hella," and she doesn't really give a shit what you think about that. She currently lives in Brooklyn, New York, where she spends her spare time drawing funny pictures in little boxes. When she grows up, she plans on living alone in a little cabin along the Oregon coastline where she can run a microbrewery out of her basement. She doesn't currently own any pets but she did once consider buying a tiny turtle from the dollar store. For new comics roughly thrice a week, visit www.fartparty.org.